Practical Istio

Learn Istio Service Mesh, Microservices, and Cloud-Native Architecture for Optimal Performance

Prashanth Josyula
Karanbir Singh
Anupam Mehta

Apress®

Practical Istio: Learn Istio Service Mesh, Microservices, and Cloud-Native Architecture for Optimal Performance

Prashanth Josyula
Fremont, CA, USA

Karanbir Singh
Milpitas, CA, USA

Anupam Mehta
Leesburg, VA, USA

ISBN-13 (pbk): 979-8-8688-1572-0
https://doi.org/10.1007/979-8-8688-1573-7

ISBN-13 (electronic): 979-8-8688-1573-7

Copyright © 2025 by Prashanth Josyula, Karanbir Singh, Anupam Mehta

This work is subject to copyright. All rights are reserved by the Publisher, whether the whole or part of the material is concerned, specifically the rights of translation, reprinting, reuse of illustrations, recitation, broadcasting, reproduction on microfilms or in any other physical way, and transmission or information storage and retrieval, electronic adaptation, computer software, or by similar or dissimilar methodology now known or hereafter developed.

Trademarked names, logos, and images may appear in this book. Rather than use a trademark symbol with every occurrence of a trademarked name, logo, or image we use the names, logos, and images only in an editorial fashion and to the benefit of the trademark owner, with no intention of infringement of the trademark.

The use in this publication of trade names, trademarks, service marks, and similar terms, even if they are not identified as such, is not to be taken as an expression of opinion as to whether or not they are subject to proprietary rights.

While the advice and information in this book are believed to be true and accurate at the date of publication, neither the authors nor the editors nor the publisher can accept any legal responsibility for any errors or omissions that may be made. The publisher makes no warranty, express or implied, with respect to the material contained herein.

Managing Director, Apress Media LLC: Welmoed Spahr
Acquisitions Editor: James Robinson-Prior
Editorial Project Manager: Jacob Shmulewitz

Distributed to the book trade worldwide by Springer Science+Business Media New York, 1 New York Plaza, New York, NY 10004. Phone 1-800-SPRINGER, fax (201) 348-4505, e-mail orders-ny@springer-sbm.com, or visit www.springeronline.com. Apress Media, LLC is a Delaware LLC and the sole member (owner) is Springer Science + Business Media Finance Inc (SSBM Finance Inc). SSBM Finance Inc is a **Delaware** corporation.

For information on translations, please e-mail booktranslations@springernature.com; for reprint, paperback, or audio rights, please e-mail bookpermissions@springernature.com.

Apress titles may be purchased in bulk for academic, corporate, or promotional use. eBook versions and licenses are also available for most titles. For more information, reference our Print and eBook Bulk Sales web page at http://www.apress.com/bulk-sales.

Any source code or other supplementary material referenced by the author in this book is available to readers on GitHub. For more detailed information, please visit https://www.apress.com/gp/services/source-code.

If disposing of this product, please recycle the paper

*Prashanth Josyula: Dedicated to my parents, my wife,
and both of my kids*

Karanbir Singh: Dedicated to my parents, my wife, and my son

Anupam Mehta: Dedicated to my family and my friends

Table of Contents

About the Authors .... **xv**

About the Technical Reviewers .... **xvii**

Introduction .... **xix**

Chapter 1: Introduction to Istio **1**

Introduction 1

Objective 2

Outline 2

What Are Microservices? 2

    Characteristics of Microservices 3

    Challenges of Microservices Architecture 4

What Is a Service Mesh? 5

    Traffic Management 6

    Security 6

    Observability 7

    Resilience and Reliability 7

    Policy Enforcement 7

    Platform Agnostic 7

    Extensibility 8

    Centralized Management 8

Overview of Istio 8

    Data Plane 8

    Control Plane 9

Comparing Istio and Other Service Mesh Solutions 9

Case Studies of Istio 10

    Rappi 11

v

Table of Contents

    Cash App 11

    T-Mobile 11

    Salesforce 11

    Mindtickle 12

    Airbnb 12

    Autotrader UK 12

What Is Kubernetes? 12

    Architecture 13

    Control Plane 14

    Worker Nodes 15

    Key Features of Kubernetes 16

Set Up a Local Environment 19

    Installing Prerequisites 19

    Set Up Istio 25

Conclusion 28

References 29

Chapter 2: Understanding Istio's Core Components 31

Introduction 31

The Case for Istio: Challenges in a Microservices Architecture Without a Service Mesh 32

What Is a Service Mesh, and What Does It Do? 34

What Is Istio, and Why Is It Designed As It Is? 36

Understanding Istio's Architecture: The Control Plane and Data Plane 37

Core Elements of Istio 38

    Istiod: Unified Control Plane 40

    Envoy Proxy: The Data Plane 44

    Istio's Deployment Modes 46

    Core Components of Envoy Proxy 46

    Choosing the Right Istio Deployment Mode: Sidecar vs. Ambient 57

    How Istio Manages Service Discovery and Load Balancing 73

    How Istio Manages Security and Identity Management 76

Comprehending the Telemetry and Monitoring Components of Istio	77
Istio: Advanced Traffic Management	78
Conclusion	79

Chapter 3: Fundamentals of Traffic Management with Istio 81

Introduction	81
Understanding the Importance of Traffic Management	81
Istio's Architecture for Traffic Management	82
Role of Envoy Proxy in Traffic Management	84
Overview of Istio Traffic Management APIs	84
Sample Application: Recommendation Service	85
Virtual Services and Destination Rules	92
Understanding Virtual Services	93
Working with Destination Rules	108
Traffic Routing Fundamentals	120
Route Rules and Precedence	120
Header-Based Routing	122
URI-Based Routing	123
Method-Based Routing	124
Weighted Routing	124
Subnet-Based Routing	125
Port-Based Routing	126
Conclusion	129

Chapter 4: Advanced Traffic Management Patterns and Gateway Control 131

Introduction	131
Advanced Traffic Management Techniques	131
Canary Deployments	133
Blue/Green Deployments	144
Resilience and Fault Tolerance	159
Circuit Breakers	159
Fault Injection	174
Retry and Timeout Policies	181

TABLE OF CONTENTS

Traffic Mirroring 185
    Understanding Traffic Mirroring Concepts 186
    Implementing Shadow Traffic 187
    Use Cases for Traffic Mirroring 188
    Analyzing Mirrored Traffic 189
    Testing and Validation Strategies 192

Gateway Management 193
    Ingress Gateway 194
    Egress Gateway 210

Best Practices and Common Pitfalls 219
    Traffic Management Patterns 219
    Configuration Best Practices 220
    Common Mistakes to Avoid 220
    Troubleshooting Strategies 221
    Performance Considerations 221

Conclusion 222

Chapter 5: Securing Microservices with Istio 223

Introduction 223
A Microservices Environment's Foundational Security Concepts 224
Introduction to Security in Distributed Systems 226
    The Evolution of Distributed Security 226
    Security Challenges in the Modern Distributed Architecture 226
    Security Implications for Organizations 227
    The Need for Modern Security Solutions 227
    What Is Istio's Role in Modern Security 228

Mutual TLS in Istio and Practical Implementation 228
    Introduction to Mutual TLS 228
    Service Identity and Certificate Management 229
    Transparent Encryption and Security 229
    Integration and Security Policies 230
    Example 230

Istio Authentication and Authorization Policies 242
    Authentication Policies 242
        Example 242
Role-Based Access Control (RBAC) in Istio 249
        Example 250
Securing Ingress and Egress Traffic 260
        Example 262
Auditing and Logging Security Events in Istio 273
        Example 273
Integrating Istio Security with External Systems 279
        Example 280
Handling Security in Multi-cluster Deployments 286
Overall Security Best Practices in Istio and Its Use in Production 288

Chapter 6: Establishing Observability Foundations in Istio: Infrastructure, Tracing, and Metrics 291

Introduction to Istio Telemetry 291
    The Three Pillars of Observability: Metrics, Logs, and Traces 292
    How Istio's Telemetry Architecture Works 294
    Overview of Istio's Telemetry API and Configuration 295
    Evolution from Mixer-Based to Mixerless Telemetry 296
Setting Up the Observability Stack 297
    Prerequisites and Environment Setup 297
    Installing the Observability Stack with Helm 297
    Verifying Your Observability Stack Installation 302
    Reinstalling Istio with Observability Configuration 305
    Sample Application 307
Telemetry API 314
Distributed Tracing 315
    Configuring Tracing 318
    Distributed Tracing with Jaeger 324
    Configuring Trace Sampling and Trace Tags 329

TABLE OF CONTENTS

Metrics Collection with Prometheus 332
    Understanding Istio's Metrics Architecture 333
    Standard Istio Metrics 338
    Standard Envoy Proxy Metrics 348
    Configuring Custom Metrics 355
    Best Practices for Metrics Collection in Istio 364

Conclusion 366

Chapter 7: Visualizing and Analyzing Service Mesh Data: Grafana, Kiali, and Logging 369

Introduction 369

Visualization with Grafana 370
    Setting Up Grafana with Istio 370
    Understanding Default Istio Dashboards 372
    Creating Custom Dashboards for Specific Use Cases 382
    Embracing the Power of Visualization with Grafana 392

Service Mesh Visualization with Kiali 392
    Understanding Kiali's Role in Service Mesh Management 393
    Setting Up and Configuring Kiali 394
    Service Topology Visualization 394
    Traffic Management Features 396
    Workload Management and Analysis 399
    Best Practices for Kiali Usage 402

Log Aggregation and Analysis 403
    Understanding Istio's Logging Architecture 404
    Configuring Access Logs 406
    Configuring Access Log Output and Format 413

Conclusion and Future Trends 415

Chapter 8: Deploying Istio in Production 417

Introduction 417
Objective 418
Outline 418
Single-Cluster Deployment 418
    Introduction to Amazon EKS 419
    Deploying Istio on the EKS Cluster 430
    Fine-Tuning in Single-Cluster Mode 434
Scaling Istio Beyond Single-Cluster Mode 435
    Primary–Remote Deployment Model 435
    Multi-primary Deployment Model 436
    Multi-network Deployment 437
    Determining the Best Fit 438
Conclusion 438
References 439

Chapter 9: Extending Istio with Custom Plugins 441

Introduction 441
Istio Extensibility 441
    Understanding Istio's Extension Points 442
    WebAssembly and Its Role in Istio 445
    Use Cases for Extending Istio 445
WebAssembly Plugins in Istio 446
    WebAssembly Fundamentals 448
    Introduction to Proxy-Wasm 451
    The WebAssembly Architecture in Istio 453
    How Envoy Uses WebAssembly Plugins 454
    Supported Programming Languages (C++, Rust, AssemblyScript) 456
Developing Envoy WebAssembly Plugins 457
    Setting Up the Development Environment 457
    Using the Proxy-Wasm C++ SDK 460

    Building and Deploying Plugins 466

    Deep Dive into the WebAssembly Plugin Architecture 479

  EnvoyFilter and Wasm 486

    Key Components and Architecture 487

    Deploying WebAssembly with EnvoyFilter 488

    Filter Chain Positioning and Operations 490

    Traffic Direction and Context Types 492

    WebAssembly Module Configuration and Initialization 493

    WebAssembly Binary Distribution Options 495

    Namespace Scoping and Mesh-Wide Deployment 497

    Handling Multiple EnvoyFilters and Precedence 499

    Practical Application Patterns 501

  Implementation and Troubleshooting 505

    Testing WebAssembly Plugins 506

    Monitoring and Troubleshooting 509

  Best Practices 516

    Development Best Practices 516

    Operational Best Practices 519

  Conclusion 522

Chapter 10: Emerging Trends and the Future of Istio 523

  The Current State and Future Roadmap 523

  Emerging Technologies and Integration 525

  Competitive Landscape and Market Evolution 526

  Edge Computing and IoT Integration 527

  The Role of Service Mesh in AI and Machine Learning Workloads 528

  MLOps and Istio's Role in Decentralized Machine Learning 528

  Istio's Role in Federated Learning 532

  Skills and Technologies for the Future 536

  Adapting and Transitioning for Organizations 537

  Case Studies and Research Initiatives 537

Enterprise Case Studies 537
Research and Development Initiatives 540
Emerging Research Areas 542
Future Research Directions 544
Conclusion 545

Index **547**

About the Authors

Prashanth Josyula is a seasoned IT professional based in San Francisco, USA, with over 17 years of experience in the IT industry. He specializes in AI, machine learning, Kubernetes, and service mesh technologies. As Principal Member of Technical Staff (PMTS) at Salesforce, he plays a pivotal role in architecting scalable, intelligent, and resilient cloud-native infrastructures, integrating AI-driven automation with modern distributed systems. Prashanth frequently speaks at and participates in industry-leading conferences, focusing on cutting-edge topics such as ML/AI Ops, retrieval-augmented generation (RAG), AI agents, responsible AI, and time-series analysis.

Karanbir Singh is currently Senior Software Engineer at Salesforce and, with almost a decade of experience leading AI/ML engineering and distributed systems, is an active contributor to the AI and software engineering community, frequently speaking at and participating in industry-leading conferences on cutting-edge technologies such as retrieval-augmented generation (RAG), AI agents, responsible AI, and time-series analysis.

ABOUT THE AUTHORS

Anupam Mehta is a distinguished security engineer with over a decade of expertise in threat modeling, infrastructure security, DevSecOps, and product and application security. He currently serves as Product Security Engineer at Stripe, where he leads security assessments for core and critical systems, ensuring the integrity and resilience of Stripe's infrastructure. Anupam's work involves deep-dive security evaluations of software supply chains, reinforcing the security of modern cloud-native environments.

About the Technical Reviewers

Rupesh Dabbir is a highly accomplished Engineering Leader at Google, driving critical data visualization initiatives that empower millions of users globally. With over 12 years of experience at leading organizations like PayPal and Atlassian, he specializes in engineering excellence, product innovation, and strategic leadership. His technical expertise spans frontend engineering, AI, and cloud technologies, enabling him to build and lead high-performing teams focused on user-centric outcomes.

Beyond his core engineering roles, Rupesh is a recognized thought leader and active participant in the tech community. He contributes through talks at JSConf, organized events, and mentorship, sharing his passion for web technologies and leadership best practices. A member of the Forbes Technology Council and a mentor at Plato, he is committed to fostering innovation and excellence. Rupesh's achievements include multiple hackathon victories and awards from National Geographic for his photography, demonstrating his diverse talents and commitment to excellence. Outside of work, he enjoys hiking and photography. For more insights into his professional journey, visit rupeshdabbir.com.

Faseela K is a cloud-native developer at Ericsson, CNCF Technical Oversight Committee Member, and a maintainer and Steering Committee member of Istio service mesh. She is the co-chair for KubeCon EU + NA 2025 and also the past co-chair of the KubeCon co-located Istio Days. She is CNCF Ambassador, LFX Mentor, and the winner of the prestigious CNCF "Chop Wood Carry Water" award, 2023. She is also the creator of *Izzy Saves the Birthday*, a children's illustrated book from Istio.

For more information, you can refer to `https://docs.google.com/document/d/1muzXVLrL3S7hsOjLctbwlAR77cz-69vBFDbfzq0CPvo/edit?usp=sharing`.

Introduction

What Is This Book About?

This book is a deep and structured exploration of Istio, designed to guide readers from the foundational concepts of service meshes to advanced production-ready deployments and custom integrations. With each chapter authored by a domain expert, the book blends conceptual clarity with real-world practicality. Whether you're a DevOps engineer, architect, or platform specialist, this guide equips you with the tools and patterns needed to confidently adopt, manage, and extend Istio in complex environments.

Chapter 1: Introduction to Istio

by Karanbir

This chapter introduces the concept of a service mesh and explores the rationale behind Istio's emergence. It walks through the evolution of cloud-native architectures and where Istio fits in. Readers will learn the fundamental problems Istio solves and get a high-level overview of its components. It's an ideal starting point for both beginners and decision-makers evaluating service mesh solutions.

Chapter 2: Understanding Istio's Core Components

by Anupam

A deep dive into the architecture of Istio, this chapter examines the control plane, data plane, and key components such as Envoy, Istiod, and their roles in traffic and policy management. The focus is on understanding how Istio orchestrates service discovery, configuration, and secure communication. Readers will gain clarity on the internal workings that enable Istio's powerful capabilities. Hands-on examples in a later chapter make it easier to map theory to practice.

Chapter 3: Fundamentals of Traffic Management with Istio

by Prashanth

This chapter introduces Istio's traffic routing features such as virtual services, destination rules, retries, timeouts, and circuit breakers. It explains how these features enable granular control over service-to-service communication. Through practical examples, readers will learn to implement intelligent traffic flow patterns. The chapter provides the foundation for reliability, failover, and user experience optimization.

Chapter 4: Advanced Traffic Management Patterns and Gateway Control
by Prashanth
Expanding on basic traffic control, this chapter explores progressive delivery techniques like canary deployments, traffic mirroring, and A/B testing. Readers will understand how to roll out features incrementally and validate changes in real time. The chapter also covers fault injection for chaos testing and service resilience. These advanced techniques empower teams to deploy with confidence and control.

Chapter 5: Securing Microservices with Istio
by Anupam
Security is a first-class citizen in Istio, and this chapter covers authentication, authorization, and encryption. Readers will learn how to enable mutual TLS (mTLS) and enforce and secure service-to-service communication by default. It also explores how Istio integrates with identity providers and certificate authorities. Practical guidance ensures security best practices are applied without compromising developer agility.

Chapter 6: Establishing Observability Foundations in Istio: Infrastructure, Tracing, and Metrics
by Prashanth
Observability is essential for understanding service behavior and performance. This chapter explains how Istio captures telemetry and integrates with systems like Prometheus and Jaeger. Readers will learn to configure tracing and metrics pipelines for full visibility into requests and workloads. The content lays the groundwork for proactive monitoring and root cause analysis in distributed systems.

Chapter 7: Visualizing and Analyzing Service Mesh Data: Grafana, Kiali, and Logging
by Prashanth
This chapter introduces the visualization tools that enhance Istio's observability—Kiali for topology and traffic flow, Grafana for dashboards, and logging for deep-dive diagnostics. It provides steps to deploy and configure each tool within the mesh. Readers will learn how to correlate logs, metrics, and traces for end-to-end insight. These practices improve both operational awareness and developer productivity.

Chapter 8: Deploying Istio in Production

by Karanbir

Focusing on real-world production deployments, this chapter explores scaling Istio for high-traffic environments and tuning it for optimal performance. It also explains how to integrate Istio into CI/CD pipelines for automated testing and deployment. The final section addresses multi-cluster and hybrid cloud scenarios, providing guidance for global services and multi-region architectures. This chapter is essential for platform teams.

Chapter 9: Extending Istio with Custom Plugins

by Prashanth

For teams with advanced requirements, this chapter shows how to extend Istio using WebAssembly (Wasm) plugins and Envoy filters. It walks through the use cases where native capabilities need to be enhanced or replaced. Readers will learn about the plugin lifecycle and safe practices for introducing custom behavior. This content enables deeper mesh customization tailored to business needs.

Chapter 10: Emerging Trends and the Future of Istio

by Anupam

The closing chapter looks ahead to Istio's evolving role in cloud-native infrastructure. Readers will also get insights into community developments, roadmap updates, and how Istio is adapting to the broader Kubernetes (K8s) and platform engineering movements. This chapter is both reflective and forward-looking.

CHAPTER 1

Introduction to Istio

Introduction

In the 2000s, backend systems typically utilized monolithic architectures. In this architecture, the user interface, business logic, and data access layers were tightly coupled and worked together as a cohesive application. This simplified the initial development and deployment of the application because all functionality was contained in a single codebase, and communication between components was frequently handled internally within the monolith itself. However, as applications became more intricate and popular, this method began to demonstrate significant drawbacks such as scalability, single point of failure, lack of flexibility, technical debt, etc. To mitigate these problems the microservices architecture was developed. This architecture separates an application into smaller, independent services, each in charge of a particular function. This provides higher scalability, flexibility, and resilience. Also, the ownership of these services by different teams enabled them to independently build, test, and deploy these services. However, microservices architecture came up with its drawbacks especially in designing the interactions between services. Again, to mitigate these problems, the service mesh technology was developed as an infrastructure layer to make it easier and more consistent for microservices to talk to each other. In service mesh solutions, Istio has become the market leader, thanks to its many features that meet the needs of current cloud-native environments. From advanced traffic routing to end-to-end encryption, Istio is designed to enhance the scalability, security, and reliability of microservices at scale.

CHAPTER 1   INTRODUCTION TO ISTIO

Objective

This chapter seeks to explain service mesh technology and build the foundation for its useful application. Istio is a crucial component of contemporary cloud systems. These fundamental ideas will get you ready for practical tasks and more complex Istio subjects in later chapters. After reading the chapter, you will

- Recognize the importance of a service mesh and its definition.
- Examine the distinctive architecture and characteristics of Istio.
- Set up a Kubernetes cluster locally.
- Install Istio.

Outline

In order to understand service mesh technology and its importance, it is essential to know about microservices and Kubernetes. So this chapter will first introduce microservices and challenges associated with microservices. After introducing the microservices, we will formally define a service mesh and provide an overview of the architecture, comparing different frameworks that are available. Finally, we will go over Kubernetes and its architecture as it plays a key role in deploying Istio. We will use Kind (Kubernetes IN Docker) to deploy the Kubernetes cluster in your local machine.

What Are Microservices?

Microservices architecture is a software architecture that has completely disrupted the way that applications are planned, created, and maintained. The idea is to divide the applications into smaller, independent services, which led developers to create and manage complex applications more quickly and robustly by focusing on modularity, flexibility, and scalability. In a microservices architecture, every service functions as a standalone module and focuses on a particular business functionality. Other than that, the introduction of cloud computing and modern software development processes made this architectural style the preferred choice of software engineers. As an example, an ecommerce platform can consist of independent services like product catalog service, shopping cart service, order service, recommendation system, and payment service. These services are loosely coupled and focus on one functionality, for example, the product catalog service is responsible for managing a catalog of products.

Characteristics of Microservices

The following are the key features of the microservices architecture that distinguish it from other architectural approaches.

Decentralization

Unlike monolithic systems, which share a single database, microservices enable decentralized data management. Every service has its data, which is typically stored in a database designed to fulfill its specific requirements.

Separation of Concerns

In microservices architecture, teams are not forced to use a single technology stack as different services are independently developed and deployed. Depending on the specific use case, a team may decide to use a different database, framework, or programming language that is suitable for building highly efficient service.

Scalability

Microservices enable finer-grained scalability. For example, an ecommerce application's order service can scale independently when it detects a large number of orders being placed through the website without affecting any other service in the system.

Fault Isolation

The failure of one service does not always bring down the entire system. For example, a temporary failure in a recommendation service should not interfere with an ecommerce application's checkout process.

Challenges of Microservices Architecture

While microservices have completely transformed applications by providing better scalability, flexibility, and agility, they come with their own suite of challenges. The following issues are the challenges associated with microservices.

Traffic Management Complexity

In a microservices architecture, every service may communicate with multiple services, which creates a web of interdependencies. In order to ensure that traffic is routed correctly and the load is balance across instances, management of retries and failovers without service disruptions requires intricate configuration and careful tuning. Traditional approaches depend on external load balancers, which can become bottlenecks as the system continues to scale.

Security Risks in Distributed Systems

In a zero-trust environment where services may be distributed across many clusters or cloud regions, safeguarding intercommunication among them becomes critical. Microservices require mutual TLS (mTLS) encryption, authentication, and fine-grained authorization for all interactions. Implementing and maintaining these security measures without centralized control can be error-prone and time-consuming.

Observability Gaps

To understand the health and performance of the system, it is essential to gain visibility into each service and its upstream and downstream service communication. A naive distributed architecture lacks centralized monitoring, and therefore it is harder to trace requests, diagnose issues, and improve system performance. Traditional monitoring technologies were not built to handle the dynamic and transitory nature of microservices, and therefore it leaves teams with insufficient information to mitigate issues before they turn into a bigger system-wide outage.

Resilience and Fault Tolerance

In a distributed system, service failures are inevitable, and without proper mechanisms for circuit breaking, retries, or timeouts, these failures can cascade and lead to widespread outages. Building such resilience into each service individually is both time-consuming and difficult to standardize.

Operational Overhead

In a distributed system that follows microservices architecture, each microservice manages its communication logic, and the burden on the teams increases significantly. Updating communication policies, debugging issues, or rolling out new features often requires touching multiple services, which slows down development cycles and introduces potential risks.

What Is a Service Mesh?

Now we know that services communicate frequently to fulfill business processes, which leads to the challenges mentioned above. A service mesh abstracts away the complexity of these interactions by introducing a proxy-based communication layer. So let's formally define it.

A service mesh can be defined as a dedicated infrastructure layer designed to handle service-to-service communication within a distributed application.

Service meshes are becoming essential for modern microservices architectures, providing a robust framework to manage communication between services. Figure 1-1 shows the key features of a service mesh, and we will discuss them in detail and their significance in streamlining service-to-service communication and maintaining system reliability.

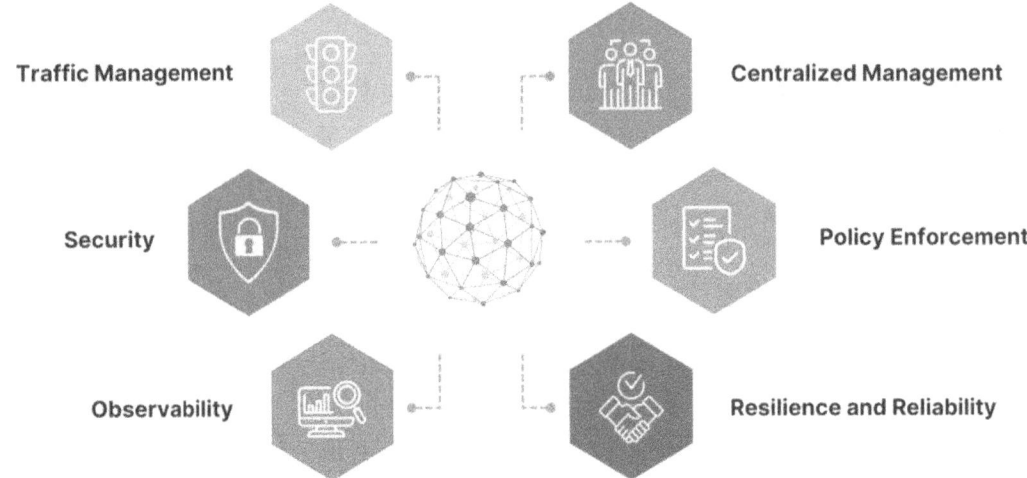

Figure 1-1. Key features of a service mesh

Traffic Management

It is a critical and the most important feature of a service mesh. It allows dynamic routing to intelligently direct requests depending on predefined policies, load, or geographical considerations. Load balancing distributes traffic evenly among service instances, improving resource usage and reducing overloads. Advanced traffic splitting capabilities enable canary deployments and A/B testing by directing a portion of traffic to new service versions or experimental features, and failover systems improve reliability by shifting traffic to healthy instances during service outages, hence resulting in minimal inconvenience to the service consumers.

Security

A service mesh follows a "never trust, always verify" strategy to secure communication even inside the same cluster. Therefore, it provides a sense of security and reliability with the help of mutual TLS (mTLS), which is responsible for encrypting communication across services while assuring confidentiality and authentication. Authentication and authorization mechanisms impose fine-grained access rules and restrict resource access to only approved users and services.

Observability

Observability tools embedded in service meshes provide complete information about system performance and health. Observability usually consists of distributed tracing, centralized logging, and real-time metrics, which helps in quicker triaging and analysis. These functionalities integrate with visualization tools such as Prometheus and Grafana to quickly build monitoring dashboards.

Resilience and Reliability

To preserve system health during unforeseen conditions, resilience and dependability are crucial components of any system. Service meshes enable retries and timeouts for unsuccessful requests, avoiding long wait times. When there is a need for an even more advanced mechanism, service meshes offer circuit breakers to maintain system stability by stopping requests and preventing cascading failures.

Policy Enforcement

In a service mesh, service policies govern communication protocols, authentication procedures, and encryption standards. Policy enforcement inside a service mesh assures compliance with organizational and operational requirements, for example, rate limiting and quotas ensure equitable resource allocation by establishing request thresholds and traffic shaping provides granular control over network traffic by applying filters or blocks based on predefined rules.

Platform Agnostic

Service meshes like Istio are platform agnostic, which enables a variety of contexts such as Kubernetes, virtual machines (VMs), and hybrid cloud infrastructures, and this flexibility makes adoption easier and provides seamless integration across diverse platforms.

Extensibility

Service meshes are built with extensibility in mind, allowing users to adapt the mesh's behavior to fit unique organizational requirements. Developers can create custom policies, extend observability capabilities, or embed custom logic into traffic flows.

Centralized Management

Last but not least, service meshes allow centralized management, which considerably minimizes operational overhead. Teams can create and enforce communication regulations, security protocols, and observability settings from a single control plane, which assures consistency and efficiency across all services.

To summarize, service meshes offer a robust framework for managing microservices, including improved traffic management, security, observability, dependability, and centralized control. Their platform independence and extensive feature set make them an invaluable resource for current software architectures.

Overview of Istio

Google, IBM, and Lyft joined forces to create Istio [10], an open source service mesh solution. It was launched in May 2017 to help organizations run microservices-based apps. Overall, it has two main components, i.e., data plane and control plane. Lyft contributed Envoy, the high-performance proxy that powers Istio's data plane. Let's briefly discuss them, and in upcoming chapters, we will discuss them in detail.

Data Plane

The data plane is responsible for managing all the actual communication between services within the mesh. It uses lightweight proxies, typically based on Envoy, to intercept and manage traffic.

Envoy Proxy

It is an open source proxy that acts as a sidecar for each service in the mesh. The sidecar is a proxy that is attached to each service instance in the mesh. It handles tasks such as traffic routing, load balancing, retries, timeouts, metrics, and log collection, and it enforces security policies.

Control Plane

It is the heart of Istio responsible for overseeing the configuration and policies that guide the behavior of the data plane. It collaborates with Envoy proxies to enforce policies, distribute configurations, and provide centralized control over the service mesh. In this book, we will be using the 1.24.2 version of Istio, and in this version, Istiod is the central component that consolidates core functionalities like service discovery, traffic management, security policies, and configuration distribution. The components that were present in previous versions like Pilot, Citadel, and telemetry are not standalone components anymore. This simplified architecture enables better performance, ease of deployment, and comprehensive control and meets the demands of modern cloud-native environments.

Comparing Istio and Other Service Mesh Solutions

There are multiple service mesh frameworks that have emerged to address the challenges of managing distributed services. Istio stands out as a feature-rich and widely adopted service mesh, and other solutions like Linkerd, Consul Connect, and AWS App Mesh offer unique capabilities tailored to different use cases. To better understand Istio, let's compare it with other leading service meshes, highlighting their strengths and differences to help you choose the best fit for their requirements. Table 1-1 depicts the key features that different service meshes support.

Table 1-1. *Comparison between different service mesh solutions*

Feature/Capability	Istio	Linkerd	Consul Connect	AWS App Mesh
Ease of use	Moderate	Easy	Moderate	Easy
Traffic management	Advanced	Basic	Basic	Moderate
Security (mTLS)	Advanced	Default	Advanced	Advanced
Observability	Comprehensive	Basic	Limited	Integrated with CloudWatch
Multi-cluster support	Yes	Limited	Yes	No
Hybrid environment	Limited	No	Yes	Limited to AWS
Performance overhead	High	Low	Moderate	Moderate
Integration	Kubernetes-first	Kubernetes-first	HashiCorp tools	AWS services
Open source	Yes	Yes	Yes	No

As shown in the table above, if you require fine-grained traffic management, robust security, and extensive observability for large-scale, complex systems, then Istio service mesh provides all these features. On the other hand, if you want to go for simplicity and lightweight needs, Linkerd is very easy to deploy and manage but lacks advanced features. For hybrid and multi-platform environments, Consul Connect works the best. For applications that are hosted in AWS, a fully managed solution AWS App Mesh is also available. To summarize, each service mesh implementation offers unique features, and the choice depends on the system's requirements, infrastructure setup, and organizational expertise.

Case Studies of Istio

Istio has been proven to significantly improve service communication, security, scalability, and dependability across multiple domains. Below are few case studies that are available over the Internet of its implementation.

Rappi [2]

A prominent Latin American super-app, active in nine countries, encountered difficulties in overseeing its swiftly growing infrastructure, comprising over 50 Kubernetes clusters and exceeding 20,000 containers. To tackle these problems, Rappi implemented Istio, which facilitated comprehensive service monitoring at scale, adaptable traffic management, and strong security features. This implementation allowed Rappi to manage more than 1,500 deployments daily while ensuring efficient, scalable, and secure connectivity among its services.

Cash App [3]

The Cash App team migrated from a proprietary Envoy service mesh to Istio to enhance the management of their microservices architecture. This action was motivated by the necessity for a more intuitive and comprehensive solution to manage service-to-service communication, security, and observability. The implementation of Istio enhanced traffic management, security protocols, and monitoring functionalities and therefore fostered a more efficient and dependable service infrastructure.

T-Mobile

T-Mobile used Istio across more than 100 clusters to facilitate their microservices for fraud detection, billing, sales, and other services. The extensive deployment necessitated meticulous evaluation of tenancy, installation, updates, feature acceptance, CI/CD integration, and architectural compromises. Istio's comprehensive capabilities allowed T-Mobile to properly encrypt and monitor microservices, guaranteeing dependable and secure communication throughout their vast infrastructure.

Salesforce [4]

Salesforce, a worldwide leader in customer relationship management (CRM), incorporated Istio and Envoy as essential elements of its service mesh design. Salesforce first created an internal control plane utilizing Envoy but later migrated to Istio because of its extensive features and community backing. This helped Salesforce to optimize service discovery, traffic management, and security, which led to enhanced operational efficiency and scalability.

Mindtickle

Mindtickle is a sales preparation platform that oversees more than 300 microservices within its AWS Elastic Kubernetes Service (EKS) infrastructure. They used Istio to guarantee high availability and resilience due to its sophisticated network management and security capabilities. The improved observability offered greater insight into measures like requests per second and latency, while topology-aware networking diminished data transfer expenses.

Airbnb [5]

Airbnb, a global online marketplace for lodging and experiences, adopted Istio to manage its complex microservices architecture. Istio's extensibility, broad feature support, and scalability made it a suitable choice for Airbnb's needs. By implementing Istio, Airbnb improved service discovery, traffic management, and security across its services, leading to enhanced operational efficiency and reliability.

Autotrader UK

Autotrader UK, a leading digital automotive marketplace, utilized Istio to streamline communication between its microservices. By adopting Istio, Autotrader achieved better traffic management, observability, and security within its service infrastructure. This implementation facilitated smoother deployments and improved overall system performance.

These instances illustrate how firms in various sectors utilize Istio to improve their service management functionalities.

What Is Kubernetes?

Google created Kubernetes (K8s), an orchestration platform that automates the deployment and management of containerized applications. Later in 2015, Kubernetes was donated to the Cloud Native Computing Foundation (CNCF). Since then it has grown in popularity to become one of the most popular open source projects. It is generally considered the industry standard for container orchestration, providing a uniform platform for managing containerized workloads. K8s is critical to Istio because it provides the infrastructure and orchestration capabilities needed for the service mesh to be deployed and managed smoothly. Therefore, before deep-diving into Istio, it is critical to gain a thorough understanding of the platform. It is not possible to provide a detailed walkthrough of the platform because it demands its own book. To obtain a complete grasp of K8s, you can reference *Kubernetes in Action* by Marko Lukša.

Architecture

Kubernetes operates on a master–slave architecture, with the control plane serving as the master responsible for managing the cluster and its state. The worker nodes are the nodes designated for the deployment of containerized applications. The control plane determines the deployment location of the application depending on available resources and additional considerations. This architecture seeks to provide a scalable, resilient, and modular foundation for managing containerized applications. Figure 1-2 depicts the platform's architecture.

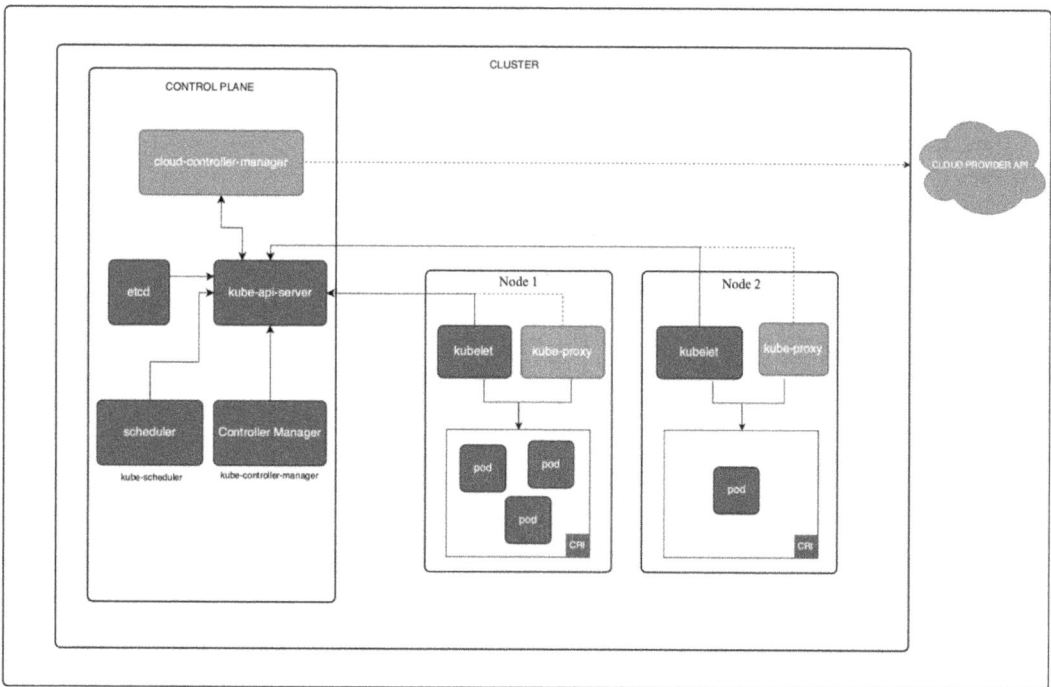

Figure 1-2. High-level architecture of K8s [1]

CHAPTER 1   INTRODUCTION TO ISTIO

Control Plane

The control plane is the most important component of the cluster, and it is responsible for overseeing the overall state of the cluster and ensuring alignment between the desired and actual states of the system. The subsequent elements are located within the control plane:

- API Server: The K8s API server functions as the interface for the control plane. It is based on the REST API framework and is responsible for all API calls from users, CLI tools (e.g., kubectl), or other components. It is also responsible for modifying the cluster state in the etcd store and guarantees security via authentication, authorization, and access control.

- etcd: It is a distributed, consistent, and highly available key-value store utilized as Kubernetes' backend store for all cluster data. It maintains configuration details, metadata, and cluster state permanently. Their elevated availability guarantees the cluster state remains uniform despite control plane failures.

- Controller Manager: The controller manager is a daemon that is responsible for managing different controllers in order to manage the cluster state. The following are some of the important controllers that are being managed by the controller manager:

  - Node Controller: It monitors the health of nodes and performs recovery actions for failed nodes.

  - Replication Controller: It ensures the desired number of pod replicas is running.

  - Endpoint Controller: It ensures proper communication between service and pods.

  - Service Account Controller: It is responsible for creating and managing service accounts for pods.

- Scheduler: The scheduler allocates tasks to worker nodes according to resource specifications, limitations, and regulations. Considered factors encompass CPU, memory, affinity rules, and node availability.

- Cloud Controller Manager: Cloud Controller Manager integrates Kubernetes with cloud provider APIs to administer resources such as load balancers, storage, and network configurations.

Worker Nodes

These are the devices (either real or virtual) that execute containerized workloads. Each node comprises the essential components to perform and oversee various workloads. Each worker node operates the containerized apps and comprises components for executing, monitoring, and managing these workloads. The following are the components that form a worker node:

- Kubelet

    The kubelet is an agent that runs on each worker node and communicates with the control plane. It ensures that the containers defined in the pod specifications are running and healthy. It monitors pod status and reports it back to the API server.

- Kube-Proxy

    It is a network proxy that operates on each worker node to regulate networking rules. It guarantees seamless communication across pods, services, etc. by establishing IP tables.

- Container Runtime

    The container runtime is the software responsible for running containers. Docker Engine is one of the most popular container runtimes, but other choices include containerd and CRI-O.

- Pods

    A pod is the smallest deployable unit in Kubernetes and represents one or more containers that share resources such as storage, network, and environment variables. Pods are created, scheduled, and managed by the control plane.

CHAPTER 1 INTRODUCTION TO ISTIO

Key Features of Kubernetes

Figure 1-3 illustrates the essential characteristics of Kubernetes that help enterprises to construct highly available and scalable systems.

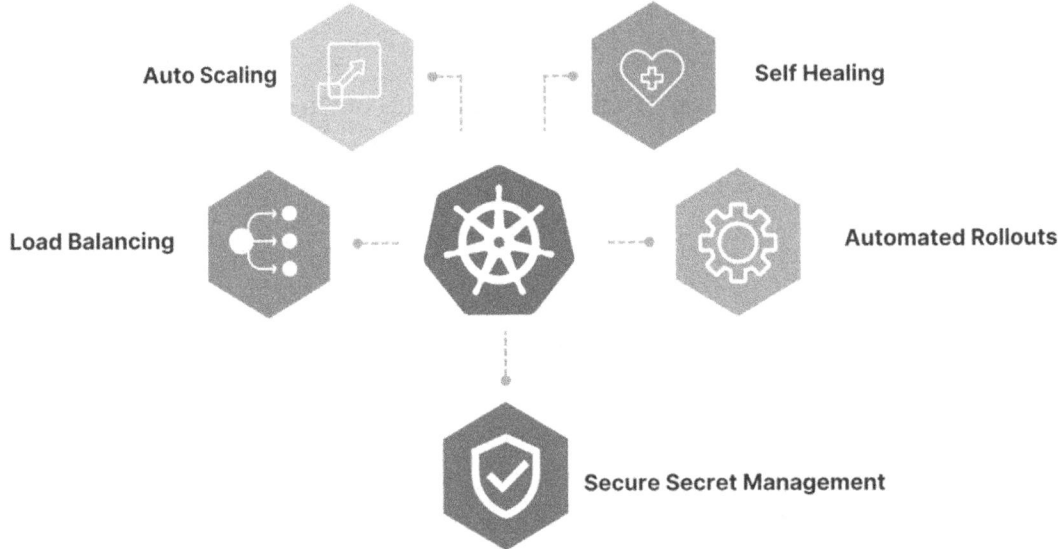

Figure 1-3. *Key features of Kubernetes*

Autoscaling

K8's notable capability is its ability to independently scale deployments according to real-time demand. Autoscaling ensures that applications maintain responsiveness during traffic spikes and cost efficiency during low-demand periods. It eliminates the need for manual intervention and also ensures that deployments scale dynamically in response to patterns of usage. Let's take a quick look at some of the Kubernetes scaling options:

Horizontal Pod Autoscaler (HPA)
The HPA adjusts the number of replicas in a deployment based on resources such as CPU and memory. For example, when CPU utilization surpasses a specified threshold, then the HPA scales up pods to manage the load.

Vertical Pod Autoscaler (VPA)
It automatically adjusts the CPU and memory resources allocated to a pod to optimize resource utilization based on the usage pattern. This particular type of scaling is less popular when using K8s, but it's still available as an option.

Cluster Autoscaler

It dynamically adds or removes worker nodes from the cluster to meet scaling demands, optimizing resource usage at the infrastructure level.

Self-Healing Capabilities

In order to keep the system highly available, self-healing characteristics are essential. It also eliminates the need for manual intervention and auto-heals the system, thus minimizing downtime. Kubernetes conducts health assessments to ascertain if a pod is operational (liveness) and prepared to handle traffic using liveness and readiness probes. The following actions can be taken to self-heal the deployments:

- Pod Restarting: When a pod malfunctions or becomes unresponsive, Kubernetes initiates a restart.

- Rescheduling: In the event of a node failure, Kubernetes reallocates pods to operational nodes to maintain application continuity.

Automated Rollouts and Rollbacks

Kubernetes streamlines application changes with automated rollouts, ensuring high availability. It ensures the secure deployment of new features without downtime and safeguards rollbacks to facilitate rapid recovery in the event of deployment failures.

- Rolling Updates: Kubernetes executes incremental, zero-downtime updates by substituting pods incrementally, i.e., it doesn't stop all the pods at once but rather initiates a pod with an updated version and then waits for it to get stable before moving the traffic to new pods and stopping older pods. This guarantees that the application remains highly available during version rollouts.

- Rollback Capability: K8s facilitates the automatic rollback to a stable version in order to minimize service interruptions.

Load Balancing

Load balancing in a distributed system guarantees the equitable distribution of workloads to prevent the overburdening of any individual resource. Kubernetes conducts liveness and readiness probes at a regular time interval to monitor pod status, ensuring that traffic is allocated to healthy pods. Unhealthy pods are automatically circumvented until they recuperate. Kubernetes enables load balancing in the following ways:

- Internal Load Balancing: Kubernetes uniformly allocates incoming requests among several pods within a service to guarantee optimal resource utilization.

- External Load Balancing: Kubernetes can deliver services to external clients by interfacing with cloud providers or ingress controllers, thereby efficiently directing traffic.

Secure Secret Management

Secure management of sensitive information is essential for modern-day applications. K8s streamlines secret management and prevents the hardcoding of sensitive information such as passwords within containers to enhance application security. It offers means for the secure management of sensitive information, including passwords, API keys, etc., through its Secrets resource. The following are the key features of the secret management in K8s:

- Encrypted Storage: Secrets are securely stored within the cluster and can be encrypted at rest to avert unauthorized access.

- Fine-Grained Access Control: Kubernetes employs role-based access control (RBAC) for fine-grained access control, ensuring that only authorized services or users can access secrets.

- Dynamic Updates: Secrets may be modified without restarting a pod, and this enables applications to adjust with changes effortlessly.

Now that we understand the internals of Kubernetes and Istio, it should be easy to figure out that they are the backbone of modern, production-level clusters. They address the critical challenges of deploying and managing distributed applications. Let's briefly recap their significance in production environments.

Orchestration and Automation with Kubernetes

Kubernetes provides the foundational layer for managing containerized workloads, ensuring applications run reliably even as demand fluctuates. Features like autoscaling, self-healing, etc. make K8s crucial to maintaining highly available and resilient applications in production environments.

Enhancing Service-to-Service Communication with Istio

Istio provides an essential standardized way of communication, enhancing security and observability in distributed systems. Features like traffic management and zero-trust security enable teams to develop and manage efficient and observable systems even in production.

Set Up a Local Environment

With this foundational understanding, it's time to translate theory into practice. Let's set up a local environment where you can experience the power of Kubernetes and Istio firsthand. This setup will enable you to

- Deploy containerized applications with Kubernetes.
- Manage service-to-service communication, security, and observability using Istio.
- Experiment with advanced traffic management and monitoring tools.

In the following steps, we'll guide you through installing Kubernetes with Kind and setting up Istio. By the end of this exercise, you'll have a fully functional environment ready for hands-on experimentation. Let's get started!

Installing Prerequisites

To begin working with Kubernetes and Istio, you'll need to install and configure the necessary tools on your local machine. Follow these step-by-step instructions to set up Docker, kubectl, Kind, and Helm.

CHAPTER 1   INTRODUCTION TO ISTIO

Install Docker

Docker is a platform that enables you to build, deploy, and manage applications in lightweight, portable containers. Containers package the application and its dependencies, ensuring it runs consistently across different environments. Docker serves as the container runtime for creating and managing Kubernetes clusters.

For macOS:

- If you are running macOS 10.10.3 (Yosemite) or later, follow these instructions to install Docker Desktop for Mac.
- Download Docker Desktop for Mac and drag and drop Docker App to the Applications folder as shown in Figure 1-4.

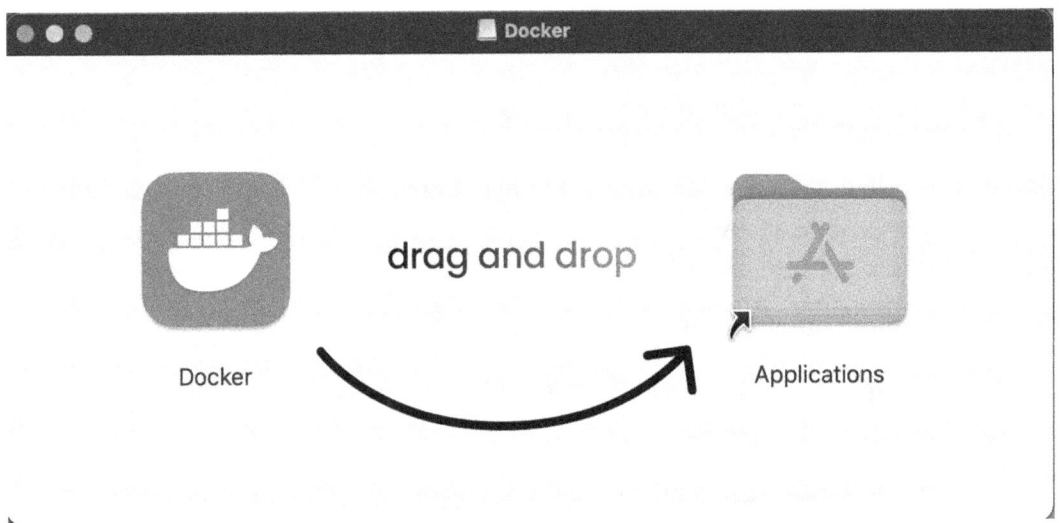

Figure 1-4. *Install Docker by dragging and dropping the Docker app to Applications*

For Linux: Use the following commands and ensure you are logged in as a user with sudo privileges [6]:

```
#Verify if curl is installed by running

which curl

#If curl is not installed, update your package manager and install it

sudo apt-get update
sudo apt-get install curl

# Use curl to download and install the latest Docker package:
```

```
curl -fsSL https://get.docker.com/ | sh
```

```
# Add your account to the docker group to run Docker commands without sudo
```

```
sudo usermod -aG docker <your_username>
```

```
# NOTE: Replace <your_username> with your Linux username. Log out and log back in for the changes to take effect.
```

```
# Run the Docker hello-world container to confirm installation:
```

```
docker run hello-world
```

If the installation is successful, you will see a message like this:

Hello from Docker.
This message shows that your installation appears to be working correctly.

Now Docker is successfully installed and ready to use on your Linux system!

Install kubectl

kubectl is the Kubernetes command-line tool for interacting with your cluster. The following are the steps to install it:

For macOS [7]:

- Download kubectl using curl as shown in Figure 1-5:

    ```
    curl -LO "https://dl.k8s.io/release/$(curl -L -s https://dl.k8s.io/release/stable.txt)/bin/darwin/arm64/kubectl"
    ```

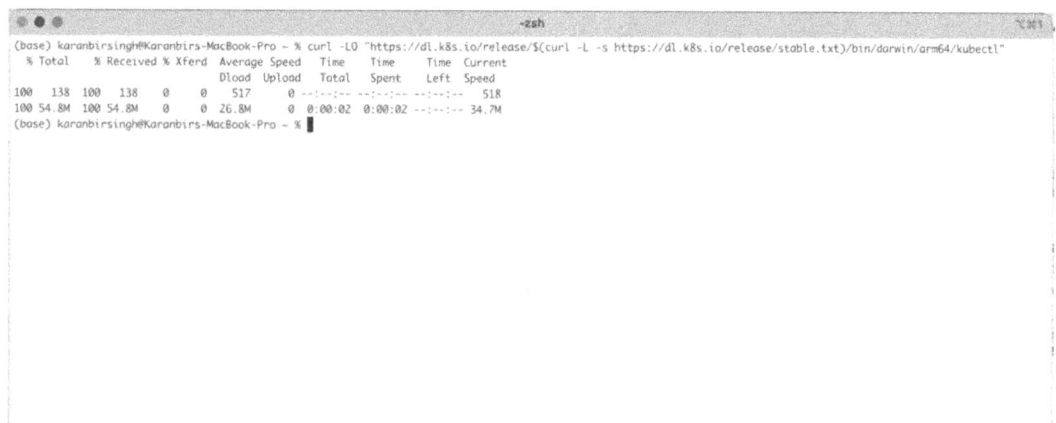

Figure 1-5. *Download kubectl using curl*

CHAPTER 1   INTRODUCTION TO ISTIO

- Validate:

    ```
    curl -LO "https://dl.k8s.io/release/$(curl -L -s https://dl.k8s.
    io/release/stable.txt)/bin/darwin/amd64/kubectl.sha256"
    echo "$(cat kubectl.sha256) kubectl" | shasum -a 256 -check
    ```

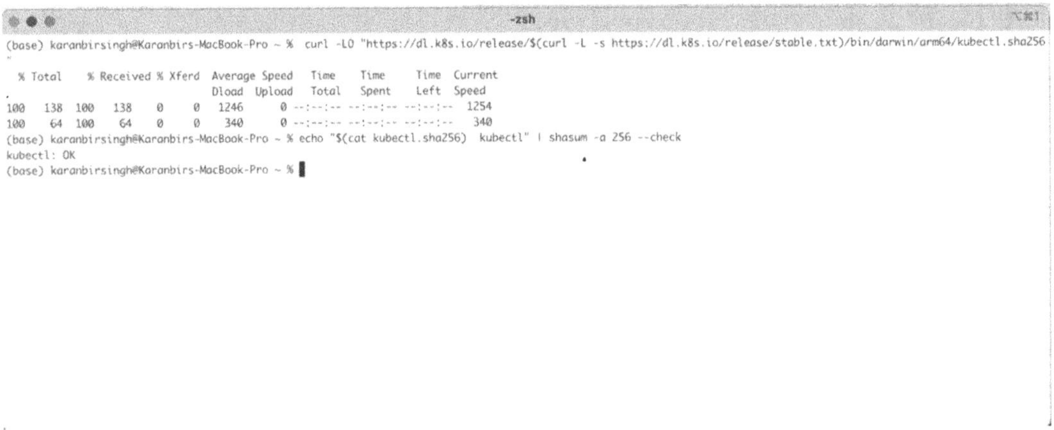

Figure 1-6. *Validate kubectl using sha256*

For Linux:

- Download kubectl:

    ```
    curl -LO "https://dl.k8s.io/release/$(curl -L -s https://dl.k8s.
    io/release/stable.txt)/bin/linux/amd64/kubectl"
    ```

- Validate:

    ```
    curl -LO "https://dl.k8s.io/release/$(curl -L -s https://dl.k8s.
    io/release/stable.txt)/bin/darwin/amd64/kubectl.sha256"
    echo "$(cat kubectl.sha256) kubectl" | sha256sum -check
    ```

If valid, the output is

kubectl ok

Install Kind

Kind (Kubernetes IN Docker) allows you to create Kubernetes clusters locally using Docker.

It was primarily designed for testing Kubernetes itself on the local system. The following are the steps to install Kind:

For Linux [8]:

- Download Kind:

  ```
  # For AMD64 / x86_64
  [ $(uname -m) = x86_64 ] && curl -Lo ./kind
  https://kind.sigs.k8s.io/dl/v0.26.0/kind-linux-amd64
  # For ARM64
  [ $(uname -m) = aarch64 ] && curl -Lo ./kind
  https://kind.sigs.k8s.io/dl/v0.26.0/kind-linux-arm64
  ```

- Move Kind to bin:

  ```
  chmod +x ./kind
  ```

  ```
  sudo mv ./kind /usr/local/bin/kind
  ```

For macOS:

- Using the package manager [9] brew is the easiest way to install Kind (The expected output of the command execution is shown in Figure 1-7):

  ```
  brew install kind
  ```

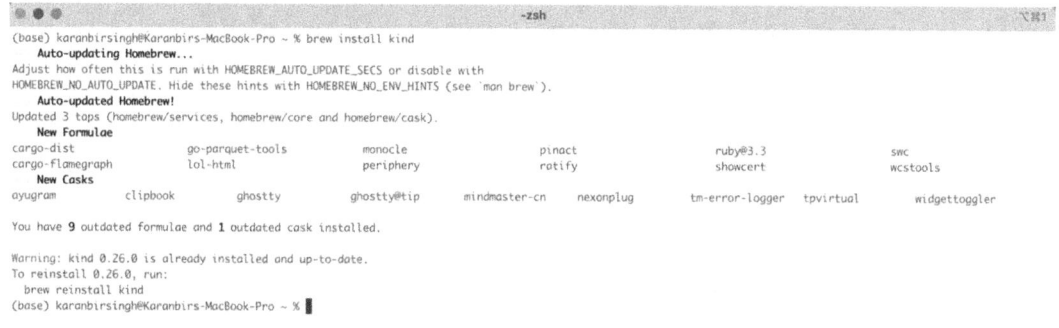

Figure 1-7. Execution of brew install kind

CHAPTER 1   INTRODUCTION TO ISTIO

To verify:

- This command will return the Kind version that is currently installed. At the time of writing this book, we are using 0.26.0 as shown in Figure 1-8:

  ```
  kind --version
  ```

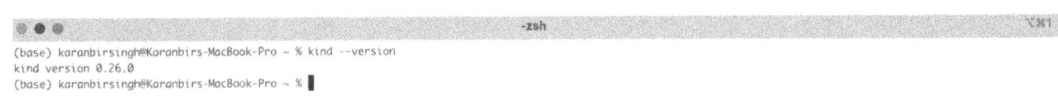

Figure 1-8. *Output of the version command showing the 0.26.0 version being used*

Install Helm

Now that we have Kind to easily set up the Kubernetes cluster, it is also a good idea to install Helm. Helm is a package manager for Kubernetes that helps users define, install, and manage applications in Kubernetes clusters. It simplifies the deployment of applications by bundling them into reusable packages called charts. Follow the underwritten steps to install Helm:

For Linux:

- Download the script and run it:

  ```
  curl -fsSL -o get_helm.sh
  https://raw.githubusercontent.com/helm/helm/main/scripts/get-helm-3
  chmod 700 get_helm.sh
  ./get_helm.sh
  ```

For macOS:

- Using the package manager brew is the easiest way to install Helm as shown in Figure 1-9:

  ```
  brew install helm
  ```

CHAPTER 1   INTRODUCTION TO ISTIO

Figure 1-9. *Installation of Helm using brew*

Set Up Istio

Now we have everything to set up Istio. The following are the steps that will create a demo Kubernetes cluster and set up Istio within the cluster. At the time of writing this book, version no. 1.24.0 is available. We will be using this version throughout the book.

Download Istio

curl -L https://istio.io/downloadIstio | sh - (expected output is shown in Figure 1-10)

cd istio-1.24.2

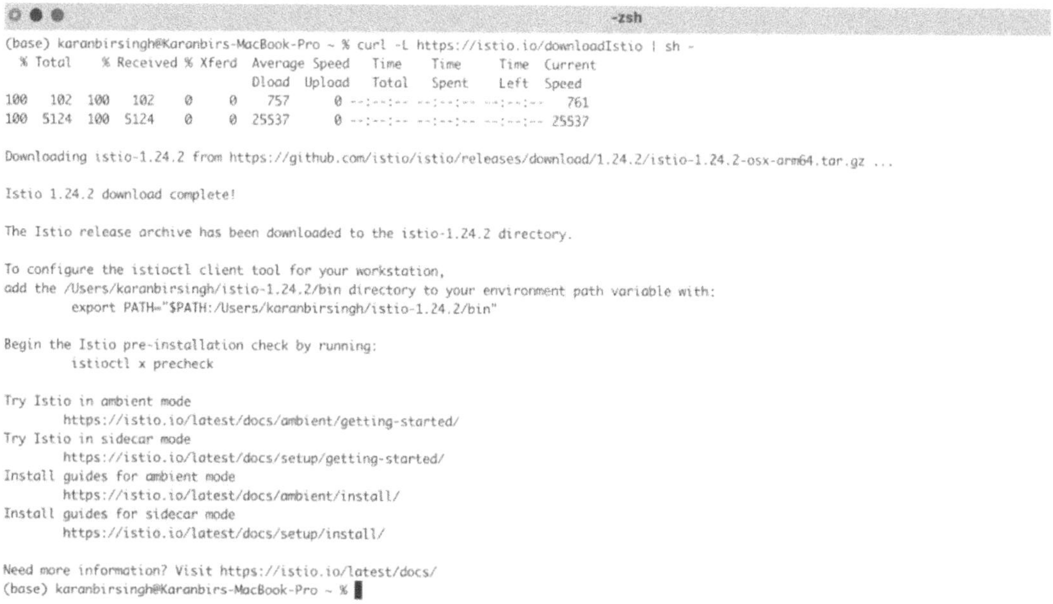

Figure 1-10. *Download Istio*

Add istioctl to PATH

export PATH=$PATH:$PWD/bin (expected output is shown in Figure 1-11)

Figure 1-11. *Add Istio bin to path*

Ideally, add this path to the .bashrc or .zshrc file to make it available in all terminal instances.

Install the Istio Control Plane

Let's create a Kubernetes cluster with the name istio-demo using Kind using the first command as shown in Figure 1-12. Kind helps in deploying the cluster seamlessly. Secondly, we will use *istioctl* to deploy Istio's control plane. The demo profile includes features like telemetry and tracing, making it suitable for experimentation:

```
kind create cluster --name istio-demo
istioctl install --set profile=demo -y
```

CHAPTER 1   INTRODUCTION TO ISTIO

Figure 1-12. *Creating a new K8s cluster using Kind and setting up Istio*

Verify Installation

Confirm Istio has been installed successfully by checking the running pods in the istio-system namespace:

```
kubectl get pods -n istio-system
```

You should see pods for Istio components like Istiod, istio-ingressgateway, and others as shown in Figure 1-13.

Figure 1-13. *Show all pods in the istio-system namespace*

Enable Namespace for Istio Injection

To allow Istio to manage traffic for applications in a namespace, enable automatic sidecar injection:

```
kubectl label namespace default istio-injection=enabled
```

Figure 1-14 shows the expected output of the execution of this command. With this step, Istio is properly set up in your system, and it is ready to be utilized in the rest of the book to understand its components.

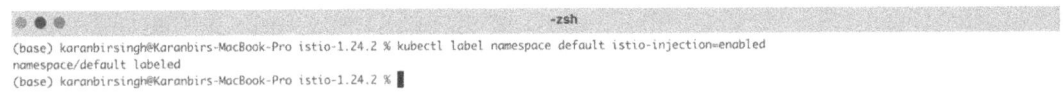

Figure 1-14. Enable Istio to manage traffic for applications

Conclusion

Istio provides a huge step forward in simplifying and improving service-to-service communication in microservices architectures. Istio helps enterprises construct durable and scalable distributed systems by solving difficulties such as traffic management, security, observability, and resilience. When combined with Kubernetes, which provides a solid basis for container orchestration, Istio allows developers and operations teams to quickly manage the intricacies of modern cloud-native applications. In this chapter, we also looked at the transition from monolithic architectures to microservices, the importance of service meshes, and Istio's features. We compared Istio with other service mesh platforms and investigated its unique features and use cases. The case studies illustrated how leading firms used Istio to improve operational efficiency and reliability at scale. Finally, we set up the local environment with Kubernetes and Istio.

We will examine Istio's architecture, parts, and sophisticated features in further detail in the next chapters. Additionally, you will learn how to encrypt your services, improve observability, create traffic controls, and optimize your apps for production-grade deployments. Now that you have this basic understanding and configuration, you are prepared to start learning Istio and how it works with contemporary cloud-native designs.

References

[1] https://kubernetes.io/docs/concepts/architecture/
[2] Rappi Case Study
[3] Cash App Case Study
[4] Salesforce Case Study
[5] Airbnb Case Study
[6] https://docs.sevenbridges.com/docs/install-docker-on-linux
[7] https://kubernetes.io/docs/tasks/tools/install-kubectl-macos/
[8] https://kind.sigs.k8s.io/docs/user/quick-start/#installing-from-release-binaries
[9] https://kind.sigs.k8s.io/docs/user/quick-start/#installing-with-a-package-manager
[10] https://istio.io/

CHAPTER 2

Understanding Istio's Core Components

Introduction

Modern cloud-native apps are largely composed of microservices, each of which handles a particular functionality. As the number of microservices increases, it becomes more difficult to ensure that they communicate safely, reliably, and clearly. Istio, as a service mesh, simplifies these complexities by adding a layer of abstraction to the microservices network.

This chapter examines Istio's architecture, specifically its core components and their roles in the service mesh. You will gain a high-level understanding of Istio's architecture and insights into Istio's service discovery, load balancing, traffic management, security, and telemetry. This chapter will go in depth from the unified control plane (Istiod) to the data plane (Envoy proxy).

By the end of this chapter, you will have the necessary knowledge of Istio's inner workings and architecture and the ability to build and configure Istio for your basic purposes. This chapter will also set the stage for establishing the groundwork for advanced subjects and configurations in setting up and deploying custom architectures with Istio.

CHAPTER 2   UNDERSTANDING ISTIO'S CORE COMPONENTS

The Case for Istio: Challenges in a Microservices Architecture Without a Service Mesh

Before we dive deep into Istio and its architecture, it's important to understand the need for Istio. Let's consider a simple microservices architecture running without it. Consider an ecommerce store that is made up of several microservices: frontend, product catalog, order service, and payment gateway. These services must interact with each other to handle user requests, process orders, and deliver notifications.

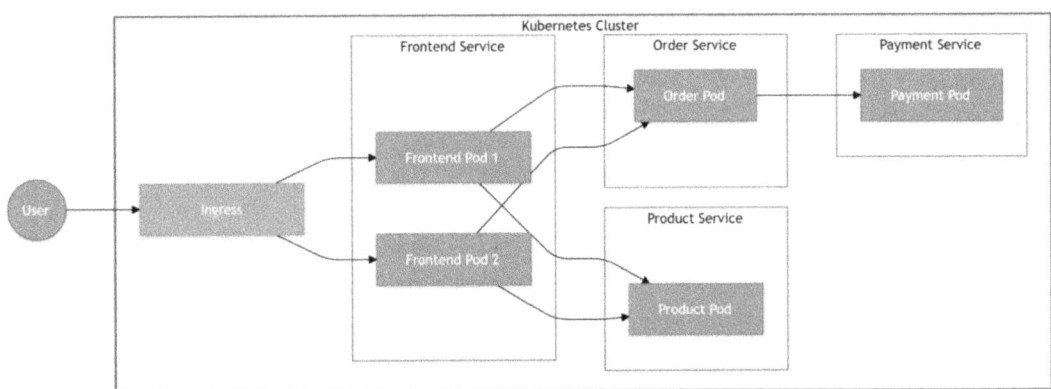

Figure 2-1. Microservices architecture without Istio

Each service is deployed independently and communicates directly with others in this setup. While Kubernetes (or similar platforms) provides basic functionalities like security, service discovery, and load balancing, various challenges arise without the support of Istio. A few of the challenges are described below:

- Manual Traffic Management: Each service needs custom logic to handle retries, timeouts, and fault tolerance. For example: If the payment gateway service is temporarily slow, the order service must handle retries and timeouts without overwhelming the gateway. Advanced traffic control scenarios like traffic shaping, weighted routing, or canary deployments are difficult to implement without writing complex custom logic or using third-party tools.

- Security Gaps: Encrypting communication between services requires the implementation and maintenance of mTLS (mutual TLS). Each service must manage and generate its TLS certificates, as well as implement authentication and authorization policies, to ensure that only trusted services communicate with each other. Without Istio, these tasks are typically carried out manually or with custom solutions that are error-prone and difficult to scale.

- Observability Challenges: Monitoring the system's health and diagnosing issues across multiple services requires consistent metrics, logs, and distributed tracing. In a setup without Istio, developers must instrument each service individually to collect telemetry data. Traces for a single request spanning multiple services (e.g., from frontend to payment gateway) are difficult to correlate, making it harder to identify performance bottlenecks or failures.

- Developer Overhead: Each service needs developers to write and maintain boilerplate code for traffic management, security, and observability. This not only slows down development but also results in inconsistent implementations, making the system extremely difficult to debug and maintain and increasing the developer overhead.

- Scaling and Resilience Challenges: Scaling specific services to meet traffic demands, along with implementing resilience patterns such as circuit breakers and failovers, requires significant effort. For example, if the notification service in our ecommerce example experiences an unexpected spike in traffic, Kubernetes can scale the pods; however, the application must still manage traffic efficiently to avoid failures. Services must manually detect unhealthy instances and reroute traffic, resulting in operational complexity.

The lack of a service mesh, such as Istio, in this architecture causes multiple operational inefficiencies. For example, developers need to create and manage unique solutions for observability, security, and traffic control. Different teams may apply these tools in various ways, producing uneven operations and inconsistencies. Managers of inter-service communication handily find it unsustainable as the system expands, leading to scalability issues, and finally without centralized fault tolerance systems, the system runs more likely to experience cascading failures.

CHAPTER 2   UNDERSTANDING ISTIO'S CORE COMPONENTS

What Is a Service Mesh, and What Does It Do?

A service mesh can be described as a microservices traffic management system. Consider a busy city with roads connecting various neighborhoods (microservices). Without traffic signals or rules, cars (requests) would collide, causing congestion and leaving no safe way to travel. Drivers would also have to navigate manually, resulting in additional errors and delays.

A service mesh is the city's primary traffic management system, comprising traffic lights (routing rules), security checks (encryption and authentication), and traffic cameras (monitoring). It ensures that cars move smoothly, securely, and efficiently while allowing city planners (operators) to make changes that do not affect the roads (application code). This abstraction simplifies and enhances city management (architecture).

A service mesh is a dedicated infrastructure layer that enables communication between microservices in a distributed application. As microservices-based systems grow in size, new challenges arise in areas such as service discovery, routing, security, and observability. A service mesh addresses these issues by abstracting and standardizing how the microservices interact without changing the underlying application code.

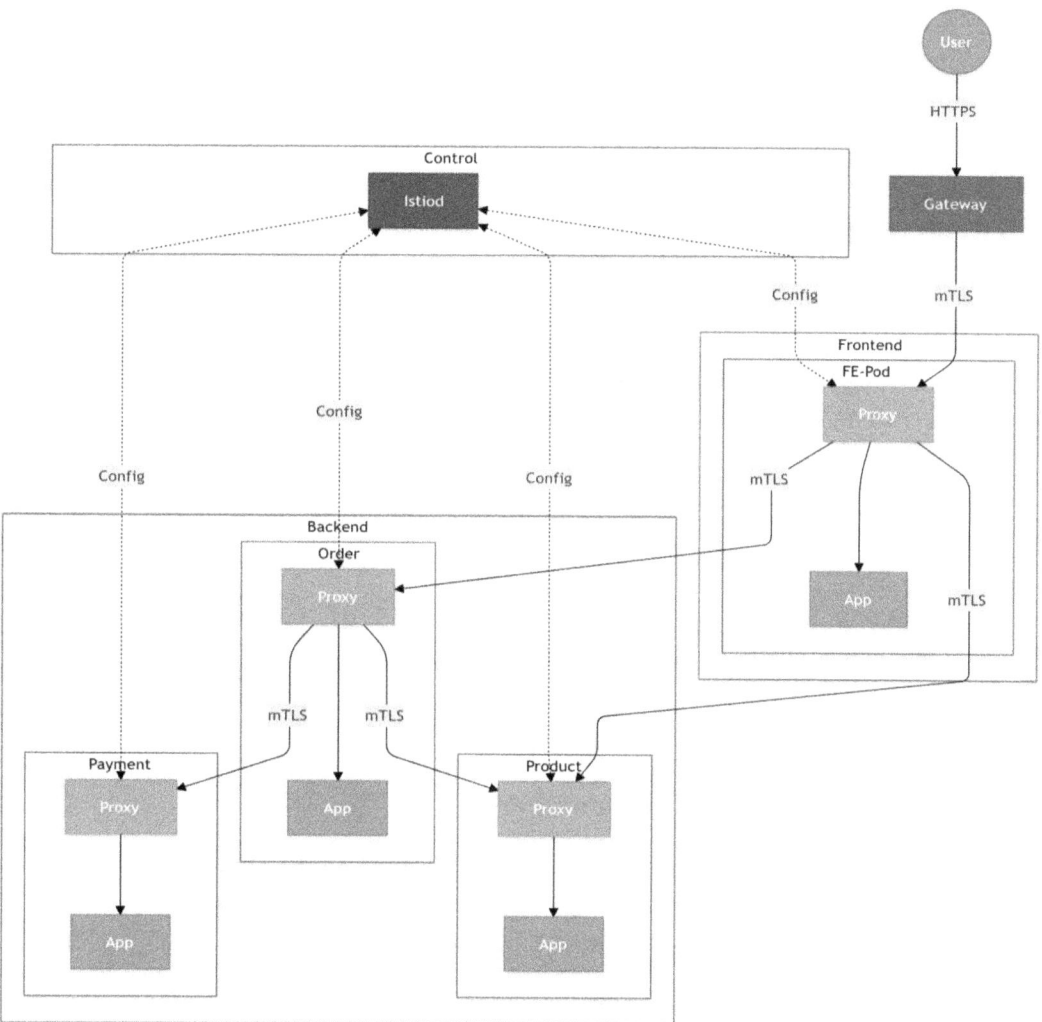

Figure 2-2. *Microservices architecture with Istio*

A service mesh comprises two primary components:

- Control Plane: Oversees the configuration, policies, and operational logic employed across the mesh. It dictates the behavior of proxies within the data plane.

- Data Plane: This element facilitates direct communication between services. This is generally accomplished through the deployment of lightweight proxies, such as Envoy proxy, alongside each service (sidecar).

In our previous ecommerce platform, we employed microservices for order management, payment processing, and shipping logistics. Without a service mesh, each service must incorporate custom logic for retries, load balancing, and security. The order service must handle retries when the payment service encounters delays. Secure communication between different services requires the manual execution of encryption and identity management. Additionally, debugging issues is challenging, as metrics and traces must be manually configured for each service.

The role of a service mesh is as follows:

- Traffic management provides load balancing, retries, and circuit breaking, along with other precise controls for directing requests between services.

- It employs mTLS for identity management and secure communication to authenticate and authorize service interactions.

- Implements fault-tolerant systems, incorporating failovers and timeouts to prevent the propagation of failures throughout the system.

- It automatically collects measurements, records, and traces to facilitate system issue monitoring and diagnosis.

- It supports extensibility through WebAssembly (Wasm) filters, enabling custom policy enforcement, logging, transformation, and other service behavior modifications without modifying core service mesh components.

A service mesh encapsulates these issues. The proxies independently handle retries, encryption, and metrics collection, ensuring consistent performance across the architecture.

What Is Istio, and Why Is It Designed As It Is?

Istio was created to address the growing challenges of managing microservices in cloud-native applications developed and deployed in dynamic environments. As discussed briefly earlier, routing, security, and monitoring are frequently resource-intensive and complex tasks in these systems, necessitating the communication of multiple services across diverse environments. Istio simplifies this by removing infrastructure tasks from developers, such as retries, timeouts, and access controls, freeing them up to focus the development efforts only on application logic. It employs dynamic routing, service discovery, and resilience features such as circuit breakers to manage intricate traffic. Istio automates identity management, enforces consistent access controls, and ensures encrypted communication via mTLS between services by utilizing its built-in security model. Additionally, Istio facilitates deep observability by collecting metrics, logs, and traces through each proxy deployed along the services. This observability enables seamless integrations with tools such as Jaeger and Prometheus for monitoring, visibility, and troubleshooting.

Organizations would often encounter difficulties with fragmented solutions and increased operational overhead in the absence of Istio. Developers often would be required to manually implement security and traffic policies for each service, which would result in inconsistencies and an increased likelihood of errors and cumbersome tasks to manage them. Additionally, the observability would be fragmented as well, which would complicate the process of identifying issues and optimizing performance. Custom-built solutions that are challenging to standardize and/or scale would be necessary to manage complex scenarios such as canary deployments or multi-cluster setups. Istio establishes this robust foundation for contemporary cloud-native architectures by consolidating these capabilities into a single platform, enhancing the security, reliability, and ease of operation of distributed systems.

Understanding Istio's Architecture: The Control Plane and Data Plane

Istio's architecture is unique and consists of a service mesh with two planes—the control plane and the data plane. Istio's design is meant to simplify microservices architecture, management, and deployments.

In charge of the control plane is Istiod, which manages certificates, centers service mesh configuration, and coordinates policy enforcement, traffic routing, and service discovery. The most recent Istio update enhances retries' management and streamlining of ambient mode's ability. Istiod oversees the control plane, which configures and maintains the service mesh. Istiod acts as a centralized brain and controls security layouts, rules, and policies.

Envoy proxies housed as sidecars or, in ambient mode, as ztunnel and waypoint proxies make up the data plane. These proxies manage all incoming and exiting service traffic by using the load balancing, security, telemetry, and traffic control configurations of the control plane. The Envoy proxies controlling the data plane intercept all network traffic between services, enforcing specified policies and collating the telemetry data.

Employing this separation of duties, Istio transparently manages service-to-service communication, so fostering increased scalability, flexibility, and security. By separating application logic from operational considerations, Istio's capabilities help developers focus on feature development while operators keep centralized control over traffic, observability, and security. It also lets teams ensure that their microservices design is strong and flexible in response to always-changing needs.

Core Elements of Istio

In the following sections, we will learn about the underlying components that facilitate the operations of a service mesh, as we have a basic understanding of the architecture and two-plane model of Istio. The data plane, i.e., Envoy proxy, and the unified control plane, Istiod, will be examined in the subsequent sections. Additionally, we will investigate how Istio manages critical functions, including observability, security, traffic management, and service discovery. This will provide a thorough understanding of how these components interact to improve and regulate service communication within a microservices framework.

CHAPTER 2　UNDERSTANDING ISTIO'S CORE COMPONENTS

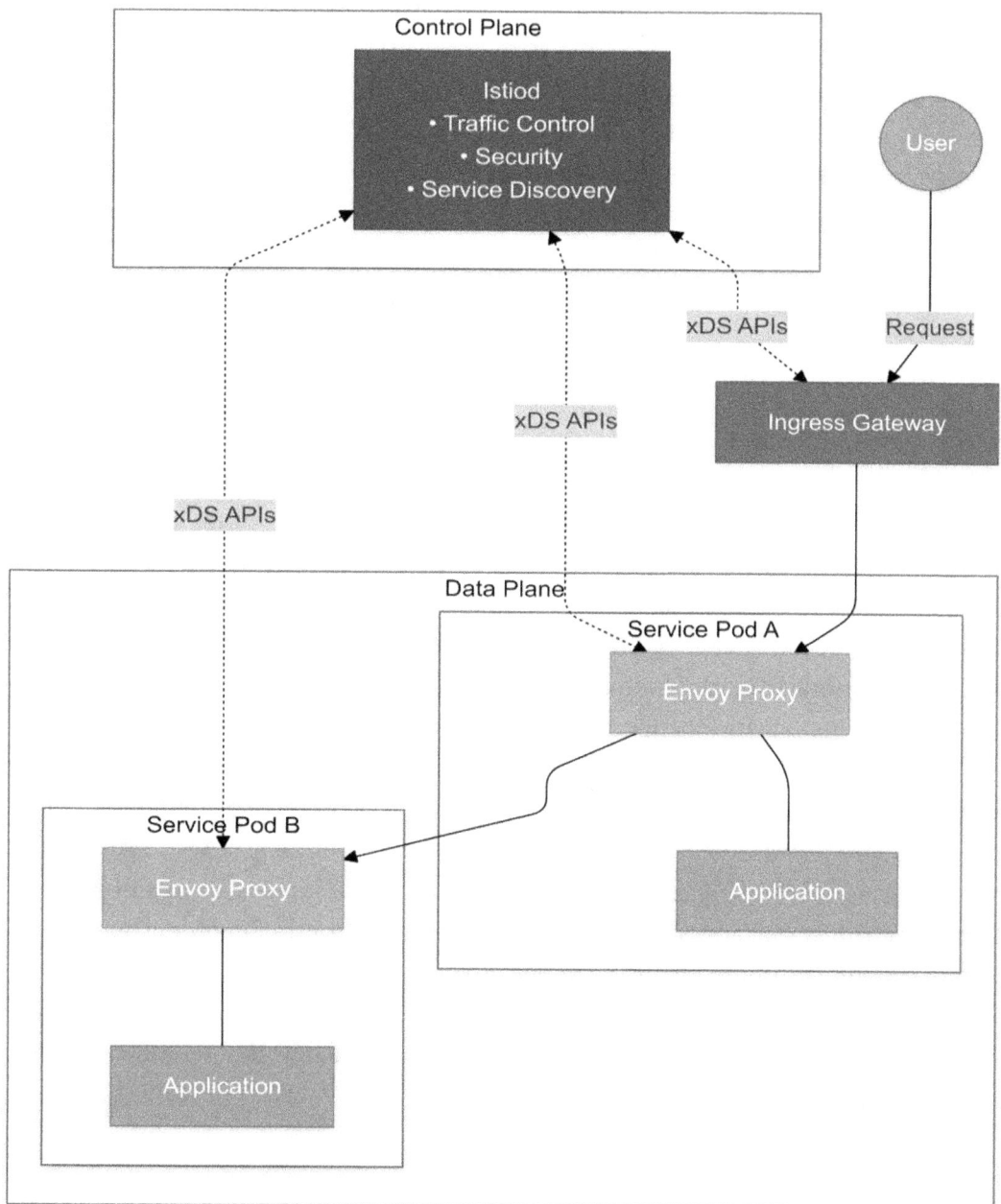

Figure 2-3.　*Control plane and data plane for Istio*

Istiod: Unified Control Plane

Istiod is the central orchestrator in Istio's architecture, managing and configuring the service mesh. By combining multiple previously separate functions into a single unified component, Istiod simplifies Istio's control plane and allows for seamless interaction across the service mesh. Its responsibilities include managing service discovery, configuration updates, security enforcement, and observability. This detailed explanation delves into each of these critical functions.

Configuration Management

Istiod is accountable for the configuration of all services within the mesh. It ensures that routing, security policies, and observability settings are applied in real time without the need for a service restart by dynamically propagating configuration updates to Envoy proxies. These configurations can be defined by developers using Istio's custom resources (e.g., a VirtualService for traffic routing and DestinationRule for load balancing, covered in later chapters). Istiod also employs declarative APIs to translate high-level intentions into actionable instructions for Envoy proxies and interpret them. This feature enables teams to incorporate sophisticated traffic control features, such as fault injection or traffic splitting, without modifying the underlying application code. Istiod interprets the user-defined configurations and policies that are defined in Istio's custom Kubernetes resources. It parses configuration by examining YAML manifests that specify access controls, fault injection policies, and traffic rules. It ensures that all services in the mesh adhere to the same rules, whether for traffic routing or policy enforcement, by distributing configurations by sending the translated configuration to Envoy proxies in the data plane. Furthermore, it facilitates dynamic updates, which enable the hot reloading of configurations, thereby guaranteeing that modifications are implemented without the need for a service restart.

Service Discovery

Istiod seamlessly handles service discovery in Istio, integrating with Kubernetes through its API server to offer robust service management capabilities. Istiod performs continuous monitoring of the lifecycle of pods and services, automatically registering them in the mesh as they are created, updated, or terminated. This automated approach eliminates the necessity for manual service registration and guarantees that the mesh consistently reflects the current state of the environment in real time. Istiod's capabilities are not just restricted to basic Kubernetes integration; it can also go beyond service discovery to support virtual machines or bare-metal services by utilizing custom resources.

Istio's capabilities in hybrid and heterogeneous environments effectively unify service management under a single control plane. Istiod also guarantees that services within the mesh can locate and communicate with each other by establishing a direct connection with the Kubernetes API server to monitor services, pods, and endpoints, thereby maintaining an accurate inventory of all mesh components. Additionally, it manages the automatic registration and deregistration of services as they are brought online or offline. Finally, it facilitates the seamless discovery of services for VMs or external services by utilizing Istio's ServiceEntry and WorkloadEntry resources. The practical impact of this advanced service discovery system is illustrated by how Istiod updates Envoy proxies in near real time in response to changes in service endpoints. This assures that the mesh accurately reflects the current network state and maintains consistent connectivity across all services, irrespective of whether they are operating in Kubernetes clusters, virtual machines, or external environments.

Security Management

Security is a cornerstone of Istiod's responsibilities. Istiod's capabilities allow it to implement and manage security policies all around the service mesh. Security is a major part of its obligations. It acts as a certificate authority (CA) and issues rotational X.509 certificates for mesh-based service providers. These certificates are needed to enable mutual TLS (mTLS), which simultaneously verifies service identities and offers strong encryption in service-to-service communication. Istiod's security features go beyond the standard certificate management, as it supports sophisticated authentication systems including JWTs for user authentication and OAuth 2.0 for safe access delegation. With the use of a wide range of techniques including mTLS, JWTs, and outside authentication providers, Istiod's authentication system verifies service identities, producing a complete and robust security framework. Istiod configures Envoy proxies with particular authorization policies, utilizing fine-grained access control. Istiod also easily connects with other security tools including Cert-Manager for automated certificate lifecycle management and Open Policy Agent (OPA) for custom policy evaluations. This integration capacity helps companies leverage Istio's mesh security features while using their current security tools. Istiod's maintenance of strong security standards across the service mesh and the automation of certificate generation and renewal and policy management drastically lower the operational overhead related to manual security management of services and identities.

Traffic Control and Routing

Istiod provides a comprehensive selection of features that enhance service control and reliability by configuring Envoy proxies to implement sophisticated traffic management strategies. It enables advanced capabilities, such as traffic mirroring, which duplicates requests to multiple destinations for testing purposes, and canary deployments, which allow teams to perform incremental feature rollouts with minimal risk. Developers can declaratively specify these behaviors, and Istiod guarantees that they are consistently enforced throughout the entire service mesh. The system employs a variety of traffic routing mechanisms, including request mirroring for production environment testing, header-based routing for various user segments, and weighted traffic shifting for canary deployments. Istiod offers support for advanced traffic policies, such as request retries, circuit breaking, and timeouts, which effectively prevent cascading failures and maintain service stability. Consequently, the application's traffic resiliency is enhanced. Furthermore, Istiod's ability to dynamically modify routing rules in real-time metrics enables the provision of services with the highest level of performance and reliability. The platform also provides granular control over service behavior by supporting sophisticated traffic policies, such as rate limiting and traffic quotas, which are based on custom-defined rules. Istiod's traffic management system is both robust and dependable, enabling organizations to implement complex deployment strategies while simultaneously guaranteeing the availability of their services, thanks to these capabilities.

Observability and Telemetry

Istiod plays a key role in making service interactions highly observable by configuring proxies to gather rich telemetry data—including metrics, logs, and traces. This data provides a clear picture of the service mesh's health and performance. By collecting detailed information like error rates, request latency, and throughput, Istiod helps teams fine-tune performance and quickly identify and troubleshoot issues.

Envoy proxies, managed by Istiod, are set up to capture in-depth request and response logs for every service interaction. This includes consistent propagation of trace context, enabling end-to-end visibility across services and seamless integration with tools like Jaeger, Zipkin, and OpenTelemetry for distributed tracing.

Istiod also integrates smoothly with monitoring systems like Prometheus for real-time metrics and Grafana for creating dashboards that highlight trends and detect anomalies. With this comprehensive observability setup, teams gain deep insights into how their systems behave, understand service dependencies, and can respond proactively to problems—keeping services reliable and performant.

Policy Enforcement

Istiod enforces wide-ranging traffic and access control policies across the service mesh to ensure system stability and security. It supports many custom rate limiting, quota management, and fault tolerance policies that are carefully applied at the proxy level for consistent enforcement. Istio's native custom resources or integration with external policy evaluation tools like Open Policy Agent can define these sophisticated policies, providing policy management flexibility. Istiod configures Envoy proxies to apply precise authorization rules for specific routes and endpoints, enables fault injection for chaos engineering experiments to test system resilience, and enforces rate limits to prevent service overload and ensure system stability as a policy enforcer. The platform's integration with external policy engines like OPA offloads complex decision-making processes, improving policy evaluation. Istio's extensible policy framework lets teams tailor their service mesh to organizational needs and compliance standards. This centralized policy enforcement approach simplifies distributed system policy management by ensuring consistent rule application across the mesh and flexibility for diverse use cases and requirements.

Multi-cluster and Hybrid Cloud Support

In hybrid cloud setups or environments that span multiple Kubernetes clusters, Istiod is essential for maintaining consistent security policies and configurations throughout the entire distributed infrastructure. Enabling seamless and secure communication between services, regardless of their physical or cloud location, it adeptly federates control across clusters. With its advanced cluster federation capabilities, Istiod simplifies service communication by ensuring consistent policy and configuration distribution across all clusters and utilizing shared control plane models. In addition to ensuring secure traffic routing between clusters, the platform's multi-cluster management also encompasses gateway connectivity. This includes the meticulous configuration of gateways to maintain secure ingress and egress points and ensure proper TLS termination. The deployment and ongoing operation of multi-cluster meshes are significantly simplified by Istiod, which addresses the complex challenges of managing distributed systems by utilizing advanced features such as intelligent gateway connectivity and remote control planes. In complex enterprise setups, this comprehensive approach to multi-cluster management guarantees both scalability and fault tolerance, enabling organizations to confidently expand their service mesh across diverse environments while maintaining consistent security and operational standards. For organizations that operate in hybrid and distributed cloud environments, the platform's capacity to seamlessly manage these intricate multi-cluster scenarios renders it an invaluable asset.

Envoy Proxy: The Data Plane

The data plane for Istio's (sidecar mode) service mesh architecture is Envoy proxy. It is a distributed proxy that operates on layers 4 (transport layer) and 7 (application layer) of the OSI model, providing high performance. Envoy is employed as a proxy in newer architectures such as ambient mode as a sidecar proxy for application workloads. Envoy supervises all inbound and outbound traffic for mesh services, guaranteeing that communication is secure, observable, and dependable.

The following is a comprehensive explanation of the core components and role of Envoy proxy.

Key Responsibilities of Envoy Proxy

Envoy proxy is essential to Istio's service mesh, as it serves as the central component of the data plane. Its obligations encompass numerous domains, guaranteeing the efficient, secure, and dependable transmission of service communications. The subsequent sections provide a comprehensive account of its primary functions.

Traffic Management

Envoy manages all aspects of traffic routing and load balancing between mesh services per the policies of the Istio control plane. The efficiency of service-to-service communication is contingent upon the system's traffic management capabilities.

- Dynamic Service Discovery: Envoy dynamically identifies available endpoints by utilizing real-time service information from Istiod. This eliminates the necessity for manual updates by enabling the proxy to adjust as services expand or contract or new instances are added.

- Advanced Load Balancing: Envoy implements sophisticated strategies to optimize traffic distribution, for example, a round-robin approach guaranteeing that each service instance receives an equitable volume of traffic, balancing the load by sending traffic to the instance with the fewest active requests, and also guarantees that traffic intended for a particular user or session is consistently directed to the same service instance, thereby enhancing the user experience for stateful applications. Additionally, other traffic strategies such as weighted least request, Maglev, Ring Hash, and Random are other traffic distribution patterns for a load balancer.

Security Enforcement

Security is a critical element in microservices architectures, and Envoy guarantees that communication within the mesh is authenticated and encrypted. Envoy ensures the security of communication by authenticating the identities of the client and server and encrypting data in transit. The dynamic issuance and rotation of certificates by the Istio control plane guarantees robust security without the need for developer intervention. Role-based access control (RBAC) is implemented by Envoy to enforce access control policies. It also collaborates with external policy engines, such as Open Policy Agent (OPA), to establish intricate policies that guarantee that data is accessible only to authorized services or users.

CHAPTER 2   UNDERSTANDING ISTIO'S CORE COMPONENTS

Telemetry Collection

Envoy is essential for ensuring that the necessary visibility is provided to monitor and maintain the health and performance of services. It provides detailed metrics, such as request counts, latency, and error rates, which are essential for the monitoring and diagnosis of system behavior and are collected by Envoy. Subsequently, these metrics are exported to observability tools, including Prometheus, for alerting and visualization. With the proxy, teams can monitor the lifecycle of requests and identify issues during debugging by generating detailed logs for each service interaction. Additionally, Envoy seamlessly integrates with distributed tracing tools, including Zipkin and Jaeger, to offer visibility into multi-service request flows. By capturing trace spans, Envoy simplifies the identification of bottlenecks or failures in distributed systems.

Istio's Deployment Modes

Istio version 1.27 and above provides users with two deployment modes: sidecar and ambient. The traditional sidecar mode injects an Envoy proxy alongside each application pod. This approach offers powerful features like fine-grained traffic control, security (mTLS), and observability by deeply integrating with each workload. However, sidecars can increase resource usage and operational complexity, especially at scale.

The newer ambient mode, introduced as a more lightweight alternative, removes the need for per-pod sidecars. Instead, it uses a shared proxy infrastructure that runs as separate DaemonSets or services in the cluster. Ambient mode simplifies operations, reduces resource overhead, and makes it easier to onboard applications to the service mesh. While it provides many core mesh capabilities such as mTLS and basic traffic policies, it may not yet support the full range of features available in sidecar mode. Ambient is ideal for users prioritizing ease of adoption and efficiency over deep traffic management.

Core Components of Envoy Proxy

Envoy proxy, a critical component of Istio's data plane, is an intricate component designed to efficiently handle service-to-service communication. Its modular and extensible architecture is composed of several core components, each with a specific purpose to ensure optimal performance, security, and observability. Feel free to skip this section as we will be talking in detail about Envoy proxy and extending Istio in Chapter 9.

CHAPTER 2   UNDERSTANDING ISTIO'S CORE COMPONENTS

However, for those who are curious and wish to explore the fundamentals of Envoy proxy now, this section provides a concise introduction to help you get started. If you're eager to understand its basics before diving into advanced topics later, feel free to continue reading!

This section provides a basic setup, installation, and peek into Envoy in action—basically, running Envoy locally on your machine.

1. Installation Options

   ```
   # Pull the official Envoy image from docker registry
   docker pull envoyproxy/envoy:v1.27-latest
   
   # Verify the installation of envoy locally
   docker run --rm envoyproxy/envoy:v1.27-latest --version
   ```

2. Basic Local Setup

   ```
   mkdir envoy-local
   cd envoy-local
   ```

3. Create a basic configuration file (envoy.yaml) and write the contents into it:

   ```
   vi envoy.yaml
   ```

   ```yaml
   admin:
     address:
         socket_address:
         address: 0.0.0.0
         port_value: 9901
   
   static_resources:
     listeners:
     - name: listener_0
       address:
         socket_address:
         address: 0.0.0.0
         port_value: 10000
         filter_chains:
         - filters:
   ```

47

```
          - name: envoy.filters.network.http_connection_manager
        typed_config:
            "@type": type.googleapis.com/envoy.extensions.
            filters.network.http_connection_manager.
            v3.HttpConnectionManager
            stat_prefix: ingress_http
            http_filters:
            - name: envoy.filters.http.router
            typed_config:
            "@type": type.googleapis.com/envoy.extensions.filters.
            http.router.v3.Router
            route_config:
            name: local_route
            virtual_hosts:
            - name: local_service
            domains: ["*"]
            routes:
            - match:
                prefix: "/"
              route:
                host_rewrite_literal: www.google.com
                    cluster: service_google
    clusters:
    - name: service_google
        connect_timeout: 0.25s
        type: LOGICAL_DNS
        dns_lookup_family: V4_ONLY
        load_assignment:
        cluster_name: service_google
        endpoints:
        - lb_endpoints:
        - endpoint:
            address:
            socket_address:
                address: www.google.com
```

                    port_value: 443
                transport_socket:
                name: envoy.transport_sockets.tls
                typed_config:
                "@type": type.googleapis.com/envoy.extensions.transport_
                sockets.tls.v3.UpstreamTlsContext

4. Run Envoy (using the Docker setup):

    ```
    docker run --rm -d \
      --name envoy \
      -p 9901:9901 \
      -p 10000:10000 \
      -v $(pwd)/envoy.yaml:/etc/envoy/envoy.yaml \
      envoyproxy/envoy:v1.27-latest
    ```

5. Check if Envoy is running:

    ```
    # Check the admin interface
    curl localhost:9901/ready

    # Check for statistics
    curl localhost:9901/stats

    # Test the proxy
    curl -v localhost:10000
    ```

6. Optional (Cleanup)

    ```
    # If using Docker
    docker stop envoy
    ```

Listener

The listener serves as the main point of entry for Envoy's incoming traffic, dictating how traffic enters the proxy and directing it to designated ports and protocols. Each listener is a highly customizable entity engineered to manage various traffic types. Envoy listeners can be configured to manage various traffic types, including HTTP/HTTPS listeners for standard web traffic with advanced features like protocol detection and TCP listeners for

CHAPTER 2   UNDERSTANDING ISTIO'S CORE COMPONENTS

non-HTTP traffic, such as database communications or custom application protocols. Envoy automatically recognizes the protocol of incoming traffic and redirects it to the corresponding handler, minimizing manual configuration and enhancing flexibility. Envoy listeners facilitate a series of filters to modify and manage traffic, allowing for capabilities such as header rewriting to implement policies or add custom metadata, alongside traffic mirroring to replicate live traffic to an alternative endpoint for testing purposes without impacting production. Envoy listeners can be configured to adapt to a variety of use cases and traffic patterns.

Below is an example of a simple HTTP listener configuration and showcases a basic HTTP listener setup in Envoy. This configuration creates a listener that accepts traffic on port 8080 and sets up HTTP connection management. It includes basic routing to a local service and is configured to handle incoming requests for all domains. This represents the entry point for all traffic flowing through your Envoy proxy:

```
static_resources:
  listeners:
  - name: http_listener
      address:
      socket_address:
      address: 0.0.0.0
      port_value: 8080
      filter_chains:
      - filters:
      - name: envoy.filters.network.http_connection_manager
      typed_config:
          "@type": type.googleapis.com/envoy.extensions.filters.network.http_connection_manager.v3.HttpConnectionManager
          stat_prefix: ingress_http
          http_filters:
          - name: envoy.filters.http.router
          typed_config:
          "@type": type.googleapis.com/envoy.extensions.filters.http.router.v3.Router
          route_config:
          name: local_route
          virtual_hosts:
```

```
        - name: local_service
          domains: ["*"]
          routes:
          - match:
              prefix: "/"
            route:
              cluster: local_service_cluster
```

Filter Chains

Filter chains are the basic building blocks of Envoy's traffic processing abilities. Each listener (briefly described earlier) gets a chain of filters, which lets traffic be changed or policies be enforced in a certain order. For example, HTTP filters set routing rules, change headers, add faults for testing resilience, and enforce rate limiting policies. TLS filters, on the other hand, can encrypt and decrypt traffic, making sure that mutual TLS (mTLS) secure communication is performed. Custom WebAssembly (Wasm) filters can be added to Envoy, making it more useful by adding service-specific telemetry, custom access control mechanisms, and request/response transformations. Filter chain capabilities allow you fine-grained control over how traffic is routed and processed, which lets Envoy adapt to the needs of large businesses.

Below is an example of a filter chain configuration with both HTTP and TLS filters, and the configuration demonstrates the power of Envoy's filter chains by implementing both HTTP and TLS filters. It includes rate limiting to control traffic flow, TLS certificate configuration for secure communication, and HTTP connection management settings. The combination of these filters allows for fine-grained control over how traffic flows through your proxy while maintaining security and performance:

```
filter_chains:
- filters:
  - name: envoy.filters.network.http_connection_manager
    typed_config:
      "@type": type.googleapis.com/envoy.extensions.filters.network.http_connection_manager.v3.HttpConnectionManager
      codec_type: auto
      stat_prefix: ingress_http
      http_filters:
```

```
        - name: envoy.filters.http.ratelimit
      typed_config:
            "@type": type.googleapis.com/envoy.extensions.filters.http.
            ratelimit.v3.RateLimit
            domain: envoy
            rate_limit_service:
            grpc_service:
            envoy_grpc:
                cluster_name: rate_limit_cluster
        - name: envoy.filters.http.router
  transport_socket:
      name: envoy.transport_sockets.tls
      typed_config:
      "@type": type.googleapis.com/envoy.extensions.transport_sockets.tls.
      v3.DownstreamTlsContext
      common_tls_context:
      tls_certificates:
      - certificate_chain: {filename: "/etc/certs/cert.pem"}
            private_key: {filename: "/etc/certs/key.pem"}
```

Cluster

In Envoy, a cluster is a logical group of upstream endpoints, such as a collection of microservices or external APIs. Dynamic service discovery and routing are determined based on clusters. Dynamic endpoint management enables Envoy to automatically adjust clusters in response to changes in services or scalability, as it receives real-time updates from Istiod. By retaining reusable connections, connection pooling optimizes resource usage, thereby reducing the overhead of creating new connections for each request. Periodic health checks are conducted by the system to ensure that only healthy endpoints receive traffic. To prevent service disruptions, unhealthy endpoints from the cluster are temporarily removed from the pool. These capabilities enhance system reliability and facilitate the management of upstream dependencies.

The below example illustrates a comprehensive service cluster configuration that incorporates several reliability features essential for production environments. It implements health checking to monitor service availability, circuit breaking to prevent cascading failures, and sophisticated load balancing for traffic distribution. The configuration also includes carefully tuned connection timeouts and retry settings to ensure optimal performance under various conditions:

```yaml
clusters:
- name: service_cluster
  type: STRICT_DNS
  connect_timeout: 0.25s
  lb_policy: ROUND_ROBIN
  load_assignment:
      cluster_name: service_cluster
      endpoints:
      - lb_endpoints:
      - endpoint:
            address:
            socket_address:
            address: service.example.com
            port_value: 80
  health_checks:
  - timeout: 1s
      interval: 5s
      unhealthy_threshold: 2
      healthy_threshold: 1
      http_health_check:
      path: "/health"
  circuit_breakers:
      thresholds:
      max_connections: 1000
      max_pending_requests: 1000
      max_requests: 1000
      max_retries: 3
```

Route

Routes define how requests are matched and handled once they reach a listener. A route is made up of matching criteria and associated actions. The matching system relies on attributes such as headers, paths, query parameters, and HTTP methods. For example, the requests to particular API endpoints can be directed to the appropriate services, while requests with specific headers may necessitate specialized processing. Routes specify the actions that should be taken in response to matched requests, including redirecting to a specific cluster, rejecting the request entirely, or forwarding it to another endpoint. Routes offer sophisticated traffic management capabilities, including traffic splitting for canary releases and path rewriting to align with backend service structures, which enables developers to effortlessly implement intricate traffic flows.

Envoy's load balancer distributes requests efficiently across service endpoints using multiple algorithms to handle varying traffic patterns. The round-robin approach distributes traffic evenly across available endpoints, whereas the least-request method routes traffic to the endpoint with the fewest active requests, ensuring dynamic load balance. Consistent hashing ensures session affinity by routing requests with identical keys to the same endpoint, which is critical for stateful applications. Envoy incorporates real-time health checks into load balancing decisions, directing traffic only to healthy instances while improving overall system reliability.

The below example configuration demonstrates Envoy's advanced routing capabilities, enabling sophisticated traffic management scenarios. It shows how to implement traffic splitting between service versions for canary deployments, utilize header-based routing for version-specific traffic, and employ path rewriting for API compatibility. The configuration includes timeout settings and showcases how to maintain backward compatibility while rolling out new service versions:

```
route_config:
  name: local_route
  virtual_hosts:
  - name: backend
      domains: ["*"]
      routes:
      - match:
      prefix: "/api/v1"
      headers:
```

```
        - name: "version"
          exact_match: "beta"
      route:
        weighted_clusters:
          clusters:
            - name: service_v1
              weight: 90
            - name: service_v2
              weight: 10
    - match:
        path: "/legacy"
      route:
        prefix_rewrite: "/api/v2"
        cluster: new_backend
        timeout: 0.5s
```

Tracing and Observability

Strong observability elements included in Envoy are essential for keeping microservices architectures under check. Envoy uses distributed tracing to spread trace context across service calls, enabling end-to-end request tracking with tools like Jaeger or Zipkin, helping teams to identify bottlenecks and grasp difficult request flows. Seamless integration with platforms like Prometheus, which shows comprehensive metrics including latency, request rates, and error counts, would be easily applicable. Tracing and observability are core for debugging, auditing, and compliance. Envoy also records detailed information on every request and response that is processed.

The below is an example configuration for tracing and metrics. This configuration sets up comprehensive observability features in Envoy, enabling detailed monitoring and troubleshooting capabilities. It integrates distributed tracing with Zipkin for request tracking, configures Prometheus metrics for monitoring, and establishes statistics collection for performance analysis. These observability features provide crucial insights into your service mesh's behavior and performance characteristics:

```
tracing:
  http:
    name: envoy.tracers.zipkin
    typed_config:
```

```
        "@type": type.googleapis.com/envoy.config.trace.v3.ZipkinConfig
        collector_cluster: zipkin
        collector_endpoint: "/api/v2/spans"
        shared_span_context: true
stats_sinks:
- name: envoy.stat_sinks.prometheus
  typed_config:
        "@type": type.googleapis.com/envoy.config.metrics.v3.PrometheusConfig
        stats_prefix: envoy
        render_clusters: true
```

Extensions and Wasm Filters

Envoy's extensibility is one of its most notable features. WebAssembly (Wasm) allows developers to add custom logic without affecting the core proxy code. Wasm filters allow organizations to add application-specific telemetry data to improve observability, implement custom access rules based on specific business needs, and extend Envoy's capabilities to support new or proprietary protocols. This modular approach permits organizations to customize Envoy to fulfill their unique operational needs, thereby securing their service mesh architecture for the future. By seamlessly integrating these components, Envoy proxy operates as a powerful data plane within Istio, facilitating reliable, secure, and high-performance microservices communication. This integration also reduces the complexity of modern architectures and enhances scalability and maintainability.

The below example is of a custom Wasm filter configuration. This configuration showcases Envoy's extensibility through WebAssembly (Wasm) filters, allowing for custom business logic integration. The example demonstrates how to implement a custom authentication filter, configure the Wasm runtime, and set up plugin loading with specific validation rules. This powerful feature enables organizations to extend Envoy's functionality while maintaining isolation and security:

```
http_filters:
- name: envoy.filters.http.wasm
  typed_config:
        "@type": type.googleapis.com/envoy.extensions.filters.http.wasm.v3.Wasm
        config:
        name: "my_plugin"
```

```
    root_id: "my_root_id"
vm_config:
vm_id: "my_vm_id"
runtime: "envoy.wasm.runtime.v8"
code:
    local:
        filename: "/etc/envoy/plugins/custom_auth.wasm"
configuration:
"@type": "type.googleapis.com/google.protobuf.StringValue"
value: |
    {
    "auth_rules": {
    "paths": ["/api/*"],
    "required_headers": ["x-custom-auth"]
    }
    }
```

Choosing the Right Istio Deployment Mode: Sidecar vs. Ambient

Choosing a suitable deployment mode is determined by the application's security, observability, resource consumption, and operational complexity. Here are some scenarios with examples to help you decide which mode is appropriate.

Scenario 1: Sidecar Mode

The critical functions in a microservices architecture such as security, observability, resource consumption, and operational complexity of the application all affect the appropriate deployment mode decision. The sidecar mode is particularly beneficial for applications that require fine-grained traffic control, extensive observability, and advanced security features like mTLS enforcement and per-pod policies. This mode is also useful for complex microservices architectures that require advanced traffic shaping features such as weighted routing or fault injection.

Consider an ecommerce platform that shows the advantages of sidecar mode deployment. In this scenario, the platform is made up of several microservices, including frontend, catalog, orders, payments, and notifications, all of which require extensive

CHAPTER 2 UNDERSTANDING ISTIO'S CORE COMPONENTS

communication. By injecting Envoy proxies into each service pod via sidecar mode, the platform gains critical capabilities: fine-grained metrics and distributed tracing enable comprehensive debugging of transaction paths (e.g., tracking requests flowing from frontend to orders to payments and finally to notifications), strict mTLS encryption ensures secure service-to-service communication, and advanced traffic management enables A/B testing and canary deployments. This deployment mode provides the strong infrastructure required to maintain and optimize complex microservice interactions while ensuring security and observability.

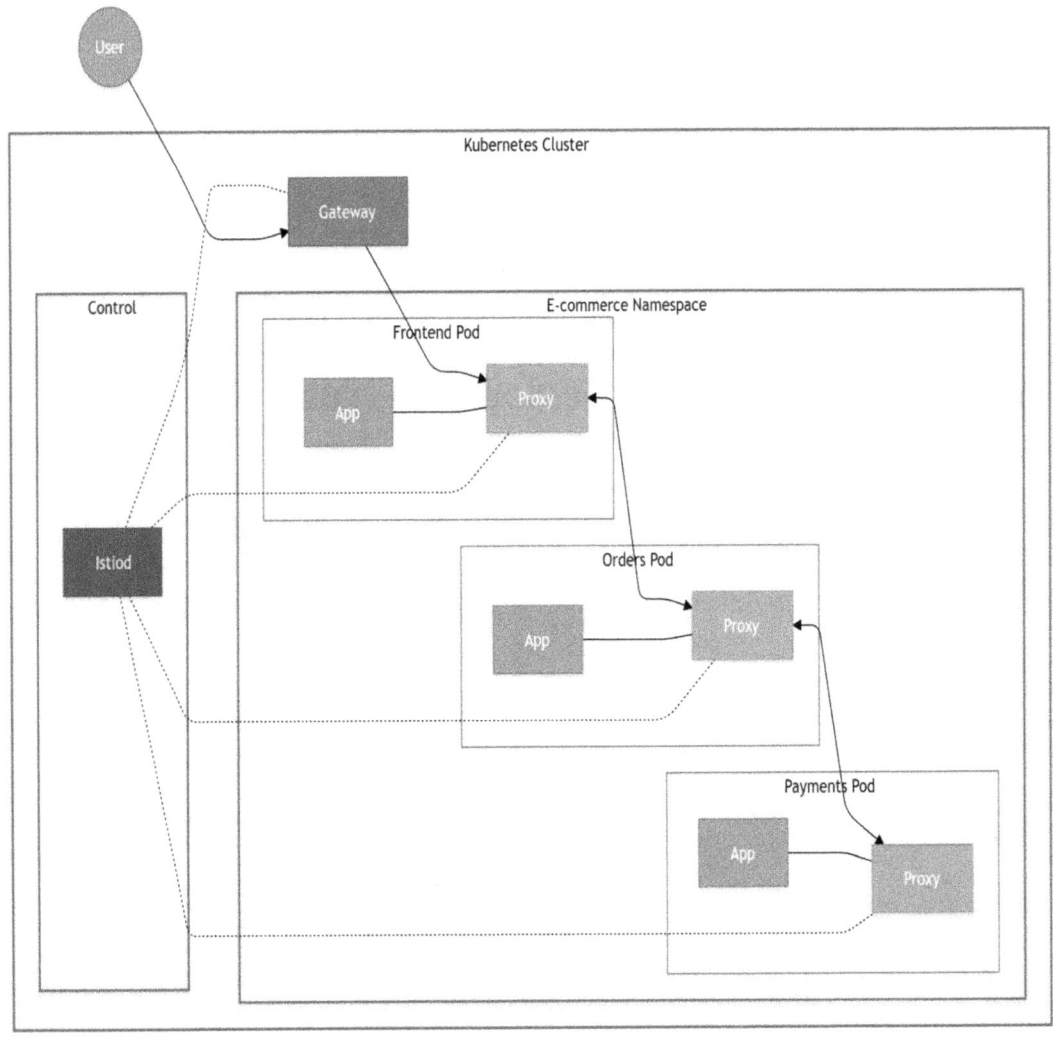

Figure 2-4. Istio's deployment in sidecar mode

CHAPTER 2   UNDERSTANDING ISTIO'S CORE COMPONENTS

Here is an example scenario:

1. First, here's the basic Kind configuration we need:

   ```yaml
   # kind-config.yaml
   kind: Cluster
   apiVersion: kind.x-k8s.io/v1alpha4
   nodes:
   - role: control-plane
     extraPortMappings:
     - containerPort: 80
         hostPort: 80
         protocol: TCP
     - containerPort: 443
         hostPort: 443
         protocol: TCP
     kubeadmConfigPatches:
     -
         kind: InitConfiguration
         nodeRegistration:
         kubeletExtraArgs:
         node-labels: "ingress-ready=true"
   - role: worker
   - role: worker
   ```

2. Here's the sample application YAML for our ecommerce services:

   ```yaml
   # sample-app.yaml
   apiVersion: v1
   kind: Service
   metadata:
     name: frontend
     labels:
         app: frontend
         service: frontend
   spec:
     ports:
   ```

```yaml
      - port: 80
        targetPort: 8080
        name: http
    selector:
        app: frontend
---
apiVersion: apps/v1
kind: Deployment
metadata:
  name: frontend
  labels:
      app: frontend
spec:
  replicas: 2
  selector:
      matchLabels:
      app: frontend
  template:
      metadata:
      labels:
      app: frontend
      annotations:
      sidecar.istio.io/inject: "true"
      spec:
      containers:
      - name: frontend
          image: ecommerce/frontend:v1
          ports:
          - containerPort: 8080
---
apiVersion: v1
kind: Service
metadata:
  name: catalog
  labels:
```

```yaml
      app: catalog
      service: catalog
spec:
  ports:
    - port: 80
      targetPort: 8080
      name: http
  selector:
      app: catalog
---
apiVersion: apps/v1
kind: Deployment
metadata:
  name: catalog
  labels:
      app: catalog
spec:
  replicas: 2
  selector:
      matchLabels:
      app: catalog
  template:
      metadata:
      labels:
      app: catalog
      annotations:
      sidecar.istio.io/inject: "true"
      spec:
      containers:
      - name: catalog
          image: ecommerce/catalog:v1
          ports:
          - containerPort: 8080
```

CHAPTER 2   UNDERSTANDING ISTIO'S CORE COMPONENTS

3. Create a Kind cluster, install Istio, and enable sidecar injection:

```
# Save the kind configuration as kind-config.yaml
kind create cluster --name istio-demo --config kind-config.yaml

# Verify cluster is running
kubectl cluster-info --context kind-istio-demo

# Download Istio
curl -L https://istio.io/downloadIstio | sh -
cd istio-*

# Add istioctl to your path
export PATH=$PWD/bin:$PATH

# Install Istio with demo profile
istioctl install --set profile=demo -y

# Verify installation
kubectl get pods -n istio-system

# Enable automatic sidecar injection for default namespace
kubectl label namespace default istio-injection=enabled

# Verify the label
kubectl get namespace -L istio-injection
```

4. Create Dockerfiles for your services:

```
# Frontend Dockerfile
FROM node:16-alpine
WORKDIR /app
COPY package*.json ./
RUN npm install
COPY . .
EXPOSE 8080
CMD ["npm", "start"]

# Catalog Dockerfile
FROM python:3.9-slim
WORKDIR /app
```

CHAPTER 2   UNDERSTANDING ISTIO'S CORE COMPONENTS

```
COPY requirements.txt .
RUN pip install -r requirements.txt
COPY . .
EXPOSE 8080
CMD ["python", "app.py"]
```

5. Build Dockerfiles for your services:

```
# Build images
docker build -t ecommerce/frontend:v1 -f frontend/Dockerfile
frontend/
docker build -t ecommerce/catalog:v1 -f catalog/Dockerfile
catalog/

# Load images into Kind
kind load docker-image ecommerce/frontend:v1 --name istio-demo
kind load docker-image ecommerce/catalog:v1 --name istio-demo
```

6. Deploy and verify deployment for our sample application:

```
# Apply the sample application YAML
kubectl apply -f sample-app.yaml

# Watch the pods come up
kubectl get pods -w

# Check all pods have 2/2 containers (app + istio-proxy)
kubectl get pods

# Check services
kubectl get svc

# Verify Istio proxy injection
kubectl describe pod -l app=frontend | grep -i proxy
```

63

Scenario 2: Ambient Mode

When deployment concerns give resource efficiency and lowered operational complexity top priority, the ambient mode is especially appropriate. For organizations working with lightweight applications that do not require pod-level fine-grained control or when security and traffic policies can be efficiently managed at the namespace or service level without sacrificing functionality, the ambient mode becomes especially valuable as a mode of deployment.

An IoT platform implementation whereby thousands of lightweight devices transmit telemetry data to a centralized backend illustrates ambient mode's efficacy. Under such conditions, using a conventional sidecar approach with proxies for every pod could cause notable resource overhead, thus affecting system performance and scalability. Organizations can significantly reduce resource usage by using the ambient mode and strategically deploying the ztunnel proxies for traffic handling and name-level encryption. This method enables the application of traffic policies at the service level, free from the complexity of managing individual pod proxies, producing a more simplified and resource-efficient infrastructure while preserving necessary security and traffic management capability.

CHAPTER 2   UNDERSTANDING ISTIO'S CORE COMPONENTS

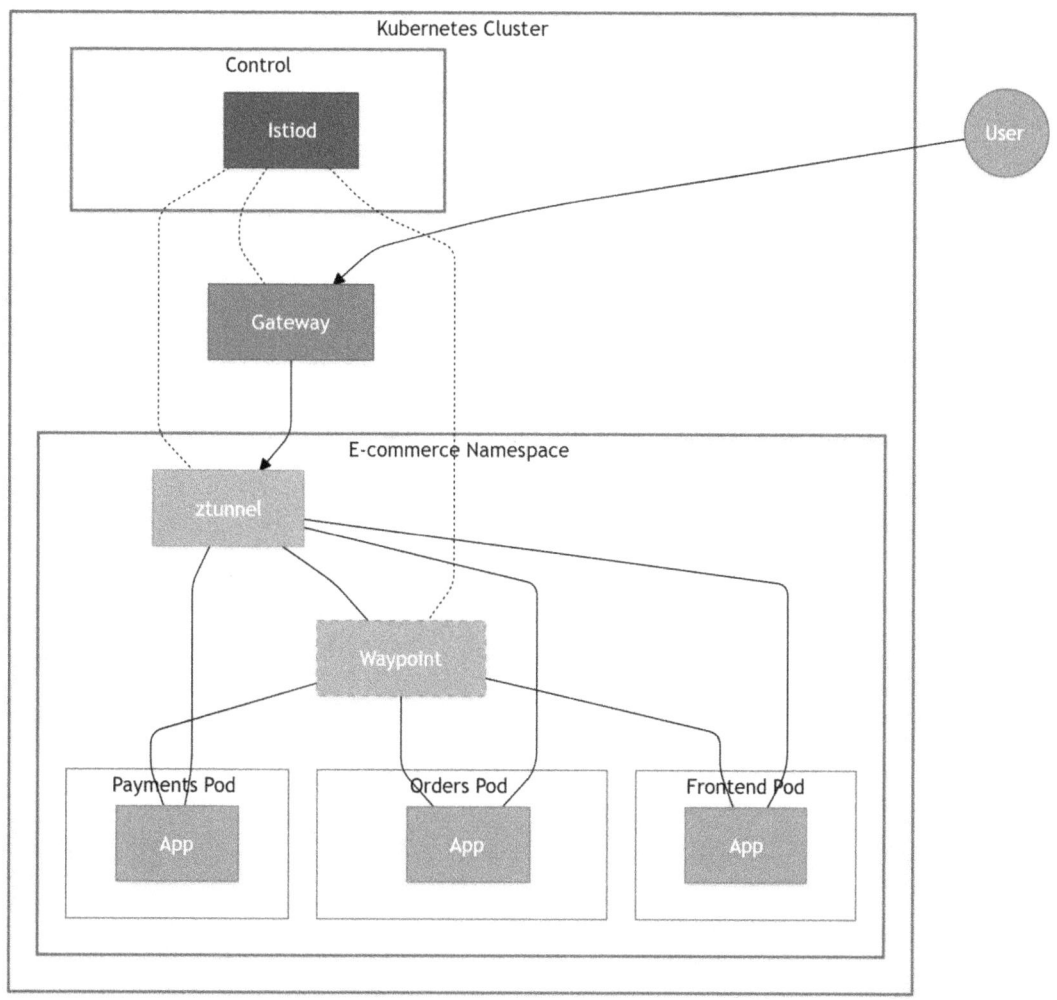

Figure 2-5. *Istio's deployment in ambient mode*

Here is an example scenario:

1. First, here's the basic Kind configuration we need:

    ```
    # kind-ambient-config.yaml
    kind: Cluster
    apiVersion: kind.x-k8s.io/v1alpha4
    nodes:
    - role: control-plane
      extraPortMappings:
      - containerPort: 80
    ```

65

```
          hostPort: 80
          protocol: TCP
        - containerPort: 443
          hostPort: 443
          protocol: TCP
      extraMounts:
      - hostPath: /var/run/cni
        containerPath: /var/run/cni
   - role: worker
     extraMounts:
     - hostPath: /var/run/cni
       containerPath: /var/run/cni
   - role: worker
     extraMounts:
     - hostPath: /var/run/cni
       containerPath: /var/run/cni
```

2. Here's the sample application YAML for our ecommerce services:

```
# ambient-app.yaml
apiVersion: v1
kind: Namespace
metadata:
  name: ecommerce
  labels:
      istio.io/dataplane-mode: ambient
---
apiVersion: v1
kind: Service
metadata:
  name: frontend
  namespace: ecommerce
spec:
  ports:
     - port: 80
       targetPort: 8080
```

```
      name: http
  selector:
      app: frontend
---
apiVersion: apps/v1
kind: Deployment
metadata:
  name: frontend
  namespace: ecommerce
spec:
  replicas: 2
  selector:
      matchLabels:
      app: frontend
  template:
      metadata:
      labels:
      app: frontend
      spec:
      containers:
      - name: frontend
          image: ecommerce/frontend:v1
          ports:
          - containerPort: 8080
---
apiVersion: v1
kind: Service
metadata:
  name: catalog
  namespace: ecommerce
spec:
  ports:
      - port: 80
      targetPort: 8080
      name: http
```

```yaml
    selector:
        app: catalog
---
apiVersion: apps/v1
kind: Deployment
metadata:
  name: catalog
  namespace: ecommerce
spec:
  replicas: 2
  selector:
      matchLabels:
      app: catalog
  template:
      metadata:
      labels:
      app: catalog
      spec:
      containers:
      - name: catalog
            image: ecommerce/catalog:v1
            ports:
            - containerPort: 8080
---
# Ambient specific configurations
apiVersion: gateway.networking.k8s.io/v1beta1
kind: Gateway
metadata:
  name: ecommerce-gateway
  namespace: ecommerce
spec:
  gatewayClassName: istio
  listeners:
  - name: http
      port: 80
```

```
      protocol: HTTP
      allowedRoutes:
        namespaces:
          from: Same
---
apiVersion: gateway.networking.k8s.io/v1beta1
kind: HTTPRoute
metadata:
  name: frontend-route
  namespace: ecommerce
spec:
  parentRefs:
  - name: ecommerce-gateway
  rules:
  - matches:
      - path:
          type: PathPrefix
          value: /
    backendRefs:
    - name: frontend
      port: 80
```

3. Create a Kind cluster, and install Istio with ambient mode:

   ```
   # Create a cluster using the ambient configuration
   kind create cluster --name istio-ambient --config kind-ambient-config.yaml

   # Verify cluster creation
   kubectl cluster-info --context kind-istio-ambient

   # Download the latest Istio
   curl -L https://istio.io/downloadIstio | sh -
   cd istio-*

   # Add istioctl to path
   export PATH=$PWD/bin:$PATH
   ```

```
# Install Istio with ambient mode enabled
istioctl install --set profile=ambient --set "ambient.
enabled=true" -y

# Verify Istio installation
kubectl get pods -n istio-system
```

4. Create Dockerfiles for your services:

```
# Frontend Dockerfile
FROM node:16-alpine
WORKDIR /app
COPY package*.json ./
RUN npm install
COPY . .
EXPOSE 8080
CMD ["npm", "start"]
```

```
# Catalog Dockerfile
FROM python:3.9-slim
WORKDIR /app
COPY requirements.txt .
RUN pip install -r requirements.txt
COPY . .
EXPOSE 8080
CMD ["python", "app.py"]
```

5. Build Dockerfiles for your services:

```
# Build the service images
docker build -t ecommerce/frontend:v1 -f frontend/Dockerfile frontend/
docker build -t ecommerce/catalog:v1 -f catalog/Dockerfile catalog/

# Load images into the Kind cluster
kind load docker-image ecommerce/frontend:v1 --name istio-ambient
kind load docker-image ecommerce/catalog:v1 --name istio-ambient
```

CHAPTER 2   UNDERSTANDING ISTIO'S CORE COMPONENTS

6. Deploy the application, enable ambient mode for services, and verify installation:

```
# Apply the ambient configuration
kubectl apply -f ambient-app.yaml

# Verify namespace is labeled for ambient mode
kubectl get namespace ecommerce --show-labels

# Label the namespace to enable ztunnel
kubectl label namespace ecommerce istio.io/dataplane-mode=ambient

# Enable L7 processing for specific services
kubectl label namespace ecommerce istio.io/ambient-services="frontend,catalog"

# Check ztunnel pods
kubectl get pods -n istio-system -l app=ztunnel

# Check waypoint proxy deployment (if L7 features are enabled)
kubectl get pods -n ecommerce -l istio.io/waypoint-proxy=true
```

7. Verify deployment for our sample application:

```
# Check all resources
kubectl get all -n ecommerce

# Output of: kubectl get all -n ecommerce
NAME                                READY   STATUS    RESTARTS   AGE
pod/frontend-75d9f6f89c-nx8p2       1/1     Running   0          2m
pod/frontend-75d9f6f89c-vk4m3       1/1     Running   0          2m
pod/catalog-86b8d7b4d5-j9x7h        1/1     Running   0          2m
pod/catalog-86b8d7b4d5-p2q3r        1/1     Running   0          2m
pod/frontend-wp-6f7d95c4-qw21p      1/1     Running   0          2m
pod/catalog-wp-5d8b9f7c-zt43n       1/1     Running   0          2m

NAME                TYPE        CLUSTER-IP      EXTERNAL-IP   PORT(S)   AGE
service/frontend    ClusterIP   10.96.45.123    <none>        80/TCP    2m
service/catalog     ClusterIP   10.96.78.234    <none>        80/TCP    2m
```

71

CHAPTER 2 UNDERSTANDING ISTIO'S CORE COMPONENTS

```
NAME                            READY   UP-TO-DATE   AVAILABLE   AGE
deployment.apps/frontend        2/2     2            2           2m
deployment.apps/catalog         2/2     2            2           2m

NAME                                      DESIRED   CURRENT   READY   AGE
replicaset.apps/frontend-75d9f6f89c       2         2         2       2m
replicaset.apps/catalog-86b8d7b4d5        2         2         2       2m

# Verify ambient mode configuration
istioctl proxy-status

# Output of: istioctl proxy-status
NAME                                         PROXY TYPE   SERIAL
IPADDRESSES        STATUS
istio-system/ztunnel-4f5gh                   Ztunnel      1.19.3
10.244.1.2         SYNCED
istio-system/ztunnel-7h9kj                   Ztunnel      1.19.3
10.244.2.2         SYNCED
istio-system/ztunnel-nt6vm                   Ztunnel      1.19.3   10.244.0.2      SYNCED
ecommerce/frontend-wp-6f7d95c4-qw21p         Waypoint     1.19.3   10.244.1.3      SYNCED
ecommerce/catalog-wp-5d8b9f7c-zt43n          Waypoint     1.19.3   10.244.2.3      SYNCED

# Check L7 routing capability
istioctl experimental ambient verify

# Output of: istioctl experimental ambient verify
✓ Verifying Ambient mesh configuration...
✓ Ztunnel DaemonSet found and running
✓ Ambient CNI DaemonSet found and running
✓ Istio discovery found and running
✓ Istio ingressgateway found and running
✓ Namespace ecommerce has ambient label
✓ Found 2 applications in mesh: frontend, catalog
✓ L7 processing enabled for services: frontend, catalog
✓ Waypoint proxies running for L7 services
```

```
✓ All required Istio CRDs are present
✓ Gateway and HTTPRoute resources are valid
✓ Authorization policies are properly configured

VERIFICATION SUCCESSFUL
Ambient mesh is properly configured and operational
```

Sidecar vs. Ambient Mode Comparison

Comprising a thorough but resource-intensive approach, sidecar mode reflects the conventional Istio implementation. Every pod in the sidecar mode gets its own proxy sidecar, allowing pod-level detailed observability and fine-grained control, and along with comprehensive metrics and distributed tracing, this architecture allows for sophisticated traffic management tools including weighted routing and exact load balancing. Teams must manage sidecar injection processes and preserve more extensive configuration sets for every microservice; thus, this granular control results in higher resource consumption and more operational complexity.

Ambient mode provides, on the other hand, a more simplified and cost-effective method of using a service mesh. It uses a shared ztunnel proxy architecture operating at the node level instead of distributing individual sidecars, so greatly lowering the total resource overhead. This mode reduces sidecar injection and centralized policy management, so simplifying the deployment and management process, and does trade some granularity in control and observability. Whereas traffic management capabilities are typically more focused on service-level rather than pod-level control, security elements like mTLS are implemented at the namespace level rather than per pod. Though still present, the observability characteristics offer a somewhat coarser perspective of the service mesh than the sidecar mode.

How Istio Manages Service Discovery and Load Balancing

Service discovery and load balancing are crucial to Istio's ability to efficiently manage service-to-service communication. This section provides a detailed explanation as to how Istio integrates with Kubernetes to enable dynamic service discovery and implements sophisticated load balancing strategies using Envoy proxies.

CHAPTER 2   UNDERSTANDING ISTIO'S CORE COMPONENTS

Service Discovery in Istio

To maintain an accurate representation of the service mesh, Istio uses Kubernetes' native service discovery mechanisms, which are enhanced by Istiod. Istiod's deep integration with Kubernetes allows it to continuously monitor the Kubernetes API server for changes in service deployments, endpoints, and pod health. It ensures that the control plane has the most recent network topology by identifying the service name, IP address, ports, and associated pods for each service. Istiod maintains a service registry, which serves as a centralized database for all services and their corresponding endpoints. Envoy proxies are dynamically configured using this registry to ensure that traffic is routed correctly. Istiod ensures continuous communication by pushing configuration updates to Envoy proxies in near real time as services are added, updated, or removed.

The following example shows how Istio discovers services within a Kubernetes cluster:

```yaml
apiVersion: v1
kind: Service
metadata:
  name: backend
  labels:
      app: backend
spec:
  selector:
      app: backend
  ports:
  - protocol: TCP
    port: 80
    targetPort: 8080
```

1. Deploy the Service:

   ```
   kubectl apply -f backend-service.yaml
   ```

2. Check Service Discovery: Verify that Istiod has detected the service:

   ```
   kubectl get endpoints backend -o yaml
   ```

3. Inspect the Service Registry: Use the `istioctl proxy-config` command to inspect the Envoy proxy configuration:

```
istioctl proxy-config endpoints <pod-name> -n <namespace>
```

Load Balancing in Istio

To optimize traffic distribution, Envoy, the data plane in Istio, which employs sophisticated load balancing strategies; round-robin, which distributes requests evenly across all available service instances; least request, which routes traffic to the instance with the fewest active connections; and weighted load balancing, which prioritizes traffic by assigning weights to different instances are among the load balancing algorithms that Istio supports. Envoy ensures that load balancing decisions are adjusted to real-time conditions by receiving updates from Istiod regarding service health and availability, and by utilizing Istio's VirtualService configuration, load balancing can be further optimized on a per-route basis.

An example of configuring a load balancing strategy in a VirtualService can be seen as follows:

```yaml
apiVersion: networking.istio.io/v1alpha3
kind: VirtualService
metadata:
  name: backend
spec:
  hosts:
  - backend.default.svc.cluster.local
  http:
  - route:
      - destination:
        host: backend.default.svc.cluster.local
        subset: v1
        port:
            number: 8080
        weight: 70
      - destination:
        host: backend.default.svc.cluster.local
        subset: v2
```

```
    port:
        number: 8080
    weight: 30
```

1. Apply the VirtualService:

   ```
   kubectl apply -f virtualservice.yaml
   ```

2. Verify Configuration: Inspect the load-balancing configuration using:

   ```
   istioctl proxy-config routes <pod-name> -n <namespace>
   ```

Consider an online shopping platform that includes several microservices: frontend, catalog, cart, and payment. During high-traffic events like Black Friday, Istio ensures that new service instances are discovered and added to the load balancer without causing any downtime. Weighted load balancing allows the service to prioritize traffic to its primary data center while routing some requests to a secondary site. Istio significantly reduces operational complexity by automating service discovery and optimizing load balancing while also keeping reliable, scalable communication between microservices.

How Istio Manages Security and Identity Management

Istio offers robust mechanisms for securing service-to-service communication and identity management within a service mesh. These capabilities are critical for modern microservices architectures, where security risks rise with the complexity and scale of interactions.

Authentication with Mutual TLS (mTLS)

Istio includes robust mechanisms for securing service-to-service communication and identity management within a service mesh. These capabilities are critical for modern microservices architectures, where security risks rise with the complexity and scale of interactions. Istio uses mutual TLS (mTLS) as its default security mechanism to ensure encrypted and authenticated communication between services. All communication between services is encrypted to prevent unauthorized data access in transit, and services are authenticated with cryptographic identities rather than traditional IP-based

CHAPTER 2   UNDERSTANDING ISTIO'S CORE COMPONENTS

mechanisms. Istiod automatically issues, rotates, and manages service certificates, significantly reducing the need for manual effort.

Authorization with Open Policy Agent (OPA)

Istio's integration with Open Policy Agent (OPA) makes it possible to control access more precisely. OPA has rules that spell out which services can talk to each other and when they can do so. For example, an organization's policy might say, "Allow the payment service to access the user service only between 8:00 a.m. and 6:00 p.m." OPA makes sure that these rules are followed by constantly checking requests and enforcing them.

Cert-Manager Integration

It is possible to connect Istio to Cert-Manager so that external certificates can be managed for traffic that goes to the Internet. Let's Encrypt. Other providers are used by Cert-Manager to automatically issue and renew certificates. Cert-Manager gives the domain an HTTPS certificate, but in the case of an ecommerce platform, an Istio gateway may let clients see the frontend. This makes sure that clients can safely talk over HTTPS without the operations team having to get involved.

The security model in Istio makes it easier to control access, authenticate users, and encrypt data in a microservices environment, which can be very complicated. Integration of mTLS, OPA, and Cert-Manager makes it possible to control who can see what, make using HTTPS for traffic from outside the network easier, and make sure that only verified services can talk to each other.

Comprehending the Telemetry and Monitoring Components of Istio

Istio offers a dependable observability stack that enables teams to comprehend and resolve their microservices architecture. Istio's fundamental functionality involves the automatic collection of comprehensive metrics regarding service-to-service communication, such as request volumes, latencies, error rates, and network behavior, through the use of Envoy proxies (sidecars). This telemetry data is particularly valuable for large-scale deployments because it is collected without necessitating changes to application code.

Three primary observability pillars are fed by the collected data: metrics (via Prometheus), distributed tracing (through systems such as Jaeger), and logging. This data can be viewed by teams through Grafana dashboards that are preconfigured with Istio, providing them with immediate insights into the health and performance of the service mesh. Operators can promptly identify issues, comprehend service dependencies, and make data-driven decisions regarding their infrastructure as a result of this comprehensive observability approach. Istio's monitoring components offer the requisite visibility into the service mesh's behavior, whether it be to investigate failures, plan capacity, or address performance bottlenecks.

Istio: Advanced Traffic Management

Istio offers advanced traffic management capabilities through Custom Resource Definitions (CRDs), which allow for precise management of service-to-service communication within your mesh, and these operators can execute critical reliability patterns, including fault injection for resilience testing, gradual traffic shifting for safe deployments, and configurable timeouts and retries for graceful failure handling, by utilizing these resources. These features are especially beneficial when testing system behavior under a variety of network conditions or when deploying new service versions with minimal risk.

The platform's core configuration is also flexible, enabling teams to customize the service mesh to meet their unique requirements, and these operators can modify Istiod's behavior and deploy custom plugins to expand its functionality beyond the default capabilities by utilizing Kubernetes ConfigMaps. The mesh's extensible architecture facilitates integration with existing infrastructure and tools, while the gateway configuration ensures secure exposure of services to external traffic. The operational consistency of Istio is maintained in that it is adaptable to various deployment scenarios due to the combination of built-in features and customization options.

Conclusion

This chapter provided a comprehensive overview of Istio's core components and their interactions. With a solid understanding of Istiod, Envoy, and the mechanisms for service discovery, security, and traffic management, you are ready to dive deeper into advanced features in the following chapters. These include traffic shaping, observability best practices, security and identity management, and multi-cluster deployments.

CHAPTER 3

Fundamentals of Traffic Management with Istio

Introduction

In modern microservices architectures, effective traffic management is fundamental to ensuring reliable, scalable, and resilient service communication. We will examine the fundamental ideas of traffic management in Istio, a powerful service mesh solution that addresses the complexities of service-to-service communication, in this chapter. We'll look at how Istio's traffic management features, which are based on Envoy proxies and managed by Istiod, allow organizations to use advanced load balancing, routing, and resilience techniques and show how Istio's virtual services, destination rules, and other resources combine to offer a fine-grained control over traffic flow while maintaining the separation between routing logic and service implementation using a real-world example of a video streaming recommendation service.

Understanding the Importance of Traffic Management

Microservices offer several advantages, such as faster development cycles, autonomous scalability, and modularity, and at the same time they also pose unique challenges to traffic flows. In a microservices context, distributed dependencies, varying workloads, and dynamic changes in service instances frequently make service-to-service communication challenging. Microservices can face several issues in the absence of robust traffic management:

- Service Failures: If there are no processes in place to handle failures gracefully, a single service outage could spread and cause disruptions to the entire system.

- Load Imbalance: Improper traffic allocation might overload certain service instances while leaving others idle, leading to inefficient and degraded performance.

- Limited Visibility: Without proper observability, it becomes challenging to understand how traffic moves across services, and it makes troubleshooting and optimization challenging.

- Deployment Challenges: Traffic routing needs to be precisely controlled for modern deployment techniques like blue/green deployments and canary releases, which are challenging to accomplish without specialized tools.

By enabling controlled routing, balancing traffic loads, and providing resilience and observability mechanisms, effective traffic management addresses these challenges.

Istio's Architecture for Traffic Management

Istio's traffic management strategy consists of two primary components: **Istiod** handles the control plane, while **Envoy proxies** represent the data plane. These components cooperate to give declarative and dynamic control over the flow of traffic between microservices. Figure 3-1 shows the overall architecture and components involved in Istio's traffic management architecture.

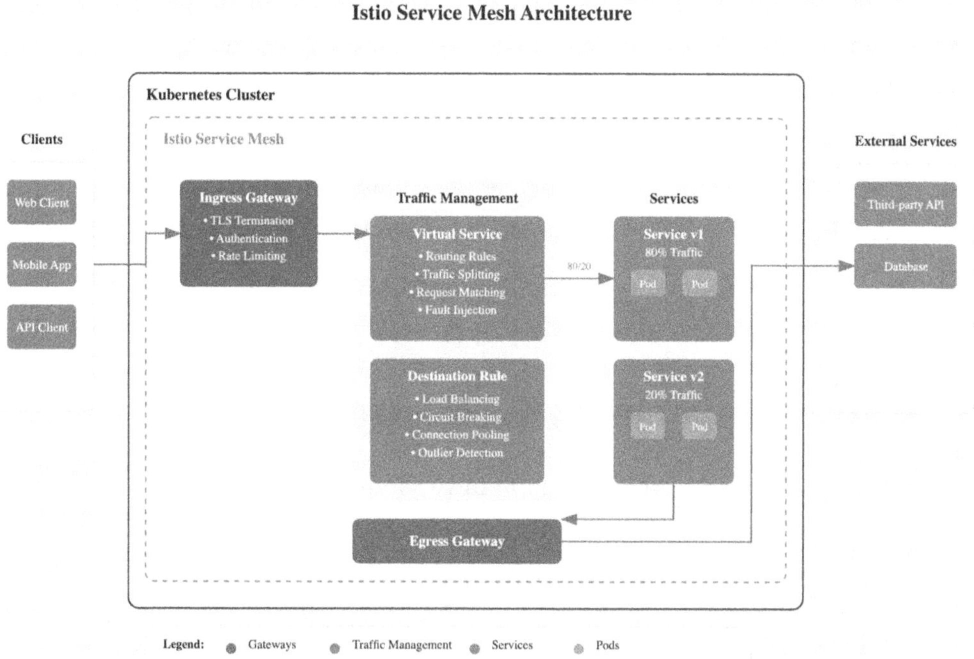

CHAPTER 3   FUNDAMENTALS OF TRAFFIC MANAGEMENT WITH ISTIO

Istio Service Mesh Architecture

Figure 3-1. The overall architecture and components involved in Istio's traffic management architecture

Traffic between services is handled by the data plane, which is powered by Envoy proxies, and by intercepting all incoming and outgoing traffic, Envoy, when deployed as a sidecar proxy alongside each pod of a service instance, enables Istio to implement traffic management policies transparently. Envoy is also responsible for observability, fault injection, load balancing, and many other features we explore in this book.

The data plane is controlled by the control plane, which is managed by Istiod. Envoy proxies can be configured using Istiod's intelligence following user-specified traffic rules. Aso, Istiod is a combination of previously distinct elements like Pilot, Citadel, and Galley into a single unified service, simplifying Istio's architecture. Istiod performs several essential functions:

- Service Discovery: Istiod locates the cluster's services and gives Envoy proxies information about them, and this guarantees that proxies are always up to date on the most recent services that are available.

- Configuration Management: Istiod distributes traffic rules that are defined by the user to Envoy proxies, and these rules dictate the flow of traffic and include resilience policies, load balancing techniques, and routing decisions.

- Security: By issuing and rotating mTLS certificates, Istiod ensures encrypted traffic and authentication while managing secure connectivity between services.

- Telemetry and Monitoring: By integrating with observability technologies, Istiod makes it possible to collect metrics, logs, and distributed traces offering deep insights into traffic behavior.

Istio can keep its traffic management framework very flexible, scalable, and resilient due to the separation of the data and control planes.

Role of Envoy Proxy in Traffic Management

A key component of Istio's traffic management capabilities is Envoy proxies. These instances are deployed alongside each service container and function as sidecar proxies, and this design is the reason Istio can implement traffic management policies without requiring modifications to the application and guarantees that all traffic both incoming and outgoing is routed through Envoy.

Envoy handles traffic interception and routing based on rules defined in Istio's configuration objects, for example, it can use HTTP headers, request routes, or other metadata to route traffic to particular service instances, and to guarantee the best use of available resources, Envoy additionally offers sophisticated load balancing techniques including round-robin, least request, and locality-aware routing.

Envoy allows traffic shaping in addition to load balancing and routing, which involves dividing traffic between service versions for canary deployments, mirroring requests to shadow services for validation, and creating artificial delays or faults for resilience testing. Metrics and distributed tracing, two of Envoy's observability capabilities, provide customers with in-depth insights into traffic patterns and facilitate quick identification of issues.

Overview of Istio Traffic Management APIs

Several declarative APIs are used by Istio's traffic management framework to enable users to specify and regulate traffic behavior at a granular level. These APIs include

1. VirtualService: This is the core API for creating traffic routing rules. A VirtualService specifies how requests should be routed to various service versions or subsets based on conditions such as

CHAPTER 3   FUNDAMENTALS OF TRAFFIC MANAGEMENT WITH ISTIO

request headers, URIs, or methods. For example, a VirtualService can direct 90% of traffic to one version of a service while sending 10% to another, enabling canary deployments.

2. DestinationRule: Supplementing a VirtualService is a DestinationRule that establishes guidelines for handling traffic when it arrives at its destination, and it helps increase service reliability, build load balancing strategies, apply connection pooling settings, and perform outlier detection mechanisms.

3. Gateway: The Gateway API allows us to control the external traffic entering or leaving the service mesh, including configuring ingress and egress gateways for tasks such as exposing services to external clients, terminating TLS connections, or applying host-based routing rules. Please note that Istio now also supports the usage of the standard Kubernetes Gateway API. We will not be covering this as part of this book as much of the industry still uses Istio's ingress and egress gateways; however, the interested readers can refer to https://istio.io/latest/docs/tasks/traffic-management/ingress/gateway-api/ and https://gateway-api.sigs.k8s.io/ for more details.

4. ServiceEntry: Istio can apply traffic policies to services outside the cluster; by using this API, it can add external services to the mesh. For example, a ServiceEntry can manage and secure communication by controlling access to an external database or API.

By effectively managing traffic in a modern microservices environment by establishing progressive delivery strategies, ensuring fair request distribution, and evaluating resilience through fault injection, Istio's traffic management architecture and APIs let users easily control complex traffic patterns.

Sample Application: Recommendation Service

To illustrate how Istio's traffic management features work, we'll use a sample **recommendation service** as the running example throughout this section. This simple

CHAPTER 3   FUNDAMENTALS OF TRAFFIC MANAGEMENT WITH ISTIO

microservice mimics a video streaming platform's recommendation engine, with two versions (v1 and v2) deployed as separate Kubernetes pods:

- Version 1 (v1): Represents the stable and currently deployed recommendation service. It returns a basic list of recommendations.

- Version 2 (v2): Represents an AI-enhanced version of the recommendation service under testing. It provides a more personalized list of recommendations.

We'll build the sample application, containerize it using Docker, and deploy both versions to Kubernetes. Then, we'll use Istio to implement traffic management features like **traffic splitting**, **fault injection**, and **protocol-specific routing** to manage traffic between these versions.

Here is the simple file structure of our application. We will try to keep the application as simple as possible and focus on the Istio configuration. We will go through the entire process of creating an application and deploying it to Kubernetes:

```
recommendation-service/
├── Dockerfile
├── recommendation_v1.py
├── recommendation_v2.py
└── requirements.txt
```

The recommendation service is developed with Python and Flask, providing a straightforward REST API featuring a single endpoint, /recommendations, which delivers a list of movie recommendations in JSON format, and the behavior varies between version 1 and version 2:

- Version 1: Returns a static list of popular and trending recommendations

- Version 2: Simulates an AI-enhanced recommendation engine with a more dynamic and personalized list

Version 1 provides a basic set of recommendations:

```python
from flask import Flask, jsonify

app = Flask(__name__)

@app.route("/recommendations", methods=["GET"])
```

```python
def get_recommendations():
    recommendations = [
        {"id": 1, "title": "Movie A", "type": "Popular"},
        {"id": 2, "title": "Movie B", "type": "Trending"},
        {"id": 3, "title": "Movie C", "type": "Top Rated"}
    ]
    return jsonify({"version": "v1", "recommendations": recommendations})

if __name__ == "__main__":
    app.run(host="0.0.0.0", port=8080)
```

Version 2 simulates an advanced recommendation engine:

```python
from flask import Flask, jsonify, request

app = Flask(__name__)

@app.route("/recommendations", methods=["GET", "POST"])
def handle_recommendations():
    if request.method == "GET":
        # Original GET logic
        recommendations = [
            {"id": 1, "title": "Movie X", "type": "AI-Enhanced"},
            {"id": 2, "title": "Movie Y", "type": "Personalized"},
            {"id": 3, "title": "Movie Z", "type": "Recently Watched"}
        ]
        return jsonify({"version": "v2", "recommendations":
        recommendations})

    elif request.method == "POST":
        # Get the JSON data from the request
        user_data = request.get_json()

        # Generate personalized recommendations based on user data
        # This is a simple example - you would typically use the user_data
        # to customize the recommendations
        recommendations = [
            {"id": 1, "title": f"Movie X for user {user_data.get('userId',
            'unknown')}",
```

```
            "type": "AI-Enhanced"},
           {"id": 2, "title": "Movie Y", "type": "Personalized"},
           {"id": 3, "title": "Movie Z", "type": "Recently Watched"}
       ]

       return jsonify({
           "version": "v2",
           "recommendations": recommendations,
           "userPreferences": user_data
       })
if __name__ == "__main__":
   app.run(host="0.0.0.0", port=8080)
```

We will use Docker to build the image:

```
ARG CMD

# Base image
FROM python:3.9-slim

ARG CMD

# Convert ARG to ENV so it's available at runtime
ENV SCRIPT_NAME=${CMD}

# Set working directory
WORKDIR /app

# Copy application code
COPY . .

# Install dependencies
RUN pip install --no-cache-dir -r requirements.txt

# Default command
CMD python ${SCRIPT_NAME}
```

For Version 1:

```
docker build -t recommendation:v1 --build-arg CMD=recommendation_v1.py .
```

CHAPTER 3   FUNDAMENTALS OF TRAFFIC MANAGEMENT WITH ISTIO

For Version 2:

```
docker build -t recommendation:v2 --build-arg CMD=recommendation_v2.py .
```

We push these images to a container registry:

```
docker tag recommendation:v1 <your-docker-repo>/recommendation:v1
docker push <your-docker-repo>/recommendation:v1
docker tag recommendation:v2 <your-docker-repo>/recommendation:v2
docker push <your-docker-repo>/recommendation:v2
```

Now that we have built the Docker images of different versions of our recommendation service, let's deploy these into our Kubernetes cluster, create the deployments with each of these versions, and apply them using `kubectl apply -f <file-name>`:

```yaml
apiVersion: apps/v1
kind: Deployment
metadata:
  name: recommendation-v1
  labels:
    app: recommendation
    version: v1
spec:
  replicas: 2
  selector:
    matchLabels:
      app: recommendation
      version: v1
  template:
    metadata:
      labels:
        app: recommendation
        version: v1
    spec:
      containers:
        - name: recommendation
          image: <your-docker-repo>/recommendation:v1
```

```
        imagePullPolicy: Always
        ports:
          - containerPort: 8080
---
apiVersion: apps/v1
kind: Deployment
metadata:
  name: recommendation-v2
  labels:
    app: recommendation
    version: v2
spec:
  replicas: 1
  selector:
    matchLabels:
      app: recommendation
      version: v2
  template:
    metadata:
      labels:
        app: recommendation
        version: v2
    spec:
      containers:
        - name: recommendation
          image: <your-docker-repo>/recommendation:v2
          imagePullPolicy: Always
          ports:
            - containerPort: 8080
```

We will create a LoadBalancer service that redirects the traffic to the pods created by these deployments.

CHAPTER 3   FUNDAMENTALS OF TRAFFIC MANAGEMENT WITH ISTIO

In Kind, to create a service of type LoadBalancer, we need to install cloud-provider-kind. More information about this can be found in the Kind documentation (https://kind.sigs.k8s.io/docs/user/loadbalancer/):

```
cloud-provider-kind can be installed using golang
go install sigs.k8s.io/cloud-provider-kind@latest
```

This will install the binary in $GOBIN (typically ~/go/bin); you can make it available elsewhere if appropriate:

```
sudo install ~/go/bin/cloud-provider-kind /usr/local/bin
```

Once the cloud-provider-kind is installed, we must keep running the binary in the other window:

```
sudo cloud-provider-kind
```

Now let's create our service and apply it:

```
apiVersion: v1
kind: Service
metadata:
  name: recommendation
  labels:
    app: recommendation
spec:
  type: LoadBalancer
  externalTrafficPolicy: Cluster
  ports:
    - port: 80
      targetPort: 8080
  selector:
    app: recommendation
```

As show in Figure 3-2 this will install the service of type LoadBalancer on your cluster, and you will be assigned an external IP. For my local Kind Kubernetes cluster, I see an external IP address assigned as below.

TYPE	CLUSTER-IP	EXTERNAL-IP
ClusterIP	10.96.0.1	
LoadBalancer	10.96.199.182	172.18.0.4
LoadBalancer	10.96.219.133	172.18.0.3

Figure 3-2. *The service of type LoadBalancer installation on the cluster with assigned external IP*

The service should now be available at http://172.18.0.4/recommendations. Trying to hit the service multiple times will cause the request to randomly go to the pods:

curl -X GET http://172.18.0.4/recommendations -H "connection:close"

We recommend starting with a fresh Kubernetes namespace for all the examples that follow. We give instructions wherever possible to delete all the resources that were created in the previous section so that you continue creating new resources for the current section:

Note Please delete all the resource configurations that were created in previous sections before starting a new one. This will keep things from going wrong.

```
kubectl delete deployments      --all -n <namespace>
kubectl delete services         --all -n <namespace>
kubectl delete virtualservice   --all -n <namespace>
kubectl delete gateway          --all -n <namespace>
kubectl delete destinationrule  --all -n <namespace>
```

Virtual Services and Destination Rules

Istio's traffic management capabilities are built on the foundation of virtual services and destination rules. They serve as the basis of Istio's ability to control and shape traffic patterns within a service mesh. While virtual services define how traffic is routed to services based on policies and conditions, destination rules decide what happens to traffic when it reaches its destination.

Together these two resources offer strong traffic management capabilities like intelligent routing, load balancing, failure resilience, retries, and timeouts. By separating concerns between destination configurations and routing logic, Istio offers a versatile and modular approach to managing microservices at scale.

CHAPTER 3   FUNDAMENTALS OF TRAFFIC MANAGEMENT WITH ISTIO

We will examine each resource in depth in this part, beginning with virtual services, to understand how they empower developers and operators to achieve fine-grained control over service-to-service communication.

> **Note**   The basic examples in the following sections will be under the CHAPTER-3/basic/ folder. Please clean up the resources in your namespace as mentioned at the beginning of the chapter. We will continue indicating the appropriate GitHub repo configuration folders wherever applicable.

Understanding Virtual Services

One of Istio's primary configuration resources, virtual services, provides you with control over the routing of requests inside your service mesh. Virtual Services enable dynamic, fine-grained traffic control without requiring changes to the application code by decoupling the implementation of services from routing rules, and they are essential for traffic management use cases like traffic shifting, canary deployments, blue-green rollouts, and A/B testing.

The rules for directing traffic to particular services within your mesh are defined by a virtual service, and these rules include specifying conditions for matching requests and using those conditions to determine the appropriate destination. Header-based routing, weight-based traffic splitting, and fault injection are some of the advanced features enabled by virtual services offering a powerful mechanism for customizing traffic behavior.

We will delve deeper into the role, advantages, and setup of virtual services in the following sections, examining their structure, key fields, and how they integrate with other Istio resources like destination rules.

Purpose and Benefits

Virtual services serve as the foundation for Istio's traffic management capabilities, offering precise control over how requests are routed within a service mesh. By defining routing rules independent of service implementation, virtual services enable dynamic traffic shaping and operational agility, which are critical for managing microservices at scale. Let's look at why we need them and what are the benefits of these.

Purpose of Virtual Services

- Dynamic Traffic Routing: With virtual services, you can specify how requests are sent to different service versions or subsets based on criteria like query parameters, URI paths, or request headers. This enables the creation of customized traffic flows for various use cases, like geographic routing or A/B testing.

- Separation of Concerns: Because routing logic and service code are separated, developers can focus on application logic while Istio operators handle traffic and routing.

- Resilience and Observability: Virtual services help create resilient microservices and help in simulating failures for testing using features like fault injection, timeouts, and retries.

- Granular Control: They provide conditional routing and exact targeting of traffic to particular service subsets, permitting incremental rollouts and regulated testing.

Benefits of Virtual Services

- Simplified Traffic Management: Virtual services make it easier to manage microservices-based applications by streamlining the creation of complex traffic patterns including traffic shifting, weighted splits, and canary deployments.

- Improved Agility: The frequency of application redeployments will be greatly reduced with centralized traffic control as changes can be made quickly and consistently across the service mesh.

- Enhanced Stability: By reducing the impact of service failures, Istio's features like outlier detection and retry policies can improve the overall system's reliability.

- Operational Efficiency: Teams can now test different kinds of traffic strategies such as routing specific set of users to a service's beta version, without affecting the wider production environments.

CHAPTER 3   FUNDAMENTALS OF TRAFFIC MANAGEMENT WITH ISTIO

Going back to the video streaming platform example, you can use virtual services to

- Keep the majority of users on recommendation-v1 and send a subset to test the AI-enhanced recommendation-v2 service.

- Inject artificial delays or simulate errors to test the resilience of the recommendation service under adverse conditions.

- Automatically retry failed requests based on predefined policies to enhance the user experience.

Basic Structure and Configuration

A Kubernetes Custom Resource Definition (CRD), which was installed into the cluster when we installed Istio, is used to define a virtual service in Istio, and by defining rules for how requests are matched and directed to one or more destinations, it gives you control over traffic routing. The basic structure of a virtual service includes fields for describing the host (destination service), routing rules, and optional policies like fault injection or retries. Usually, a virtual service manifest contains the following sections (you can also find the complete list of attributes at https://istio.io/latest/docs/reference/config/networking/virtual-service/):

- Metadata: Includes the name and namespace of the virtual service.

- Spec:

    - Hosts: Identifies the virtual service's host or destination services

    - Gateways (Optional): Defines the gateways through which the virtual service can be accessed

    - HTTP/TCP/TLS (Protocol-Specific Routing): Contains rules to match requests and define routing behavior

    - Policies (Optional): Additional configurations like retries, timeouts, fault injection, or mirroring

Here's an example of the basic structure:

```
apiVersion: networking.istio.io/v1beta1
kind: VirtualService
metadata:
```

```yaml
  name: recommendation-virtualservice
spec:
  hosts:
    - "*"
  gateways:
    - recommendation-gateway
  http:
    - match:
        - uri:
            prefix: /recommendations
      rewrite:
        uri: "/recommendations"
      route:
        - destination:
            host: recommendation-service
            subset: v2
          weight: 20
        - destination:
            host: recommendation-service
            subset: v1
          weight: 80
    - match:
        - uri:
            prefix: /v1
      rewrite:
        uri: "/recommendations"
      route:
        - destination:
            host: recommendation-service
            subset: v1
```

We will explore the meaning and significance of each of these fields as we progress through this chapter.

CHAPTER 3   FUNDAMENTALS OF TRAFFIC MANAGEMENT WITH ISTIO

Key Fields and Their Significance

With fine-grained traffic routing provided by Istio's virtual services, developers can design complex routing rules for their respective applications. Every field available in a virtual service serves a different purpose and enhances the general operation of the service. Let's examine the importance of these fields and see their pragmatic applications:

1. The hosts field indicates the DNS or service name the virtual service corresponds to. This can include mesh-based services as well as those reachable via gateways. For instance, the below example shows how a virtual service can control all traffic directed to the recommendation service:

   ```
   hosts:
     - recommendation-service
   ```

2. The virtual service can control traffic entering or exiting the mesh through specific ingress or egress gateways by using the optional gateways field. For example, the below illustrated configuration ensures that only traffic going through the specified gateway is subject to the virtual service rules. If the gateways field is omitted, the virtual service applies solely to in-mesh traffic:

   ```
   gateways:
     - recommendation-gateway
   ```

3. Depending on the kind of traffic, routing rules are protocol-specific and are described under fields like http, tcp, and tls, and these sections allow you to specify advanced features like load balancing, fault injection, retries, and URL-based routing. For instance, you can set rules under http that will route requests to a particular version of the recommendation service when they contain URIs that start with /recommendations, and the following configuration is used to accomplish this:

   ```
   http:
     - match:
         - uri:
   ```

```
        prefix: "/recommendations"
  route:
    - destination:
        host: recommendation-service
        subset: v1
```

4. The `match` field within a protocol section enables conditional routing based on specific request characteristics, such as URI prefixes, headers, or query parameters. The following example guarantees that only requests with URIs starting with /recommendations are routed accordingly. This functionality is crucial for implementing features such as A/B testing, canary deployments, or user segmentation:

```
match:
  - uri:
      prefix: "/recommendations"
```

5. Once traffic is matched, the `route` field determines where the traffic should be directed. It allows specifying one or more destinations along with their traffic weights, which is particularly useful for load balancing or canary releases. For example, the below configuration distributes 80% of the traffic to version v1 and 20% to version v2 of the recommendation service. The destinations are further defined using the `destination` field, which specifies the target service and its subset. Below is an example where we can see subsets such as v1 and v2 defined in a destination rule:

```
route:
  - destination:
      host: recommendation-service
      subset: v1
    weight: 80
  - destination:
```

```
      host: recommendation-service
      subset: v2
    weight: 20
```

6. The `weight` field, which allocates a percentage of traffic to each destination, is used to accomplish traffic splitting. In scenarios like testing new features or releasing updates gradually, this feature is pivotal. For example, if weight is set to 20, 20% of the traffic will be directed to the specified location.

7. Istio also provides options to enhance reliability through the `retries` field, which defines retry behavior for failed requests. For example, configuring retries for failed requests up to three times, with a timeout of two seconds for each attempt, improves the resilience of applications by handling transient errors gracefully:

```
retries:
  attempts: 3
  perTryTimeout: 2s
```

8. The `fault` field enables the simulation of delays or the introduction of defects into traffic for testing and resilience research, and this is beneficial for evaluating service performance under adverse conditions. The following example implements a fixed delay of five seconds for 50% of the traffic, allowing developers to assess service performance under high-latency circumstances:

```
fault:
  delay:
    fixedDelay: 5s
    percentage: 50
```

9. Finally, the `mirror` field enables duplicating live traffic to a secondary service or version for testing purposes. For example, mirroring traffic to version v2 of the recommendation service

allows developers to test new versions without affecting production traffic:

```
mirror:
  host: recommendation-service
  subset: v2
```

When used effectively, these fields give you power for managing traffic in a service mesh, and you can make virtual services that meet the requirements of your application by understanding and using them. This will ensure high availability, reliability, and traffic routing flexibility.

Field	Purpose	Significance
hosts	Defines target service(s)	Determines where the virtual service rules apply
gateways	Specifies ingress/egress gateways	Controls traffic entering or exiting the mesh
http, tcp, tls	Manages protocol-specific traffic	Enables advanced features like routing, retries, and fault injection
match	Matches incoming request conditions	Enables conditional routing
route	Defines destinations for traffic	Supports traffic splitting and load balancing
destination	Specifies target service/subset	Links to destination rules for version control
weight	Sets traffic distribution	Facilitates canary deployments and load testing
retries	Configures retry behavior	Enhances reliability by retrying failed requests
fault	Simulates errors or delays	Tests service resilience under adverse conditions
mirror	Duplicates traffic for testing	Enables non-intrusive validation of new services or versions

CHAPTER 3   FUNDAMENTALS OF TRAFFIC MANAGEMENT WITH ISTIO

At this point, don't worry if these fields appear overwhelming or unfamiliar. In this chapter, we will explore each of these fields in further detail, analyzing their configuration, functionality, and real-world applications. You will have a greater understanding of these fields by the end of the chapter and feel more at ease using them to develop reliable and effective traffic management strategies for your service mesh. Think of this as the fundamental framework; each concept will be described and backed up by examples to help you understand its importance and use it successfully in real-world applications.

Match Conditions and Routing Rules

Match conditions and routing rules are the foundation of Istio's traffic management capabilities, which offer users precise control over request routing within the service mesh. The combination of these two components outlines the process of identifying and subsequently managing incoming traffic. Ultimately, these features enable the development of complicated routing strategies that can be customized to the specific requirements of your application.

Istio will be able to identify specific traffic flows based on the attributes of incoming requests, as match conditions are determined by those attributes. The URI path, HTTP headers, query parameters, and HTTP methods are among the numerous elements that can be included in these attributes. For example, consider a situation in which the traffic is routed differently based on whether or not the request URI begins with /recommendations. To accomplish this, the virtual service configuration provided below can be used:

```
http:
 - match:
    - uri:
        prefix: "/recommendations"
      headers:
        user-agent:
          regex: ".*Chrome.*"
   route:
    - destination:
        host: recommendation-service
        subset: v1
```

101

In this scenario, requests with the URI prefix /recommendations are matched and sent to version v1 of the recommendation service. Such match criteria allow developers to divide traffic and carefully control how requests are processed.

When traffic patterns match, routing rules determine where and how it should be processed and sent. Routing rules can divide traffic among many service versions, direct traffic to particular subsets of a service, and even change request attributes like headers. For example, assume you want to send 70% of traffic to the /recommendations route of the service and the remaining 30% to version v2. Then we can use the below configuration to achieve this:

```
http:
  - match:
      - uri:
          prefix: "/recommendations"
    route:
      - destination:
          host: recommendation-service
          subset: v1
        weight: 70
      - destination:
          host: recommendation-service
          subset: v2
        weight: 30
```

This setting is especially helpful for canary deployments, in which a new version of a service is gradually available to a small group of users. By carefully watching the traffic split, you can keep an eye on how stable and performant the new version is, without affecting the majority of your users.

Istio can support complex traffic control rules that combine both match conditions and routing rules. For instance, you might want to send premium users, who can be identified by a user-type header, to a version of the service that works best with paid features. Normal users, on the other hand, can be sent to a more general version, and one way to put this scenario into configuration is as follows:

```
http:
  - match:
      - uri:
```

```
          prefix: "/recommendations"
        headers:
          user-type:
            exact: "premium"
      route:
        - destination:
            host: recommendation-service
            subset: premium-v1
    - match:
        - uri:
            prefix: "/recommendations"
      route:
        - destination:
            host: recommendation-service
            subset: standard-v1
```

The user-type: premium header tells you that the request is from a premium user, and the standard-v1 header tells you that a request is from any other user. Based on the user profile, this approach makes sure that the experience is tailored and optimized for each user.

Routing rules and match conditions are also important for making systems more resilient and reliable. For example, fault injection can be used to mimic failures or delays that let developers test how their app behaves when things go wrong. When set up this way, 50% of the flow will be held up for five seconds:

```
http:
  - match:
      - uri:
          prefix: "/recommendations"
    fault:
      delay:
        fixedDelay: 5s
        percentage: 50
    route:
      - destination:
          host: recommendation-service
          subset: v1
```

Similarly, retry behavior can be defined to handle transient failures gracefully. For instance, retrying failed requests up to three times with a timeout of two seconds for each attempt can be configured as follows:

```
http:
  - match:
      - uri:
          prefix: "/recommendations"
    retries:
      attempts: 3
      perTryTimeout: 2s
    route:
      - destination:
          host: recommendation-service
          subset: v1
```

By mastering the interplay between match conditions and routing rules, you unlock Istio's full potential to manage traffic with unparalleled flexibility and precision. These features enable you to design routing mechanisms that are not only intelligent but also adaptable to the evolving needs of your applications, ensuring optimal performance, scalability, and user satisfaction.

We will dive deeper into the concept of destinations in the upcoming section, where we will explore their structure, purpose, and how they interact with virtual services. For now, you can think of destinations as the specific endpoints or subsets of a service that traffic is routed to. These endpoints define where matched requests are ultimately directed, enabling precise control over traffic flow. As we progress, we will break down the key components of destinations, such as subsets, load balancing, and their configuration, to provide a comprehensive understanding. Until then, assume destinations represent the target services specified in the routing rules.

Protocol-Specific Routing Features

Beyond basic routing, Istio's traffic management features offer protocol-specific features that give users fine-grained control over how traffic is handled for the TCP, TLS, and HTTP protocols. These features allow developers to fine-tune routing behaviors based on the unique requirements of each protocol, making Istio a versatile solution for diverse application architectures. This section explores the routing capabilities offered by each protocol and provides examples to show how to use them.

The most often used protocol in microservices is HTTP, and Istio provides a wealth of features to manage HTTP traffic. These include routing according to HTTP methods, query parameters, headers, and URL routes. Rules can be put in place, for example, to route requests using specific URI prefixes to different service versions. We have already seen examples of http routine in the previous section.

Istio offers features to effectively route and manage TCP traffic for services that depend on raw TCP connection, like databases or legacy systems. TCP allows for advanced traffic control even if it does not have the same level of detail as HTTP (such as headers or query parameters). Properties like IP addresses and ports can be used to redirect traffic.

For example, if your stateful database communicates over TCP, you can use port numbers or application tiers to send traffic to different database replicas. In the following configuration, you can see a simple TCP routing rule:

```
tcp:
  - match:
      - port: 3306
    route:
      - destination:
          host: db-service
          subset: read-replica
  - match:
      - port: 3307
    route:
      - destination:
          host: db-service
          subset: write-master
```

In this case, the database service's read-replica subset receives traffic on port 3306, while the write-master subset receives traffic on port 3307. By doing this, you can optimize the database load by separating read and write activities.

For services to communicate securely, TLS is essential. Both mutual TLS (mTLS) and Server Name Indication (SNI)–based routing scenarios are supported by Istio for TLS traffic routing. Depending on the requested server name, SNI (Server Name Indication) is particularly useful for routing encrypted traffic to specific locations.

CHAPTER 3   FUNDAMENTALS OF TRAFFIC MANAGEMENT WITH ISTIO

For example, you can configure a virtual service to use the SNI header to direct TLS traffic to different services:

```
tls:
  - match:
      - sniHosts:
          - "secure.recommendation.example.com"
    route:
      - destination:
          host: secure-recommendation
  - match:
      - sniHosts:
          - "secure.analytics.example.com"
    route:
      - destination:
          host: secure-analytics
```

In this setup

- Traffic with the SNI host secure.recommendation.example.com is routed to the secure-recommendation service.

- Traffic with the SNI host secure.analytics.example.com is routed to the secure-analytics service.

TLS routing ensures secure and precise handling of encrypted traffic, making it an essential feature for compliance and data protection requirements. We will discuss more about TLS and SNI in Chapter 4.

Istio's capacity to handle mixed-protocol setups is one of its strengths, for example, a single application can use TCP for database connections, TLS for secure transactions, and HTTP for API interactions. Istio offers seamless management across different traffic types by enabling you to implement protocol-specific rules within the same virtual service:

```
http:
  - match:
      - uri:
          prefix: "/recommendations"
```

```
    route:
      - destination:
          host: recommendation-service
          subset: v1
tcp:
  - match:
      - port: 3306
    route:
      - destination:
          host: db-service
          subset: read-replica
tls:
  - match:
      - sniHosts:
          - "secure.payment.example.com"
    route:
      - destination:
          host: secure-payment
```

In this configuration

- HTTP traffic to /recommendations is routed to version v1 of the recommendation service.

- TCP traffic on port 3306 is routed to the read-replica subset of the db-service.

- TLS traffic with the SNI host secure.payment.example.com is routed to the secure-payment service.

Istio is a powerful tool for handling various application requirements because of its routing features that are specific to each protocol and let developers tailor traffic management strategies that fit the needs of each protocol, ensuring that performance, security, and reliability are all at their best. Also, Istio's protocol-specific features give you the flexibility and control you need to support modern, complicated microservices architectures, whether you're handling encrypted communication, routing API requests, or managing database traffic.

Working with Destination Rules

In Istio's traffic management ecosystem, destination rules play a pivotal role. They enable policies like load balancing, connection pooling, and failure detection by defining how traffic behaves at its destination and controlling what happens when traffic reaches its destination, in contrast to virtual services, which dictate how traffic is routed to a destination. This section explores their purpose, connection pooling, load balancing, subsets, and outlier detection, as well as how they relate to virtual services.

Purpose and Relationship with Virtual Services

By defining policies that are applied to traffic at its destination, destination rules serve as a complement to virtual services. The destination rule controls how traffic behaves when it reaches the service, whereas a virtual service specifies how traffic is matched and routed. Applying different policies to different service subsets and splitting traffic between versions are some examples of advanced traffic control strategies that can be implemented with the help of these resources.

For instance, a virtual service can route 20% of traffic to v2 and 80% to v1 of the service, and a destination rule makes sure that traffic that reaches v1 and v2 behaves in a specific way, like controlling elements like connection pooling, load balancing, etc. This separation of routing and destination logic enables scalability and maintainability in complex microservices architectures:

```
apiVersion: networking.istio.io/v1beta1
kind: DestinationRule
metadata:
  name: recommendation-destinationrule
spec:
  host: recommendation-service
  subsets:
    - name: v1
      labels:
        version: v1
    - name: v2
      labels:
        version: v2
```

```
trafficPolicy:
  loadBalancer:
    simple: ROUND_ROBIN
```

Defining Subsets of Services

Subsets in destination rules are a fundamental notion that enables the grouping of service instances according to common attributes, usually specified by Kubernetes labels. These subsets function as logical representations of various versions or environments of a service, allowing Istio to implement customized traffic management policies for each group, and utilizing them enables precise control over traffic routing and management, making them essential for implementing deployment strategies such as canary releases, A/B testing, or blue-green deployments.

Subsets are especially useful in microservices architectures because various versions of a service can coexist simultaneously. A stable iteration of a video recommendation service (v1) may operate concurrently with a beta version (v2) that has experimental functionalities, and by utilizing subsets, one may segregate traffic for each version and implement targeted policies, such as prioritizing performance for the stable version while assessing the beta version for stability and user feedback.

Subsets are specified in the subsets section of a destination rule and are designated by a distinct name and a collection of labels that must correspond to the labels assigned to the pods in the relevant Kubernetes deployment. Below is an example configuration:

```
apiVersion: networking.istio.io/v1beta1
kind: DestinationRule
metadata:
  name: recommendation-destinationrule
spec:
  host: recommendation-service
  subsets:
    - name: v1
      labels:
        version: v1
    - name: v2
      labels:
        version: v2
```

The labels (version: v1 and version: v2) assigned to these subsets must correspond to the labels assigned to the pods in the relevant Kubernetes deployment, and you can target specific service versions with unique policies by defining subsets and ensuring controlled and predictable traffic behavior.

To have a better understanding, consider a more real-world example. Assume you want to deploy our recommendation service's beta version as a canary release. The destination rule allows you to specify subsets for stable and beta versions, and then you can set up a virtual service to route traffic accordingly:

```yaml
apiVersion: networking.istio.io/v1beta1
kind: DestinationRule
metadata:
  name: recommendation-destinationrule
spec:
  host: recommendation-service
  subsets:
    - name: stable
      labels:
        version: stable
    - name: beta
      labels:
        version: beta

apiVersion: networking.istio.io/v1beta1
kind: VirtualService
metadata:
  name: recommendation-virtualservice
spec:
  hosts:
    - recommendation
  http:
    - route:
        - destination:
            host: recommendation-service
            subset: stable
          weight: 90
```

```
    - destination:
        host: recommendation-service
        subset: beta
      weight: 10
```

In this configuration

- The `stable` subset represents the current production version of the service.

- The `beta` subset represents the canary version.

- 90% of the traffic is routed to the stable version, while 10% is routed to the beta version, ensuring a controlled exposure to the new version.

This setup is particularly valuable for testing new features in production with minimal risk.

The ability to group and manage service instances based on subsets ensures that your traffic management policies align with your deployment and operational goals, making Istio an indispensable tool for modern application development.

Load Balancing Configurations

A critical feature of Istio's traffic management system is load balancing, which makes sure that requests are distributed among service instances efficiently. Istio optimizes resource usage and boosts the overall performance and reliability of your applications by balancing the load evenly so that no one instance is overwhelmed. Also, load balancing becomes indispensable in a distributed microservices architecture, where multiple instances of the same service are deployed for failover and scalability.

Istio offers a range of load balancing algorithms, allowing you to select the one that best fits the requirements of your application. These algorithms are specified in a destination rule's `trafficPolicy.loadBalancer` field. Let's take a closer look at these configurations and provide some real-world examples.

Round-Robin Load Balancing

The simplest and widely applied load balancing technique is the round-robin algorithm. It ensures even traffic distribution by distributing incoming requests cyclically among all available service instances:

```
trafficPolicy:
  loadBalancer:
    simple: ROUND_ROBIN
```

In this configuration, Istio cycles through the list of available instances, sending one request to each instance in turn. This approach works well when all instances have similar capacities and the workload is evenly distributed.

Least-Request Load Balancing

Traffic is routed to the instance that has the fewest active requests by the least-request algorithm. This strategy works especially well when the amount of load that each instance has can vary significantly, such as when instances are working on jobs that require a lot of computing power:

```
trafficPolicy:
  loadBalancer:
    simple: LEAST_REQUEST
```

In this case, Istio directs incoming requests to the instance with the least amount of load by dynamically monitoring the number of active requests for each instance, thus preventing any instance from becoming a bottleneck. Response times under varying workloads are improved.

Random Load Balancing

For every incoming request, a service instance is chosen at random by the random algorithm. In certain situations, such as when the cost of storing extra state (such as active request counts) is prohibitive, random load balancing might aid in the efficient distribution of traffic, although it lacks the predictability of other strategies:

```
trafficPolicy:
  loadBalancer:
    simple: RANDOM
```

CHAPTER 3   FUNDAMENTALS OF TRAFFIC MANAGEMENT WITH ISTIO

This method works well in environments where service instances are homogeneous in terms of capacity and performance.

Weighted Load Balancing

Istio also supports weighted load balancing, which involves assigning predetermined weights to service instances or subsets to determine the distribution of traffic. This is especially beneficial for deployment strategies such as canary releases, which involve redirecting a small portion of traffic to a new service version for testing:

```
apiVersion: networking.istio.io/v1beta1
kind: DestinationRule
metadata:
  name: recommendation-destinationrule
spec:
  host: recommendation-service
  subsets:
    - name: stable
      labels:
        version: stable
    - name: beta
      labels:
        version: beta
  trafficPolicy:
    loadBalancer:
      simple: ROUND_ROBIN
```

In this setup, weights can be configured in the corresponding virtual service:

```
apiVersion: networking.istio.io/v1beta1
kind: VirtualService
metadata:
  name: recommendation-virtualservice
spec:
  hosts:
    - recommendation
  http:
    - route:
```

113

```yaml
    - destination:
        host: recommendation-service
        subset: stable
      weight: 90
    - destination:
        host: recommendation-service
        subset: beta
      weight: 10
```

Here, 90% of traffic is directed to the `stable` subset and 10% to the `beta` subset, allowing for a controlled introduction of the new version.

We can also do the load balancing at the `subset` level. A similar structure and syntax are valid for `loadBalancer` defined at the subset level. Selecting the appropriate load balancing strategy depends on your application's requirements:

- Use **round-robin** for simple, evenly distributed workloads.
- Opt for **least request** when instances experience varying loads or handle computationally intensive tasks.
- Choose **random** when a lightweight, stateless approach is needed.
- Employ **weighted load balancing** for progressive delivery scenarios like canary deployments.
- Consider **advanced options** like locality-based routing or consistent hashing for specialized use cases.

By configuring the right load balancing strategy in destination rules, you can ensure optimal performance, reliability, and user experience across your service mesh.

Connection Pool Settings

Connection pooling is an essential aspect of Istio's traffic management, allowing you to manage the lifecycle and utilization of connections between clients and services. Connection pooling helps optimize resource usage, stabilize application performance, and prevent service instances from getting overloaded by limiting the number of concurrent connections or requests to a service.

The `trafficPolicy.connectionPool` section of a destination rule in Istio allows you to configure connection pooling for both HTTP and TCP traffic. Limits on the number of concurrent connections, idle timeouts, and requests per connection can be precisely controlled with this configuration. Making effective use of these settings will greatly increase your services' scalability and reliability, particularly in high-traffic scenarios.

Connection pooling settings are defined in a destination rule and categorized into HTTP-specific and TCP-specific configurations:

```
trafficPolicy:
  connectionPool:
    http:
      http1MaxPendingRequests: 100
      maxRequestsPerConnection: 50
      idleTimeout: 15s
```

In this example

- `http1MaxPendingRequests` sets the maximum number of pending requests for HTTP/1.1 connections to 100.
- `maxRequestsPerConnection` limits the number of requests that can be made over a single connection to 50.
- `idleTimeout` specifies the amount of time an idle connection remains open before being closed, set here to 15 seconds.

These parameters keep a balance between performance and stability by making sure that connection resources are used effectively without overloading service instances. Below is an example of the TCP configuration that shows one of the ways to accomplish this task:

```
trafficPolicy:
  connectionPool:
    tcp:
      maxConnections: 100
      connectTimeout: 5s
```

`maxConnections` limits the total number of concurrent TCP connections to 100.

`connectTimeout` sets the maximum time to wait while establishing a connection to five seconds.

These settings are particularly useful for applications that rely on persistent TCP connections, such as database services or message brokers.

CHAPTER 3   FUNDAMENTALS OF TRAFFIC MANAGEMENT WITH ISTIO

Use Cases for Connection Pooling

1. Limiting Resource Consumption

   Connection pooling ensures that services don't consume all of the available resources such as memory and CPU, by limiting the number of active connections and requests. This is particularly crucial in situations where spikes in traffic could overwhelm backend services.

2. Improving Scalability

   Pooling lets applications handle more users at once without degrading performance by controlling the flow of traffic at the connection level, for instance, in a video recommendation service, connection pooling can limit the number of requests that can be sent at the same time to the backend recommendation engines. This keeps reaction times stable, even when traffic is high.

3. Enhancing Stability in High-Latency Networks

   In distributed systems, network latency can cause connections to remain idle, using up resources that aren't needed. Setting the `idleTimeout` will make sure that these connections are closed automatically, making room for current requests.

There are several other advanced configuration options `h2UpgradePolicy`, `http2MaxRequests`, etc. that are related to HTTP2 connections. Please refer to the Istio documentation (`https://istio.io/latest/docs/reference/config/networking/destination-rule/`) for these additional options.

Benefits of Connection Pooling

1. Efficient Resource Management

   By capping the number of connections and requests, connection pooling prevents resource exhaustion and ensures predictable performance across service instances.

2. Improved Resilience

    Connection pooling mitigates the impact of sudden traffic spikes or network instability, helping maintain service reliability under adverse conditions.

3. Scalability and Flexibility

    The ability to configure connection pooling separately for HTTP and TCP traffic allows Istio to cater to diverse application requirements, supporting a wide range of use cases.

One of the most effective tools in Istio's traffic management toolbox is connection pooling. You can improve your microservices' performance and resilience by adjusting these settings, which will ensure a seamless user experience and efficient service mesh operation.

Outlier Detection

Istio's outlier detection is a robust feature that improves the reliability and resilience of distributed applications, and this works by perpetually monitoring the behavior of individual instances (e.g., Kubernetes pods) of a service to identify and isolate problematic instances. Istio can autonomously remove an instance from the pool of healthy endpoints when it experiences abnormal behavior, such as frequent connection failures, excessive latency, or high error rates, and this guarantees that users and other services interact exclusively with healthy instances and prevents the defective instance from adversely affecting the overall performance.

In microservices architectures, this feature is indispensable, as it enables the deployment of multiple replicas of a service to accommodate fluctuating traffic volumes. A single misbehaving instance could destabilize the service mesh, degrade the user experience, or cause cascading failures in the absence of outlier detection.

In this context, an instance is a unique Kubernetes pod that is running a specific application and is a deployment of a service, and each replica is regarded as a distinct instance if your video recommendation service is deployed with three replicas.

Each instance is independently monitored by Istio. If one instance begins returning errors or responding too slowly, Istio can isolate it, ensuring that traffic is routed only to healthy and performant instances. This ensures that transient or localized issues do not affect the overall stability of the system.

CHAPTER 3   FUNDAMENTALS OF TRAFFIC MANAGEMENT WITH ISTIO

The `trafficPolicy.outlierDetection` section of a destination rule is where outlier detection is configured, and you can establish thresholds for what constitutes abnormal behavior," establish monitoring time frames, and specify the duration of time for which an instance should be ejected if it exceeds the thresholds. Let's look at an example:

```
apiVersion: networking.istio.io/v1beta1
kind: DestinationRule
metadata:
  name: recommendation-destinationrule
spec:
  host: recommendation-service
  trafficPolicy:
    outlierDetection:
      consecutive5xxErrors: 5
      interval: 10s
      baseEjectionTime: 30s
      maxEjectionPercent: 50
```

We will review each element in this configuration:

- The number of consecutive 5xx errors (note the 5 in this instance) that must occur before an instance is considered unhealthy is defined by `consecutive5xxErrors`.

- `interval` sets the time window (ten seconds here) during which Istio monitors the behavior of instances.

- The `baseEjectionTime` parameter tells the required amount of time (30 seconds) for which the misbehaved instance should be removed from the pool.

- `maxEjectionPercent` constrains the number of instances that can be removed simultaneously, thereby guaranteeing that there is sufficient capacity to process requests.

Suppose that your video recommendation service is deployed with five instances (pod-1, pod-2, pod-3, pod-4, and pod-5) and a memory leak has resulted in one of these instances (pod-3) returning errors. Given this scenario let's try to understand how outlier detection can help.

How does outlier detection help?

1. Outlier detection facilitates the constant monitoring of the behavior of all five instances.

2. Pod-3 surpasses the limit of five consecutive faults within a ten-second timeframe.

3. Istio designates pod-3 as unhealthy and removes it from the pool for 30 seconds.

4. The remaining four instances continue to process traffic throughout this time.

5. After 30 seconds, Istio lets pod-3 back into the pool and checks it again to see if the issue still persists.

These settings are very helpful for applications that need to keep TCP connections open, like database services or message brokers.

Benefits of Outlier Detection

1. Improved Resilience

    Outlier detection isolates problematic instances before they cause significant disruption, helping maintain the stability of services even under adverse conditions.

2. Proactive Fault Management

    By identifying and ejecting faulty instances, Istio prevents issues from escalating into broader failures, reducing the need for manual intervention.

3. Enhanced User Experience

    Users interact with healthy instances, ensuring consistent and reliable service delivery.

4. Fault Recovery

    Ejected instances are reintroduced into the pool after a defined period, allowing transient issues to resolve without permanent exclusion.

By effectively utilizing outlier detection, it is possible to construct a service mesh that is resilient and automatically reduces the impact of faulty instances. With this proactive approach, your services can scale seamlessly while maintaining high availability, ensuring consistent performance and reliability.

We don't cover all the settings here. We have a dedicated chapter in this book that talks about circuit breakers, where we will try to cover each of these settings in more detail.

Traffic Routing Fundamentals

Traffic routing is a crucial part of Istio's ability to regulate and improve service-to-service communication inside a service mesh. Istio makes it possible to have precise control over the rules and constraints that dictate how requests are routed between services and you can easily adjust to diverse deployment strategies with Istio's extensive toolkit for implementing different routing techniques, and also in this section we will also examine the core ideas of Istio traffic routing, including weighted routing, subnet-based routing, port-based routing, header-based routing, URI-based routing, method-based routing, and route precedence. We'll base our examples on a video streaming recommendation service to better appreciate the features that we have already introduced in earlier sections.

This service has two versions:

- v1: A stable version, serving most of the traffic.
- v2: A new version is being tested with partial traffic.

In this section, we will briefly cover the different kinds of routing techniques. We will try to explore these ideas in more detail and go deeper into them in the subsections that follow. Let's begin by understanding the essential components of Istio traffic routing. You can find all the examples under the CHAPTER3/routing-fundamentals folder of the source code attached with this book.

Route Rules and Precedence

Route rules specify how traffic should be processed and sent to a destination service or any of its subsets in Istio. URI paths, HTTP headers, request methods, and other request attributes can all serve as the basis for rules. When multiple rules apply, **precedence** determines which rule takes effect. Istio evaluates route rules in the order they are specified in the VirtualService, with the first match taking precedence.

CHAPTER 3 FUNDAMENTALS OF TRAFFIC MANAGEMENT WITH ISTIO

Requests that start with /v2 are sent to version v2 in this configuration. Version v1 is where the requests that start with /v1 are routed to. The order in the configuration tells what comes first:

```
apiVersion: networking.istio.io/v1beta1
kind: VirtualService
metadata:
  name: recommendation-virtualservice
spec:
  hosts:
    - '*'
  gateways:
    - recommendation-gateway
  http:
    - match:
        - uri:
            prefix: /v2
      rewrite:
        uri: /recommendations
      route:
        - destination:
            host: recommendation-service
            subset: v2
    - match:
        - uri:
            prefix: /v1
      rewrite:
        uri: /recommendations
      route:
        - destination:
            host: recommendation-service
            subset: v1
```

CHAPTER 3   FUNDAMENTALS OF TRAFFIC MANAGEMENT WITH ISTIO

Header-Based Routing

Headers in the request will be used to decide how to route the request with header-based routing. This is useful when requests are sent to different routes based on user roles, feature flags, or A/B testing.

Example: Routing Based on User-Agent Header

```yaml
http:
  - match:
    - headers:
        user-agent:
          regex: ".*Chrome.*"
      uri:
        prefix: "/recommendations"
    route:
      - destination:
          host: recommendation-service
          subset: v2
  - match:
    - headers:
        user-type:
          exact: "premium"
    route:
      - destination:
          host: recommendation-service
          subset: v2
  - route:
    - destination:
        host: recommendation-service
        subset: v1
```

Requests from Chrome users (based on User-Agent) are routed to the v2 subset.

Requests from premium users based on header user-type are routed to the v2 subset, and finally, all other users are routed to the v1 subset.

URI-Based Routing

Routing based on the request URI is one of the simplest and most commonly used mechanisms. It enables routing specific endpoints or API paths to distinct service subsets. In the following example, exact matches (/v1/recommendations) are routed to the v1 subset, and prefix matches (/v2/recommendations) are routed to the v2 subset:

```
http:
 - match:
   - uri:
       exact: "/v1/recommendations"
   rewrite:
     uri: "/recommendations"
   route:
   - destination:
       host: recommendation-service
       subset: v1
 - match:
   - uri:
       prefix: "/v2/recommendations"
   rewrite:
     uri: "/recommendations"
   route:
   - destination:
       host: recommendation-service
       subset: v2
 - match:
   - uri:
       regex: ".*recommendations/premium.*"
   rewrite:
     uri: "/recommendations"
   route:
   - destination:
       host: recommendation-service
       subset: v2
```

Method-Based Routing

In addition to headers and URIs, routing can also be performed based on the HTTP method (e.g., GET, POST). This is useful for separating read and write operations or applying distinct policies for different methods.

Example: Routing Based on HTTP Methods

```
http:
- match:
  - method:
      exact: GET
    uri:
      prefix: "/recommendations"
  route:
  - destination:
      host: recommendation-service
      subset: v1
- match:
  - method:
      exact: POST
    uri:
      prefix: "/recommendations"
  route:
  - destination:
      host: recommendation-service
      subset: v2
```

- GET requests are routed to a v1 subset.
- POST requests are routed to a v2 subset.

Weighted Routing

We already discussed weighted routing in earlier sections. It enables gradual traffic shifting between versions of a service or subsets, a feature critical for rolling updates or canary deployments. For completeness in this section, let's take a look at an example.

Example: Weighted Traffic Splitting

```
http:
  - match:
      - uri:
          prefix: /recommendations
    rewrite:
      uri: "/recommendations"
    route:
      - destination:
          host: recommendation-service
          subset: v2
        weight: 20
      - destination:
          host: recommendation-service
          subset: v1
        weight: 80
  - match:
      - uri:
          prefix: /v1
    rewrite:
      uri: "/recommendations"
    route:
      - destination:
          host: recommendation-service
          subset: v1
```

Subnet-Based Routing

You can set up routing for certain client subnets, which lets you segment data into groups based on the source IP address range. In this case, only traffic from the 192.168.1.0/24 address is sent to internal users, and the remaining traffic is sent to external users.

Example: Subnet-Based Routing

```
apiVersion: networking.istio.io/v1beta1
kind: VirtualService
metadata:
  name: subnet-routing
spec:
  hosts:
    - recommendation-service
  http:
    - match:
        - sourceSubnet: ["192.168.1.0/24"]
      route:
        - destination:
            host: recommendation-service
            subset: internal-users
    - match:
        - sourceSubnet: ["0.0.0.0/0"]
      route:
        - destination:
            host: recommendation-service
            subset: external-users
```

Port-Based Routing

Port-based routing is useful when multiple services or subsets are exposed on different ports. For instance, in this example traffic to port 9001 is routed to the v1 subset and 9002 is routed to the v2 subset.

Example: Port-Based Routing

```
http:
  - match:
    - port: 9001
      uri:
        prefix: "/recommendations"
```

```
      route:
      - destination:
          host: recommendation-service
          subset: v1
          port:
            number: 80
    - match:
      - port: 9002
        uri:
          prefix: "/recommendations"
      route:
      - destination:
          host: recommendation-service
          subset: v2
          port:
            number: 80
    - route:
      - destination:
          host: recommendation-service
          subset: v1
```

For setting up the port-based routing, we have to follow a sequence of steps. Let's go through them in detail:

1. Since we are using Kind to set up the local Kubernetes cluster, it is necessary that we open ports 9001 and 9002 so that we can route the traffic to Gateway and then further to the VirtualServices. If you already have created the Kind cluster, you should delete the cluster and create it again with a custom config:

   ```
   kind delete cluster

   kind create cluster --config kind-config.yaml
   ```

2. The following is the kind-config file that we have used above. You can also find this file under the CHAPTER3 source folder:

```
kind: Cluster
apiVersion: kind.x-k8s.io/v1alpha4
nodes:
- role: control-plane
  extraPortMappings:
  - containerPort: 80
    hostPort: 80
    protocol: TCP
    listenAddress: "0.0.0.0"
  - containerPort: 9001
    hostPort: 9001
    protocol: TCP
    listenAddress: "0.0.0.0"
  - containerPort: 9002
    hostPort: 9002
    protocol: TCP
    listenAddress: "0.0.0.0"
```

3. Finally, we have to expose these ports in our ingress gateway, so that it allows the traffic through these ports:

```
apiVersion: install.istio.io/v1alpha1
kind: IstioOperator
spec:
 components:
   ingressGateways:
     - namespace: istio-system
       name: istio-ingressgateway
       enabled: true
       k8s:
         service:
           ports:
             - port: 80
               targetPort: 8080
```

```
          name: http2
          protocol: TCP
        - port: 443
          targetPort: 8443
          name: https
          protocol: TCP
        - port: 9001
          targetPort: 9001
          name: http2-9001
          protocol: TCP
        - port: 9002
          targetPort: 9002
          name: http2-9002
          protocol: TCP
```

You must use this config file while installing Istio into your cluster (at least applying this file after creating the gateway didn't work for us). The following is the command to install Istio with this modified ingress gateway:

`istioctl install -f gateway-patch.yaml`

You can find this file under the CHAPTER3/routing-fundamentals/port-routing folder.

Conclusion

Understanding the fundamentals of traffic management in Istio is crucial for building robust microservices architectures. Through this chapter, we've explored how Istio's key components—virtual services and destination rules—work together to provide comprehensive traffic control capabilities. From basic routing mechanisms to sophisticated traffic shaping strategies, Istio offers the flexibility and control needed to handle complex service communication patterns. By mastering these fundamental concepts, development teams can effectively implement various routing strategies, ensure proper load distribution, and maintain service reliability. The practical examples using the recommendation service demonstrate how these concepts translate into real-world applications, providing a solid foundation for more advanced traffic management patterns. As organizations continue to adopt microservices architectures, these foundational traffic management capabilities become increasingly essential for building scalable, resilient, and maintainable systems.

CHAPTER 4

Advanced Traffic Management Patterns and Gateway Control

Introduction

Building upon the fundamental traffic management concepts covered in the previous chapter, we now venture into more advanced patterns and gateway control mechanisms in Istio. As organizations scale their microservices architecture, basic routing and load balancing often prove insufficient for complex deployment scenarios and advanced traffic control requirements. This chapter explores advanced deployment methodologies like canary and blue/green deployments, resilience patterns, and comprehensive gateway management strategies. Understanding these advanced patterns is crucial for DevOps teams facing the challenges of managing complex service deployments, implementing sophisticated testing strategies, and ensuring robust service-to-service communication in production environments.

Advanced Traffic Management Techniques

One of the most important problems DevOps teams continue to encounter in the constantly changing world of microservices architecture is the secure and efficient deployment of new service versions. The stakes for every deployment get higher as the complexity and user base of your applications increase. Service disruptions, revenue losses, and eroded user confidence might result from a poor rollout. This section examines how Istio offers enhanced deployment methodologies and tools for handling these challenges.

In Istio, percentage-based traffic distribution is arguably the simplest yet most effective type of traffic splitting. Imagine that you are directing traffic at a fork in the road, but you have exact control over the percentage of cars that go in each direction rather than having to choose at random. This is exactly what percentage-based traffic distribution allows you to do with your service requests. We have already discussed weight-based routing in the previous chapter.

What's particularly powerful about this approach is its precision and flexibility. Istio ensures that the traffic split remains accurate over time, maintaining the specified percentages across all requests. This is more sophisticated than it might initially appear. Consider these aspects:

- Session Persistence: While the split is 80/20 overall, individual users might need consistent routing to the same version to maintain the session state. We'll cover how to handle this with header-based routing shortly.

- Load Balancing: Istio handles the complexities of maintaining the specified split even when instances are added or removed from either version.

- Health Checking: If instances of either version become unhealthy, Istio automatically adjusts the routing while maintaining the specified ratios among healthy instances.

While percentage-based splitting gives us control over the overall traffic distribution, header-based splitting provides an even finer level of control. This approach allows us to make routing decisions based on specific attributes of the request, such as user identity, device type, or geographic location.

Think of header-based splitting as having a sophisticated filtering system at your traffic control point. Instead of simply directing a percentage of all traffic, you can now make routing decisions based on specific characteristics of each request. This is particularly powerful for

- Testing new features with specific user segments

- Implementing sophisticated A/B testing scenarios

- Managing different API versions
- Debugging issues with specific clients or users

Canary Deployments

The phrase "canary deployment" comes from a bygone era of coal mining in which miners would bring canary birds into the mines. Due to their heightened sensitivity to harmful gases, these birds would cease singing—or worse—if they sensed hazardous vapors, giving the miners an early warning system. This similar idea is used in contemporary software deployment: we first release a new version to a limited group of users while closely observing for any signs of issues before expanding the rollout. Please refer to the source code attached to the chapter (CHAPTER-3/canary) for a full list of examples.

Implementing Progressive Rollouts

The foundation of effective canary deployments is progressive rollouts. You're testing the waters (in this example, the stability and performance of your new version) before making a full commitment. Think of it as dipping your toe in the water before jumping in. We can execute this plan with amazing accuracy using Istio.

Let's go over how we're going to roll out our recommendation service gradually:

```yaml
# Initial DestinationRule (Pre-Switch)
apiVersion: networking.istio.io/v1beta1
kind: DestinationRule
metadata:
 name: recommendation-destinationrule
spec:
 host: recommendation-service
 trafficPolicy:
   loadBalancer:
     simple: LEAST_REQUEST
   connectionPool:
     tcp:
       maxConnections: 100
     http:
```

```
        http1MaxPendingRequests: 25
        maxRequestsPerConnection: 10
    outlierDetection:
      consecutive5xxErrors: 5
      interval: 30s
      baseEjectionTime: 30s
  subsets:
  - name: stable
    labels:
      version: v1
      env: v1
  - name: canary
    labels:
      version: v2
      env: v2
```

This configuration establishes two critical subsets of our service: the stable version (v1) and our canary version (v2). The trafficPolicy section includes several crucial safety mechanisms:

1. The LEAST_REQUEST load balancer ensures even distribution while favoring less busy instances.

2. Connection pooling prevents any single instance from being overwhelmed.

3. Outlier detection automatically removes problematic instances from the pool.

Now comes the critical part—implementing the actual progressive rollout. We'll do this in carefully measured stages:

Stage 1—Initial Exposure (1% Traffic)

```
  - route:
    - destination:
        host: recommendation-service
        subset: canary
      weight: 1
    - destination:
```

```
      host: recommendation-service
      subset: stable
    weight: 99
```

Only 1% of traffic is redirected to our new version from this original setup. Why is the percentage so low? Because even this small amount of exposure could limit potential impact while revealing critical issues. One percent of a service that processes millions of requests every day nevertheless yields useful information for analysis.

Stage 2—Confidence Building (5% Traffic)

```
- route:
  - destination:
      host: recommendation-service
      subset: canary
    weight: 5
  - destination:
      host: recommendation-service
      subset: stable
    weight: 95
```

At this stage, we've gained some confidence from our initial deployment and are ready to expose more users to the new version. The 5% threshold provides a broader dataset while still maintaining a safety margin.

Stage 3—Expanded Validation (20% Traffic)

```
- route:
  - destination:
      host: recommendation-service
      subset: canary
    weight: 20
  - destination:
      host: recommendation-service
      subset: stable
    weight: 80
```

By this point, we're exposing a significant portion of our traffic to the new version. This stage provides substantial data about how the new version performs under varied conditions while still maintaining the stable version as the primary path.

Figure 4-1 shows one more way in which one can achieve progressive rollout.

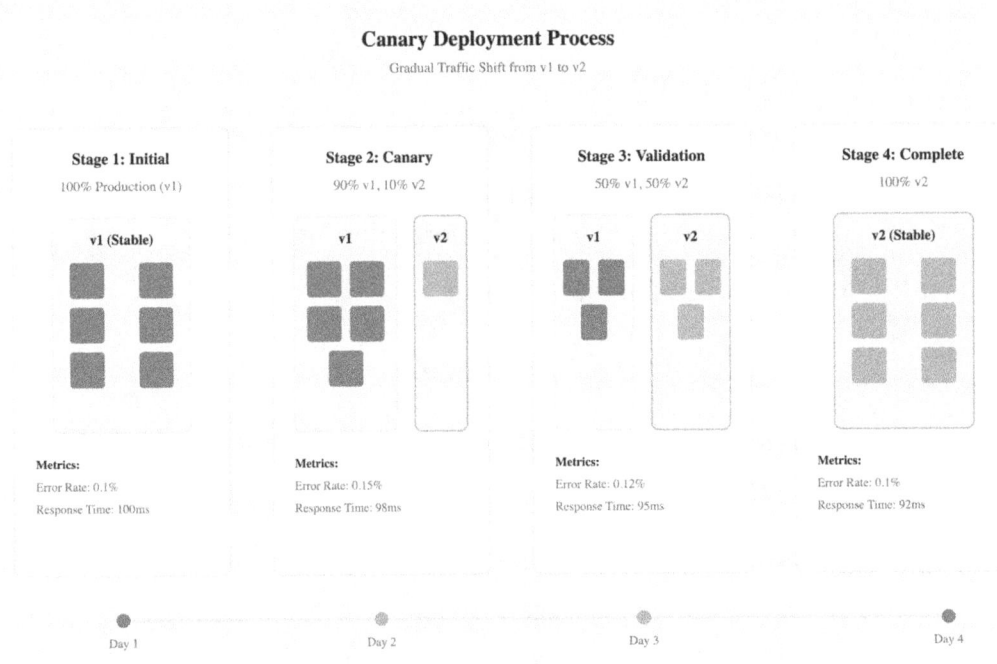

Figure 4-1. *One way to achieve progressive rollout*

Monitoring and Validating Canary Releases

Monitoring is not limited to observing metrics during a canary deployment; it also involves interpreting the narrative that these indicators convey regarding the health of your deployment. We should establish a comprehensive monitoring strategy that considers both technical and business metrics. Before we begin, we will collect some basic metrics using the below monitoring configuration:

```
apiVersion: telemetry.istio.io/v1alpha1
kind: Telemetry
metadata:
  name: recommendation-monitoring
spec:
  metrics:
    - providers:
        - name: prometheus
      overrides:
```

```
    - match:
        metric: REQUEST_DURATION
        mode: CLIENT_AND_SERVER
    - match:
        metric: REQUEST_COUNT
        mode: CLIENT_AND_SERVER
    - match:
        metric: RESPONSE_SIZE
        mode: CLIENT_AND_SERVER
```

With this configuration, Istio is told to get three important metrics from both the client and server sides. Think of REQUEST_DURATION as a stopwatch that keeps track of how long each request lasts, REQUEST_COUNT as a counter that keeps track of how many requests there are, and RESPONSE_SIZE as a tape measure that keeps track of the size of replies and the mode. The CLIENT_AND_SERVER setting is very important because it can find problems that might only show up on one side of the conversation by getting data from both sides. For instance, if the client has long latency and the server says replies are quick, this could mean that there is a problem with the network between the two. Let's take a look at what we watch and why.

Response time distribution (p50, p95, p99) is like measuring how long customers wait in line. p50 tells us the typical wait time (median), while p95 and p99 show us how bad it gets for the unlucky customers who wait longer. Here's how we measure it:

```
histogram_quantile(0.95, sum(rate(istio_request_duration_
milliseconds_bucket{
  destination_service="recommendation"
}[5m])) by (le))
```

This query looks complex, but think of it as a way to say "Show me the response time that 95% of requests are faster than." The rate(...)[5m] part means we're looking at data over the last five minutes to smooth out temporary spikes.

```
sum(rate(istio_requests_total{
  destination_service="recommendation",
  response_code=~"5.*"
}[5m]))
/
```

```
sum(rate(istio_requests_total{
  destination_service="recommendation"
}[5m]))
* 100
```

This query calculates what percentage of requests are failing (getting 5xx errors). It's like tracking how often our kitchen sends out the wrong order. We divide the number of errors by total requests and multiply by 100 to get a percentage.

For business metrics, we need to be more creative since Istio doesn't directly track business outcomes. Instead, we infer them from the patterns of requests, for example:

```
sum(rate(istio_requests_total{
  destination_service="recommendation",
  path="/recommendations/accept"
}[5m]))
/
sum(rate(istio_requests_total{
  destination_service="recommendation",
  path="/recommendations"
}[5m]))
* 100
```

This query tracks how often users accept our recommendations by comparing requests to the accept endpoint vs. total recommendation requests. It's like measuring how often customers take our waiter's suggestions.

To make all this monitoring actionable, we set up alerts:

```
apiVersion: monitoring.coreos.com/v1
kind: PrometheusRule
metadata:
  name: canary-alerts
spec:
  groups:
  - name: recommendation.rules
    rules:
    - alert: HighLatency
      expr: |
```

```
histogram_quantile(0.95,
  sum(rate(istio_request_duration_milliseconds_bucket{
    destination_service="recommendation",
    destination_version="v2"
  }[5m])) by (le)
) > 500
```

This alert is like having an automatic system that notifies the kitchen if too many orders are taking longer than expected. The alert triggers if 95% of requests to our new version (v2) take longer than 500 milliseconds.

One crucial detail: Notice how we specifically look at destination_version="v2" in our alerts. This helps us compare the performance of our canary (new version) against the stable version. If the canary shows worse metrics, we might need to roll back or fix issues before expanding the rollout.

Remember, monitoring isn't just about collecting numbers—it's about telling a story about how our service is performing. Each metric we collect helps paint part of that picture, from technical stability to business success. By watching all these metrics during a canary deployment, we can make informed decisions about whether to proceed with the rollout or roll back to the previous version.

If you don't understand this section fully, it's fine. We have the complete Chapter 6 dedicated to observability and monitoring, and we will go through all these configurations in detail.

Rolling Back Canary Deployments

Even with the best planning and monitoring, things don't always happen as planned. The ability to roll forward successfully is only one aspect of a robust deployment plan; another is how well it can handle failures. The technical and user experience aspects of the process must be carefully considered when rolling back a canary deployment in Istio.

Let's investigate the implementation of a comprehensive rollback plan for our recommendation service. Making the rollback process as seamless and quick as possible without sacrificing system stability is crucial.

Let's start by putting in place an instant rollback configuration that we can use as soon as we identify critical issues:

```
# Step 1: Immediate Traffic Switch VirtualService
apiVersion: networking.istio.io/v1beta1
```

```
kind: VirtualService
metadata:
 name: recommendation-virtualservice
spec:
 hosts:
 - recommendation
 http:
 - route:
   - destination:
       host: recommendation-service
       subset: v1     # Immediately route all traffic back to v1 version
   retries:
     attempts: 3
     perTryTimeout: "2s"
     retryOn: "connect-failure,refused-stream,unavailable,cancelled,retriab
le-status-codes"
   timeout: "3s"
```

This configuration does several important things:

- Immediately routes 100% of traffic back to the stable version
- Implements retry logic to handle any transient issues during the transition
- Maintains availability during the rollback process

However, simply routing traffic back to the stable version isn't enough. We need to implement a proper rollback procedure that considers all aspects of the system. Here's a comprehensive rollback strategy:

```
# Step 1: Immediate Traffic Switch VirtualService
apiVersion: networking.istio.io/v1beta1
kind: VirtualService
metadata:
 name: recommendation-virtualservice
spec:
 hosts:
 - recommendation
```

```yaml
    http:
    - route:
      - destination:
          host: recommendation-service
          subset: v1     # Immediately route all traffic back to v1 version
      retries:
        attempts: 3
        perTryTimeout: "2s"
        retryOn: "connect-failure,refused-stream,unavailable,cancelled,
        retriable-status-codes"
      timeout: "3s"      # Strict timeout to prevent hanging requests
# Step 2: Implement connection draining
---
apiVersion: networking.istio.io/v1beta1
kind: DestinationRule
metadata:
  name: recommendation-destinationrule
spec:
  host: recommendation
  subsets:
  - name: v2
    labels:
      version: v2
      env: v2
    trafficPolicy:
      connectionPool:
        tcp:
          maxConnections: 0      # Prevent new TCP connections
        http:
          http2MaxRequests: 0         # Prevent new HTTP requests
          maxRequestsPerConnection: 1
      outlierDetection:
        consecutive5xxErrors: 1
        interval: 1s
        baseEjectionTime: 1h     # Keep ejected for a long time
```

Chapter 4 Advanced Traffic Management Patterns and Gateway Control

```yaml
# Step 3: Apply safeguard policies
---
apiVersion: networking.istio.io/v1beta1
kind: PeerAuthentication
metadata:
  name: recommendation-rollback-security
spec:
  selector:
    matchLabels:
      app: recommendation
      version: v2
  mtls:
    mode: STRICT
  portLevelMtls:
    8080:
      mode: STRICT
```

A safe and systematic return to the stable version is ensured by this three-step rollback setup. Let's understand the significance of each step:

1. Users are shielded from further issues with the problematic version by the instant traffic change. During the transition, the additional outlier detection offers an additional layer of protection.

2. By blocking incoming connections to the canary version, connection draining makes sure that ongoing sessions are permitted to finish organically. For our recommendation service, where users may be in the middle of browsing suggestions, this is very crucial. To stop the service from receiving any more requests, we set the maximum connections and maximum requests to zero.

3. During and after the rollback, the safeguard measures stop any unintentional traffic leaks to the faulty version. `PeerAuthentication` will be covered in full in Chapter 5.

Please refer to the chapter examples for how we can add circuit breaker configuration and enhancements for v1 traffic after we rolled back. Additionally, we should implement automated rollback triggers based on our monitoring metrics. Here's how we can set up automated rollback conditions:

```yaml
apiVersion: monitoring.coreos.com/v1
kind: PrometheusRule
metadata:
  name: rollback-triggers
  namespace: istio-system
spec:
  groups:
  - name: recommendation.rules
    rules:
    - alert: HighErrorRate
      expr: |
        sum(rate(istio_requests_total{
          response_code=~"5.*",
          destination_service="recommendation"
        }[5m])) /
        sum(rate(istio_requests_total{
          destination_service="recommendation"
        }[5m])) > 0.05
      for: 5m
      labels:
        severity: critical
    - alert: HighLatency
      expr: |
        histogram_quantile(0.95, sum(rate(istio_request_duration_
        milliseconds_bucket{
          destination_service="recommendation"
        }[5m])) by (le)) > 2000
      for: 5m
      labels:
        severity: warning
```

Our automated systems should have the ability to initiate the rollback procedure when these criteria are breached. Maintaining service reliability, particularly outside of regular business hours, depends on this automation. In Chapter 6, we will go into greater detail on observability and monitoring.

Blue/Green Deployments

Blue/Green deployment stands out for its simplicity and beauty in the world of deployment strategies. In contrast to the incremental strategy of canary deployments, blue/green deployments maintain two identical production environments, one hosting the new version (green) and the other serving live traffic (blue). With this approach, handling multiple live versions at once is no longer complicated, and instant rollback options are provided.

Using Istio's traffic management capabilities, let's explore how we can use blue/green deployments for our recommendation service.

Setting Up Blue/Green Environments

Setting up blue/green environments in Istio requires careful consideration of several key components: the deployments themselves, the service that will expose them, and the Istio resources that will manage the traffic. Your current version (v1) will live in one of the parallel universes set up by this configuration, while your new version (v2) will dwell in the other.

We must set up two separate deployments for our recommendation service, which will be used as our green (v2) and blue (v1) environments. We will create two deployments that will differ in labels and the version of the container image. Here are the key elements of the configuration that make blue/green deployment possible, while the full deployment configuration would also include several additional elements. Please refer to the source code attached to the chapter (CHAPTER-3/blue_green) for a full list of examples:

```
# Blue deployment (v1)
metadata:
  name: recommendation-blue
  labels:
    app: recommendation
    version: blue     # This label is crucial for traffic routing
# Green deployment (v2)
```

CHAPTER 4 ADVANCED TRAFFIC MANAGEMENT PATTERNS AND GATEWAY CONTROL

```
metadata:
  name: recommendation-green
  labels:
    app: recommendation
    version: green     # This label differentiates the Green deployment
```

A single Kubernetes service will act as the entry point for both deployments. The service uses label selectors that match both versions, allowing Istio to control which version receives traffic:

```
spec:
  selector:
    app: recommendation     # Matches both v1 and v2 deployments
```

Implementation Strategies

Blue/green deployments in Istio necessitate a carefully thought-out approach that extends beyond simple traffic switching. Imagine it like directing a carefully choreographed dance in which two versions of your service coexist, but only one is presented to viewers at a time. We'll look at how to successfully apply this strategy for our recommendation service. Figure 4-2 shows the different phases the blue-green deployment goes through.

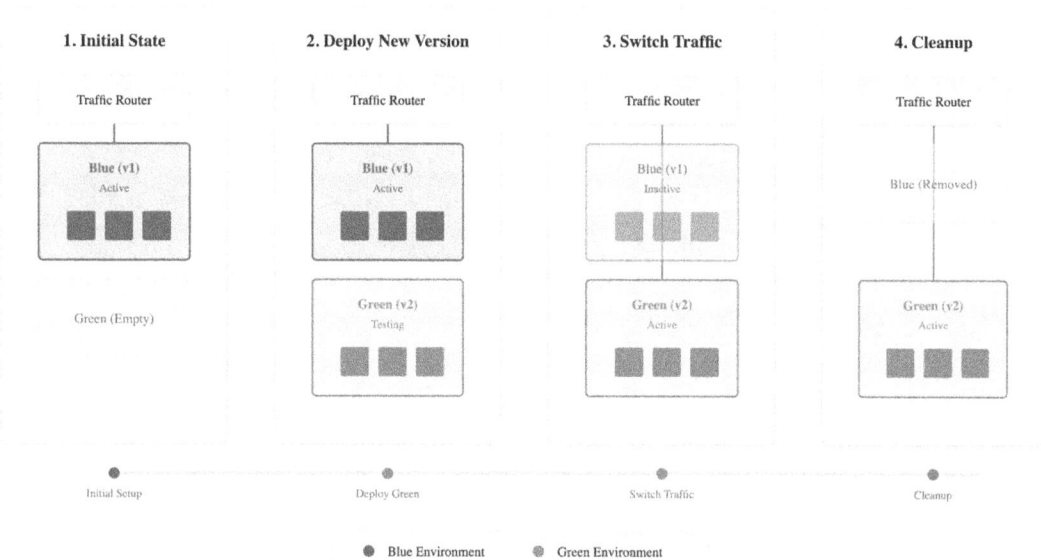

Figure 4-2. The different phases the blue-green deployment goes through

CHAPTER 4   ADVANCED TRAFFIC MANAGEMENT PATTERNS AND GATEWAY CONTROL

Phase 1: Foundation Setup

Laying the foundation for your blue/green deployment is the first step, and we have to build separate environments for each version while maintaining their resources and identical configurations.

First, create a DestinationRule that defines both versions of your service:

```
apiVersion: networking.istio.io/v1beta1
kind: DestinationRule
metadata:
 name: recommendation-destinationrule
spec:
 host: recommendation-service
 subsets:
   - name: blue
     labels:
       version: blue
   - name: green
     labels:
       version: green
 trafficPolicy:
   loadBalancer:
     simple: ROUND_ROBIN
   connectionPool:
     tcp:
       maxConnections: 100
     http:
       http1MaxPendingRequests: 25
       maxRequestsPerConnection: 10
   outlierDetection:
     consecutive5xxErrors: 5
     interval: 30s
     baseEjectionTime: 30s
     maxEjectionPercent: 100
```

As part of our blue/green deployment strategy, this configuration fulfills two essential functions. First, by carefully managing labels, the deployment creates a separate boundary between your service versions. These labels serve as identity cards for your pods, making it possible for Istio to differentiate between different versions of your service. Istio will not be able to precisely route traffic to your target version without this separation, and the configuration guarantees that traffic is split evenly between pods in each version by applying a consistent load balancing policy across both versions. Regardless of which version is managing the traffic, this consistent approach to load balancing is essential since it preserves predictable performance characteristics and makes sure that the new version and the current production version adhere to the same traffic management rules and makes the transition between them more reliable and predictable. Together, these aspects create a foundation for controlled and reliable version management in your service mesh.

Phase 2: Pre-deployment Validation

Use header-based routing to carry out a validation strategy before exposing any production traffic to v2. This allows regular users to continue using v1 while your testing team has access to v2. Here's how to set this up:

```yaml
apiVersion: networking.istio.io/v1beta1
kind: VirtualService
metadata:
  name: recommendation-virtualservice
spec:
  hosts:
    - recommendation
  http:
    - match:
        - headers:
            x-test-version:
              exact: "v2"
      route:
        - destination:
            host: recommendation-service
            subset: green
```

```yaml
    - route:
        - destination:
            host: recommendation-service
            subset: blue
```

Before committing to a full switch, this configuration unlocks powerful testing capabilities that enable comprehensive validation of your new version. While the rest of your users continue to utilize v1 of the service without interruption, your QA teams can methodically test v2 by using header-based routing, and you can also stress-test v2 using simulated traffic patterns with this tailored access, which allows you to collect useful performance metrics without running the risk of affecting your production traffic flowing to v1. Most importantly, this setup gives key stakeholders a means to test and assess v2's functionality in an actual environment. Consider this as an independent preview environment that runs concurrently with your production service, allowing stakeholders to see the updated version as it will behave in production, making informed decisions about the readiness of v2 for general release. This controlled exposure approach significantly reduces the risk of unexpected issues when you eventually switch all traffic to the new version.

Phase 3: Health Check Implementation

Implementing robust health checks is crucial before proceeding with the switch. Configure health checks for both versions:

```yaml
spec:
  template:
    spec:
      containers:
        - name: recommendation
          livenessProbe:
            httpGet:
              path: /health
              port: 8080
          readinessProbe:
            httpGet:
              path: /ready
              port: 8080
```

Additionally, implement outlier detection in your DestinationRule:

```
trafficPolicy:
  outlierDetection:
    consecutive5xxErrors: 5
    interval: 30s
    baseEjectionTime: 30s
```

Phase 4: Preparation for Traffic Switch

Before executing the switch, set up monitoring and alerting thresholds. Configure telemetry to track key metrics:

```
apiVersion: telemetry.istio.io/v1alpha1
kind: Telemetry
metadata:
  name: recommendation-metrics
spec:
  metrics:
    - providers:
        - name: prometheus
      overrides:
        - match:
            metric: REQUEST_DURATION
            mode: SERVER
```

The foundation of a successful switch lies in understanding your service's behavior through multiple lenses. Start by monitoring response time distributions across your service—this tells you not just about average performance, but reveals important patterns in how different users experience your service. For instance, in our recommendation service, you'll want to know if some users are experiencing significantly slower recommendation generation than others. During the switch, error rates serve as your early warning system, helping you to detect issues before they have a substantial impact on a large percentage of your users. Resource utilization metrics are especially important to monitor since they could identify potential bottlenecks before they become problems that affect users. For example, if v2 of our recommendation service starts consuming more memory than expected during pre-switch testing, you'll want to investigate before proceeding with the full transition. Perhaps above all, keep an eye on business metrics that directly represent the value of your service. For our recommendation service, these metrics include the frequency with which users click recommended items, the variety of recommendations that are provided, and the duration of user sessions. By verifying that the technical transition results in real business benefit, these business metrics operate as your north star. By establishing baseline measurements for all these metrics before the switch, you create a clear reference point for evaluating the success of your transition.

Phase 5: Traffic Management Strategy

In this phase we will put into practice a traffic strategy that allows quick rollbacks and switches. Creating multiple VirtualService configurations is required to achieve this:

For Initial Validation with a Small Percentage of Traffic:

```
spec:
  http:
    - route:
        - destination:
            host: recommendation-service
            subset: green
          weight: 1
        - destination:
            host: recommendation-service
            subset: blue
          weight: 99
```

For the Final Switch:

```
spec:
  http:
    - route:
        - destination:
            host: recommendation-service
            subset: green
```

Phase 6: Contingency Planning

Implement circuit breakers to protect against cascading failures during the switch:

```
spec:
  trafficPolicy:
    connectionPool:
      tcp:
        maxConnections: 100
      http:
        http1MaxPendingRequests: 100
        maxRequestsPerConnection: 10
    outlierDetection:
      consecutive5xxErrors: 5
      interval: 30s
      baseEjectionTime: 30s
```

Phase 7: Post-deployment Strategy

After the switch, maintain both versions for a predetermined period. This allows for

- Quick rollback if issues are detected
- Gradual decommissioning of v1
- Collection of comparative metrics

Consider implementing a mirror traffic policy to validate v2's behavior with production traffic before the switch:

```
spec:
  http:
    - route:
        - destination:
            host: recommendation-service
            subset: v1
      mirror:
        host: recommendation-service
        subset: v2
      mirrorPercentage:
        value: 100.0
```

This comprehensive strategy for execution guarantees a safe and controlled blue/green deployment. A robust framework for managing version transitions is created by each phase building on the one before it. Maintaining complete control over traffic flow while being confident in your ability to undo changes if necessary is key.

Remember that automation and monitoring are critical to the success of blue/green deployments. Think about putting these configurations into practice using GitOps practices, which use CI/CD pipelines to automatically deploy and version control infrastructure changes.

Switching Traffic Between Versions

The process of switching traffic between versions in a blue/green deployment is a critical operation that requires careful planning and execution. Blue/green deployments usually entail a decisive change from one version to another, in contrast to canary deployments where traffic changes gradually. Let's explore how to use Istio's traffic management features to accomplish this.

Istio's traffic switching is fundamentally managed by VirtualService resources. Consider a virtual service as an advanced traffic controller that can route requests according to several different parameters. We'll look at a few different strategies for handling the switch for our recommendation service.

Changing the VirtualService configurations to reroute all traffic from blue to green is the basic traffic switch. The starting configuration for v1 is as follows:

```
spec:
  http:
    - route:
        - destination:
            host: recommendation-service
            subset: blue
```

When we're ready to switch to v2, we modify the configuration:

```
spec:
  http:
    - route:
        - destination:
            host: recommendation-service
            subset: green
```

Progressive Switching Strategies

While blue/green deployments typically involve a complete switch, we can implement more sophisticated switching strategies for additional safety, and here are several approaches:

Header-Based Validation Switch: Using HTTP headers, we can validate v2 before performing the full switch. While everyone else keeps using v1, this enables specific users or testing teams to access v2:

```
spec:
  http:
  - match:
    - headers:
        x-version:
          exact: "green"
        user-type:
          exact: "tester"
    route:
    - destination:
        host: recommendation-service
        subset: green
  - route:
    - destination:
        host: recommendation-service
        subset: blue
```

Cookie-Based Switch: Additionally, cookies can be used to preserve session affinity during the switch, guaranteeing a consistent user experience:

```
spec:
  http:
  - match:
    - headers:
        cookie:
          regex: ".*version=v2.*"
    route:
    - destination:
```

```
            host: recommendation-service
            subset: green
    - route:
        - destination:
            host: recommendation-service
            subset: blue
```

Pre-switch Validation

Before executing the switch, implement validation rules to ensure v2 is ready:

```
spec:
  http:
    - match:
        - uri:
            prefix: "/recommendations"
      route:
        - destination:
            host: recommendation
            subset: green
      fault:
        delay:
          fixedDelay: 1s
          percentage:
            value: 100
```

By adding a synthetic delay to v2, this configuration allows us to observe how it behaves under pressure before the full switching.

Keep in mind that effective planning and monitoring are critical to the success of traffic switching in blue/green installations, and the secret is to ensure a seamless transition to v2 while ensuring the option to swiftly return to v1. Make sure your monitoring systems can give you real-time information on the health of both versions throughout the switch, and always test your switching procedures in a non-production environment first.

Rollback Procedures

The ability to quickly roll back when problems occur is one of the most alluring features of blue/green deployments. If things don't work out as intended, you can use a rollback as your safety net. Even though we hope to never have to use it, an effective rollback plan is essential to preserving user confidence and system reliability.

Three key factors need to be taken into account while implementing rollbacks in Istio: managing system state throughout the transition, handling in-flight requests gracefully, and immediately reverting traffic. Using our recommendation service as an example, let's take a closer look at each of these features.

Your first line of defense is the instant traffic reversion, and when problems are found with our recommendation service's version 2, you'll want to quickly redirect all traffic back to v1. This is accomplished through Istio's VirtualService resource. Here's how we would configure this immediate reversion:

```
apiVersion: networking.istio.io/v1beta1
kind: VirtualService
metadata:
  name: recommendation-rollback
spec:
  hosts:
    - recommendation-service
  http:
    - route:
        - destination:
            host: recommendation-service
            subset: blue
          weight: 100
```

But merely rerouting traffic is not sufficient. What happens to consumers who are in the middle of their v2 sessions is something we need to think about. Enter "connection draining." Draining the connection is similar to allowing users to complete their ongoing tasks before shutting down. This can be accomplished by configuring a DestinationRule:

```
apiVersion: networking.istio.io/v1beta1
kind: DestinationRule
metadata:
```

CHAPTER 4   ADVANCED TRAFFIC MANAGEMENT PATTERNS AND GATEWAY CONTROL

```
  name: recommendation-drain
spec:
  host: recommendation-service
  subsets:
    - name: green
      labels:
        version: green
      trafficPolicy:
        connectionPool:
          tcp:
            maxConnections: 0
          http:
            maxRequests: 0
        outlierDetection:
          consecutive5xxErrors: 1
          interval: 1s
          baseEjectionTime: 3600s

apiVersion: networking.istio.io/v1beta1
kind: DestinationRule
metadata:
  name: recommendation-drain
spec:
  host: recommendation-service
  subsets:
    - name: green
      labels:
        version: green
      trafficPolicy:
        connectionPool:
          tcp:
            maxConnections: 0
          http:
            maxRequests: 0
        outlierDetection:
          consecutive5xxErrors: 1
```

```
        interval: 1s
        baseEjectionTime: 3600s
```

Monitoring plays a crucial role during rollbacks. We can configure automated rollback triggers based on metrics using Istio's telemetry features:

```
apiVersion: telemetry.istio.io/v1alpha1
kind: Telemetry
metadata:
  name: rollback-monitoring
spec:
  metrics:
    - providers:
        - name: prometheus
      overrides:
        - match:
            metric: REQUEST_COUNT
            mode: CLIENT_AND_SERVER
        - match:
            metric: REQUEST_DURATION
            mode: CLIENT_AND_SERVER

apiVersion: monitoring.coreos.com/v1
kind: PrometheusRule
metadata:
  name: rollback-triggers
  namespace: istio-system
spec:
  groups:
  - name: recommendation.rules
    rules:
    - alert: HighErrorRate
      expr: |
        sum(rate(istio_requests_total{
          response_code=~"5.*",
          destination_service="recommendation"
        }[3m])) /
```

```
      sum(rate(istio_requests_total{
        destination_service="recommendation"
      }[3m])) > 0.02
    for: 3m
    labels:
      severity: critical
  - alert: HighLatency
    expr: |
      histogram_quantile(0.95, sum(rate(istio_request_duration_
      milliseconds_bucket{
        destination_service="recommendation"
      }[3m])) by (le)) > 1000
    for: 3m
    labels:
      severity: warning
```

For our recommendation service, we might also want to add circuit breakers to protect the system during rollback. In the next section, we will go over circuit breakers in further detail. It is equally important to test your rollback processes as it is to test the deployment itself. Practicing the rollbacks regularly in lower-level environments that mimic different failure and error scenarios is something we advise. To make sure the automatic rollback triggers function properly, you can, for example, write a test script that purposefully introduces errors in v2.

Keep in mind that rollbacks indicate a mature deployment process rather than failure. We can proceed with new deployments with confidence when you have strong rollback procedures in place because you know you can swiftly revert if necessary, and teams will also be able to innovate and introduce new features at much faster pace while preserving system stability and reliability because of this safety net.

When putting rollback processes into place for your services, start by identifying your critical metrics and establishing clear thresholds for when a rollback should be triggered. When making a decision, take into account both technical and business processes. Document your processes, automate where you can, and test your rollback mechanisms regularly. Above all, take advantage of every rollback as a chance to learn and enhance your deployment and rollback processes.

Resilience and Fault Tolerance

The complexity of service interactions in contemporary distributed systems, especially microservices architectures, leads to a great deal of failure potential, and these failures can show up as data center outages, service breakdowns, network latency spikes, or resource exhaustion. The challenge isn't just handling these failures—it's preventing them from cascading through your system and causing widespread disruption.

Building systems that can tolerate and recover from errors gracefully is made easier with Istio's extensive suite of resilience and fault tolerance features. Using our recommendation service as a real-world example, let's examine these aspects in more detail.

Circuit Breakers

Circuit breakers represent one of the most fundamental patterns in building resilient distributed systems. Circuit breakers in software systems monitor for signs of trouble and stop sending requests to problematic services, giving them time to recover. The idea is modeled after electrical circuit breakers, which protect your home by cutting power when they detect dangerous conditions.

Think of a circuit breaker as a watchful guardian standing between your services. When it notices that a particular service is struggling and perhaps responding too slowly or returning too many errors, then it temporarily redirects traffic away from that service. This is the same way that taking a break helps you recover when you're feeling overwhelmed. This keeps the struggling service from getting overwhelmed and gives it time to recuperate.

As shown in Figure 4-3, three key ideas driving the circuit breaker configuration in Istio are load balancer settings, connection pools, and outlier identification. Connection pools manage the number of connections and requests that can be made to a service. Outlier detection determines when a service instance should be removed from the load balancing pool. Load balancer settings determine how traffic should be distributed among healthy instances.

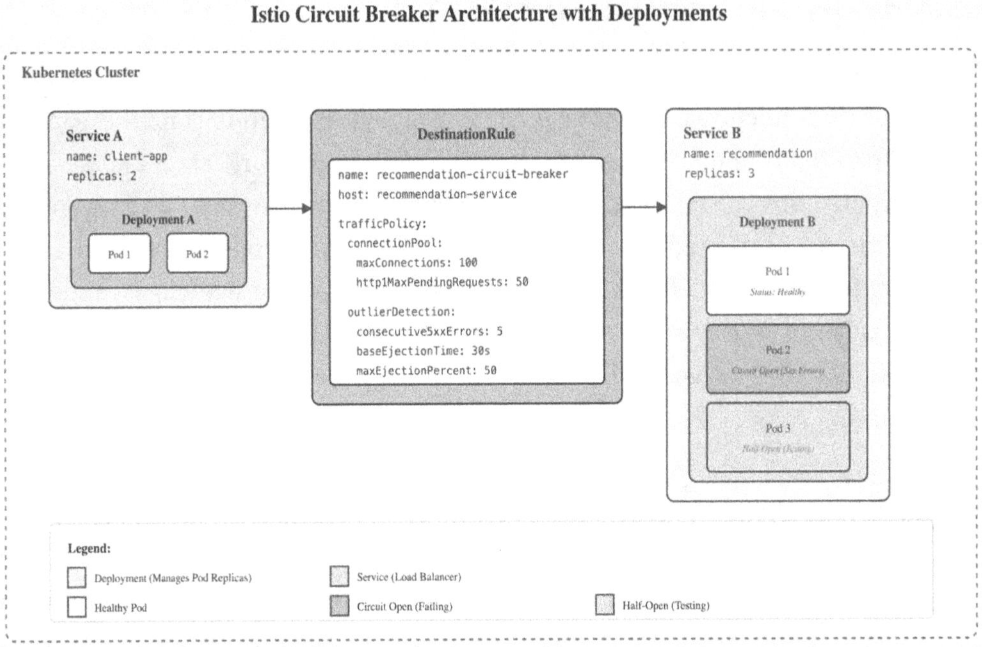

CHAPTER 4   ADVANCED TRAFFIC MANAGEMENT PATTERNS AND GATEWAY CONTROL

Figure 4-3. The three key ideas driving circuit breaker configuration in Istio: load balancer settings, connection pools, and outlier identification

Configuration Parameters

The power of Istio's circuit breakers is their configurability, and by carefully tuning certain parameters, you can specify precisely what behavior is wrong and how the system should react. The DestinationRule resource defines these settings, which can be set globally, for particular subsets or even for individual ports. TCP and HTTP connection parameters are the two primary categories into which Istio's circuit breakers' connection parameters fall, and each type of parameter has a specific function in maintaining system stability and averting cascading failures.

Let's examine a comprehensive circuit breaker configuration for our recommendation service:

```
apiVersion: networking.istio.io/v1beta1
kind: DestinationRule
metadata:
  name: recommendation-circuit-breaker
```

```
spec:
  host: recommendation-service
  trafficPolicy:
    connectionPool:
      tcp:
        maxConnections: 100          # Maximum concurrent connections
        connectTimeout: 30ms         # Connection establishment timeout
        tcpKeepalive:                # TCP keepalive settings
          time: 7200s
          interval: 75s
          probes: 10
      http:
        http1MaxPendingRequests: 1   # Max requests waiting for an
                                     #   available connection
        maxRequestsPerConnection: 1  # Max requests on a single connection
        maxRetries: 3                # Maximum number of retries
        idleTimeout: 15s             # How long to keep idle connections
        h2MaxRequests: 1000          # Max concurrent HTTP/2 requests
```

TCP Connection Parameters

The TCP connection pool settings form the foundation of our circuit breaker configuration. These parameters operate at the transport layer, controlling the basic networking aspects of our service communications:

- maxConnections represents the maximum number of TCP connections allowed to a destination service. Think of this as controlling how many parallel conversations your service can have at once. If your service tries to establish more connections than this limit, Istio will queue new connection attempts until existing connections close. For our recommendation service, we might set this to 100 connections.

- connectTimeout determines how long Istio will wait when trying to establish a new TCP connection before giving up. This is crucial for preventing your service from hanging while waiting for unresponsive instances. A typical setting might be 30 milliseconds.

- The tcpKeepalive settings help maintain healthy connections over time. These settings are particularly important in cloud environments where network issues can create "zombie" connections—connections that appear active but are dead.

HTTP Connection Parameters

HTTP connection parameters provide a more fine-grained control over HTTP traffic. These settings are crucial for services that communicate via HTTP/1.1 or HTTP/2 protocols, like our recommendation service:

- http1MaxPendingRequests controls how many requests can queue up waiting for an available connection. Think of this as a waiting room for requests. If the waiting room is full, additional requests will be rejected immediately rather than queuing up indefinitely.

- maxRequestsPerConnection limits how many requests can be multiplexed over a single HTTP connection. This is particularly relevant for HTTP/2 connections where multiple requests can share the same connection.

- maxRetries defines how many times Istio will retry a failed request before giving up. While retries can improve reliability, too many retries can make problems worse by increasing load during periods of stress.

- idleTimeout specifies how long Istio will keep an idle connection open. This helps clean up resources when connections aren't being actively used.

- For HTTP/2-specific settings, we have h2MaxRequests, which controls the maximum number of concurrent HTTP/2 streams that can be active on a single connection.

Here's how we might put all these parameters together for our recommendation service in the DestinationRule, with different settings for our stable and experimental versions:

CHAPTER 4   ADVANCED TRAFFIC MANAGEMENT PATTERNS AND GATEWAY CONTROL

```yaml
trafficPolicy:
  connectionPool:
    tcp:
      maxConnections: 100
      connectTimeout: 30ms
      tcpKeepalive:
        time: 7200s
        interval: 75s
        probes: 10
    http:
      http1MaxPendingRequests: 50
      maxRequestsPerConnection: 10
      maxRetries: 3
      idleTimeout: 15s
      h2MaxRequests: 1000
subsets:
  - name: v1   # Stable version
    labels:
      version: v1
    trafficPolicy:
      connectionPool:
        http:
          http1MaxPendingRequests: 100      # More generous limits for
                                            stable version
          maxRequestsPerConnection: 50
          maxRetries: 5
  - name: v2   # Experimental version
    labels:
      version: v2
    trafficPolicy:
      connectionPool:
        http:
          http1MaxPendingRequests: 25       # More conservative limits for
                                            the new version
          maxRequestsPerConnection: 20
          maxRetries: 2
```

CHAPTER 4 ADVANCED TRAFFIC MANAGEMENT PATTERNS AND GATEWAY CONTROL

In this comprehensive configuration, we're implementing different levels of protection for our stable and experimental versions. The stable version (v1) gets more generous limits since we have confidence in its performance characteristics. The experimental version (v2) gets more conservative limits to protect the system while we validate its behavior under load.

This careful tuning of connection parameters helps ensure our recommendation service remains stable and responsive even under challenging conditions. By understanding and properly configuring these parameters, we can build resilient systems that gracefully handle the various types of stress they might encounter in production.

Threshold Settings

Threshold settings in Istio's circuit breakers act as the decision-making logic that determines when to trip the circuit and how to handle subsequent recovery, and these settings are particularly crucial because they define the fine line between maintaining service availability and preventing cascading failures. Consider them your service mesh's nervous system; they are always on the lookout for warning signs and, when necessary, initiate protective responses.

Let's start by examining a comprehensive threshold configuration:

```
apiVersion: networking.istio.io/v1beta1
kind: DestinationRule
metadata:
  name: recommendation-thresholds
spec:
  host: recommendation-service
  trafficPolicy:
    outlierDetection:
      consecutive5xxErrors: 5
      interval: 10s
      baseEjectionTime: 30s
      maxEjectionPercent: 50
      minHealthPercent: 50
      consecutiveGatewayErrors: 3
      consecutiveLocalOriginFailures: 3
```

Error Detection Mechanisms

The heart of threshold settings lies in their error detection mechanisms. Istio provides several ways to identify problematic instances, each serving a specific purpose in maintaining system health.

`consecutive5xxErrors` is perhaps the most straightforward threshold, and when a service instance returns five consecutive HTTP 5XX errors (in our example), Istio marks that instance as unhealthy and temporarily removes it from the load balancing pool. Consider this scenario with our recommendation service:

```
Request 1: 500 Internal Server Error
Request 2: 503 Service Unavailable
Request 3: 500 Internal Server Error
Request 4: 502 Bad Gateway
Request 5: 500 Internal Server Error
Result: Instance is ejected from the load balancing pool
```

`consecutiveGatewayErrors` focuses specifically on errors that occur at the gateway level. These could be TLS handshake failures, HTTP 502 replies, or connection timeouts, and this is especially important when our recommendation service is exposed via an Istio gateway.

`consecutiveLocalOriginFailures` tracks errors that originate from the local proxy itself, such as connection timeouts or circuit breaker trips. This helps identify network-level issues that might not manifest as HTTP errors.

The timing parameters in threshold settings control how quickly Istio responds to problems and how long it maintains protective measures.

`interval` defines how often Istio evaluates the error conditions. In our example, every ten seconds, Istio checks if any instances have exceeded their error thresholds.

`baseEjectionTime` specifies the minimum amount of time an instance must "cool down" before it can receive traffic again, as well as how long an unhealthy instance stays ejected from the load balancing pool. For our recommendation service, we might set this to 30 seconds, and what makes this particularly interesting is that Istio implements a progressive backoff mechanism. If an instance continues to fail after being readmitted to the pool, its ejection time doubles, for example:

```
First ejection: 30 seconds
Second ejection: 60 seconds
Third ejection: 120 seconds
```

Protection Limits

Istio employs protection limits using two crucial settings to stop the system from ejecting too many instances and perhaps leading to capacity problems.

maxEjectionPercent defines the maximum percentage of instances that can be ejected at any time. This is essential to avoid situations in which the pool is cleared of an excessive number of instances. This means that, even if more instances are exhibiting issues, no more than five instances can be evicted at once in our recommendation service with ten instances.

minHealthPercent serves as a last line of defense, guaranteeing that some capacity is still available even in the worst-case situation by ensuring that a minimal percentage of instances stay in the pool regardless of their health status.

Let's look at a complete example that implements different threshold settings for our development and production environments:

```
# Development Environment
apiVersion: networking.istio.io/v1beta1
kind: DestinationRule
metadata:
  name: recommendation-dev
spec:
  host: recommendation-service
  trafficPolicy:
    outlierDetection:
      consecutive5xxErrors: 10      # More tolerant of errors in
                                    #   development
      interval: 30s                 # Longer evaluation interval
      baseEjectionTime: 60s         # Longer cooling-off period
      maxEjectionPercent: 50        # Can eject more instances
      minHealthPercent: 30          # Lower minimum health requirement
# Production Environment
apiVersion: networking.istio.io/v1beta1
kind: DestinationRule
metadata:
  name: recommendation-prod
```

```yaml
spec:
  host: recommendation-service
  trafficPolicy:
    outlierDetection:
      consecutive5xxErrors: 5      # Stricter error threshold
      interval: 10s                # Faster evaluation
      baseEjectionTime: 30s        # Shorter initial ejection
      maxEjectionPercent: 25       # More conservative ejection limit
      minHealthPercent: 75         # Higher minimum health requirement
```

Circuit Breaker Patterns

When it comes to distributed systems, circuit breaker patterns are examples of sophisticated strategies for dealing with service failures. In spite of the fact that the fundamental idea behind a circuit breaker is to prevent traffic from reaching services that are malfunctioning, the actual implementation patterns might vary greatly depending on the requirements that you have. Using our recommendation service as a real-world example, let's examine these patterns in more detail.

Simple Circuit Breaking Pattern

The most basic circuit breaker pattern is one that focuses on providing protection at the connection level. When there are an excessive number of connections or requests attempting to pass through at the same time, this pattern acts similarly to a basic fuse that is installed in your electrical system. Listed below is one possible implementation for our recommendation service that we could use:

```yaml
apiVersion: networking.istio.io/v1beta1
kind: DestinationRule
metadata:
  name: recommendation-simple-breaker
spec:
  host: recommendation-service
  trafficPolicy:
    connectionPool:
      tcp:
        maxConnections: 100
```

```
    http:
      http1MaxPendingRequests: 50
      maxRequestsPerConnection: 10
```

This simple pattern is particularly effective when your main concern is protecting against resource exhaustion. For instance, a circuit breaker limits both TCP connections and HTTP requests to keep our recommendation service from becoming overloaded if it begins to receive more requests than it can handle.

Outlier Detection Pattern

The outlier detection pattern represents a more sophisticated approach to circuit breaking. Istio can do more than just count connections. It can also keep an eye on how service instances behave and eliminate problematic ones from the load balancing pool. Think of this as having a smart circuit breaker that can identify which specific circuit in your house is causing problems:

```
apiVersion: networking.istio.io/v1beta1
kind: DestinationRule
metadata:
  name: recommendation-outlier
spec:
  host: recommendation-service
  trafficPolicy:
    outlierDetection:
      consecutive5xxErrors: 5
      interval: 10s
      baseEjectionTime: 30s
      maxEjectionPercent: 50
```

This pattern is particularly valuable when you have multiple instances of your service and want to isolate failures to specific instances. For example, if one instance of our recommendation service starts returning errors due to a memory leak, this pattern ensures that the instance is temporarily removed while other healthy instances continue serving traffic.

Progressive Circuit Breaking Pattern

The progressive circuit breaking pattern has multiple layers of safety, with each layer getting stricter than the last. This is like having different types of safety systems in a nuclear power plant, each one protecting in a different way:

```
apiVersion: networking.istio.io/v1beta1
kind: DestinationRule
metadata:
  name: recommendation-progressive
spec:
  host: recommendation-service
  trafficPolicy:
    connectionPool:
      tcp:
        maxConnections: 100
        connectTimeout: 30ms
      http:
        http1MaxPendingRequests: 50
        maxRequestsPerConnection: 10
    outlierDetection:
      consecutive5xxErrors: 5
      interval: 10s
      baseEjectionTime: 30s
      maxEjectionPercent: 50
    loadBalancer:
      simple: LEAST_CONN
```

In this pattern, we have three layers of protection:

1. Connection pool limits prevent resource exhaustion.

2. Outlier detection removes problematic instances.

3. Load balancing ensures even distribution of traffic among healthy instances.

CHAPTER 4   ADVANCED TRAFFIC MANAGEMENT PATTERNS AND GATEWAY CONTROL

Version-Aware Circuit Breaking Pattern

For services that maintain multiple versions, like our recommendation service, we can implement version-aware circuit breaking. This pattern recognizes that different versions might have different stability characteristics and need different protection levels:

```yaml
apiVersion: networking.istio.io/v1beta1
kind: DestinationRule
metadata:
  name: recommendation-version-aware
spec:
  host: recommendation-service
  subsets:
    - name: v1
      labels:
        version: v1
      trafficPolicy:
        connectionPool:
          http:
            maxRequestsPerConnection: 50
        outlierDetection:
          consecutive5xxErrors: 10
          baseEjectionTime: 30s
    - name: v2
      labels:
        version: v2
      trafficPolicy:
        connectionPool:
          http:
            maxRequestsPerConnection: 20
        outlierDetection:
          consecutive5xxErrors: 5
          baseEjectionTime: 60s
```

In this example, we're more lenient with our stable v1 version (allowing more requests per connection and more errors before ejection) while being more protective of our newer v2 version. This pattern is particularly useful during canary deployments or when testing new features.

Monitoring Circuit Breaker Status

Understanding how your circuit breakers behave in production is crucial for maintaining a healthy service mesh, and without proper monitoring, circuit breakers are like safety systems operating in the dark—you won't know if they're working effectively or potentially causing problems themselves. Let's explore how to implement comprehensive monitoring for our circuit breakers.

Metrics Collection

Istio provides a rich set of metrics that help us understand circuit breaker behavior. These metrics are exposed through Istio's telemetry system and can be collected by Prometheus. Here's how we configure metrics collection for our recommendation service:

```
apiVersion: telemetry.istio.io/v1alpha1
kind: Telemetry
metadata:
  name: recommendation-metrics
spec:
  metrics:
    - providers:
        - name: prometheus
      overrides:
        - match:
            metric: REQUEST_COUNT     # Instead of CIRCUIT_BREAKER_STATUS
            mode: SERVER
        - match:
            metric: TCP_CLOSED_CONNECTIONS  # Instead of UPSTREAM_
            EJECTIONS_ACTIVE
            mode: SERVER
```

```
        - match:
            metric: TCP_OPENED_CONNECTIONS  # Instead of CONNECTION_
            POOL_METRICS
            mode: SERVER
```

The key metrics we want to monitor fall into several categories:

1. Circuit State Metrics

    - `istio_requests_total`: Total number of requests handled

2. Connection Pool Metrics

    - `istio_upstream_cx_overflow`: Times the connection pool overflowed

    - `istio_upstream_rq_pending_overflow`: Number of requests rejected due to max pending

    - `istio_upstream_rq_timeout`: Number of requests that timed out

3. Outlier Detection Metrics

    - `istio_upstream_ejections_active`: Currently ejected instances

    - `istio_upstream_ejections_total`: Total number of ejection events

Real-Time Monitoring Dashboard

To make these metrics actionable, we can create a monitoring dashboard that provides real-time visibility into our circuit breakers. Here's an example of how to query these metrics using PromQL (Prometheus Query Language):

```
# Circuit Breaker Trips
rate(istio_circuit_breakers{destination_service="recommendation"}[5m])

# Active Ejections
sum(istio_upstream_ejections_active{destination_service="recommendation"})
by (pod)
```

```
# Connection Pool Saturation
rate(istio_upstream_cx_overflow{destination_service="recommendation"}[5m])
```

Health Status Visualization

Understanding the health status of your circuit breakers is easier with proper visualization. Here's how we might structure a Grafana dashboard for our recommendation service:

Circuit Breaker Overview Panel:

```
panels:
  - title: "Circuit Breaker Status"
    type: "stat"
    targets:
      - expr: |
          sum(istio_circuit_breakers{
            destination_service="recommendation"
          }) by (version)
```

Connection Pool Saturation Panel:

```
panels:
  - title: "Connection Pool Usage"
    type: "gauge"
    targets:
      - expr: |
          sum(rate(istio_upstream_cx_overflow{
            destination_service="recommendation"
          }[5m])) by (version)
```

Finally for our recommendation service, we might create a troubleshooting script:

```
#!/bin/bash
SERVICE_NAME="recommendation"

echo "Checking Circuit Breaker Status..."
kubectl get destinationrule ${SERVICE_NAME} -o yaml | grep -A 10 outlierDetection
```

```
echo "Checking Active Ejections..."
istioctl proxy-status | grep ${SERVICE_NAME}

echo "Analyzing Recent Circuit Breaker Events..."
kubectl logs -l app=${SERVICE_NAME} -c istio-proxy | grep "ejection" |
tail -n 10
```

If all these feel completely new, you can skip this section for now. We will discuss more about observability and monitoring in Chapter 6. You can always come back and refer to this section after going through that chapter.

Fault Injection

For your microservices architecture, fault injection is like conducting a fire drill. Fault injection helps us understand how our services react under adverse circumstances, much like regular fire drills help organizations prepare for actual emergencies. We can validate our resilience mechanisms including the circuit breakers we just covered—by deliberately introducing controlled failures into our system.

Delay Injection

Network delays are one of the most common issues in distributed systems. Sometimes these delays are brief and manageable; other times, they can cascade into system-wide problems. Istio allows us to simulate these delays through its fault injection capabilities.

Think of delay injection as artificially making a service slower to respond, and this is particularly valuable for testing timeout configurations and understanding how delays in one service affect others. Let's see how we can implement delay injection for our recommendation service:

```
apiVersion: networking.istio.io/v1beta1
kind: VirtualService
metadata:
  name: recommendation-delays
spec:
  hosts:
    - recommendation-service
  http:
```

```
      - fault:
          delay:
            fixedDelay: 7s
            percentage:
              value: 25
        route:
          - destination:
              host: recommendation-service
              subset: v1
```

In this configuration, we're introducing a seven-second delay to 25% of all requests to our recommendation service. This helps in the resolution of critical queries such as the following:

- Are slow responses appropriately detected and handled by our circuit breakers?

- When recommendations are slow, how do downstream services behave?

- Do we have the right timeout settings?

Think about a real-world situation: due to increased traffic, our recommendation service may have higher latency during Black Friday deals. By injecting delays now, we can verify that our system handles such situations gracefully:

```
apiVersion: networking.istio.io/v1beta1
kind: VirtualService
metadata:
  name: recommendation-peak-load
spec:
  hosts:
    - recommendation-service
  http:
    - match:
        - headers:
            user-type:
              exact: "premium"
```

```
      fault:
        delay:
          fixedDelay: 2s
          percentage:
            value: 10
      route:
        - destination:
            host: recommendation-service
  - route:
      - destination:
          host: recommendation-service
```

This configuration simulates occasional delays for premium users, helping us validate that our service-level objectives (SLOs) are still met even under degraded conditions.

Abort Injection

While delays test our system's ability to handle slow responses, abort injection tests how well our system handles complete failures. Abort injection simulates scenarios where a service fails outright, returning error responses instead of valid ones.

Let's implement abort injection for our recommendation service:

```
apiVersion: networking.istio.io/v1beta1
kind: VirtualService
metadata:
  name: recommendation-failures
spec:
  hosts:
    - recommendation-service
  http:
    - fault:
        abort:
          httpStatus: 503
          percentage:
            value: 10
```

```
route:
  - destination:
      host: recommendation-service
      subset: v1
```

Ten percent of calls fail with a 503 Service Unavailable error because of this configuration. This helps us check a number of things about our system. Do our circuit breakers know about these failures and act in the right way? If something fails, do our retry rules handle it well? How do our frontend apps handle these mistakes and show them to users?

```
apiVersion: networking.istio.io/v1beta1
kind: VirtualService
metadata:
  name: recommendation-chaos
spec:
  hosts:
    - recommendation-service
  http:
    - match:
        - headers:
            user-agent:
              regex: ".*Mobile.*"
      fault:
        delay:
          fixedDelay: 5s
          percentage:
            value: 15
        abort:
          httpStatus: 503
          percentage:
            value: 5
      route:
        - destination:
            host: recommendation-service
            subset: v1
```

The above setup assumes that mobile users are in a challenging situation where 15% of requests are late and 5% fail. This kind of testing helps us make sure that our mobile apps can work well even when service is slow.

Testing Service Resilience

Like stress-testing a bridge, testing the robustness of microservices lets us see if our system can handle different kinds of stress without breaking. When we test service resilience, we're not just making sure that individual parts work; we're also making sure that our whole system can stay stable and recover from problems.

Testing for resilience is especially important for our recommendation service because the recommendations work with many other parts of our system. If the recommendation service isn't very reliable, it could ruin the whole shopping experience, even if the core shopping features stay the same.

Building a Resilience Test Plan

To begin, we should establish a methodical approach to evaluating the resilience of our service. A comprehensive test plan should evaluate the behavior of isolated components and system-wide interactions. Consider it a test of the bridge's individual support beams and the overall structure's ability to withstand stress.

First, let's create a basic fault injection scenario that we'll use for testing:

```
apiVersion: networking.istio.io/v1beta1
kind: VirtualService
metadata:
  name: recommendation-test-suite
spec:
  hosts:
    - recommendation-service
  http:
    - name: "periodic-failures"
      fault:
        abort:
          httpStatus: 503
          percentage:
            value: 15
```

```yaml
      fault:
        delay:
          fixedDelay: 3s
          percentage:
            value: 20
      route:
        - destination:
            host: recommendation-service
            subset: v1
```

This configuration causes both delays and failures, which makes things hard for our service. But adding faults isn't enough; we also need to regularly check how our system responds.

Progressive Load Testing Under Fault Conditions

Let's come up with a way to test that gradually puts more stress on the system while faults are still present. Let's say we're slowly adding weight to our bridge and creating bad weather at the same time:

```bash
#!/bin/bash
# resilience-test.sh

# Stage 1: Baseline monitoring
echo "Establishing baseline metrics..."
baseline_error_rate=$(kubectl exec -it $PROMETHEUS_POD -n monitoring -- \
  curl -s 'http://localhost:9090/api/v1/query' \
  --data-urlencode 'query=rate(istio_requests_total{response_
  code="503"}[5m])')

# Stage 2: Introduce faults
kubectl apply -f recommendation-test-suite.yaml

# Stage 3: Progressive load increase
for load in 10 25 50 75 100; do
  echo "Testing with ${load}% load..."
  hey -n 1000 -c $load http://recommendation.default.svc.cluster.local/v1/
  recommendations
```

```
# Monitor circuit breaker status
kubectl exec -it $PROMETHEUS_POD -n monitoring -- \
  curl -s 'http://localhost:9090/api/v1/query' \
  --data-urlencode 'query=istio_circuit_breakers{destination_
  service="recommendation"}'

  sleep 30
done
```

In this test script, we're gradually increasing the load while monitoring how our circuit breakers and other resilience mechanisms respond. The key is not just applying load but understanding system behavior at each stage.

Validating Recovery Patterns

One of the most critical aspects of resilience testing is validating that our service can recover properly after failures. Let's create a test scenario that verifies recovery behavior:

```
apiVersion: networking.istio.io/v1beta1
kind: VirtualService
metadata:
  name: recommendation-recovery-test
spec:
  hosts:
    - recommendation-service
  http:
    - name: "catastrophic-failure"
      fault:
        abort:
          httpStatus: 503
          percentage:
            value: 100
      route:
        - destination:
            host: recommendation-service
            subset: v1
```

This configuration simulates a complete service failure. We then monitor recovery using a series of checks:

Circuit Breaker Response:

```
watch 'istioctl proxy-status | grep recommendation'
```

Service Recovery:

```
while true; do
  curl -s -o /dev/null -w "%{http_code}\n" \
    http://recommendation.default.svc.cluster.local/v1/recommendations
  sleep 1
done
```

Performance During Recovery:

```
hey -n 1000 -c 10 http://recommendation.default.svc.cluster.local/v1/recommendations
```

Retry and Timeout Policies

Request failures in distributed microservices architectures can be caused by resource constraints, network issues, and brief service outages. If not managed appropriately, even transient failures can have a major effect on the user experience. Istio offers powerful timeout and retry methods to efficiently handle these failures. Take a look at our recommendation service. Users want to receive personalized recommendations as soon as they surf your video streaming platform. This experience could be interrupted by network glitches or transient service issues, and this is where Istio's retry and timeout policies become crucial since they maintain user satisfaction and service reliability even in the event of a problem.

Configuring Retry Policies

Ensuring application resilience requires properly configuring Istio's retry policies, which specify how frequently and under what conditions a failed request should be retried:

```
apiVersion: networking.istio.io/v1beta1
kind: VirtualService
```

```
metadata:
  name: recommendation-retry
spec:
  hosts:
    - recommendation-service
  http:
    - route:
        - destination:
            host: recommendation-service
      retries:
        attempts: 3
        perTryTimeout: 2s
        retryOn: "connect-failure,refused-stream,unavailable,cancelled,resource-exhausted,5xx"
```

The retry configuration includes three key components:

1. `attempts`: Specifies the maximum number of retry attempts. Setting this to 3 in our example indicates that Istio will make up to three further attempts once the first one fails.

2. `perTryTimeout`: Every time a retry attempt is made, perTryTimeout sets a timeout. Our two-second timeout makes sure that retries don't take too long.

3. `retryOn`: Defines the conditions that trigger a retry. Istio supports several retry conditions:

    - `connect-failure`: Network connection failures
    - `refused-stream`: When the upstream service refuses the connection
    - `unavailable`: Service unavailable errors (HTTP 503)
    - `cancelled`: When the client cancels the request
    - `resource-exhausted`: Resource exhaustion errors
    - 5xx: Any server-side error (500–599)

Timeout Settings

When services are slow or unresponsive, timeouts prevent requests from hanging indefinitely, and by serving as a safety valve, they make sure that resources aren't wasted waiting for responses that might never come.

For the duration of the request, including any retries, the timeout field in this example sets a global timeout of ten seconds. The request will be terminated if it is not completed within this time frame, and also you can combine timeouts with retries for comprehensive error handling:

```
apiVersion: networking.istio.io/v1beta1
kind: VirtualService
metadata:
  name: recommendation-resilient
spec:
  hosts:
    - recommendation-service
  http:
    - route:
        - destination:
            host: recommendation-service
      timeout: 15s
      retries:
        attempts: 3
        perTryTimeout: 2s
        retryOn: "connect-failure,5xx"
```

Backoff Configurations

While Istio doesn't provide explicit backoff configuration in VirtualServices, it implements an internal backoff strategy in its proxy (Envoy) when handling retries. This innate behavior keeps overwhelming potentially struggling services.

To help avoid "thundering herd" issues, which occur when many unsuccessful requests retry simultaneously, the proxy automatically applies progressive delays between retry attempts, which is comparable to an exponential backoff strategy, and this means that each subsequent retry attempt will wait a little longer before trying again.

When a service experiences failures, Istio's proxy automatically implements progressive delays between retry attempts, and like a smart elevator system if the first attempt to call an elevator fails, it doesn't immediately try again. Instead, it waits a moment and then tries again, with each subsequent attempt waiting a bit longer.

This internal backoff mechanism follows certain principles. After the first failure, there's a brief initial delay before the first retry, and each subsequent retry waits longer than the previous one, and small random variations in timing prevent multiple services from retrying simultaneously.

For example, if our recommendation service fails, the retry timing can look like the first retry might have an ~100 ms delay, the second retry will have an ~200 ms delay, and finally the third retry might have an ~400 ms delay.

This progression helps prevent what's known as the "thundering herd" problem, where many failed requests retry simultaneously and potentially overwhelm the recovering service.

Best Practices

When implementing retry and timeout policies, consider these best practices:

1. Set Reasonable Timeout Values:

    - Base timeouts on your service's actual performance characteristics.

    - Account for network latency, especially in distributed deployments.

    - Make the global timeout longer than (perTryTimeout × attempts).

    - Monitor and adjust timeouts based on real-world performance data.

2. Configure Retries Carefully:

    - Keep retry attempts low (two to three maximum) to prevent cascading failures.

    - Be selective with retry conditions—only retry on truly transient errors.

    - Consider the impact on downstream services.

    - Implement circuit breakers alongside retries.

3. Monitor and Adjust:

    - Track retry metrics to identify problematic services.
    - Monitor timeout occurrences to identify performance issues.
    - Use distributed tracing to understand retry patterns.
    - Set up alerts for excessive retries or timeouts.

Here's a production-ready example incorporating these best practices:

```
apiVersion: networking.istio.io/v1beta1
kind: VirtualService
metadata:
  name: recommendation-production
spec:
  hosts:
    - recommendation-service
  http:
    - route:
        - destination:
            host: recommendation-service
      timeout: 15s
      retries:
        attempts: 2
        perTryTimeout: 2s
        retryOn: "connect-failure,503,504"
```

This configuration provides a balanced approach to handling transient failures while protecting both the service and its clients from cascading issues.

Traffic Mirroring

Traffic mirroring, also known as shadow traffic, is one of Istio's most powerful yet underutilized features for safely testing new service versions in production environments. Like a two-way mirror in a detective movie, traffic mirroring allows you to observe real production traffic behavior without affecting the actual users. Figure 4-4 illustrates the basic setup of traffic mirroring.

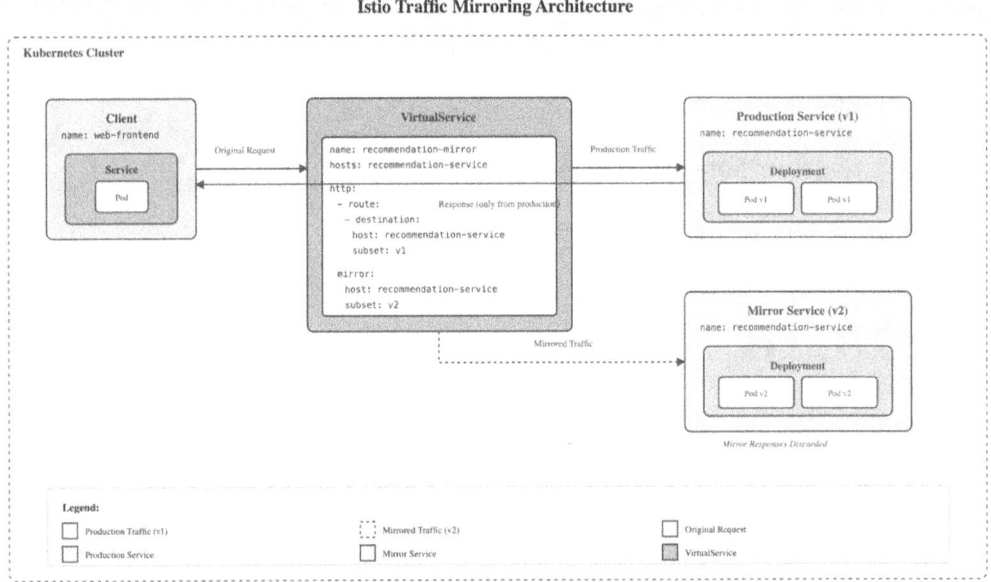

Figure 4-4. The basic setup of traffic mirroring

Understanding Traffic Mirroring Concepts

With Istio, traffic mirroring copies incoming requests to a mirrored service and only returns responses from the primary service; you can test new versions of your service using actual production traffic in a shadow environment without impacting real customers. You can imagine this as your practice stage that runs in parallel to a main stage where actors can rehearse with the same script but without a crowd.

Let's say we want to test a new AI-powered recommendation algorithm (v2) in the context of our recommendation service without risking the user experience. We can examine how the new algorithm might function in real-world scenarios by using traffic mirroring that sends a copy of every request made to our experimental v2 service from our stable v1 service.

The key concepts of traffic mirroring include

1. Source Service: The original service receiving production traffic (v1 of our recommendation service).

2. Mirror Service: The service receiving the copied traffic (v2 of our recommendation service).

CHAPTER 4 ADVANCED TRAFFIC MANAGEMENT PATTERNS AND GATEWAY CONTROL

3. Mirror Percentage: The percentage of traffic to mirror (can be 0–100%).

4. Shadow Responses: Responses from the mirrored service are discarded to prevent impact on users.

Implementing Shadow Traffic

We have to carefully configure Istio's VirtualService resource to implement traffic mirroring, and we can set it for our recommendation service as below:

```
apiVersion: networking.istio.io/v1beta1
kind: VirtualService
metadata:
  name: recommendation-mirror
spec:
  hosts:
    - recommendation-service
  http:
    - route:
        - destination:
            host: recommendation-service
            subset: v1
      mirror:
        host: recommendation-service
        subset: v2
      mirrorPercentage:
        value: 100.0     # Mirror 100% of traffic
```

This configuration accomplishes several important tasks:

- Routes all primary traffic to the v1 subset
- Creates an exact copy of the traffic and sends it to the v2 subset
- Discards responses from the v2 subset to prevent user impact
- Preserves headers, body, and other request characteristics in the mirrored traffic

For more granular control, we can implement conditional mirroring based on specific criteria:

```
apiVersion: networking.istio.io/v1beta1
kind: VirtualService
metadata:
  name: recommendation-selective-mirror
spec:
  hosts:
    - recommendation-service
  http:
    - match:
        - headers:
            user-type:
              exact: "premium"
      route:
        - destination:
            host: recommendation-service
            subset: v1
      mirror:
        host: recommendation-service
        subset: v2
      mirrorPercentage:
        value: 100.0
```

Use Cases for Traffic Mirroring

In modern service deployment strategies, traffic mirroring serves several crucial purposes. Let us get into each use case in detail:

> Performance Testing: Performance characteristics can be evaluated risk-free under real-world scenarios by mirroring production traffic to a new version. This entails comparing the response times of the AI-enhanced version and the present algorithm for our recommendation service.

Behavior Validation: Mirroring helps in confirming that new versions manage every edge case seen in real-world traffic. Given how erratic user behavior can be, this is very helpful for our recommendation system.

Capacity Planning: By analyzing how mirrored services handle production load, you can better understand resource requirements for new versions, and for instance, in real-world scenarios, we might discover that our AI-enhanced v2 requires more CPU resources.

Regression Testing: By comparing responses across versions, traffic mirroring can help in identifying potential regressions. We can verify that none of the critical recommendations made by the existing version of the recommendation system are overlooked by our new updated algorithm.

Machine Learning (ML) Model Validation: For services like our recommendation engine that might use ML models, mirroring allows us to validate new models with production data before deployment.

Analyzing Mirrored Traffic

Understanding how your new service version operates in real-world scenarios requires proper analysis when deploying traffic mirroring in a microservices architecture. Imagine that we are updating our recommendation service from a simple algorithm to one that is driven by artificial intelligence (AI). In this case, we have to fully understand how the new version handles real user requests without affecting the user experience. This can be achieved by closely examining mirrored traffic patterns, performance metrics, and system behavior.

For example, when a user requests movie recommendations through our service, the current version (v1) might use a simple collaborative filtering algorithm based on user ratings. The new version (v2) could employ a sophisticated machine learning model that considers viewing history, time of day, and trending content. Through traffic mirroring, we can analyze how both versions handle the same request:

Chapter 4   Advanced Traffic Management Patterns and Gateway Control

```yaml
apiVersion: telemetry.istio.io/v1alpha1
kind: Telemetry
metadata:
  name: recommendation-mirror-analysis
spec:
  metrics:
    - providers:
        - name: prometheus
      overrides:
        - match:
            metric: REQUEST_COUNT
          mode: CLIENT_AND_SERVER
        - match:
            metric: REQUEST_DURATION
          mode: CLIENT_AND_SERVER
        - match:
            metric: RESPONSE_SIZE
          mode: SERVER
```

This configuration enables us to track essential metrics about both versions of our service, including request patterns, latency measurements, and error rates.

Performance Monitoring and Analysis

By analyzing behavior in the real world under identical settings, performance comparison provides important insights about your service versions. Using basic genre matching "user 123 enjoys action films," as an example, we can see that v1 of our recommendation system consistently produces results in 100 ms—since it suggests well-known action films—and the new AI-powered v2 takes 150 ms to react, but it provides more complex recommendations by examining the user's whole viewing history, current trends, and even time-based viewing patterns.

Let's examine a real-world example of how both versions handle the same request:

```
// V1 Response (100ms)
GET /recommendations?user_id=123
{
  "recommendations": [
```

```
    "Die Hard",
    "Mission Impossible",
    "The Matrix"
  ]
}

// V2 Response (150ms)
GET /recommendations?user_id=123
{
  "recommendations": [
    "John Wick",          // Based on recent viewing history
    "Top Gun: Maverick",  // Currently trending
    "Inception"           // Matches evening viewing preference
  ]
}
```

Resource utilization analysis reveals another crucial dimension of performance. For example, our monitoring might show that while v1 operates efficiently with two CPU cores and 2 GB of memory, v2 requires three CPU cores and 3 GB of memory to support its AI model. Understanding these differences becomes crucial for capacity planning and infrastructure scaling decisions.

Real-Time Analysis and Automation

Real-time monitoring serves as our early warning system for potential issues or anomalies, and we can implement automated alerts to notify teams when key metrics deviate from expected ranges. For example, our monitoring system might trigger alerts under these conditions. If you don't understand what is PrometheusRule here, don't worry. We will be talking about it more in Chapter 6:

```
apiVersion: monitoring.coreos.com/v1
kind: PrometheusRule
metadata:
  name: recommendation-alerts
spec:
  groups:
    - name: recommendation.rules
```

```
      rules:
      - alert: HighLatency
        expr: rate(istio_request_duration_milliseconds_sum{destination_
        service="recommendation-v2"}[5m]) > 200
```

By using this systematic approach to traffic monitoring and mirroring, teams can confidently test new service versions in real-world scenarios while preserving system stability and improving user satisfaction. Effective service upgrades are guaranteed by the combination of comprehensive monitoring, automated alerts, and detailed performance analysis. Every insight obtained from mirrored traffic analysis contributes to improving the deployment strategy and service implementation, which eventually results in reliable systems and improved user experiences.

Testing and Validation Strategies

The efficient use of traffic mirroring is ensured by a systematic testing and validation process. Here is a comprehensive strategy.

Gradual Mirror Implementation:

```
apiVersion: networking.istio.io/v1beta1
kind: VirtualService
metadata:
  name: recommendation-gradual-mirror
spec:
  hosts:
    - recommendation
  http:
    - route:
        - destination:
            host: recommendation-service
            subset: v1
      mirror:
        host: recommendation-service
        subset: v2
      mirrorPercentage:
        value: 25.0    # Start with 25% traffic mirroring
```

For automated validation, implement alerts for key metrics:

```
apiVersion: monitoring.coreos.com/v1
kind: PrometheusRule
metadata:
  name: recommendation-alerts
spec:
  groups:
    - name: recommendation.rules
      rules:
        - alert: HighLatency
          expr: rate(istio_request_duration_milliseconds_sum{destination_service="recommendation-v2"}[5m]) > 200
```

Through this systematic approach to traffic mirroring and analysis, teams can confidently evaluate new service versions under real-world conditions. The combination of comprehensive monitoring, automated alerts, and detailed performance analysis ensures successful service upgrades while maintaining system stability and improving user satisfaction. Each insight gained through mirrored traffic analysis helps refine both the service implementation and the deployment strategy, ultimately leading to better user experiences and more reliable systems.

Gateway Management

Controlling and managing the flow of traffic into and out of your service mesh is very important in modern microservices architectures. Istio's gateway management offers this important feature through two primary components: ingress gateways, which handle incoming traffic, and egress gateways, which handle outgoing traffic. These gateways are like high-tech border patrols for your microservices ecosystem as they control what comes in and goes out, enforce policies, handle security, and make sure all the traffic goes to the right place, and before we get into the specifics of setting up the gateway, it is important to know why it's so important to handle the gateway correctly in a microservices architecture.

1. Security: Gateways are the central point where security rules, SSL/TLS termination, and access control can all be set up from one place.

2. Monitoring: By channeling traffic through gateways, you gain better visibility into the communication patterns between your services and the outside world.

3. Protocol Support: Gateways can handle more than one protocol and perform the conversion between them when necessary.

4. Load Balancing: Different algorithms and rules can be used to split traffic between different service instances.

5. Version Management: Gateways make it easier to use advanced deployment techniques like blue-green deployments and canary releases.

Ingress Gateway

The main way that traffic from outside your service mesh gets in is through the ingress gateway. It is different from other Kubernetes ingress resources as it manages traffic more effectively and has more advanced routing, load balancing, and security features. Figure 4-5 shows the architecture and the components involved in routing a request through Ingress gateway.

CHAPTER 4   ADVANCED TRAFFIC MANAGEMENT PATTERNS AND GATEWAY CONTROL

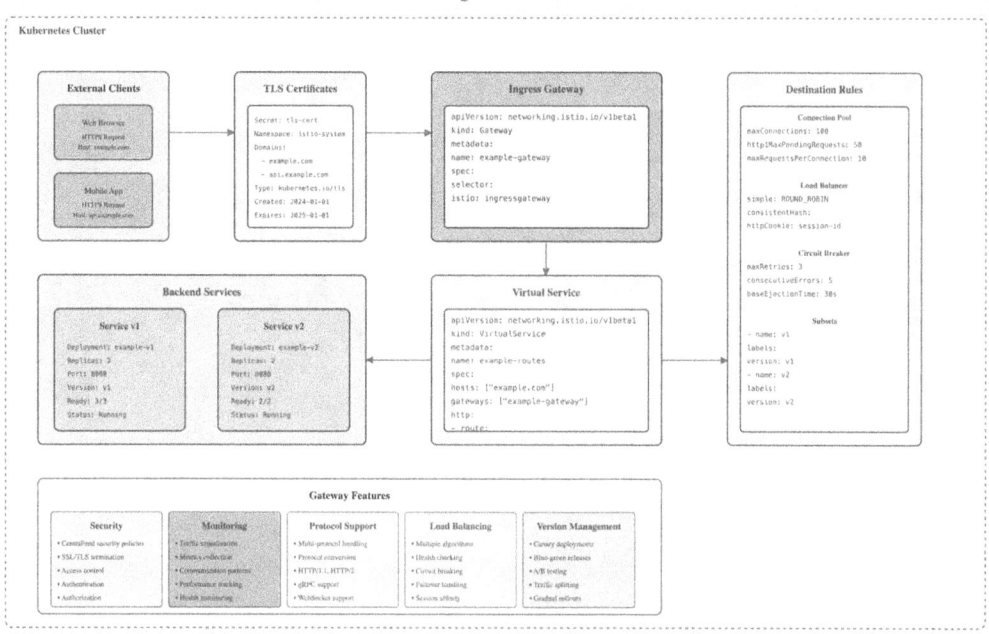

Figure 4-5. *The architecture and components involved in routing a request through Ingress gateway*

Let's examine how we can leverage these capabilities for our recommendation service.

Gateway Configuration

To configure an ingress gateway, it is necessary to have various critical components collaborate with one another. Let's dissect each component and have a better understanding of what it does. The first thing that has to be done is to create a Gateway resource that will tell our mesh on how to receive traffic:

```
apiVersion: networking.istio.io/v1beta1
kind: Gateway
metadata:
  name: recommendation-gateway
spec:
  selector:
    istio: ingressgateway
  servers:
  - port:
```

195

CHAPTER 4   ADVANCED TRAFFIC MANAGEMENT PATTERNS AND GATEWAY CONTROL

```
    number: 80
    name: http
    protocol: HTTP
  hosts:
  - "recommendations.example.com"
- port:
    number: 443
    name: https
    protocol: HTTPS
  tls:
    mode: SIMPLE
    credentialName: recommendations-cert
  hosts:
  - "recommendations.example.com"
```

Let's examine each part of this configuration:

- `selector`: Determines which Istio ingress gateway pod will handle the traffic. The default Istio installation creates a gateway with the label `istio: ingressgateway`.

- `servers`: Defines one or more server configurations for handling incoming traffic.

- `port`: Specifies the ports and protocols the gateway will listen on.

- `hosts`: Lists the hosts that this gateway will accept traffic for.

Virtual Service Configuration: After defining the gateway, we need to configure how traffic should be routed once it enters our mesh:

```
apiVersion: networking.istio.io/v1beta1
kind: VirtualService
metadata:
  name: recommendation-routes
spec:
  hosts:
  - "recommendations.example.com"
  gateways:
  - recommendation-gateway
```

```yaml
  http:
  - match:
    - uri:
        prefix: "/api/v1/recommendations"
    route:
    - destination:
        host: recommendation-v1
        port:
          number: 8080
  - match:
    - uri:
        prefix: "/api/v2/recommendations"
    route:
    - destination:
        host: recommendation-v2
        port:
          number: 8080
```

This virtual service configuration

- Associates with our gateway using the gateway name
- Defines specific URI-based routing rules
- Routes different API versions to different service versions

Destination Rules: We also need to configure DestinationRules to define how traffic should be handled once it reaches our services. We already went over the DestinationRule configurations in the previous chapter:

```yaml
apiVersion: networking.istio.io/v1beta1
kind: DestinationRule
metadata:
  name: recommendation-destinations
spec:
  host: recommendation-v1
  trafficPolicy:
    loadBalancer:
      simple: ROUND_ROBIN
```

```
    connectionPool:
      tcp:
        maxConnections: 100
      http:
        http1MaxPendingRequests: 25
        maxRequestsPerConnection: 10
  subsets:
  - name: v1
    labels:
      version: v1
```

Complete Setup to Implement the Gateway Configuration: Apply these resources in order:

```
# Create the gateway
kubectl apply -f recommendation-gateway.yaml

# Create the virtual service
kubectl apply -f recommendation-vs.yaml

# Create the destination rule
kubectl apply -f recommendation-dr.yaml

# Verify the configuration
kubectl get gateway recommendation-gateway -o yaml
kubectl get virtualservice recommendation-routes -o yaml
```

Exposure Patterns

When deploying microservices in production, how you expose your services to the outside world can significantly impact your application's security, maintainability, and user experience. Istio's ingress gateway offers a variety of advanced service exposure patterns, each tailored to a specific use case or necessity. Let us investigate these patterns in depth.

Path-Based Routing Pattern

Path-based routing is one of the most basic and popular techniques for exposing microservices. This pattern checks the URL path to see which backend service should handle the request. Consider it a sophisticated postal sorting system in which packages (requests) are routed to different departments (services) according to their address (URL path).

For our recommendation service, path-based routing enables us to handle different versions of our API while maintaining a clean and consistent URL structure. Here's how we implement this pattern:

```
apiVersion: networking.istio.io/v1beta1
kind: VirtualService
metadata:
  name: path-based-routes
spec:
  hosts:
  - "api.recommendations.com"
  gateways:
  - recommendation-gateway
  http:
  - match:
    - uri:
        prefix: "/v1/recommendations"
    route:
    - destination:
        host: recommendation-v1
        port:
          number: 8080
    rewrite:
      uri: "/recommendations"  # Removes the version prefix before
      forwarding
  - match:
    - uri:
        prefix: "/v2/recommendations"
```

```
        route:
        - destination:
            host: recommendation-v2
            port:
              number: 8080
          rewrite:
            uri: "/recommendations"
```

This configuration shows a number of important ideas. First, `prefix` matching lets us catch all requests that begin with a specific path segment, and in this case, the first rule will catch any request sent to `/v1/recommendations/user/123`. The `rewrite` field changes the URL and eliminates the version prefix before it gets to the backend service, and this is very helpful because it means our backend services don't have to know about the versioning in the URL—they can just handle calls to `/v1/recommendations/user/123`.

A real-world scenario helps illustrate this pattern's value. Imagine we're rolling out a new AI-powered recommendation algorithm. We can expose it under the `/v2` path while keeping the existing algorithm at `/v1`. This allows us to

- Maintain backward compatibility for existing clients
- Gradually migrate users to the new version
- A/B test different algorithms
- Provide a clear upgrade path for API consumers

Features-Based Routing Pattern

We can use a more advanced pattern that groups routes around business features to extend the path-based routing. This method is very similar to domain-driven design ideas, and it helps clients understand how the API is structured better and can be used in our recommendation service in the following way:

```
apiVersion: networking.istio.io/v1beta1
kind: VirtualService
metadata:
  name: feature-based-routes
spec:
```

```yaml
hosts:
- "api.recommendations.com"
gateways:
- recommendation-gateway
http:
- match:
  - uri:
      prefix: "/recommendations/personalized"
  route:
  - destination:
      host: personalized-recommendations
      port:
        number: 8080
- match:
  - uri:
      prefix: "/recommendations/trending"
  route:
  - destination:
      host: trending-recommendations
      port:
        number: 8080
- match:
  - uri:
      prefix: "/recommendations/collaborative"
  route:
  - destination:
      host: collaborative-recommendations
      port:
        number: 8080
```

This pattern shines in complex applications where different teams might own different features. Each team can deploy and manage their service independently, while the gateway provides a unified entry point for clients. For instance, the personalization team can focus on improving the AI models for personalized recommendations without affecting the trending recommendation system.

CHAPTER 4   ADVANCED TRAFFIC MANAGEMENT PATTERNS AND GATEWAY CONTROL

Environment Segregation Pattern

Managing the different environments (development, staging, and production) gets harder as apps get bigger. The Istio gateway can help separate traffic based on the location while maintaining consistent routing rules. Here's a comprehensive implementation:

```
apiVersion: networking.istio.io/v1beta1
kind: Gateway
metadata:
  name: multi-env-gateway
spec:
  selector:
    istio: ingressgateway
  servers:
  - port:
      number: 443
      name: https-dev
      protocol: HTTPS
    tls:
      mode: SIMPLE
      credentialName: dev-cert
    hosts:
    - "*.dev.recommendations.com"
  - port:
      number: 443
      name: https-staging
      protocol: HTTPS
    tls:
      mode: SIMPLE
      credentialName: staging-cert
    hosts:
    - "*.staging.recommendations.com"
  - port:
      number: 443
      name: https-prod
```

```
    protocol: HTTPS
  tls:
    mode: SIMPLE
    credentialName: prod-cert
  hosts:
  - "*.prod.recommendations.com"
```

For businesses that use GitOps or strictly segregate their environments, this strategy is especially helpful as each environment has the same underlying gateway infrastructure but receives its own subdomain and TLS certificate. This strategy has a number of advantages:

1. Every environment is separated at the DNS level, ensuring a clear separation of concerns.

2. Environment-specific certificates for enhanced security.

3. Ability to apply different routing rules per environment.

4. Simplified debugging and monitoring.

5. Easy implementation of environment-specific features or configurations.

SSL/TLS Termination

SSL/TLS termination is a critical aspect of secure communication in microservices architectures, ensuring that data transmitted between clients and services remains encrypted and protected from unauthorized access. In Istio, this process is efficiently handled by the ingress gateway, which offloads the computational overhead of encryption and decryption from individual services. This section explores how SSL/TLS termination works in Istio and provides guidance on configuring it for secure traffic management.

When external clients communicate with services within a Kubernetes cluster, their traffic often needs to be encrypted using HTTPS. SSL/TLS termination refers to the process of decrypting this traffic at a designated gateway before routing it to the appropriate internal services. This approach centralizes the management of SSL/TLS certificates and simplifies security compliance.

CHAPTER 4 ADVANCED TRAFFIC MANAGEMENT PATTERNS AND GATEWAY CONTROL

Istio's ingress gateway acts as the termination point for HTTPS traffic, decrypting incoming requests and forwarding them to services within the mesh. By handling SSL/TLS at the gateway, Istio reduces the complexity for individual services, which no longer need to manage certificates or encryption configurations.

Configuring SSL/TLS Termination in Istio

To set up SSL/TLS termination, you need to create a Gateway resource in Istio. This resource specifies the ports, protocols, and certificates to be used for secure communication. Below is a step-by-step guide:

Create a Kubernetes Secret for Certificates: Certificates and private keys required for HTTPS are stored as Kubernetes secrets, for example:

```
kubectl create secret tls my-credential --cert=/path/to/tls.crt --key=/path/to/tls.key -n istio-system
```

Here, `my-credential` is the name of the secret, and the certificate and key files are specified.

Define a Gateway Resource: The Gateway resource configures the ingress gateway to handle HTTPS traffic using the certificates stored in the secret:

```
apiVersion: networking.istio.io/v1beta1
kind: Gateway
metadata:
  name: ingress-gateway
  namespace: istio-system
spec:
  selector:
    istio: ingressgateway
  servers:
  - port:
      number: 443
      name: https
      protocol: HTTPS
    tls:
      mode: SIMPLE
      credentialName: my-credential
```

```
hosts:
- "example.com"
```

- `port`: Specifies the HTTPS port (443)
- `tls.mode`: Set to SIMPLE for standard HTTPS termination
- `credentialName`: References the Kubernetes secret containing the SSL/TLS certificate
- `hosts`: Defines the domain name(s) for which the gateway will handle traffic

Benefits of SSL/TLS Termination

1. Centralized Certificate Management: By handling SSL/TLS at the ingress gateway, certificates can be managed in one location, simplifying updates and renewals. This reduces the risk of certificate mismanagement and ensures consistent security practices across the service mesh.

2. Reduced Service Complexity: Individual services do not need to handle SSL/TLS configurations, making them easier to deploy and maintain. Developers can focus on application logic without being burdened by encryption and decryption concerns.

3. Improved Performance: Putting encryption and decryption in the hands of the gateway helps to reduce the amount of computational work that is required by individual services, and this guarantees that services can function effectively without being influenced by cryptographic operations when they are being performed.

4. Enhanced Security: To make sure the communication remains secure, all incoming traffic is encrypted, and by placing SSL/TLS termination in a central location, security vulnerabilities that could have been caused by different services having inconsistent configurations are eliminated.

5. Ease of Compliance: Centralized administration and consistent enforcement of SSL/TLS policies facilitate compliance with regulatory mandates, including GDPR, HIPAA, and PCI-DSS. At the same time a unified point of control simplifies the auditing process.

6. Seamless Integration with Monitoring: The ingress gateway can be integrated with monitoring tools to provide visibility into encrypted traffic patterns, identifying anomalies and potential security threats.

7. Scalability: The ingress gateway can scale independently to handle increasing encrypted traffic, ensuring the system remains performant under high loads.

These benefits make SSL/TLS termination at the ingress gateway a foundational practice for securing modern microservices architectures.

Best Practices

1. Use Automated Certificate Management: Integrate tools like Cert-Manager to automate certificate issuance and renewal. This minimizes manual effort, reduces the risk of errors, and ensures uninterrupted service by proactively handling certificate expiration.

2. Enable Mutual TLS (mTLS): Configure mTLS between services to ensure strong authentication and end-to-end encryption within the service mesh. This prevents unauthorized access and safeguards sensitive data during transit.

3. Monitor Certificate Expiry: Regularly monitor and set up alerts for expiring certificates to avoid service disruptions. Combine this with automated renewal processes for seamless operations.

4. Implement Fine-Grained Access Control: Use Istio's authorization policies to enforce granular access control between services. This ensures that only authorized services can communicate, reducing the attack surface.

5. Scale Gateway Resources Dynamically: Configure autoscaling policies for the ingress gateway to handle traffic spikes efficiently without performance degradation.

6. Enable Observability: Use Istio's telemetry capabilities to observe SSL/TLS traffic metrics, including handshake failures, latency, and throughput as this allows for the proactive identification and resolution of possible issues

7. Adopt Security Audits: Conduct regular security audits of SSL/TLS configurations to verify compliance with current best practices and regulatory standards, including PCI-DSS and HIPAA.

8. Centralized Policy Management: Manage all SSL/TLS policies centrally at the ingress gateway to ensure consistency and simplify updates across the mesh.

9. Rate Limiting and DDoS Protection: Configure rate limiting and implement DDoS protection at the gateway level to safeguard backend services from abusive traffic patterns.

10. Use Latest Protocols: Ensure the use of up-to-date SSL/TLS protocols (e.g., TLS 1.3) for improved security and performance.

By adhering to these best practices, Istio users can ensure robust, secure, and efficient traffic management while simplifying operations and enhancing system reliability.

By implementing SSL/TLS termination at the ingress gateway, Istio simplifies secure traffic management and ensures encrypted communication between external clients and internal services. This approach aligns with modern security practices, making it an essential part of Istio's traffic management capabilities.

Host-Based Routing

Host-based routing is a versatile feature of Istio that allows traffic routing decisions to be determined using the HTTP Host header. This capability is especially beneficial in multi-tenant situations or scenarios in which multiple domains use the same ingress gateway. By defining routing rules based on hostnames, Istio enables precise traffic management for different services or applications hosted under the same gateway.

CHAPTER 4   ADVANCED TRAFFIC MANAGEMENT PATTERNS AND GATEWAY CONTROL

In an HTTP request, the Host header specifies the domain name of the target server. Istio uses this header to direct traffic to the appropriate destination service. For instance, traffic intended for example.com can be directed to one service, whilst traffic for api.example.com is directed to another, and this functionality is implemented using the Gateway and VirtualService resources. The Gateway delineates the domains managed by the ingress gateway, whereas the VirtualService establishes the routing protocols for each domain. Let's try to understand the detailed flow with the help of an example.

The Gateway resource is configured to listen for traffic on specific domains:

```
apiVersion: networking.istio.io/v1beta1
kind: Gateway
metadata:
  name: host-based-gateway
  namespace: istio-system
spec:
  selector:
    istio: ingressgateway
  servers:
  - port:
      number: 80
      name: http
      protocol: HTTP
    hosts:
    - "example.com"
    - "api.example.com"
```

In this configuration

- hosts defines the domains the gateway will handle.
- Additionally, this gateway will be responsible for processing traffic for example.com as well as api.example.com.

Create separate VirtualService resources for each domain to route traffic to the appropriate services:

```
apiVersion: networking.istio.io/v1beta1
kind: VirtualService
metadata:
```

208

```yaml
  name: example-route
  namespace: istio-system
spec:
  hosts:
  - "example.com"
  gateways:
  - host-based-gateway
  http:
  - match:
    - uri:
        prefix: "/"
    route:
    - destination:
        host: example-service
        port:
          number: 80
apiVersion: networking.istio.io/v1beta1
kind: VirtualService
metadata:
  name: api-route
  namespace: istio-system
spec:
  hosts:
  - "api.example.com"
  gateways:
  - host-based-gateway
  http:
  - match:
    - uri:
        prefix: "/"
    route:
    - destination:
        host: api-service
        port:
          number: 80
```

In this setup

- Requests to `example.com` are routed to the example-service.
- Requests to `api.example.com` are routed to the api-service.

Egress Gateway

Just as important as managing incoming traffic in a contemporary microservices architecture is managing how your services interact with the outside world. An egress gateway serves as a dedicated point of departure for traffic leaving your service mesh and going to external systems outside of the service mesh. Think of it like a security checkpoint at the international departure terminal of an airport: before departing the nation (our service mesh), all travelers (in our case, network requests) must go through this regulated exit point. Figure 4-6 shows the architecture of Egress Gateway. Imagine a situation in which our recommendation system must interface with third-party analytics services or retrieve movie data from external APIs such as TMDB (The Movie Database) and it would be challenging to monitor, secure, and control these communications if each service connects directly to these external endpoints in the absence of an egress gateway. We obtain centralized control, increased security, and better observability of external dependencies by directing all outgoing traffic through an egress gateway. Consider a scenario where our recommendation service needs to fetch trending movies from TMDB's API, and below is an example of how we can configure an egress gateway to manage this external traffic:

```
apiVersion: networking.istio.io/v1beta1
kind: Gateway
metadata:
  name: movies-egress-gateway
spec:
  selector:
    istio: egressgateway
  servers:
  - port:
      number: 443
      name: https
```

```
    protocol: HTTPS
hosts:
- "api.themoviedb.org"
```

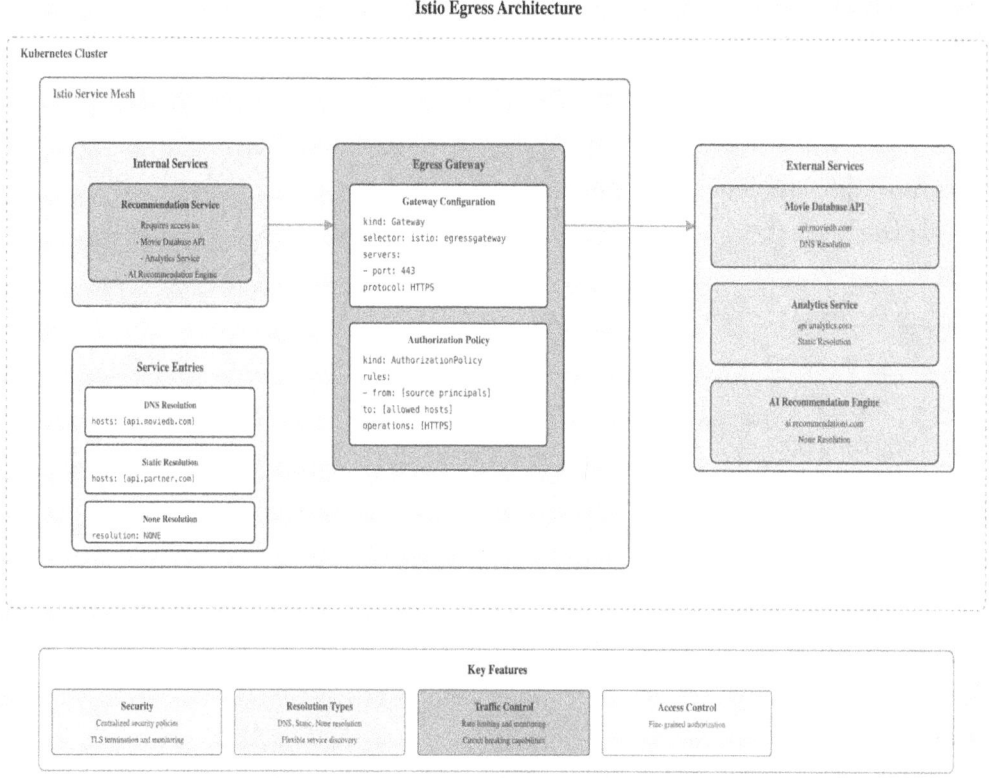

Figure 4-6. *The architecture of Egress Gateway*

This configuration establishes a dedicated gateway that handles all outbound traffic to TMDB's API and acts as an intermediary, allowing us to implement security policies, monitor traffic patterns, and maintain compliance requirements at a single point.

Controlling Outbound Traffic

Controlling outbound traffic through an egress gateway is more complicated than just creating a way for external communications to pass. Routing rules, traffic policies, and security measures must all be carefully thought out. This control is necessary for maintaining security, managing the costs of external API calls, and making sure the service works reliably.

CHAPTER 4   ADVANCED TRAFFIC MANAGEMENT PATTERNS AND GATEWAY CONTROL

Let's think about a real-world scenario where our recommendation service needs to talk to several outside APIs: a movie database to get content, an AI-powered recommendation engine to make recommendations, and an analytics service to keep track of how users behave. Taking care of these external interactions needs a well-planned strategy.

We need to define precise routing rules that determine how traffic flows from our services to these external endpoints. This is where VirtualService configurations become crucial:

```
apiVersion: networking.istio.io/v1beta1
kind: VirtualService
metadata:
  name: external-routing-rules
spec:
  hosts:
  - api.moviedb.com
  gateways:
  - recommendation-egress-gateway
  - mesh
  http:
  - match:
    - gateways:
      - mesh
      sourceLabels:
        app: recommendation-service
    route:
    - destination:
        host: istio-egressgateway.istio-system.svc.cluster.local
        subset: moviedb-route
        port:
          number: 443
    timeout: 5s
    retries:
      attempts: 3
      perTryTimeout: 2s
```

```
        retryOn: "connect-failure,refused-stream,unavailable,cancelled,resour
ce-exhausted"
```

The VirtualService defines a two-stage routing process. The egress gateway is the first place where traffic from our recommendation service goes, and the gateway forwards it to the external service. We can implement centralized control policies with this two-stage process, and using source labels, we can tell which services are able to connect to external endpoints. This prevents unauthorized services from making external calls:

```
apiVersion: security.istio.io/v1beta1
kind: AuthorizationPolicy
metadata:
  name: egress-access-control
  namespace: istio-system
spec:
  selector:
    matchLabels:
      app: istio-egressgateway
  rules:
  - from:
    - source:
        principals: ["cluster.local/ns/default/sa/recommendation-service"]
    to:
    - operation:
        hosts: ["api.moviedb.com"]
```

Note If the VirtualService has a list of gateways specified in the top-level gateways field, it must include the reserved gateway mesh for the sourceLabels field to be applicable.

We will talk more about different kinds of security configurations in Chapter 5.

We have already discussed a lot of details about virtual services and destination rules in the previous sections. All of those configurations are applicable for components associated with egress gateways. We will omit them for the sake of brevity, and we refer the readers to the previous sections.

This multifaceted method of managing outbound traffic guarantees that external service communications are secure, observable, and reliable. By employing these controls, we can guarantee that our services can interact with the external world in a reliable manner when necessary while also maintaining strict governance over external dependencies.

Service Entry Configuration

In the service mesh architecture of Istio, ServiceEntry resources are essential for connecting your mesh-internal services to the external world. ServiceEntries can be viewed as a directory of external services that your mesh must communicate with, similar to the way a company maintains a vetted inventory of approved external vendors and partners.

At its foundation, a ServiceEntry adds an entry to Istio's internal service registry, enabling the discovery and management of external dependencies within your mesh. This is especially crucial for our recommendation service, as it has to interact with external movie databases, recommendation engines, and analytics services.

Let's start with a basic ServiceEntry configuration:

```
apiVersion: networking.istio.io/v1beta1
kind: ServiceEntry
metadata:
  name: moviedb-ext
spec:
  hosts:
  - api.moviedb.com
  ports:
  - number: 443
    name: https
    protocol: HTTPS
  resolution: DNS
  location: MESH_EXTERNAL
```

This configuration tells Istio about an external service, but there's much more we can do to enhance and control this external communication. Let's look at all components of the ServiceEntry resource.

CHAPTER 4   ADVANCED TRAFFIC MANAGEMENT PATTERNS AND GATEWAY CONTROL

The hosts component forms the cornerstone of a ServiceEntry configuration, defining the addressable destinations for your service. These can be domain names that your mesh services will use to locate and communicate with the external service. The hosts field supports both exact domain names and wildcard prefixes, providing flexibility in how services can be addressed within your mesh.

The addresses component enables you to designate virtual IP addresses for your service. Although this component is optional, it is essential when you require precise control over service routing or when implementing specific networking policies, and Istio can utilize these addresses as virtual identifiers for policy enforcement and routing.

The ports component specifies the communication channels that are accessible to your service. Three key elements are necessary for each port definition: a protocol specification that specifies the manner of communication, a unique name for identification within the mesh, and a port number for the actual network port. This component guarantees that services can communicate via the appropriate protocols and channels.

The location component serves as a critical indicator to Istio about how to treat the service within the mesh. By specifying either MESH_EXTERNAL or MESH_INTERNAL, you determine the level of mesh features and controls applied to the service. This choice affects everything from security policies to monitoring capabilities.

Istio's method of discovering and connecting to service endpoints is determined by the resolution component. Apart from providing flexibility in the process of service discovery, this component offers the option of DNS, STATIC, or NONE resolution, and the overall reliability of service connections and the dynamic or static nature of your service communication are influenced by the resolution method selected.

The endpoints component is indispensable when static resolution is implemented. It specifies the precise network locations from which your service can be accessed along with sophisticated routing strategies and load balancing configurations. These can be achieved by incorporating specific addresses, ports, and identifiers into each endpoint.

At the same time, Istio is able to guarantee security, reliability, and observability by maintaining precise control over external service communication through this comprehensive combination of components, and together, these components establish a strong framework for managing external service access within your service mesh, with each component playing a critical role in determining the dynamics of service interaction.

CHAPTER 4 ADVANCED TRAFFIC MANAGEMENT PATTERNS AND GATEWAY CONTROL

Resolution and Mesh Control in Istio

The fundamental mechanism for locating and connecting to services is represented by resolution in Istio's service mesh. In the same way that your GPS must comprehend how to locate a destination, Istio must comprehend how to locate services when communication is necessary, and this resolution system is especially important when interacting with external services that are located outside of your Kubernetes cluster.

The most prevalent and adaptable approach is DNS resolution, and when a service entry is configured with DNS resolution, Istio performs dynamic DNS lookups to determine the actual IP addresses of external services. This method is indispensable when collaborating with contemporary cloud services that frequently modify their fundamental infrastructure. In the event that your app connects to a cloud-based database, DNS resolution makes sure that it always finds the right address, even if the database provider moves or expands their infrastructure. Let's take a look at how DNS resolution really works. If you want a recommendation service to get information from an external movie database API, then you can set up the service entry in the following way:

```
apiVersion: networking.istio.io/v1beta1
kind: ServiceEntry
metadata:
  name: moviedb-service
spec:
  hosts:
  - api.moviedb.com
  ports:
  - number: 443
    protocol: HTTPS
    name: https
  resolution: DNS
  location: MESH_EXTERNAL
```

In contrast, static resolution offers a more structured method of service discovery. Static resolution enables you to explicitly specify the IP addresses of your external services, as opposed to relying on DNS lookups. This method is especially beneficial when dealing with legacy systems or when you require guaranteed connectivity to

CHAPTER 4   ADVANCED TRAFFIC MANAGEMENT PATTERNS AND GATEWAY CONTROL

specific endpoints. Consider it as having a direct phone line to your service, as opposed to having to search up the number each time:

```
apiVersion: networking.istio.io/v1beta1
kind: ServiceEntry
metadata:
  name: external-api
spec:
  hosts:
  - api.partner.com
  addresses:
  - 192.0.2.10
  ports:
  - number: 443
    protocol: HTTPS
    name: https
  resolution: STATIC
  endpoints:
  - address: 192.0.2.10
  location: MESH_EXTERNAL
```

The third resolution type, NONE, serves specialized use cases where you want Istio to be aware of the service but delegate the actual resolution to another system, and this approach is like telling your GPS about a destination but letting another navigation system handle the actual routing details:

```
apiVersion: networking.istio.io/v1beta1
kind: ServiceEntry
metadata:
  name: abstract-service
spec:
  hosts:
  - my-abstract-service.com
  ports:
  - number: 443
    protocol: HTTPS
```

CHAPTER 4 ADVANCED TRAFFIC MANAGEMENT PATTERNS AND GATEWAY CONTROL

```
    name: https
  resolution: NONE
  location: MESH_EXTERNAL
```

The manner in which Istio manages and monitors services within its ecosystem is determined by mesh control, which is implemented through the location field in service entries. By specifying MESH_EXTERNAL, you are essentially informing Istio that this service is located outside of the mesh's direct control. This designation influences the manner in which Istio applies security policies, manages mutual TLS authentication, and monitors traffic patterns. To illustrate mesh control for an external analytics service, consider the following example:

```
apiVersion: networking.istio.io/v1beta1
kind: ServiceEntry
metadata:
  name: analytics-service
spec:
  hosts:
  - api.analytics.com
  location: MESH_EXTERNAL
  ports:
  - number: 443
    protocol: HTTPS
    name: https
  resolution: DNS
```

MESH_INTERNAL, on the other hand, instructs Istio to treat an external service as though it were part of your mesh. This approach enables you to apply the full range of Istio's capabilities—from detailed metrics collection to sophisticated traffic management—to services that might physically reside outside your cluster. It's particularly useful when working with trusted external services that require the same level of control and monitoring as your internal services.

The combination of resolution types and mesh control creates a flexible system for managing external service communication. For instance, you might use DNS resolution with MESH_EXTERNAL for public APIs, but opt for static resolution with MESH_INTERNAL for crucial business services that require strict control and monitoring. This flexibility allows you to build robust, secure, and observable systems that can effectively interact with the external world while maintaining appropriate levels of control and visibility.

Understanding these concepts thoroughly enables you to make informed decisions about how your services interact with external dependencies. Whether you're building a new system or integrating with existing services, the proper configuration of resolution and mesh control ensures reliable, secure, and observable service communication within your Istio environment.

Best Practices and Common Pitfalls

In order to effectively manage traffic in Istio, it is necessary to strike a balance between complexity and flexibility. Although Istio offers robust tools for managing service-to-service communication, organizations frequently encounter difficulties in effectively implementing these features, and this is the reason it is essential to comprehend both the recommended approaches and potential pitfalls in order to establish a dependable service mesh infrastructure. The secret to success is to begin with straightforward, well-understood patterns and progressively refine them in response to operational feedback and specific requirements as this enables teams to develop confidence in their traffic management strategies while avoiding common issues, such as insufficient failure handling mechanisms or excessively complex routing rules. Also, teams can develop traffic management configurations that are scalable, maintainable, and robust and that complement their microservices architecture rather than complicating it, by adhering to established best practices and learning from common errors.

Traffic Management Patterns

There are a few patterns that have come up as particularly useful for managing traffic in Istio. A method called "progressive deployment" is the key to managing traffic well. Instead of putting in place all the complicated traffic rules at once, you should start with simple routing setups and add more complex patterns over time. For example, when you launch a new version of your service, start with a small amount of traffic (maybe 1–2%) and slowly increase it while keeping an eye on key data. This pattern, which is sometimes called "progressive delivery," lets you find problems early on while keeping risk to a minimum.

Circuit breakers and retry rules are used together, which is another important pattern. Retries can help with short-term problems, but they need to be paired with circuit breakers to stop failures that start one after another. For example, if your recommendation service fails sometimes, set up retries with exponential backoff, and make sure there are circuit breakers to keep the system from being overloaded during recovery times. And when you put these patterns together, you get a strong and reliable traffic management strategy.

Configuration Best Practices

Maintainability and scalability should be your main concerns when setting up Istio's traffic management features. First, make sure that all of your Istio tools have clear names. As an example, use prefixes to show the environments (e.g., prod-, dev-, or staging-) and suffixes to show the type of resource (e.g., -vs for VirtualServices or -dr for DestinationRules). As your service mesh grows, this makes it easier to keep track of configurations.

Do not put your VirtualService and DestinationRule settings together in one YAML file. Instead, keep them separate. This separation of concerns makes it easier to keep your traffic rules up to date on your own. Also, never use the latest tags in your configuration; always use explicit versions instead. This makes sure that the same thing happens again and again and makes it easier to see how your traffic management setup has changed.

Version your Istio configurations alongside your application code in source control. This practice ensures that traffic management changes are reviewed, and tracked, and can be rolled back if necessary. Consider using GitOps practices where possible, allowing you to manage your traffic configurations declaratively through version control.

Common Mistakes to Avoid

Setting up route rules that are too complicated from the start is one of the most common mistakes people make when managing Istio traffic. This often results in configurations that are hard to fix and keep up to date. Instead, add your traffic management rules one layer at a time and test each one before adding more. Not properly scoping service mesh resources to specific namespaces is another common mistake that can cause strange behavior and vulnerabilities.

A lot of teams make the mistake of not setting up proper backup systems in their traffic management plans. For instance, when you set up a "canary" deployment, make sure that your rollback processes and monitoring thresholds are very clear. Also, don't give in to the urge to use too many retries without the right circuit breakers. This can cause a chain of failures when the system is under a lot of stress.

Troubleshooting Strategies

When problems happen with your traffic management configuration, you need to take a methodical approach to fix them. Check the basics first, and make sure that all of the necessary Istio CRDs are applied correctly and that your service mesh is healthy. You can find possible configuration problems with `isioctl analyze` before they become a problem in production. The command can find common configuration errors and give detailed advice on how to fix them. With tools like Kiali and Jaeger, you can use Istio's built-in monitoring features to see how data flows and find bottlenecks, and when you are trying to figure out what the problem is, you can focus on it by briefly making your traffic rules less strict. For instance, if you're having trouble with a complicated canary deployment, send all traffic to the stable version until you can figure out what's wrong.

Performance Considerations

The performance of your service mesh can be substantially influenced by the configuration of traffic management. Maintain the simplicity of your routing rules while still satisfying your needs. Complex matches and excessive route rules can result in an increase in latency, as each request must be evaluated against these rules. To alleviate the burden on your services, consider the implementation of caching mechanisms at the gateway level for frequently accessed resources.

Monitor the resource utilization of your Istio proxies, as the implementation of complex traffic management policies may result in an increase in CPU and memory consumption. At the same time pay close attention to the effects of circuit breakers and retry policies on system resources. For instance, when you use request mirroring, you need to be aware that this practically doubles the load on your target service, so make sure that your capacity is planned accordingly. Lastly, it's important to keep checking your configuration's performance under different types of traffic as your service mesh grows to make sure it stays effective.

Conclusion

Throughout this chapter, we've elevated our understanding of Istio's traffic management capabilities beyond the basics, exploring sophisticated patterns and controls that enable robust microservices deployments. From implementing progressive canary releases to managing complex gateway configurations, these advanced patterns provide the tools necessary for handling real-world deployment scenarios. The combination of resilience patterns, fault tolerance mechanisms, and comprehensive gateway controls creates a robust framework for managing modern service architectures. While the basic patterns covered in the previous chapter form the foundation, these advanced techniques enable organizations to implement production-grade traffic management strategies that can scale with their growing microservices ecosystem. Success in implementing these patterns requires careful consideration of monitoring, testing, and best practices, ultimately leading to more reliable and maintainable service deployments in production environments.

CHAPTER 5

Securing Microservices with Istio

Introduction

Security is a paramount concern in any distributed system, and Istio offers robust features to ensure secure service-to-service communication. In Chapter 2, we introduced Istio's security architecture as one of its fundamental pillars, where we explored the basic components like Istiod's role in certificate management, authentication, and authorization. We learned how Istio's security features work together to create a secure service mesh environment, touching upon concepts like mutual TLS, service identity, and basic access control. Building upon that foundation, this chapter takes a deep dive into Istio's comprehensive security framework. We'll explore advanced security configurations, examine real-world implementation strategies, and understand how to leverage Istio's security features to their full potential. From setting up robust authentication mechanisms to implementing fine-grained authorization policies, this chapter will equip you with the knowledge needed to secure your microservices architecture effectively. Whether you're dealing with internal service-to-service communication or external traffic through ingress and egress gateways, you'll learn how to implement security best practices that align with zero-trust principles and modern security requirements.

CHAPTER 5   SECURING MICROSERVICES WITH ISTIO

A Microservices Environment's Foundational Security Concepts

Transport Layer Security (TLS): A cryptographic protocol that ensures end-to-end security for data transmitted between applications via networks. It guarantees confidentiality using encryption, integrity through message authentication codes, and authenticity using digital certificates and public key infrastructure (PKI).

Mutual TLS (mTLS): Is an extension of TLS in which both the client and server present X.509 certificates to establish bidirectional authentication. This creates a cryptographically verified identity for each service, ensuring zero-trust networking since both endpoints can validate each other's identity. This process establishes higher trust.

Authentication: In Istio is a comprehensive process of verifying claimed identities within the service mesh using cryptographic methods. To guarantee secure service-to-service and end user interactions, the platform implements numerous authentication mechanisms. At its core, Istio uses SPIFFE-compatible X.509 certificates to establish service identity, providing a cryptographically secure method for discovering and validating services in the service mesh. For end user authentication, Istio supports JWT validation, allowing for seamless integration with existing identity management systems. The platform manages certificate lifecycle management automatically using Istiod, which automates certificate rotation and renewal. Furthermore, Istio's authentication framework supports flexible integration with external identity providers, allowing organizations to manage identities consistently across their infrastructure.

Authorization: Authorization in Istio provides a robust framework for implementing access control through detailed policy definition and enforcement mechanisms. The platform offers a multi-level approach to authorization, implementing

CHAPTER 5 SECURING MICROSERVICES WITH ISTIO

RBAC policies that can be applied at both namespace and service levels, providing granular control over service-to-service communication. Organizations can define custom authorization policies using YAML configuration, making it easy to implement and maintain complex access control requirements. Istio's fine-grained access control system can make authorization decisions based on multiple factors, including service identity, source and destination properties of the communication, HTTP- and gRPC-level attributes, and JWT claims. This comprehensive approach allows organizations to implement precise access control policies that align with their security requirements while maintaining flexibility and ease of management.

Public Key Infrastructure (PKI): Forms the backbone of modern secure communications, providing a comprehensive framework for managing digital certificates and encryption. At its core, PKI encompasses the hardware, software, and procedures necessary for creating, distributing, and managing digital certificates, enabling secure data transmission and authentication across networks. Digital certificates, following the X.509 standard, serve as electronic identity documents that bind public keys to specific entities, containing essential information like the owner's identity, validity period, and usage restrictions.

Certificate Authorities (CAs): Are the trusted entities that underpin the entire PKI ecosystem by issuing and managing these digital certificates. CAs handle critical tasks including certificate issuance, validation, and revocation while maintaining Certificate Revocation Lists (CRL) and providing Online Certificate Status Protocol (OCSP) responses. In the context of Istio's service mesh, Istiod functions as the CA (Istio also supports use of custom CAs), automatically managing certificates for secure service-to-service communication and implementing robust key management protocols to maintain the mesh's security posture.

These mechanisms form the foundation of Istio's zero-trust security model, enabling granular control over service-to-service communication within the mesh.

CHAPTER 5 SECURING MICROSERVICES WITH ISTIO

Introduction to Security in Distributed Systems

The Evolution of Distributed Security

The evolution of software architecture from monolithic applications to distributed systems has fundamentally transformed how we approach security. As organizations break down their applications into microservices, the traditional security perimeter dissolves, creating a complex web of service interactions that must be protected. Each microservice represents a potential entry point, every service-to-service communication channel a possible attack vector, and every API endpoint a security boundary to defend. This shift demands a sophisticated, multi-layered security approach that goes beyond traditional network security measures.

Security Challenges in the Modern Distributed Architecture

The transition to distributed architectures introduces significant complexity in security management. The expanded attack surface presents a primary concern, as distributed systems contain multiple entry points across services, increased network communication paths, and complex inter-service dependencies. These systems often employ diverse technology stacks and protocols, further complicating the security landscape. Identity and trust become paramount concerns, as organizations must manage service identities, handle dynamic service creation and destruction, and ensure robust cross-service authentication. The challenge extends to credential management at scale, requiring sophisticated solutions for secret management and access control.

Network security in distributed systems takes on new dimensions, encompassing both east–west traffic protection between services and north–south traffic control for external communications. Organizations must implement comprehensive protocol-level security measures and enforce network policies that adapt to the dynamic nature of modern applications. This complexity requires automated solutions that can scale with the growing number of services and interactions.

Security Implications for Organizations

The distributed nature of modern applications profoundly impacts organizational operations and security practices. Operational challenges emerge in managing complex security policies, handling certificate lifecycles, and coordinating security monitoring and incident response across distributed services. Organizations must maintain comprehensive audit trails while ensuring compliance with various data protection regulations and industry-specific standards. This often requires implementing sophisticated logging and monitoring solutions that can track security events across the entire service mesh.

The development process itself undergoes significant transformation, as security becomes an integral part of the software development lifecycle. Organizations must adopt security-first development practices, implement continuous security testing, and integrate automated security controls into their CI/CD pipelines. The adoption of DevSecOps practices becomes crucial, ensuring that security considerations are addressed throughout the development process rather than being treated as an afterthought.

The Need for Modern Security Solutions

Modern distributed systems demand comprehensive security measures that address multiple aspects of system protection. Service-to-service communication security forms the foundation, requiring robust authentication between services, encrypted data transmission, and carefully managed protocol security. Traffic management policies must be implemented to control and secure service interactions, ensuring that only authorized communications occur within the system.

Access control mechanisms must provide fine-grained authorization capabilities, implementing role-based access control systems that can scale with the growing number of services. Policy enforcement needs to be automated and consistent across the entire service mesh, while identity management must handle both service and user identities effectively. Traffic protection extends to both ingress and egress points, requiring sophisticated API gateway protection and DDoS mitigation strategies.

Traditional security approaches prove inadequate in addressing the challenges of distributed systems. Conventional perimeter security measures fail to provide sufficient protection for internal service communication and cannot handle dynamic service scaling. These traditional approaches offer limited visibility into service interactions and cannot provide the granular control required in modern architectures. Manual security management becomes unsustainable as systems scale, leading to configuration errors and slow response times to security threats.

What Is Istio's Role in Modern Security

Istio addresses these modern security challenges by providing a comprehensive and unified security framework. Through centralized policy management and automated certificate handling, Istio ensures consistent security enforcement across the entire service mesh. Its built-in security features implement zero-trust architecture principles, starting with default deny-all policies and enforcing strong service identity through mutual TLS encryption.

From an operational perspective, Istio excels in automating security operations and providing comprehensive monitoring capabilities. Its scalable security policies adapt to growing systems, while integrated compliance tools help organizations meet regulatory requirements. The platform's approach to security automation reduces the operational burden on teams while maintaining robust security controls.

This comprehensive approach to security in distributed systems ensures that organizations can build and maintain secure, scalable, and compliant microservices architectures. By leveraging Istio's security capabilities effectively, organizations can address the complex security challenges of modern distributed systems while maintaining operational efficiency and development agility.

Mutual TLS in Istio and Practical Implementation
Introduction to Mutual TLS

In the realm of service mesh security, mutual TLS (mTLS) stands as a fundamental pillar of Istio's security architecture. While traditional TLS provides one-way authentication where a client verifies the server's identity, mTLS elevates security by establishing bidirectional authentication between communicating services. This two-way authentication ensures that both the client and server verify each other's identities before establishing a secure communication channel.

In Istio's implementation, every service gets its own identity in the form of a service account. When a service starts, Istio automatically provisions it with a certificate containing this identity. These certificates are automatically rotated by Istio to maintain security. The mTLS handshake process involves several steps: identity verification, key exchange, and establishing an encrypted channel.

Istio offers three modes of mTLS operation: STRICT, PERMISSIVE, and DISABLED. STRICT mode ensures that all traffic must be mTLS, providing the highest security but requiring all clients to support mTLS. PERMISSIVE mode allows both plain text and mTLS traffic, useful during migration. DISABLED mode turns off mTLS completely, though this is not recommended for production environments.

Service Identity and Certificate Management

Service identity in Istio is implemented through a robust certificate management system. Each service receives a unique X.509 certificate that encapsulates its identity attributes, including namespace, service account, and workload information. The control plane continuously monitors these certificates, automatically handling rotation and renewal to maintain security without service interruption. This automated certificate lifecycle management eliminates the operational burden typically associated with certificate handling in distributed systems.

Transparent Encryption and Security

One of Istio's most powerful features is its ability to implement transparent encryption across the service mesh. When mTLS is enabled, all service-to-service communication within the mesh is automatically encrypted, regardless of whether the applications themselves implement any security measures. This encryption happens at the proxy level through Envoy sidecars, which handle all TLS negotiations and certificate validations. The beauty of this approach lies in its transparency—the application code remains unchanged while gaining robust security capabilities.

CHAPTER 5 SECURING MICROSERVICES WITH ISTIO

Integration and Security Policies

The effectiveness of mTLS in Istio extends beyond mere encryption. It integrates with Istio's broader security framework, including authentication and authorization policies. Administrators can define granular access controls based on service identities, ensuring that only authorized services can communicate with each other. This integration creates a comprehensive security model that addresses both transport security and access control requirements in modern microservices architectures.

Example

Implementing mTLS in Istio involves several coordinated components working together seamlessly. The process begins with the deployment of services into the mesh, where Istio automatically injects Envoy proxies as sidecars. These proxies establish secure connections with their peers using the certificates provided by the control plane. Through configuration policies, administrators can define the strictness of mTLS enforcement, allowing for gradual adoption in existing environments or strict security in new deployments.

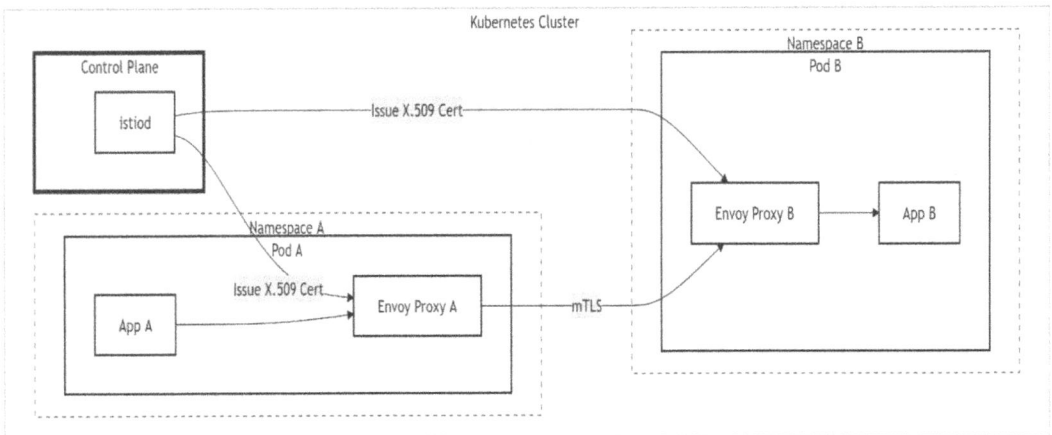

Figure 5-1. *Microservices in separate namespaces communicating over mTLS*

CHAPTER 5   SECURING MICROSERVICES WITH ISTIO

Implementation Steps

1. Set up certificate infrastructure. In this step we will create a directory and create a certificate authority with a root certificate and intermediate certificate. The parameters for the command-line arguments (openssl) can be looked at the man page for openssl (https://docs.openssl.org/3.0/man7/migration_guide/#synopsis). These steps will also require us to create a Kubernetes secret.

> **Note** *OpenSSL* is a cryptographic toolkit implementing SSL/TLS protocols for secure communication and certificate management.

```
# Create a directory for certificates
mkdir -p certs

# Generate root certificate
openssl req -x509 -sha256 -nodes -days 365 -newkey rsa:2048 \
    -subj '/O=Example Inc./CN=Example Root CA' \
    -keyout certs/root-key.pem \
    -out certs/root-cert.pem

# Create an intermediate certificate
openssl req -newkey rsa:2048 -nodes \
    -subj '/CN=Example Intermediate CA' \
    -keyout certs/ca-key.pem \
    -out certs/ca-cert.csr

openssl x509 -req -days 365 -sha256 \
    -in certs/ca-cert.csr \
    -CA certs/root-cert.pem \
    -CAkey certs/root-key.pem \
    -CAcreateserial \
    -out certs/ca-cert.pem
```

CHAPTER 5   SECURING MICROSERVICES WITH ISTIO

```
# Create Kubernetes secret for certificates
kubectl create namespace istio-system
kubectl create -n istio-system secret generic cacerts \
  --from-file=certs/root-cert.pem \
  --from-file=certs/ca-cert.pem \
  --from-file=certs/ca-key.pem \
  --from-file=certs/root-cert.pem
```

2. Install Cert-Manager charts using Helm from the Helm repository. Next, Install Istio with custom certificates.

```
# Add cert-manager helm repository
helm repo add jetstack https://charts.jetstack.io
helm repo update
# Install cert-manager
helm install cert-manager jetstack/cert-manager \
  --namespace cert-manager \
  --create-namespace \
  --version v1.14.0 \
  --set installCRDs=true

# Create ClusterIssuer
cat <<EOF | kubectl apply -f -
apiVersion: cert-manager.io/v1
kind: ClusterIssuer
metadata:
  name: selfsigned-issuer
spec:
  selfSigned: {}
EOF

# Download Istio
curl -L https://istio.io/downloadIstio | ISTIO_VERSION=1.25.0 sh -

# Move to Istio directory
cd istio-1.25.0

# Add istioctl to PATH
```

```
export PATH=$PWD/bin:$PATH

# Create Istio installation configuration
cat <<EOF > istio-config.yaml
apiVersion: install.istio.io/v1alpha1
kind: IstioOperator
metadata:
  namespace: istio-system
spec:
  values:
    global:
      caAddress: istiod.istio-system.svc:15012
      certificatesDir: /etc/cert-manager/istio
    pilot:
      env:
        ENABLE_CA_SERVER: "false"
    k8s:
      overlays:
        - kind: Deployment
          name: istiod
          patches:
          - path: spec.template.spec.containers.
            [name:discovery].volumeMounts
              value:
              - name: istio-ca
                mountPath: /etc/cert-manager/istio
          - path: spec.template.spec.volumes
              value:
              - name: istio-ca
                secret:
                  secretName: istio-ca
EOF

# Install Istio
istioctl install -f istio-config.yaml
```

CHAPTER 5   SECURING MICROSERVICES WITH ISTIO

3. Create and set up an application namespace, and then create a frontend and a backend service certificate.

```
# Create namespace
kubectl create namespace mtls-demo

# Enable Istio injection
kubectl label namespace mtls-demo istio-injection=enabled

# Create a certificate for backend service
cat <<EOF | kubectl apply -f -
apiVersion: cert-manager.io/v1
kind: Certificate
metadata:
  name: backend-service-cert
  namespace: mtls-demo
spec:
  secretName: backend-service-tls
  duration: 2160h # 90 days
  renewBefore: 360h # 15 days
  subject:
      organizations:
      - Example Inc.
  commonName: backend-service.mtls-demo.svc
  dnsNames:
      - backend-service
      - backend-service.mtls-demo.svc
      - backend-service.mtls-demo.svc.cluster.local
  issuerRef:
      name: selfsigned-issuer
      kind: ClusterIssuer
---
apiVersion: cert-manager.io/v1
kind: Certificate
metadata:
  name: frontend-service-cert
  namespace: mtls-demo
```

CHAPTER 5 SECURING MICROSERVICES WITH ISTIO

```
      spec:
        secretName: frontend-service-tls
        duration: 2160h
        renewBefore: 360h
        subject:
            organizations:
            - Example Inc.
        commonName: frontend-service.mtls-demo.svc
        dnsNames:
            - frontend-service
            - frontend-service.mtls-demo.svc
            - frontend-service.mtls-demo.svc.cluster.local
        issuerRef:
            name: selfsigned-issuer
            kind: ClusterIssuer
    EOF
```

4. Deploy the application services created above in a cluster.

```
    # Backend Service
    cat <<EOF | kubectl apply -f -
    apiVersion: v1
    kind: ServiceAccount
    metadata:
      name: backend-service
      namespace: mtls-demo
    ---
    apiVersion: v1
    kind: Service
    metadata:
      name: backend-service
      namespace: mtls-demo
      labels:
          app: backend-service
    spec:
      ports:
```

```yaml
      - port: 8080
        name: http
    selector:
      app: backend-service
---
apiVersion: apps/v1
kind: Deployment
metadata:
  name: backend-service
  namespace: mtls-demo
spec:
  replicas: 1
  selector:
      matchLabels:
      app: backend-service
  template:
      metadata:
      labels:
      app: backend-service
      spec:
      serviceAccountName: backend-service
      containers:
      - name: backend
            image: gcr.io/google-samples/hello-go-gke:1.0
            ports:
            - containerPort: 8080
            volumeMounts:
            - name: cert
            mountPath: /etc/certs
            readOnly: true
      volumes:
      - name: cert
            secret:
            secretName: backend-service-tls
EOF
```

Frontend Service
```bash
cat <<EOF | kubectl apply -f -
apiVersion: v1
kind: ServiceAccount
metadata:
  name: frontend-service
  namespace: mtls-demo
---
apiVersion: v1
kind: Service
metadata:
  name: frontend-service
  namespace: mtls-demo
  labels:
    app: frontend-service
spec:
  ports:
    - port: 80
      name: http
  selector:
    app: frontend-service
---
apiVersion: apps/v1
kind: Deployment
metadata:
  name: frontend-service
  namespace: mtls-demo
spec:
  replicas: 1
  selector:
    matchLabels:
      app: frontend-service
  template:
    metadata:
```

CHAPTER 5 SECURING MICROSERVICES WITH ISTIO

```
          labels:
          app: frontend-service
          spec:
          serviceAccountName: frontend-service
          containers:
          - name: frontend
               image: nginx:1.21
               ports:
               - containerPort: 80
               volumeMounts:
               - name: cert
               mountPath: /etc/certs
               readOnly: true
          volumes:
          - name: cert
               secret:
               secretName: frontend-service-tls
     EOF
```

5. Configure mTLS policies in STRICT mode and verify and monitor the communication over mTLS.

```
# Enable Strict mTLS
cat <<EOF | kubectl apply -f -
apiVersion: security.istio.io/v1beta1
kind: PeerAuthentication
metadata:
  name: default
  namespace: mtls-demo
spec:
  mtls:
      mode: STRICT
EOF

# Create Authorization Policy
cat <<EOF | kubectl apply -f -
apiVersion: security.istio.io/v1beta1
```

```yaml
kind: AuthorizationPolicy
metadata:
  name: backend-policy
  namespace: mtls-demo
spec:
  selector:
    matchLabels:
      app: backend-service
  rules:
  - from:
    - source:
      principals: ["cluster.local/ns/mtls-demo/sa/frontend-service"]
    to:
    - operation:
      methods: ["GET"]
EOF

# Verify Service Deployment
# Check pods
kubectl get pods -n mtls-demo

# Check certificates
kubectl get certificates -n mtls-demo

# Verify mTLS Status

# Check PeerAuthentication policy
istioctl analyze -n mtls-demo

# Verify certificates in proxies
istioctl proxy-config secret deploy/backend-service.mtls-demo

# Monitor Certificate Status

# Watch certificate events
kubectl get events -n mtls-demo --field-selector reason=Certificate
```

CHAPTER 5   SECURING MICROSERVICES WITH ISTIO

```
# Check certificate rotation
for pod in $(kubectl get pods -n mtls-demo -o jsonpath='{.
items[*].metadata.name}'); do
  kubectl exec -n mtls-demo $pod -c istio-proxy -- pilot-agent
  request GET /debug/certs
done

# Test Service Communication
# Test from frontend to backend (should succeed)
kubectl exec -n mtls-demo deploy/frontend-service -c frontend --
curl http://backend-service:8080

# Test from external pod (should fail)
kubectl run -n mtls-demo test-pod --image=curlimages/curl -i --
tty -- sh
curl http://backend-service:8080
```

6. The below steps will show you how to view details on certificate rotation and monitoring.

```
# Set Up Monitoring
# Install Prometheus and Grafana
kubectl apply -f samples/addons/prometheus.yaml
kubectl apply -f samples/addons/grafana.yaml

# Access Grafana dashboard
istioctl dashboard grafana

# Monitor Certificate Lifecycle
# View certificate expiration
istioctl proxy-config secret deploy/backend-service.mtls-demo

# Check cert-manager logs
kubectl logs -n cert-manager -l app=cert-manager -c cert-manager
```

CHAPTER 5　SECURING MICROSERVICES WITH ISTIO

Useful Troubleshooting Steps

1. Certificate Issues and mTLS Connection Problems

    ```
    # Check certificate status
    kubectl describe certificate -n mtls-demo

    # Verify secret creation
    kubectl get secrets -n mtls-demo

    # sample-output
    NAME
    TYPE                                                       DATA    AGE
    default-token-abcde
    kubernetes.io/service-account-token       3        1d
    istio.default
    istio.io/key-and-cert                                         3        1d
    istio-ingressgateway-service-account-token-xyz12
      kubernetes.io/service-account-token                3        1d
    httpbin-token-12345
    kubernetes.io/service-account-token       3        1d

    # Check proxy configuration
    istioctl proxy-config listeners deploy/backend-service.mtls-demo

    # View proxy logs
    kubectl logs deploy/backend-service -n mtls-demo -c istio-proxy

    # Verify policies
    istioctl experimental authz check deploy/backend-service.mtls-demo
    ```

Cleanup

```
# Remove application resources
kubectl delete namespace mtls-demo

# Remove cert-manager (optional)
helm delete cert-manager -n cert-manager
kubectl delete namespace cert-manager
```

```
# Remove Istio (optional)
istioctl uninstall --purge
```

All components work together to provide a secure, production-ready service mesh with proper certificate management and mTLS communication.

Istio Authentication and Authorization Policies

Authentication Policies

Authentication in Istio operates at two levels: peer authentication and request authentication. Peer authentication deals with service-to-service communication, primarily through mTLS. Request authentication handles end user authentication, typically through JWTs.

Peer authentication policies can be applied at different levels: mesh-wide, namespace-level, or workload-level. This hierarchical approach allows for flexible security configurations. When multiple policies apply to the same workload, Istio follows a well-defined precedence order to determine which policy takes effect.

Request authentication supports various JWT providers and can be configured to validate tokens from multiple issuers. This flexibility allows integration with existing identity providers while maintaining security. Token validation includes checking the signature, expiration, and claims according to the configured rules.

Istio's authentication policies define how services validate client identities. These policies are used to enforce

- mTLS
- JWT-based authentication

Example

The example demonstrates a secure microservices architecture with a frontend service handling public and admin endpoints and a backend service for data operations. The security implementation includes mTLS for service-to-service communication, JWT authentication for external requests, and granular authorization policies that restrict access based on user roles and service identities. The frontend service can access /public/* endpoints openly while /admin/* endpoints require authentication,

CHAPTER 5 SECURING MICROSERVICES WITH ISTIO

and the backend service is only accessible from the authenticated frontend service, implementing defense in depth and least privilege access principles in a practical microservices environment.

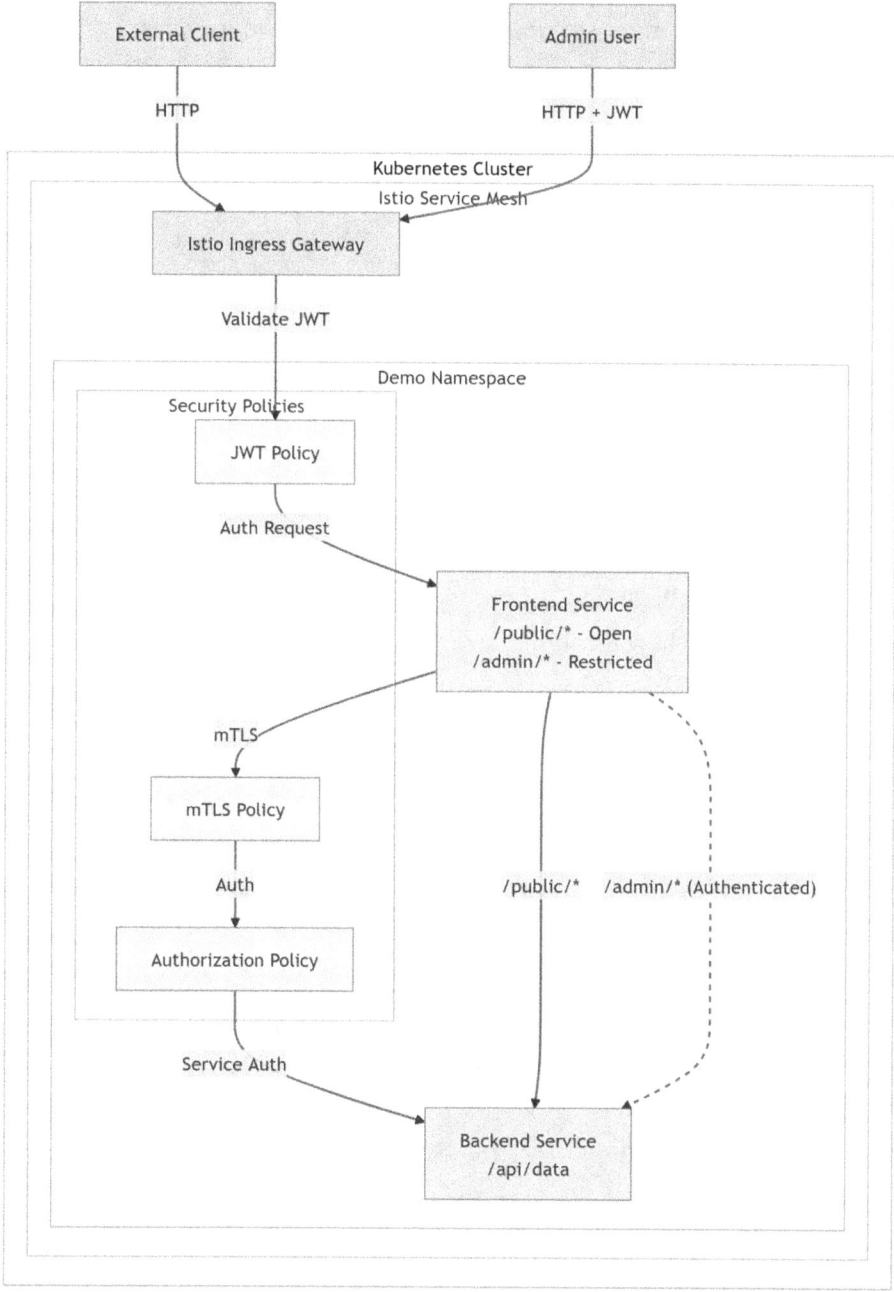

Figure 5-2. *Authentication and authorization between services in a given namespace*

CHAPTER 5   SECURING MICROSERVICES WITH ISTIO

Implementation Steps

1. To implement Istio, follow the prerequisite and installation steps outlined earlier in Chapter 1. Then, add it to the path.

2. Create a sample microservices application with two services:

    - Frontend service (public-facing)

    - Backend service (internal)

    ```yaml
    # backend-deployment.yaml
    apiVersion: apps/v1
    kind: Deployment
    metadata:
      name: backend
      namespace: demo
    spec:
      replicas: 1
      selector:
          matchLabels:
          app: backend
      template:
          metadata:
          labels:
          app: backend
          spec:
          containers:
          - name: backend
            image: nginx:alpine
            ports:
            - containerPort: 80
    ---
    apiVersion: v1
    kind: Service
    metadata:
      name: backend
      namespace: demo
    ```

```yaml
spec:
  ports:
  - port: 80
      targetPort: 80
    selector:
      app: backend
# frontend-deployment.yaml
apiVersion: apps/v1
kind: Deployment
metadata:
  name: frontend
  namespace: demo
spec:
  replicas: 1
  selector:
      matchLabels:
      app: frontend
    template:
      metadata:
      labels:
      app: frontend
      spec:
      containers:
      - name: frontend
        image: nginx:alpine
        ports:
        - containerPort: 80
---
apiVersion: v1
kind: Service
metadata:
  name: frontend
  namespace: demo
spec:
  ports:
```

CHAPTER 5 SECURING MICROSERVICES WITH ISTIO

```
      - port: 80
        targetPort: 80
    selector:
      app: frontend
```

3. Create a demo namespace and enable Istio injection. Next, deploy the application.

```
kubectl create namespace demo
kubectl label namespace demo istio-injection=enabled
kubectl apply -f backend-deployment.yaml
kubectl apply -f frontend-deployment.yaml
```

4. Configure authentication and authorization policies in YAML and apply/implement them.

```yaml
# Enable mTLS for the entire namespace:
# peer-authentication.yaml
apiVersion: security.istio.io/v1beta1
kind: PeerAuthentication
metadata:
  name: default
  namespace: demo
spec:
  mtls:
    mode: STRICT

# Set up JWT authentication for the frontend service:

# jwt-authentication.yaml
apiVersion: security.istio.io/v1beta1
kind: RequestAuthentication
metadata:
  name: jwt-config
  namespace: demo
spec:
  selector:
    matchLabels:
      app: frontend
```

```yaml
  jwtRules:
  - issuer: "https://accounts.google.com"
    jwksUri: "https://www.googleapis.com/oauth2/v3/certs"

# frontend-authorization.yaml
apiVersion: security.istio.io/v1beta1
kind: AuthorizationPolicy
metadata:
  name: frontend-policy
  namespace: demo
spec:
  selector:
    matchLabels:
      app: frontend
  rules:
  - from:
    - source:
        requestPrincipals: ["*"]
    to:
    - operation:
        methods: ["GET"]
        paths: ["/public/*"]
  - from:
    - source:
        requestPrincipals: ["accounts.google.com/admin@example.com"]
    to:
    - operation:
        methods: ["POST", "PUT", "DELETE"]
```

```yaml
# backend-authorization.yaml
apiVersion: security.istio.io/v1beta1
kind: AuthorizationPolicy
metadata:
  name: backend-policy
  namespace: demo
```

```yaml
spec:
  selector:
      matchLabels:
      app: backend
  rules:
  - from:
      - source:
      principals: ["cluster.local/ns/demo/sa/frontend"]
      to:
      - operation:
      methods: ["GET", "POST"]
```

```
kubectl apply -f peer-authentication.yaml
kubectl apply -f jwt-authentication.yaml
kubectl apply -f frontend-authorization.yaml
kubectl apply -f backend-authorization.yaml
```

5. Test the entire setup.

```
# Check mTLS status
istioctl x authz check <pod-name>

# Verify PeerAuthentication
kubectl get peerauthentication -n demo

# Test JWT Authentication
#Get a test token (replace with your actual token)

TOKEN=$(curl https://your-auth-server/token)

# Test authenticated request
curl -H "Authorization: Bearer $TOKEN" http://frontend-service/public/hello

# Test unauthenticated request (should fail)
curl http://frontend-service/public/hello

# Test Authorization
# Test allowed path with a  valid token
```

```
curl -H "Authorization: Bearer $TOKEN" http://frontend-service/
public/hello

# Test restricted path (should fail)
curl -H "Authorization: Bearer $TOKEN" http://frontend-service/
admin/config
```

Cleanup

```
#Remove all resources:

kubectl delete namespace demo
kubectl delete -f peer-authentication.yaml
kubectl delete -f jwt-authentication.yaml
kubectl delete -f frontend-authorization.yaml
kubectl delete -f backend-authorization.yaml
istioctl x uninstall --purge
```

Role-Based Access Control (RBAC) in Istio

RBAC in Istio extends the traditional RBAC model to control access at the service mesh level. Role-based access control (RBAC) in Istio provides fine-grained access control for service-to-service communication within your service mesh. This guide walks through implementing RBAC for a practical microservices scenario.

RBAC in Istio provides fine-grained access control for service-to-service communication. It operates through authorization policies that define who can access what under what conditions. These policies support both ALLOW and DENY rules, with DENY taking precedence.

Authorization policies can be based on various factors: service identity, namespace, IP addresses, JWT claims, and request properties like HTTP methods and paths. This flexibility allows for sophisticated access control scenarios. Policies can be applied at different scopes: mesh-wide, namespace-wide, or workload-specific.

The RBAC system supports role aggregation, allowing for hierarchical role structures. This enables organizations to implement the principle of least privilege effectively. Policies can also include conditions based on request attributes, enabling context-aware access control decisions.

CHAPTER 5 SECURING MICROSERVICES WITH ISTIO

Example

In this practical implementation of role-based access control (RBAC) in Istio, we'll create a microservices-based ecommerce system that demonstrates real-world service-to-service communication patterns. The system consists of three core microservices: the product service, which serves as the central repository for all product-related information including inventory, pricing, and product details; the order service, which manages the entire order lifecycle from creation to fulfillment, processing customer transactions and maintaining order history; and the analytics service, which aggregates data from both the product and order services to generate valuable business insights, sales reports, and inventory analytics. Each service needs specific access permissions—for example, the order service requires read access to product information to validate orders, while the analytics service needs read access to both product and order data to generate comprehensive reports. By implementing RBAC with Istio, we'll ensure that each service has precisely the permissions it needs, following the principle of least privilege, while maintaining secure and controlled communication between services.

CHAPTER 5 SECURING MICROSERVICES WITH ISTIO

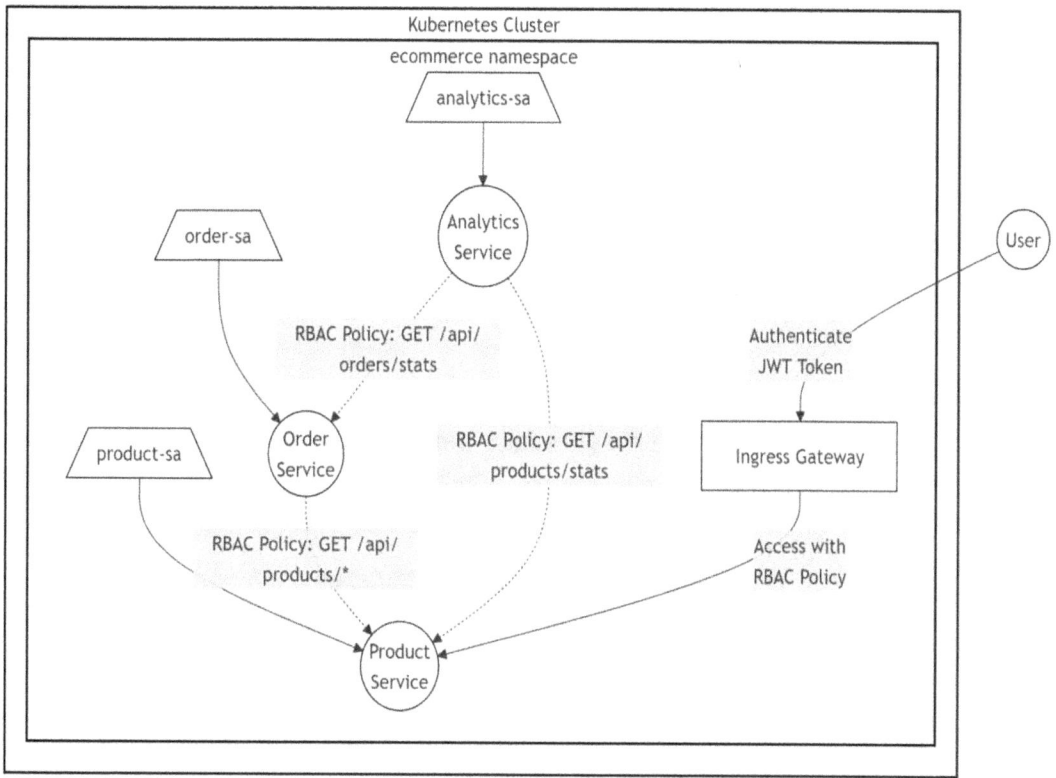

Figure 5-3. *RBAC policies controlling access to various services*

Implementation Steps

1. To install Istio, follow the prerequisite and installation steps outlined earlier in Chapter 1. Then, add it to the path. Create a demo profile and verify the installation.

   ```
   # Install Istio with demo profile
   istioctl install --set profile=demo -y
   ```

   ```
   # Verify installation
   kubectl get pods -n istio-system
   ```

2. Create and label a namespace for our ecommerce example.

   ```
   # Create namespace
   kubectl create namespace ecommerce
   ```

CHAPTER 5 SECURING MICROSERVICES WITH ISTIO

```
# Enable Istio injection
kubectl label namespace ecommerce istio-injection=enabled

# Verify label
kubectl get namespace ecommerce --show-labels
```

3. Create sample applications such as product, order, and analytics services. These are node applications for the purpose of this example.

```
# Create simple node applications for testing
mkdir -p ecommerce-demo/{product-service,order-service,analytics-service}

# Create product service
cat << EOF > ecommerce-demo/product-service/server.js
const express = require('express');
const app = express();
app.get('/api/products/*', (req, res) => res.json({ message: 'Product data' }));
app.get('/api/products/stats', (req, res) => res.json({ message: 'Product stats' }));
app.listen(8080);
EOF

# Create order service
cat << EOF > ecommerce-demo/order-service/server.js
const express = require('express');
const app = express();
app.get('/api/orders/stats', (req, res) => res.json({ message: 'Order stats' }));
app.post('/api/orders', (req, res) => res.json({ message: 'Order created' }));
app.listen(8080);
EOF

# Create analytics service
cat << EOF > ecommerce-demo/analytics-service/server.js
```

CHAPTER 5　SECURING MICROSERVICES WITH ISTIO

```
const express = require('express');
const app = express();
app.get('/api/analytics', (req, res) => res.json({ message:
'Analytics data' }));
app.listen(8080);
EOF
```

4. Create Kubernetes resources.

```
# Create Service Accounts
# service-accounts.yaml
apiVersion: v1
kind: ServiceAccount
metadata:
  name: product-service
  namespace: ecommerce
---
apiVersion: v1
kind: ServiceAccount
metadata:
  name: order-service
  namespace: ecommerce
---
apiVersion: v1
kind: ServiceAccount
metadata:
  name: analytics-service
  namespace: ecommerce

# Create Services
# services.yaml
apiVersion: v1
kind: Service
metadata:
  name: product-service
  namespace: ecommerce
spec:
```

253

```yaml
      selector:
          app: product-service
      ports:
          - port: 8080
          targetPort: 8080
---
apiVersion: v1
kind: Service
metadata:
  name: order-service
  namespace: ecommerce
spec:
  selector:
      app: order-service
  ports:
      - port: 8080
      targetPort: 8080
---
apiVersion: v1
kind: Service
metadata:
  name: analytics-service
  namespace: ecommerce
spec:
  selector:
      app: analytics-service
  ports:
      - port: 8080
      targetPort: 8080

# Create Deployments
# deployments.yaml
apiVersion: apps/v1
kind: Deployment
metadata:
  name: product-service
  namespace: ecommerce
```

CHAPTER 5   SECURING MICROSERVICES WITH ISTIO

```
spec:
  replicas: 1
  selector:
      matchLabels:
      app: product-service
  template:
      metadata:
      labels:
      app: product-service
      spec:
      serviceAccountName: product-service
      containers:
      - name: product-service
      image: node:16-alpine
      command: ["node", "/app/server.js"]
      volumeMounts:
      - name: app-code
            mountPath: /app
      volumes:
      - name: app-code
      configMap:
            name: product-service-code
---
apiVersion: apps/v1
kind: Deployment
metadata:
  name: order-service
  namespace: ecommerce
spec:
  replicas: 1
  selector:
      matchLabels:
      app: order-service
  template:
      metadata:
      labels:
```

CHAPTER 5   SECURING MICROSERVICES WITH ISTIO

```
            app: order-service
            spec:
            serviceAccountName: order-service
            containers:
            - name: order-service
            image: node:16-alpine
            command: ["node", "/app/server.js"]
            volumeMounts:
            - name: app-code
                mountPath: /app
            volumes:
            - name: app-code
            configMap:
                name: order-service-code
---
apiVersion: apps/v1
kind: Deployment
metadata:
  name: analytics-service
  namespace: ecommerce
spec:
  replicas: 1
  selector:
      matchLabels:
      app: analytics-service
    template:
      metadata:
      labels:
      app: analytics-service
      spec:
      serviceAccountName: analytics-service
      containers:
      - name: analytics-service
      image: node:16-alpine
      command: ["node", "/app/server.js"]
      volumeMounts:
```

CHAPTER 5   SECURING MICROSERVICES WITH ISTIO

```
      - name: app-code
          mountPath: /app
    volumes:
    - name: app-code
      configMap:
          name: analytics-service-code

# Apply service account resources
kubectl apply -f service-accounts.yaml

# Apply services
kubectl apply -f services.yaml

# Apply deployment resource
kubectl apply -f deployments.yaml

# Create ConfigMaps for each service
kubectl create configmap product-service-code --from-file=server.js=ecommerce-demo/product-service/server.js -n ecommerce
kubectl create configmap order-service-code --from-file=server.js=ecommerce-demo/order-service/server.js -n ecommerce

kubectl create configmap analytics-service-code --from-file=server.js=ecommerce-demo/analytics-service/server.js -n ecommerce
```

5. Create RBAC policies for authentication and authorization.

```
# Create Product Service Policy
# product-policy.yaml
apiVersion: security.istio.io/v1beta1
kind: AuthorizationPolicy
metadata:
  name: product-service-policy
  namespace: ecommerce
spec:
  selector:
     matchLabels:
        app: product-service
```

257

CHAPTER 5   SECURING MICROSERVICES WITH ISTIO

```yaml
  rules:
  - from:
      - source:
          principals: ["cluster.local/ns/ecommerce/sa/order-service"]
      to:
      - operation:
          methods: ["GET"]
          paths: ["/api/products/*"]
  - from:
      - source:
          principals: ["cluster.local/ns/ecommerce/sa/analytics-
            service"]
      to:
      - operation:
          methods: ["GET"]
          paths: ["/api/products/stats"]
# Create Order Service Policy
# order-policy.yaml
apiVersion: security.istio.io/v1beta1
kind: AuthorizationPolicy
metadata:
  name: order-service-policy
  namespace: ecommerce
spec:
  selector:
      matchLabels:
      app: order-service
  rules:
  - from:
      - source:
          principals: ["cluster.local/ns/ecommerce/sa/analytics-
            service"]
      to:
      - operation:
          methods: ["GET"]
```

CHAPTER 5 SECURING MICROSERVICES WITH ISTIO

```
      paths: ["/api/orders/stats"]
  - from:
    - source:
      namespaces: ["ecommerce"]
    to:
    - operation:
      methods: ["POST"]
      paths: ["/api/orders"]

# Apply policy resources
kubectl apply -f product-policy.yaml
kubectl apply -f order-policy.yaml
```

6. Verify Setup: Check all resources.

```
# Check all resources
kubectl get all -n ecommerce

# Check service accounts
kubectl get serviceaccounts -n ecommerce

# Check authorization policies
kubectl get authorizationpolicy -n ecommerce

# Wait for pods to be ready
kubectl wait --for=condition=ready pod -l app=product-service -n
ecommerce
kubectl wait --for=condition=ready pod -l app=order-service -n
ecommerce
kubectl wait --for=condition=ready pod -l app=analytics-service -n
ecommerce
```

7. Test the RBAC rules defined above between the services:

```
# Test Order Service accessing Product Service (should succeed)
kubectl exec -n ecommerce deploy/order-service -c order-
service -- \
  curl -s http://product-service:8080/api/products/1
```

259

```
# Test Analytics Service accessing Order Stats (should succeed)
kubectl exec -n ecommerce deploy/analytics-service -c analytics-service -- \
  curl -s http://order-service:8080/api/orders/stats

# Test unauthorized access (should fail)
kubectl exec -n ecommerce deploy/analytics-service -c analytics-service -- \
  curl -s http://product-service:8080/api/products/1
```

8. Cleanup all resources.

```
# Delete authorization policies
kubectl delete authorizationpolicy -n ecommerce --all

# Delete deployments
kubectl delete deployment -n ecommerce --all

# Delete services
kubectl delete service -n ecommerce --all

# Delete service accounts
kubectl delete serviceaccount -n ecommerce --all

# Delete configmaps
kubectl delete configmap -n ecommerce --all

# Delete namespace
kubectl delete namespace ecommerce

# Optional: Uninstall Istio
istioctl uninstall --purge
kubectl delete namespace istio-system
```

Securing Ingress and Egress Traffic

The primary objective of ingress traffic security is to safeguard services from external access. Istio's Gateway resource offers the ability to terminate TLS, manage certificates, and upgrade the protocols. It is capable of integrating with external certificate managers to facilitate the automated provisioning and rotation of certificates.

Istio offers a variety of security mechanisms for egress traffic. All outbound traffic can be monitored and controlled by egress gateways. They have the ability to enforce TLS origination, which guarantees that external communication is encrypted, even if internal services communicate in plain text. A whitelist-based security model is established by ServiceEntry resources, which specify which external services may be accessed.

Advanced security features, such as traffic routing, circuit breaking, and rate limiting, are supported by both ingress and egress configurations. These capabilities serve to safeguard against both internal service vulnerabilities and external threats. This guide illustrates the process of establishing secure ingress and egress traffic patterns through the use of Istio service mesh. We will address the origination and termination of TLS, authentication, authorization, and monitoring of both incoming and outgoing traffic.

As discussed, earlier TLS termination and origination are also possible at the sidecar level. In Istio, TLS origination (initiating outbound TLS connections) and TLS termination (handling inbound TLS connections) are not limited to ingress or egress gateways; they can also occur directly at the sidecar proxy level. This is a powerful and widely used feature that enables secure communication between services, especially when integrating with external systems or services that require TLS.

TLS handling at the sidecar level is particularly useful in scenarios where

- A service within the mesh needs to connect to an external service over HTTPS.

- An internal service expects encrypted traffic, even from peers within the mesh.

- Fine-grained control is needed over TLS behavior, such as custom certificates, specific ports, or strict validation rules.

To achieve this, Istio provides mechanisms via

- **Sidecar resources** to configure the scope of traffic captured and managed by Envoy.

- **DestinationRules** to specify how Envoy should handle TLS when sending traffic to a specific service or host. For instance, you can configure `tls.mode: SIMPLE` for TLS origination or `tls.mode: ISTIO_MUTUAL` for mTLS within the mesh.

CHAPTER 5   SECURING MICROSERVICES WITH ISTIO

Here's a high-level example:

- You define a `ServiceEntry` to allow outbound traffic to an external HTTPS service.

- Then, you configure a `DestinationRule` to enable TLS origination by the sidecar.

- Optionally, an `EnvoyFilter` or `Sidecar` resource can be used to fine-tune behavior if needed.

This flexibility ensures secure and policy-driven communication while offloading complex TLS management from the applications themselves to the sidecar proxies.

Example

This example illustrates a comprehensive system for securing both incoming (ingress) and outgoing (egress) traffic in a Kubernetes cluster by utilizing Istio service mesh. To enable HTTPS termination at the gateway level, we initiate the process of creating TLS certificates and storing them as Kubernetes secrets for ingress traffic. The Gateway resource serves as the entry point, determining how external traffic enters the cluster on port 443 with TLS enabled. The VirtualService subsequently directs this traffic to specific services based on URL patterns (such as /api/v1). Security is enforced through a multi-layered approach. Initially, an AuthenticationPolicy is implemented to ensure that all communication is encrypted and authenticated by implementing mutual TLS (mTLS) between services and JWT validation. The AuthorizationPolicy adds fine-grained access control by specifying which service accounts are permitted to access specific API endpoints and by incorporating JWT claim validation. The implementation employs an egress gateway to regulate and supervise all outbound connections for egress traffic. The ServiceEntry specifies which external services are accessible, while the egress Gateway and VirtualService regulate how internal services connect to these external endpoints. This establishes a secure tunnel for external communication, guaranteeing that all outbound traffic is monitored and regulated. The example also includes a sample application deployment to illustrate the practical functionality of these configurations, as well as monitoring and troubleshooting tools such as Kiali for visualizing the service mesh traffic patterns. The entire setup adheres to zero-trust principles, which require that each connection be explicitly authorized and authenticated, regardless of whether it is incoming or outgoing traffic.

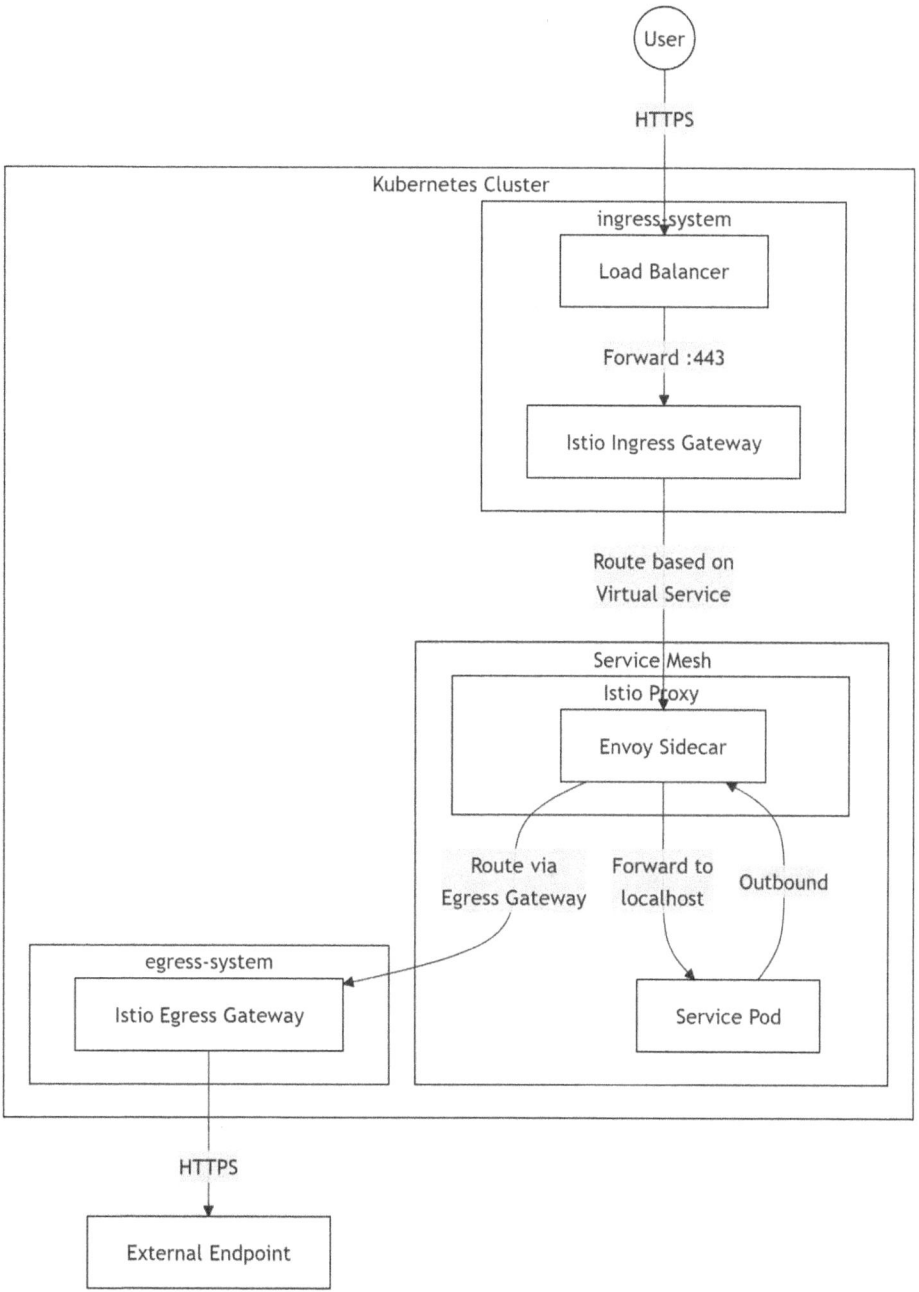

Figure 5-4. *Ingress and egress communication in a cluster with Istio*

Implementation Example
Part 1: Securing Ingress Traffic

1. Generate TLS certificates. First, let's create a self-signed certificate for our ingress gateway.

Note *OpenSSL* is a cryptographic toolkit implementing SSL/TLS protocols for secure communication and certificate management.

```
openssl req -x509 -sha256 -nodes -days 365 -newkey rsa:2048 \
  -subj '/O=Example Inc./CN=example.com' \
  -keyout example.com.key \
  -out example.com.crt
```

2. To implement Istio, follow the prerequisite and installation steps outlined earlier in Chapter 1. Then, add it to the path.

3. Create a Kubernetes secret with the certificate.

```
kubectl create -n istio-system secret tls example-credential \
  --key=example.com.key \
  --cert=example.com.crt
```

4. Define the Gateway resource.

```yaml
apiVersion: networking.istio.io/v1beta1
kind: Gateway
metadata:
  name: secure-gateway
  namespace: default
spec:
  selector:
      istio: ingressgateway
  servers:
  - port:
      number: 443
      name: https
```

CHAPTER 5   SECURING MICROSERVICES WITH ISTIO

```
      protocol: HTTPS
      tls:
      mode: SIMPLE
      credentialName: example-credential
      hosts:
      - "api.example.com"
```

5. Configure VirtualService for routing.

```
apiVersion: networking.istio.io/v1beta1
kind: VirtualService
metadata:
  name: api-routes
spec:
  hosts:
  - "api.example.com"
  gateways:
  - secure-gateway
  http:
  - match:
      - uri:
      prefix: "/api/v1"
      route:
      - destination:
      host: api-service
      port:
            number: 8080
```

6. Implement an authentication policy.

```
apiVersion: security.istio.io/v1beta1
kind: AuthenticationPolicy
metadata:
  name: api-auth-policy
  namespace: default
spec:
  selector:
```

265

CHAPTER 5   SECURING MICROSERVICES WITH ISTIO

```
      matchLabels:
        app: api-service
    peers:
    - mtls:
        mode: STRICT
    origins:
    - jwt:
        issuer: "https://accounts.example.com"
        jwksUri: "https://accounts.example.com/.well-known/
   jwks.json"
    principalBinding: USE_ORIGIN
```

7. Define an authorization policy.

```
   apiVersion: security.istio.io/v1beta1
   kind: AuthorizationPolicy
   metadata:
     name: api-authz-policy
     namespace: default
   spec:
     selector:
        matchLabels:
        app: api-service
     rules:
     - from:
        - source:
        principals: ["cluster.local/ns/default/sa/api-client"]
        to:
        - operation:
        methods: ["GET", "POST"]
        paths: ["/api/v1/*"]
        when:
        - key: request.auth.claims[groups]
        values: ["api-users"]
```

CHAPTER 5 SECURING MICROSERVICES WITH ISTIO

Part 2: Securing Egress Traffic

1. Enable the egress gateway.

    ```
    apiVersion: install.istio.io/v1alpha1
    kind: IstioOperator
    spec:
      components:
          egressGateways:
          - name: istio-egressgateway
            enabled: true
    ```

2. Create ServiceEntry for external services.

    ```
    apiVersion: networking.istio.io/v1beta1
    kind: ServiceEntry
    metadata:
      name: external-api
    spec:
      hosts:
      - api.external-service.com
      ports:
      - number: 443
        name: https
        protocol: HTTPS
      resolution: DNS
      location: MESH_EXTERNAL
    ```

3. Configure the egress gateway.

    ```
    apiVersion: networking.istio.io/v1beta1
    kind: Gateway
    metadata:
      name: external-service-gateway
    spec:
      selector:
          istio: egressgateway
      servers:
      - port:
    ```

267

```
      number: 443
      name: https
      protocol: HTTPS
    hosts:
    - api.external-service.com
```

4. Define egress VirtualService.

```
apiVersion: networking.istio.io/v1beta1
kind: VirtualService
metadata:
  name: external-service-vs
spec:
  hosts:
  - api.external-service.com
  gateways:
  - mesh
  - external-service-gateway
  http:
  - match:
      - gateways:
      - mesh
      port: 443
    route:
    - destination:
      host: istio-egressgateway.istio-system.svc.cluster.local
      port:
          number: 443
  - match:
      - gateways:
      - external-service-gateway
      port: 443
    route:
    - destination:
      host: api.external-service.com
      port:
          number: 443
```

CHAPTER 5 SECURING MICROSERVICES WITH ISTIO

5. Implement a network security policy.

   ```
   apiVersion: security.istio.io/v1beta1
   kind: AuthorizationPolicy
   metadata:
     name: egress-gateway-policy
     namespace: istio-system
   spec:
     selector:
       matchLabels:
         app: istio-egressgateway
     rules:
     - from:
       - source:
         principals: ["cluster.local/ns/default/sa/application"]
       to:
       - operation:
         hosts: ["api.external-service.com"]
   ```

Part 3: Let's Implement a Complete Example with a Sample Application

1. Deploy the sample application.

   ```
   apiVersion: apps/v1
   kind: Deployment
   metadata:
     name: sample-app
     labels:
       app: sample-app
   spec:
     replicas: 2
     selector:
       matchLabels:
         app: sample-app
     template:
       metadata:
         labels:
           app: sample-app
   ```

269

```yaml
    spec:
      serviceAccountName: application
      containers:
      - name: sample-app
        image: sample-app:1.0
        ports:
        - containerPort: 8080
---
apiVersion: v1
kind: Service
metadata:
  name: sample-app-service
spec:
  selector:
    app: sample-app
  ports:
  - port: 8080
    targetPort: 8080
```

2. Apply all configurations.

   ```
   # Apply Gateway and VirtualService
   kubectl apply -f secure-gateway.yaml
   kubectl apply -f api-routes.yaml

   # Apply Authentication and Authorization policies
   kubectl apply -f api-auth-policy.yaml
   kubectl apply -f api-authz-policy.yaml

   # Apply Egress configurations
   kubectl apply -f external-service-entry.yaml
   kubectl apply -f external-service-gateway.yaml
   kubectl apply -f external-service-vs.yaml
   kubectl apply -f egress-gateway-policy.yaml
   ```

3. Verify the configuration.

   ```
   # Check Gateway status
   kubectl get gateway secure-gateway -o yaml

   # Verify VirtualService
   kubectl get virtualservice api-routes -o yaml

   # Check Authentication Policy
   kubectl get authenticationpolicy api-auth-policy -o yaml

   # Verify Egress Gateway
   kubectl -n istio-system get pod -l istio=egressgateway
   ```

Testing

1. Test ingress.

   ```
   curl -v -HHost:api.example.com \
     --resolve api.example.com:443:$INGRESS_IP \
     --cacert example.com.crt \
     https://api.example.com/api/v1/test
   ```

2. Test egress.

   ```
   kubectl exec -it $POD_NAME -c sample-app -- curl \
     https://api.external-service.com/test
   ```

Monitoring

1. Check Istio proxy logs.

   ```
   kubectl logs $POD_NAME -c istio-proxy
   ```

2. View metrics in Grafana:

   - Navigate to the Istio Dashboard.
   - Check "Istio Service Dashboard."
   - Monitor inbound/outbound traffic.
   - Use Kiali for visualization:

CHAPTER 5 SECURING MICROSERVICES WITH ISTIO

```
istioctl dashboard kiali
```

Cleanup

```
# Remove application resources
kubectl delete deployment sample-app
kubectl delete service sample-app-service

# Remove Istio ingress configurations
kubectl delete gateway secure-gateway
kubectl delete virtualservice api-routes
kubectl delete secret -n istio-system example-credential

# Remove security policies
kubectl delete authenticationpolicy api-auth-policy
kubectl delete authorizationpolicy api-authz-policy
kubectl delete authorizationpolicy egress-gateway-policy

# Remove egress configurations
kubectl delete serviceentry external-api
kubectl delete gateway external-service-gateway
kubectl delete virtualservice external-service-vs

# Optional: Remove monitoring resources
kubectl delete -n istio-system gateway monitoring-gateway
kubectl delete -n istio-system virtualservice grafana-vs
kubectl delete -n istio-system virtualservice kiali-vs

# Verify cleanup
kubectl get gateway --all-namespaces
kubectl get virtualservice --all-namespaces
kubectl get authenticationpolicy --all-namespaces
kubectl get authorizationpolicy --all-namespaces
kubectl get serviceentry --all-namespaces
```

Auditing and Logging Security Events in Istio

Istio provides comprehensive auditing and logging capabilities for security events. Every request passing through the mesh generates detailed logs including source, destination, protocol, response codes, and timing information. These logs can be customized to include specific security-relevant fields.

The logging system integrates with popular backends like Prometheus and Grafana for metrics collection and visualization. Security metrics include mTLS connection statistics, authentication failures, authorization denials, and certificate rotation events.

Istio's telemetry system allows for real-time monitoring of security posture. Operators can set up alerts for suspicious patterns like sudden increases in authentication failures or unauthorized access attempts.

Example

In this section, we will describe an end-to-end setup for Istio security logging and monitoring.

Implementation Steps

1. To implement Istio, follow the prerequisite and installation steps outlined earlier in Chapter 1. Then, add it to the path.

2. Create directories and files.

   ```
   mkdir istio-security-monitoring
   cd istio-security-monitoring
   ```

3. Create configuration files.

   ```
   # namespace.yaml
   apiVersion: v1
   kind: Namespace
   metadata:
     name: monitoring
     labels:
         istio-injection: enabled
   ---
   apiVersion: v1
   ```

CHAPTER 5 SECURING MICROSERVICES WITH ISTIO

```yaml
kind: Namespace
metadata:
  name: logging
  labels:
      istio-injection: enabled

# prometheus-config.yaml
apiVersion: monitoring.coreos.com/v1
kind: ServiceMonitor
metadata:
  name: istio-metrics
  namespace: monitoring
spec:
  selector:
      matchLabels:
        istio: ingressgateway
  endpoints:
  - port: http-monitoring
      interval: 15s

# telemetry-config.yaml
apiVersion: telemetry.istio.io/v1alpha1
kind: Telemetry
metadata:
  name: access-logging
  namespace: istio-system
spec:
  accessLogging:
      - providers:
      - name: envoy
      filters:
      - expression: "response.code >= 400 || request.headers['x-custom-header'] == 'audit'"

# authorization-policy.yaml
apiVersion: security.istio.io/v1beta1
kind: AuthorizationPolicy
```

```
metadata:
  name: audit-policy
  namespace: default
spec:
  action: AUDIT
  rules:
  - from:
      - source:
      notNamespaces: ["trusted-namespace"]
    to:
    - operation:
      methods: ["POST", "PUT", "DELETE"]
#Fluentd-config.yaml
apiVersion: v1
kind: ConfigMap
metadata:
  name: fluentd-config
  namespace: logging
data:
  fluent.conf: |
      <source>
      @type tail
      path /var/log/containers/*.log
      pos_file /var/log/fluentd-containers.log.pos
      tag kubernetes.*
      <parse>
      @type json
      </parse>
      </source>

      <match kubernetes.**>
      @type elasticsearch
      host elasticsearch-logging
      port 9200
      logstash_format true
```

CHAPTER 5   SECURING MICROSERVICES WITH ISTIO

```
      </match>
---
apiVersion: apps/v1
kind: DaemonSet
metadata:
  name: fluentd
  namespace: logging
spec:
  selector:
      matchLabels:
      app: fluentd
  template:
      metadata:
      labels:
      app: fluentd
      spec:
      containers:
      - name: fluentd
      image: fluent/fluentd-kubernetes-daemonset:v1.11-debian-
      elasticsearch7-1
```

4. Installation Script (install.sh)

```
#!/bin/bash

# Create namespaces
kubectl apply -f namespace.yaml

# Install Prometheus & Grafana
helm repo add prometheus-community https://prometheus-community.
github.io/helm-charts
helm repo add grafana https://grafana.github.io/helm-charts
helm repo update

helm install prometheus prometheus-community/kube-
prometheus-stack \
  --namespace monitoring
```

```
helm install grafana grafana/grafana \
  --namespace monitoring \
  --set datasources."datasources\.yaml".apiVersion=1 \
  --set datasources."datasources\.yaml".datasources[0].
    name=Prometheus \
  --set datasources."datasources\.yaml".datasources[0].
    type=prometheus \
  --set datasources."datasources\.yaml".datasources[0].url=http://
    prometheus-server

# Apply Istio configurations
kubectl apply -f telemetry-config.yaml
kubectl apply -f authorization-policy.yaml
kubectl apply -f prometheus-config.yaml
kubectl apply -f fluentd-config.yaml

# Wait for pods to be ready
kubectl wait --for=condition=ready pod -l app=fluentd -n logging
--timeout=300s
```

5. Verification Script (verify.sh)

```
#!/bin/bash

# Get credentials
GRAFANA_PASSWORD=$(kubectl get secret grafana -n monitoring -o
jsonpath="{.data.admin-password}" | base64 --decode)
echo "Grafana admin password: $GRAFANA_PASSWORD"

# Port forwarding
kubectl port-forward svc/prometheus-server 9090:9090 -n
monitoring &
kubectl port-forward svc/grafana 3000:3000 -n monitoring &
kubectl port-forward svc/elasticsearch-logging 9200:9200 -n
logging &

# Generate test traffic
curl -H "x-custom-header: audit" http://your-gateway-url/api/test
```

```
# View logs
echo "Envoy Logs:"
kubectl logs -l app=istio-ingressgateway -n istio-system --tail=10

echo "Elasticsearch Logs:"
curl -X GET "localhost:9200/logstash-*/_search" -H 'Content-Type: application/json' -d'
{
  "query": {
      "bool": {
      "must": [
      { "match": { "audit.event_type": "authorization_denied" } }
      ]
      }
    }
}'
```

6. Run the setup.

   ```
   chmod +x install.sh verify.sh
   ./install.sh
   ./verify.sh
   ```

7. Observe the output.

   ```
   {
     "timestamp": "2024-01-23T10:15:30.000Z",
     "request": {
         "method": "POST",
         "url": "/api/test",
         "source": {
         "ip": "10.0.0.1",
         "service": "frontend"
         }
     },
     "response": {
         "code": 403,
   ```

```
        "duration_ms": 50
    },
    "security": {
        "auth_status": "JWT_INVALID",
        "policy_status": "DENY"
    }
}
```

8. Access the dashboards available on localhost, for example:

    - The Prometheus dashboard is available at `http://localhost:9090`.

    - The Grafana dashboard is available at `http://localhost:3000`. (admin:$GRAFANA_PASSWORD)

    - The Elasticsearch dashboard is available at `http://localhost:9200`.

Integrating Istio Security with External Systems

Istio's security features allow interaction with external security systems using a variety of mechanisms. It uses JWT validation to authenticate external identity providers. For certificate management, it can collaborate with external certificate authorities and management systems.

External authorization systems can be integrated using the external authorization feature, allowing organizations to use existing policy engines. This allows for more complex authorization scenarios, such as access to external data or business logic.

Integration with security information and event management (SIEM) systems is possible, thanks to Istio's logging and monitoring features. This enables security teams to maintain centralized visibility across the infrastructure.

Extend Istio's capabilities by integrating with

- Certificate authorities (e.g., Cert-Manager)
- Identity providers for OIDC or LDAP
- External WAFs or API gateways

Example

This example shows how to integrate Istio with Open Policy Agent (OPA) as an external authorization system. OPA is a general-purpose policy engine that allows for consistent, context-aware policy enforcement across the entire stack. In this configuration, we'll set Istio to delegate authorization decisions to OPA, which will serve as an external decision point. The workflow starts with installing Istio and OPA in a Kubernetes cluster and then configures OPA policies and Istio's external authorization framework. We will also deploy a test application to ensure that the integration works properly. When a request arrives at a service mesh endpoint, Istio will consult OPA to make authorization decisions based on custom policies. This integration enables advanced authorization scenarios that can include external data and complex business logic in addition to Istio's built-in RBAC capabilities.

CHAPTER 5   SECURING MICROSERVICES WITH ISTIO

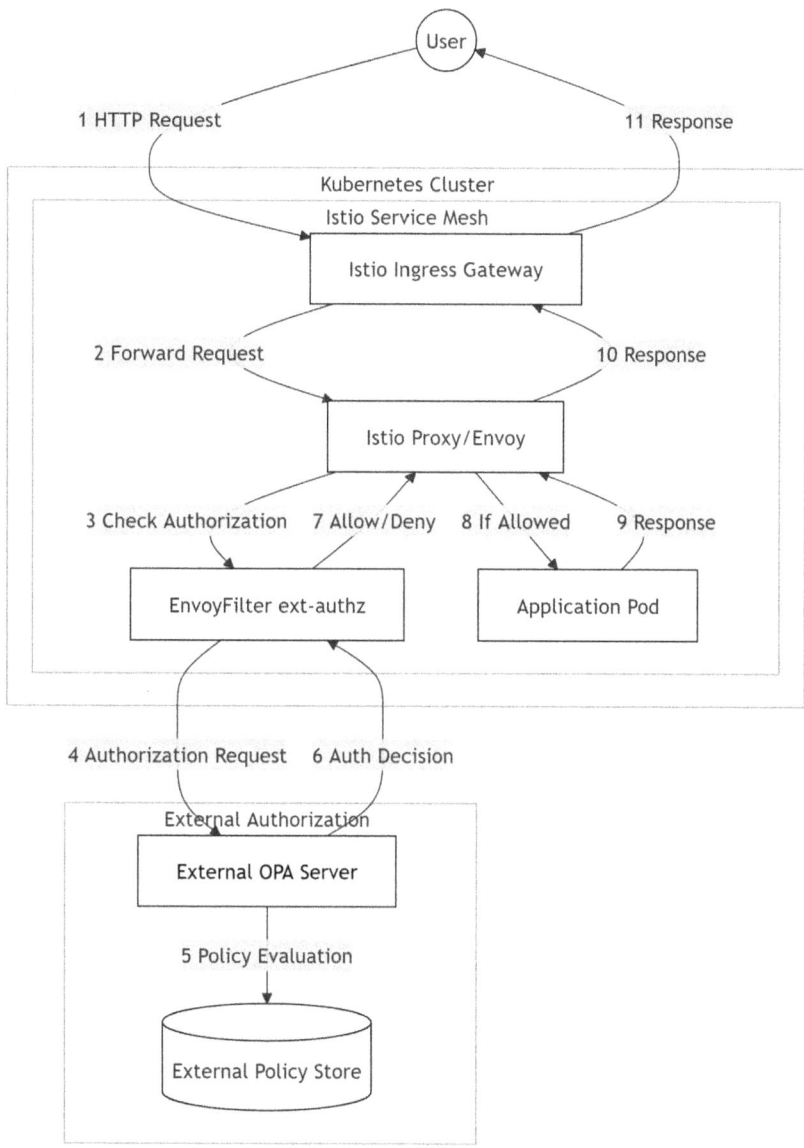

Figure 5-5. *External integration of Istio with OPA*

CHAPTER 5   SECURING MICROSERVICES WITH ISTIO

Implementation Steps

1. To implement Istio, follow the prerequisite and installation steps outlined in Chapter 1. Next, add it to the path, and create a demo profile with injection enabled.

   ```
   # Install Istio with demo profile
   kubectl create namespace istio-system
   istioctl install --set profile=demo -y

   # Enable sidecar injection
   kubectl label namespace default istio-injection=enabled
   ```

2. Verify Istio installation.

   ```
   # Check Istio components
   kubectl get pods -n istio-system

   # Check injection functionality
   kubectl get mutatingwebhookconfiguration
   ```

3. Install OPA.

   ```
   # opa-deployment.yaml
   apiVersion: apps/v1
   kind: Deployment
   metadata:
     name: opa
   spec:
     replicas: 1
     selector:
         matchLabels:
           app: opa
     template:
         metadata:
         labels:
           app: opa
         spec:
           containers:
   ```

282

```
    - name: opa
      image: openpolicyagent/opa:latest
      ports:
      - containerPort: 8181
      args:
      - "run"
      - "--server"
      - "--addr=:8181"
---
apiVersion: v1
kind: Service
metadata:
  name: opa
spec:
  selector:
      app: opa
  ports:
  - port: 8181
```

4. Install the OPA policy.

```
# policy.rego
package istio.authz

default allow = false

allow {
    # Allow requests from authenticated users
    input.attributes.request.http.headers["authorization"]
    # Add your custom authorization logic here
}
```

5. Configure Istio external authorization.

```
apiVersion: security.istio.io/v1beta1
kind: AuthorizationPolicy
metadata:
```

```yaml
  name: ext-authz
spec:
  action: CUSTOM
  provider:
     name: opa-external-authz
  rules:
  - to:
     - operation:
        paths: ["/*"]
---
apiVersion: networking.istio.io/v1alpha3
kind: EnvoyFilter
metadata:
  name: ext-authz
spec:
  workloadSelector:
     labels:
        app: myapp
  configPatches:
  - applyTo: HTTP_FILTER
     match:
     context: SIDECAR_INBOUND
     listener:
     filterChain:
        filter:
        name: "envoy.filters.network.http_connection_manager"
     patch:
     operation: INSERT_BEFORE
     value:
     name: envoy.filters.http.ext_authz
     typed_config:
        "@type": type.googleapis.com/envoy.extensions.filters.
        http.ext_authz.v3.ExtAuthz
        grpc_service:
        google_grpc:
```

CHAPTER 5 SECURING MICROSERVICES WITH ISTIO

```
            target_uri: opa:8181
            stat_prefix: ext_authz
            timeout: 0.5s
```

6. Deploy the test application.

```
apiVersion: apps/v1
kind: Deployment
metadata:
  name: test-app
spec:
  replicas: 1
  selector:
      matchLabels:
      app: test-app
  template:
      metadata:
      labels:
      app: test-app
      spec:
      containers:
      - name: nginx
        image: nginx
---
apiVersion: v1
kind: Service
metadata:
  name: test-app
spec:
  selector:
      app: test-app
  ports:
  - port: 80
```

7. Test and verify.

```
# Apply configurations
kubectl apply -f opa-deployment.yaml
kubectl apply -f policy.rego
kubectl apply -f external-authz.yaml
kubectl apply -f test-app.yaml

# Test authorization
curl -H "Host: test-app" http://test-app/  # Should fail
curl -H "Host: test-app" -H "Authorization: Bearer token123" http://test-app/  # Should succeed

# Monitor
kubectl logs -l app=opa
kubectl logs <pod-name> -c istio-proxy
```

Handling Security in Multi-cluster Deployments

In addition to the fundamental mTLS enforcement, Istio's network policies necessitate thorough configuration. Organizations should combine Kubernetes NetworkPolicies with Istio authorization policies to implement defense in depth. This dual-layer approach assures that workloads are safeguarded even in the event that one security control is compromised. In accordance with the principle of least privilege, network policies should be configured to explicitly specify the permitted communication paths. Performing routine audits of these policies assists in the identification and elimination of any excessively permissive regulations that may have been implemented during the development or troubleshooting phases.

Organizations ought to consider the implementation of a robust public key infrastructure (PKI) strategy, despite the fact that Istio offers built-in certificate management. This encompasses the establishment of distinct certificate authorities for distinct environments (development, staging, and production), the implementation of automated certificate rotation schedules, and the preservation of appropriate backup and recovery procedures for root certificates. Additionally, organizations should contemplate the utilization of hardware security modules (HSMs) to store root certificates in production environments. The prevention of service disruptions

CHAPTER 5   SECURING MICROSERVICES WITH ISTIO

is facilitated by the regular monitoring of certificate expiration dates and the implementation of automated alerts for approaching expiration.

Additional security measures are necessary for the Istio control plane in addition to the default configurations. Organizations should establish rigorous RBAC policies for control plane access, periodically rotate control plane credentials, and maintain distinct service accounts for distinct control plane components. In order to prevent denial-of-service attacks, the control plane API server should be configured with rigorous authentication requirements and rate limiting. Furthermore, the attack surface is reduced by implementing network segregation for control plane components.

Identity management in Istio encompasses more than just basic service accounts. A comprehensive workload identity strategy involves the consistent rotation of service account credentials and the implementation of pod security policies to prevent privilege escalation. Organizations should conduct regular audits of service account permissions and integrate with external identity providers to unify access management, thereby eliminating unused identities. The security posture is further improved by the implementation of just-in-time credential issuance for ephemeral workloads.

Particular attention must be paid to security details in the context of configuration management in Istio. Organizations are required to conduct automated security scanning and implement version control for all Istio configurations prior to deployment. In addition to rigorous change management protocols for security-critical configurations, it is imperative to conduct routine security audits of custom resources and CRDs. The implementation of configuration validation webhooks should be complemented by the maintenance of appropriate backup and disaster recovery procedures for Istio configurations.

Organizations should implement comprehensive security monitoring solutions in addition to basic monitoring. This encompasses the integration of anomaly detection for traffic patterns and the implementation of security information and event management (SIEM) systems. It is imperative to conduct routine security scans of container images in the mesh and monitor control plane audit logs for any suspicious activity. Additionally, it is recommended that organizations conduct routine penetration testing of the service mesh infrastructure and implement automated responses to security events.

In addition to transport encryption, data protection in Istio necessitates additional consideration. End-to-end encryption should be implemented by organizations for sensitive workloads, and encryption keys should be rotated on a regular basis. Comprehensive data protection is guaranteed by the implementation of data classification and handling policies, in addition to the secure storage and management of secrets. The security posture is further fortified by the implementation of data loss prevention (DLP) measures and the regular auditing of data access patterns.

Regular backups of mesh configurations and certificates, as well as the implementation of cross-region failover procedures, are security considerations for disaster recovery. Organizations should conduct regular recovery procedure tests and ensure security during failover scenarios. The preparation for a variety of disaster scenarios is guaranteed by the regular updating of recovery playbooks and the documentation of emergency access procedures.

Organizations are required to maintain comprehensive compliance programs that encompass the regular assessment of security against industry standards and the preservation of detailed audit logs. The ongoing adherence to security requirements is guaranteed by the regular review of security policies and procedures and the implementation of compliance monitoring tools. The organization's security culture is sustained through the regular training of team members on security procedures and the documentation of security controls and their effectiveness.

Overall Security Best Practices in Istio and Its Use in Production

The implementation of security in a service mesh environment using Istio represents a fundamental shift in how organizations approach application and infrastructure security. Through the comprehensive security features and capabilities discussed, Istio provides organizations with the tools necessary to build and maintain zero-trust architectures that can withstand modern cyber threats while supporting business agility and innovation.

The multi-layered security approach offered by Istio addresses the complex challenges faced in distributed systems. By implementing strong identity management through service accounts and workload identity, organizations can ensure that every service interaction is authenticated and authorized. The platform's robust mTLS implementation, coupled with fine-grained authorization policies, creates a secure communication fabric that protects both data in transit and service-to-service interactions.

Certificate management in Istio demonstrates the platform's maturity in handling complex security requirements. The automated certificate rotation, integration with

CHAPTER 5 SECURING MICROSERVICES WITH ISTIO

external certificate authorities, and comprehensive PKI management capabilities ensure that organizations can maintain strong cryptographic security without operational overhead. This automation is crucial for maintaining security at scale, where manual certificate management would be impractical and error-prone.

Network security implementation in Istio goes beyond traditional perimeter-based approaches. The combination of network policies, authorization policies, and gateway controls provides defense in depth that is essential in modern cloud-native environments. The ability to implement microsegmentation at the service level, rather than network level, enables organizations to create highly granular security policies that align with application requirements rather than network topology.

The platform's approach to configuration management and security policy enforcement demonstrates an understanding of modern DevSecOps practices. By supporting policy as code and providing robust API-driven configuration capabilities, Istio enables organizations to implement security controls that can keep pace with rapid application development and deployment cycles. The ability to version control security policies and automate their deployment ensures consistent security posture across environments.

Monitoring and observability capabilities in Istio provide the visibility needed to maintain strong security posture. The integration with external monitoring systems, comprehensive audit logging, and anomaly detection capabilities enable organizations to detect and respond to security incidents quickly. This visibility is crucial for maintaining compliance requirements and supporting incident response activities.

Disaster recovery and business continuity considerations in Istio reflect the platform's enterprise readiness. The ability to maintain security controls during failover scenarios, coupled with comprehensive backup and recovery capabilities, ensures that organizations can maintain security even during adverse conditions. The support for cross-cluster and multi-cluster scenarios enables organizations to implement robust disaster recovery strategies without compromising security.

Integration capabilities with external security systems and tools demonstrate Istio's role in a broader security ecosystem. The platform's ability to integrate with external identity providers, security information and event management (SIEM) systems, and compliance tools enables organizations to maintain consolidated security operations while leveraging Istio's powerful security features.

The future of service mesh security will likely see continued evolution in areas such as zero-trust implementation, automated security response, and integration with emerging security technologies. Istio's architecture and extensibility position it well to adapt to these changes while maintaining backward compatibility and operational stability.

Organizations implementing Istio should approach security implementation as a journey rather than a destination. Regular security assessments, continuous monitoring, and ongoing policy refinement are essential for maintaining strong security posture. The platform's comprehensive security features provide the foundation, but success requires ongoing attention to security operations, policy management, and threat response.

Success in implementing Istio security requires a balanced approach that combines technical controls with operational processes. Organizations should invest in training, documentation, and process development alongside technical implementation. Regular security exercises, including penetration testing and disaster recovery drills, help ensure that both technical controls and operational procedures are effective.

In conclusion, Istio's security capabilities provide organizations with the tools needed to implement comprehensive security in modern distributed systems. The platform's approach to security, combining strong technical controls with operational flexibility, enables organizations to maintain robust security posture while supporting business agility. As threats continue to evolve and application architectures become more complex, Istio's security features and extensibility will continue to play a crucial role in organizational security strategies.

CHAPTER 6

Establishing Observability Foundations in Istio: Infrastructure, Tracing, and Metrics

Introduction to Istio Telemetry

In today's cloud-native landscape, applications are increasingly being created as collections of microservices, each responsible for a distinct business function; this architectural approach has several benefits, including enhanced scalability, shorter deployment times, and improved fault isolation. However, it adds tremendous complexity to understanding system behavior. When dozens or hundreds of services interact to satisfy a single user request, typical monitoring methods fail.

Observability becomes critical in this context because it provides the deep insights needed to understand, manage, and troubleshoot complex distributed systems. Unlike traditional monitoring, which focuses on known failure modes and predefined metrics, observability enables teams to ask new questions about their system's behavior and get meaningful answers, even for previously unknown scenarios.

The transition from monolithic to microservices architectures has profoundly altered how we approach system visibility. Most interactions in a monolithic application occur within a single process, making system behavior relatively easy to comprehend. In contrast, microservices introduce many network borders, asynchronous communications, and complex dependency chains. As systems get more complicated, teams require more sophisticated tools and ways to maintain visibility into them.

Imagine the challenge of operating the traffic system of a massive city without the use of cameras, sensors, or other monitoring technologies. You would be completely unaware of the locations where traffic accumulates, the most efficient routes, or when accidents occur. Similarly, operating a microservices architecture without sufficient observability is equivalent to flying blind. This is when Istio's telemetry tools serve as your eyes and ears within the service mesh, offering critical insights into service behavior, performance, and interactions.

The Three Pillars of Observability: Metrics, Logs, and Traces

Observability in Istio rests on three fundamental pillars, each serving a distinct purpose in understanding your system.

Metrics

Metrics provide a numerical depiction of your system's behavior across time as they provide the quantitative foundation required for understanding system performance, resource use, and business outcomes. Their ability to display trends and patterns over time is what makes metrics so essential, allowing teams to discover both slow degradation and unexpected changes in system behavior.

Metrics in Istio can be broadly categorized into several key types:

1. Traffic Metrics: These determine the number of requests that are flowing through your service mesh as well as the characteristics of those requests and include request rates, error rates, and success rates, offering valuable information into the overall health of communication between service providers and recipients.

2. Resource Metrics: Consumption of system resources such as the CPU cores, memory, and network bandwidth is monitored by these metrics. When it comes to capacity planning and performance optimization, it is necessary to have a solid understanding of these resource consumption patterns.

3. Performance Metrics: Response times, latency distributions, and queue depths are examples of metrics used to assess the performance of your services. At the same time these metrics can help in identifying performance bottlenecks and validating service-level objectives.

4. Business Metrics: This is not something Istio offers directly, but the telemetry system can be expanded to track business-critical data such as conversion rates, user interaction, and transaction values.

Logs

Logs give a complete account of what happens within your service mesh. Unlike metrics, which aggregate numerical data, logs contain detailed contextual information about specific events. This full record is invaluable for investigating issues or understanding particular user experiences.

The logging system in Istio captures various types of information:

1. Access Logs: These record details about every request processed by the service mesh, including source and destination services, response codes, timing information, and request metadata.

2. Error Logs: They are used to record specific information about what failed when anything goes wrong. This information includes stack traces, error messages, and related context.

3. Audit Logs: These track security-relevant events, such as authentication attempts, authorization decisions, and configuration changes.

4. Application Logs: Although application logs are not directly managed by Istio, they can be combined with the telemetry data that Istio collects to provide a comprehensive picture of how the system is behaving.

Traces

When it comes to observability, distributed tracing is the most advanced pillar since it offers visibility into request flows across services from beginning to end. The history of a single request is communicated through each trace as it travels through your system, illustrating the entirety of the request's path across service boundaries.

Tracing in Istio captures several critical aspects of request processing:

1. Latency Information: Traces provide an accurate representation of the amount of time that each service spent processing a request, which assists in identifying performance bottlenecks and opportunities for optimization.

2. Service Dependencies: By tracking request flows, traces reveal the actual service dependency patterns in your system, which may differ from the designed architecture.

3. Error Propagation: When failures occur, traces show how errors propagate through the system and which services are affected.

4. Request Context: Traces capture important metadata about requests, including headers, payload sizes, and user information.

How Istio's Telemetry Architecture Works

In distributed systems, Istio's telemetry architecture offers a sophisticated approach to gathering and processing observability data. The architecture was designed to be powerful and efficient, reducing the performance impact while offering complete visibility.

Fundamentally, Istio's telemetry system runs using a distributed network of proxies (Envoy) automatically injected alongside every service instance. In the telemetry system, these proxies fulfill several important roles:

1. Data Collection: The proxies intercept all incoming and outgoing traffic, collecting detailed information about each request and response.

2. Data Processing: Raw telemetry data is processed at the proxy level, including aggregating metrics, formatting log entries, and generating trace spans.

3. Data Export: Processed telemetry data is exported to various backend systems for storage, analysis, and visualization.

Overview of Istio's Telemetry API and Configuration

At the heart of Istio's observability capabilities is its Telemetry API, a sophisticated system that gives you precise control over how observability data is gathered, analyzed, and transmitted within your service mesh. This API offers a significant departure from traditional monitoring systems, providing a declarative mechanism to manage telemetry that is completely consistent with cloud-native principles and practices.

The Telemetry API is built using Kubernetes custom resources, which provides mesh operators with both familiarity and power. Istio makes telemetry configuration feel natural to Kubernetes-experienced teams while also delivering the comprehensive features required for sophisticated observability scenarios. The integration with Kubernetes goes beyond syntax; it allows teams to manage observability configurations with the same tools and workflows they use for other infrastructure components.

The provider configuration portion of the API specifies where telemetry data is sent and how it is structured. This adaptability is critical in current situations, when organizations frequently need to deliver observability data to several backend systems, each with a different purpose or different stakeholder needs. Whether you're sending metrics to Prometheus, traces to Jaeger, or logs to a centralized logging system, the provider setup gives you the control you need to guarantee data arrives at its intended destination in the proper format.

Istio's Telemetry API uses a hierarchical paradigm for configuration, providing mesh operators with both flexibility and control. Mesh-wide parameters set a baseline for telemetry collection across all services. These can then be tweaked or overridden at the namespace level, allowing teams to use multiple observability techniques across different areas of their application, and workload-level configurations provide the most granular control over telemetry gathering for specific services or deployments.

The evolution of the Telemetry API reflects the overall evolution of Istio. The current v1alpha1 version reflects the convergence of lessons learned from real-world deployments, providing a consistent approach to configuring all areas of telemetry collection. This version combines metrics, traces, and access logs into a single, cohesive configuration architecture, simplifying the operator experience while retaining the flexibility required for complex scenarios.

CHAPTER 6 ESTABLISHING OBSERVABILITY FOUNDATIONS IN ISTIO: INFRASTRUCTURE, TRACING, AND METRICS

The Telemetry API does not exist in isolation. One of the important features of the telemetry system is its ability to integrate with other Istio APIs. This creates a comprehensive service mesh solution complementing Istio's security and traffic management capabilities. The integration is especially important when exploring how security policies can affect telemetry collecting or how traffic routing decisions may impact the observability data you collect.

The successful implementation of Istio's Telemetry API typically follows a pattern of gradual enhancement, where teams usually start with mesh-wide defaults, which enable basic observability across all services; they are later supplemented with specific settings as needed, driven by operational requirements or organizational priorities. This strategy guarantees that teams keep full visibility while also providing the flexibility to add more specific telemetry collection where it is most useful.

Evolution from Mixer-Based to Mixerless Telemetry

The evolution of Istio's telemetry architecture marks a significant advancement in service mesh technology, and understanding this evolution gives important background for working with modern Istio deployments and explains critical design decisions in the current architecture.

Telemetry collection was formerly handled by a centralized component known as Mixer in Istio, and this component served as the primary hub for policy enforcement and telemetry collecting, processing data from all proxies in the mesh. While this system provided strong centralized control, it had considerable downsides. The Mixer-based architecture had multiple challenges. Each request required more network hops to deliver telemetry data to Mixer, which added latency. The centralized design of Mixer resulted in a possible bottleneck and single point of failure. As mesh deployments grew in size, Mixer's resource requirements increased significantly, creating scaling issues.

Modern Istio versions have moved to a Mixerless architecture, with telemetry processing taking place directly within the Envoy proxies. This architectural adjustment profoundly alters the way telemetry data is collected and processed. Instead of transmitting raw telemetry data to a central component, each proxy now processes it locally before passing it on to backend systems.

This transition brought numerous substantial benefits. The elimination of additional network hops has greatly enhanced system performance. Resource consumption has improved when processing is distributed across the mesh. The removal of Mixer as a central component improved system reliability while simplifying the overall architecture.

Setting Up the Observability Stack

Setting up the underlying infrastructure correctly is the first step toward successful observability in a service mesh, and this section will cover how to build a robust observability stack, create an example application that demonstrates its capabilities, and make sure everything works as it should. We will concentrate on developing a production-ready environment that offers a comprehensive understanding of the behavior of your service mesh.

Prerequisites and Environment Setup

Before we start the installation process, it's important to make sure that your system meets all the requirements. You need a Kubernetes cluster with version 1.21 or higher because it has the stability and features that our observability stack needs. You should have Helm 3.x on your machine because we'll be using it to deploy the configuration files bundled as Helm charts. You should have Istio version 1.12 or later installed and make sure that your kubectl tool is set up correctly to communicate with your cluster. These requirements ensure that everything works together and lets you use the newest observability features.

For this chapter, we need to install Istio with a custom mesh configuration using an IstioOperator CRD. We will be talking about this right after we install the observability stack.

We will quickly skim through the installation of several observability components in this section. Remember that there are multiple ways in which we can get these components to work on your cluster, and we will be choosing Helm to install them into our Kubernetes cluster.

Installing the Observability Stack with Helm

Following a systematic approach, we will be using Helm, the de facto package manager for Kubernetes, to install our observability stack, and we'll be deploying several essential components that work together to provide thorough insights into your service mesh: Grafana for visualization, Prometheus for metrics gathering, Jaeger for distributed tracing, and Kiali for service mesh observability.

CHAPTER 6 ESTABLISHING OBSERVABILITY FOUNDATIONS IN ISTIO: INFRASTRUCTURE, TRACING, AND METRICS

To get started, let's begin by adding the required Helm repositories. All of the charts that we will want for our installation are contained within these repositories:

```
# Add the Helm repositories
helm repo add prometheus-community https://prometheus-community.github.io/helm-charts
helm repo add grafana https://grafana.github.io/helm-charts
helm repo add jaegertracing https://jaegertracing.github.io/helm-charts            helm repo add kiali https://kiali.org/helm-charts

helm repo update
```

With our repositories in place, we'll create a separate namespace for all our observability components. This separation in the form of namespaces offers clear boundaries and simplifies resource management:

```
kubectl create namespace istio-observability
```

We can now proceed to install each component. We will begin with Prometheus, the foundation of our metrics collection system. The configuration we'll use includes persistent storage and reasonable retention periods:

```
helm install prometheus prometheus-community/prometheus \
  --namespace istio-observability \
  --set server.persistentVolume.size=10Gi \
  --set server.retention=15d \
  --set server.global.scrape_interval=15s
```

Following Prometheus, we'll install Grafana, our visualization platform. Grafana needs to be configured with Prometheus as a data source, and we'll set up persistent storage to maintain our dashboards and configurations.

For Grafana, create a file named `grafana-values.yaml`. We just show a portion of the file, but please refer to the source code attached to the chapter for the full file:

```
...
datasources:
 datasources.yaml:
   apiVersion: 1
   datasources:
   - name: Prometheus
```

```
      type: prometheus
      url: http://prometheus-server.istio-observability.svc.cluster.local
      isDefault: true
      access: proxy
      editable: true

# Configure dashboard providers
dashboardProviders:
 dashboardproviders.yaml:
    apiVersion: 1
    providers:
    - name: 'istio'
      orgId: 1
      folder: 'Istio'
      type: file
      disableDeletion: false
      editable: true
      options:
        path: /var/lib/grafana/dashboards

# Configure dashboard sidecar
sidecar:
 dashboards:
    enabled: true
    label: grafana_dashboard
    searchNamespace: ALL
    provider:
      allowUiUpdates: true
      foldersFromFilesStructure: true

# Add Istio dashboards ConfigMap
...
```

Install Grafana using this configuration:

```
helm install grafana grafana/grafana \
  --namespace istio-observability \
  -f grafana-values.yaml
```

For Jaeger, create a file named `jaeger-values.yaml`:

```yaml
allInOne:
 enabled: true
 name: jaeger
 image:
   repository: jaegertracing/all-in-one
   tag: "1.45.0"
   pullPolicy: IfNotPresent
 args:
   - "--memory.max-traces=100000"
   - "--query.base-path=/jaeger"
 ports:
   - name: jaeger-agent
     port: 6831
     protocol: UDP
     targetPort: 6831
   - name: jaeger-collector
     port: 14268
     protocol: TCP
     targetPort: 14268
   - name: jaeger-query
     port: 16686
     protocol: TCP
     targetPort: 16686

storage:
 type: memory

service:
 type: ClusterIP
 ports:
   - name: agent-udp
     port: 6831
     protocol: UDP
     targetPort: 6831
   - name: collector-http
```

```yaml
      port: 14268
      protocol: TCP
      targetPort: 14268
    - name: query-http
      port: 16686
      protocol: TCP
      targetPort: 16686
```

Now let us Install Jaeger using this configuration:

```
helm install jaeger jaegertracing/jaeger \
  --namespace istio-observability \
  -f jaeger-values.yaml
```

Here are few important notes about this setup:

1. We're using the "all-in-one" image, which combines all Jaeger components into a single deployment. This is simpler to manage and perfect for development and small to medium deployments.

2. In-memory storage means that traces will be lost if the pod restarts. For production environments, you might want to use Elasticsearch instead. Here's how that configuration would look:

    ```yaml
    # jaeger-values-elasticsearch.yaml
    allInOne:
      enabled: false  # Disable all-in-one since we'll use separate
      components

    storage:
      type: elasticsearch

    elasticsearch:
      enabled: true
      image: docker.elastic.co/elasticsearch/elasticsearch:7.17.3
      resources:
        requests:
          cpu: "500m"
          memory: "1Gi"
        limits:
    ```

```
      cpu: "1"
      memory: "2Gi"
  minimumMasterNodes: 1
  clusterName: "jaeger-elasticsearch"
  nodeGroup: "data"
```

For Kiali, create a file named kiali-values.yaml:

```
auth:
  strategy: anonymous  # For testing. Use 'token' in production
deployment:
  view_only_mode: false
  accessible_namespaces: ["**"]
external_services:
  prometheus:
    url: http://prometheus-server.istio-observability.svc.
    cluster.local
  grafana:
    url: http://grafana.istio-observability.svc.cluster.local
  tracing:
    url: http://jaeger-query.istio-observability.svc.cluster.
    local:16686
server:
  web_root: /kiali
```

Install Kiali now with Helm:

```
helm install kiali kiali/kiali-server \
  --namespace istio-observability \
  -f kiali-values.yaml
```

Verifying Your Observability Stack Installation

After we've installed our components, we need to ensure that everything works properly. This verification method is similar to performing a health check on our observability system. Let us divide this down into multiple steps:

CHAPTER 6   ESTABLISHING OBSERVABILITY FOUNDATIONS IN ISTIO: INFRASTRUCTURE, TRACING, AND METRICS

```
# Check pod status
kubectl get pods -n istio-observability
```

A healthy deployment should show output similar to this:

```
NAME                                                   READY   STATUS    RESTARTS   AGE
grafana-f88cc454d-qs7pt                                1/1     Running   0          23m
jaeger-7566cfbd68-ldpdx                                1/1     Running   0          4m1s
prometheus-alertmanager-0                              1/1     Running   0          38m
prometheus-kube-state-metrics-88947546-vsbnj           1/1     Running   0          38m
prometheus-prometheus-node-exporter-hbr7d              1/1     Running   0          38m
prometheus-prometheus-pushgateway-9f8c968d6-p8d9c      1/1     Running   0          38m
prometheus-server-6b884dc7f6-9lm99                     2/2     Running   0          38m
kiali-6b587b5559-zspjx                                 1/1     Running   0          10m
```

The READY column indicates if all containers in each pod are running. For example, Prometheus displays 2/2 since it operates both the server and configuration reloader containers, and if any pods indicate a status other than Running or if the READY count differs from the expected number of containers, we'll need to investigate further. By looking at the pod logs, we will be able to investigate any problems in greater depth:

```
# For Prometheus
kubectl logs -n istio-observability deploy/prometheus-server

# For Grafana
kubectl logs -n istio-observability deploy/grafana
```

```
# For Jaeger
kubectl logs -n istio-observability deploy/jaeger

# For Kiali
kubectl get pods -n istio-observability -l app=kiali
```

Next, let's verify network connectivity by setting up port forwarding to access each service's web interface:

```
# Create port forwarding for all services
kubectl port-forward -n istio-observability svc/grafana 3000:80 &
kubectl port-forward -n istio-observability svc/prometheus-server 9090:80 &
kubectl port-forward -n istio-observability svc/jaeger-query 16686:16686 &
kubectl port-forward -n istio-observability svc/kiali 20001:20001
```

With these ports forwarded, we can now verify each component's functionality.

As shown in Figure 6-1, Prometheus can be found at http://localhost:9090, and the UI should be operational, and Kiali can be found at http://localhost:20001. Similarly, with Grafana, go to http://localhost:3000 and the default login credentials can be retrieved as follows:

- Username: admin

- Password: (Retrieve using the following command)

    ```
    kubectl get secret -n istio-observability grafana -o jsonpath="{.data.admin-password}" | base64 --decode ; echo
    ```

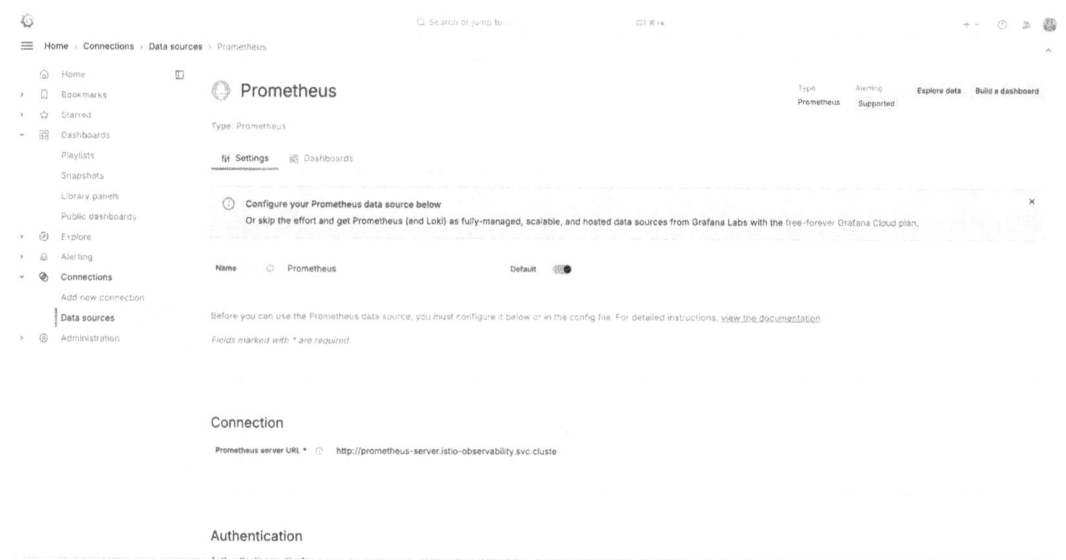

Figure 6-1. *Prometheus web interface showing functional setup and query results*

Once logged in, verify that the Prometheus data source is configured correctly by navigating to Connections ➤ Data Sources. You should see Prometheus listed. Click the Prometheus data source and click "Save & test." You should see a response "Successfully queried the Prometheus API."

For Jaeger, navigate to `http://localhost:16686`. The interface should load and display the available services in the dropdown menu; if no services appear, this is normal until we generate trace data.

Reinstalling Istio with Observability Configuration

As mentioned earlier we need to reinstall Istio with a custom configuration so that it can interact with the observability components we created in the previous section. You can find the custom mesh configuration file under the CHAPTER-6 folder with name mesh-config.yaml:

```
istioctl uninstall -y --purge
```

```
istioctl install -f mesh-config.yaml
```

The IstioOperator is a core custom resource in Istio that acts as the primary configuration interface for controlling and modifying your service mesh installation. Consider it a primary control panel where you can specify how your entire mesh should operate and what features should be enabled. When you build an IstioOperator resource, you can customize several features of Istio, such as core mesh settings, component installations, feature gates, and extension providers like monitoring and tracing systems. One of its most significant features is that it takes a declarative approach: you declare the desired state of your mesh, and Istio's operator controller works continuously to preserve that state, making it ideal for GitOps processes. The IstioOperator resource allows you to adjust everything from fundamental settings like enabling and disabling capabilities to more complicated configurations like designing custom profiles, setting resource restrictions, configuring gateways, and establishing observability pipelines, allowing you to carefully tune your service mesh to your individual requirements, whether you're running a tiny development environment or a large-scale production system. This configuration is version-controlled and readily reproducible across different environments, which makes it an indispensable tool for ensuring consistency in your Istio installations. You can read more about IstioOperator at https://istio.io/latest/docs/reference/config/istio.operator.v1alpha1/.

The following snippet from `mesh-config.yaml` captures the important details that we will discuss more:

```yaml
enableTracing: true
defaultConfig:
    tracing: {} # disable MeshConfig tracing options
  extensionProviders:
  - name: jaeger
    opentelemetry:
      port: 4317
      service: jaeger-collector.istio-observability.svc.cluster.local
  - name: prometheus
    prometheus: {}
  - name: otel
    envoyOtelAls:
      service: jaeger-collector.istio-observability.svc.cluster.local
      port: 4317
  defaultProviders:
    accessLogging:
    - envoy
    - otel
```

The included IstioOperator configuration file is crucial for enabling observability in your Istio service mesh, establishing a robust monitoring and tracing infrastructure by combining two critical components, Jaeger for distributed tracing and Prometheus for collecting metrics (we will be installing these tools in the next section). The configuration starts with enabling tracing throughout the entire mesh using the enableTracing: true directive, which allows you to track requests as they pass through the microservices. The configuration creates an OpenTelemetry-based tracing pipeline that sends trace data to a Jaeger collector service operating on port 4317 within the istio-observability namespace. The use of OpenTelemetry over earlier protocols such as Zipkin reflects a forward-thinking strategy, as OpenTelemetry has become the industry standard for observability data collection. The configuration also adds Prometheus as a metrics provider for automatically collecting and storing key performance indicators from your services and thus delivering a comprehensive observability solution that allows us to monitor, debug, and understand the behavior of our distributed applications running within the service mesh.

Sample Application

To see Istio's observability features in action, we'll look at a real-world ecommerce application (the most common example in many scenarios; we believe this example makes it easier to understand the concepts of observability rather than spending time understanding the application logic itself) that demonstrates distributed tracing, metrics collection, and logging across multiple services and will show you how requests flow through a service mesh and how Istio's telemetry tools can provide insights into your system's behavior.

Architecture Overview

As shown in Figure 6-2, our sample app uses three microservices to build a simple order processing flow: order service, inventory service, and payment service. When a customer submits an order, the order service serves as the entry point, working with the inventory service to determine product availability and the payment service to complete the transaction; this design uses standard microservice patterns like service-to-service communication, synchronous API calls, and distributed transaction management.

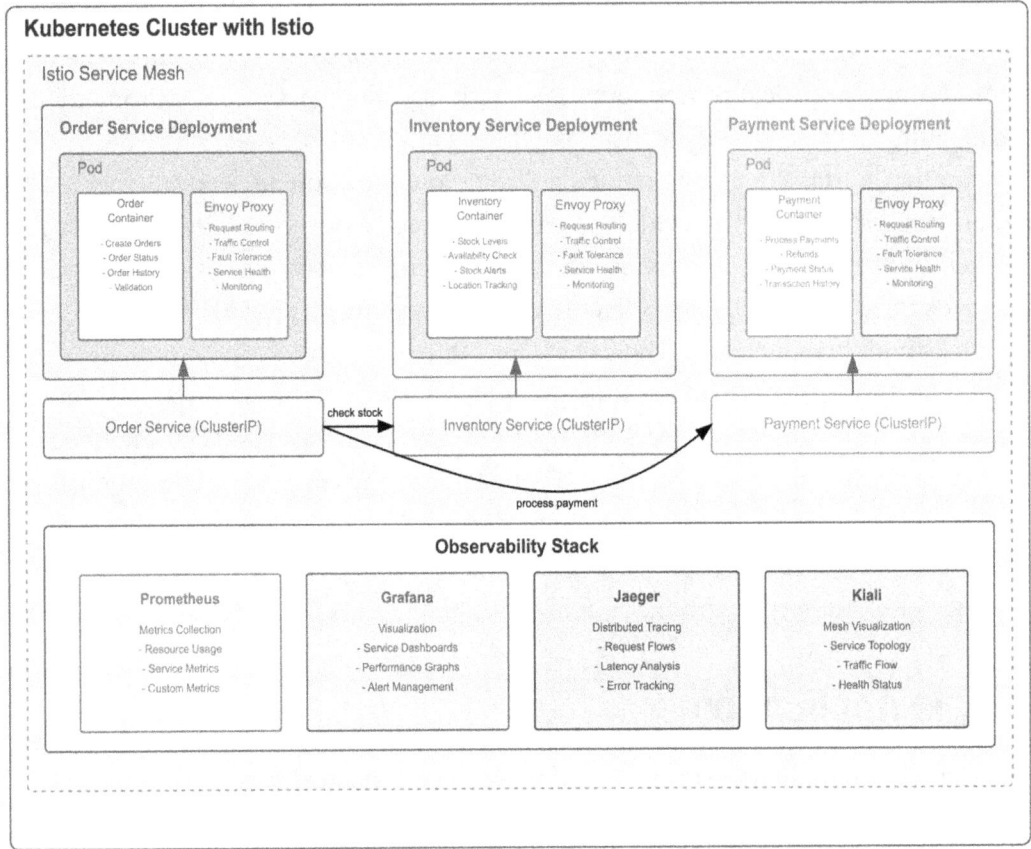

Figure 6-2. Sample ecommerce application architecture with three microservices (order service, inventory service, and payment service)

Service Implementation

The application is designed with Spring Boot, which provides a strong foundation for developing microservices, and each service is constructed as a standalone Spring Boot app, with REST controllers, service layers, and observability configurations. The order service monitors order volumes and success rates, the inventory service keeps track of stock levels and checks latencies, and the payment service measures transaction throughput and success ratios. The chapter's repository contains the whole source code for all three services.

The services use Spring's RestTemplate for inter-service communication and implement JSON-formatted logging with correlation IDs for request tracing. Each service also exposes custom metrics for business-critical operations, complementing Istio's automatically collected proxy-level metrics.

Kubernetes Deployment

We'll use Kubernetes manifests that define the deployments and services that are needed to run our sample app, and each microservice has its deployment configuration that tells it how many replicas to use, what container images to use, and how many resources it needs. These manifests have the proper labels and selectors that Istio needs to set up the service mesh and collect metrics. There are also Prometheus alert rules in the deployment files for keeping an eye on the health of the service. These rules cover error rates, response times, and resource utilization.

Rather than including the complete manifest files here, you can find them in the chapter's source code repository. The key points are the service mesh–specific annotations and labels that enable Istio's automatic sidecar injection and telemetry collection.

Deployment Process

The deployment process follows a systematic approach starting with building each Spring Boot application and creating Docker images. We make a dedicated namespace for our sample application, enable Istio injection, and apply the Kubernetes manifests. Also, the deployment comprises defining Prometheus alert rules for service health monitoring, enabling log aggregation, and establishing metrics collecting endpoints.

Observing the Application

Once deployed, you can view the application's activity through various lenses. Jaeger offers a distributed tracing visualization that displays the whole path of each request, Prometheus captures both service-level data (order volumes and payment success rates) and proxy-level information (request latencies and error rates), the structured logs provide a rich context for debugging, and finally customized alarms inform you of any service health issues, business irregularities, or resource limits.

CHAPTER 6   ESTABLISHING OBSERVABILITY FOUNDATIONS IN ISTIO: INFRASTRUCTURE, TRACING, AND METRICS

Learning Objectives

This sample application serves several educational purposes:

- Demonstrates the practical implementation of distributed tracing across different services

- Demonstrates how to collect metrics at the service and mesh levels, as well as effective logging strategies using correlation and structured formats

- Shows examples of useful alert setups depending on business and technical metrics

- Provides hands-on experience using Istio's entire observability stack

Working with this sample application will provide you with hands-on experience of Istio's observability features and help you learn how to apply them to your microservices architectures. The full source code, metric configurations, logging settings, and alert definitions are available in the GitHub repository of the book.

Finally, before wrapping up this section, let's quickly review the setup and code structure that is attached with this chapter:

1. We have built three microservices, and they can be found under the `ecommerce-istio` folder of the chapter-3 source code folder. All the three microservices are built using Spring Boot and Maven and can be imported into your favorite IDE. Do a `mvn clean install` to set up the project. To simplify things all these services use the in-memory database H2. Remember a restart of the deployment/pod/containers will erase the database.

2. Once you have set up the project, you can build the respective images using the below Docker commands and push them into your Docker repo:

   ```
   docker build -t order-service:2.0.4 -f order-service/Dockerfile .
   docker tag order-service:2.0.4 <docker-repo>/order-service:2.0.4
   docker push <docker-repo>/order-service:2.0.4
   ```

   ```
   docker build -t inventory-service:2.0.4 -f inventory-service/Dockerfile .
   ```

CHAPTER 6   ESTABLISHING OBSERVABILITY FOUNDATIONS IN ISTIO: INFRASTRUCTURE, TRACING, AND METRICS

```
docker tag inventory-service:2.0.4 <docker-repo>/inventory-
service:2.0.4
docker push <docker-repo>/inventory-service:2.0.4

docker build -t payment-service:2.0.4 -f payment-service/
Dockerfile .
docker tag payment-service:2.0.4 <docker-repo>/payment-
service:2.0.4
docker push <docker-repo>/payment-service:2.0.4
```

3. You can deploy all these images into Kubernetes using the manifest files under the kubernetes-manifests folder by running the below kubectl command once you are inside the folder:

```
kubectl create namespace ecommerce
```

```
kubectl label namespace ecommerce istio-injection=enabled
```

```
kubectl apply -f payment-service/.
```

```
kubectl apply -f inventory-service/.
```

```
kubectl apply -f order-service/.
```

4. Do a port-forward and check if you are able to access the services at the respective health endpoints:

```
kubectl port-forward -n ecommerce service/order-service
8080:8080 &
kubectl port-forward -n ecommerce service/payment-service
8082:8082 &
kubectl port-forward -n ecommerce service/inventory-service
8081:8081
```

You should find the order service at http://localhost:8080/actuator/health, the inventory service at http://localhost:8081/actuator/health, and finally the payment service at http://localhost:8083/actuator/health.

5. We have also included sample database scripts in the database folder. You can copy the SQL and run it in the H2 Console. The H2 Console will be accessible at the /h2-console for each of the services. Your database URI for connecting to H2 DB is jdbc:h2:mem:orderdb, jdbc:h2:mem:paymentdb, and jdbc:h2:mem:inventorydb and the password is "password".

6. To test all the microservices, let's call our order service using curl. After you do the curl, feel free to explore the Jaeger traces, Prometheus metrics, and Kiali for your service:

```
curl -X POST 'http://localhost:8080/api/orders' \
-H 'Content-Type: application/json' \
-d '{
    "customerId": "CUST-001",
    "items": [
        {
            "productId": "PROD-001",
            "quantity": 1,
            "unitPrice": 1299.99,
            "productName": "Dell XPS 13 Laptop",
            "productCategory": "Electronics"
        },
        {
            "productId": "PROD-008",
            "quantity": 2,
            "unitPrice": 49.99,
            "productName": "Java Programming Guide",
            "productCategory": "Books"
        }
    ],
    "customerNote": "Please deliver during business hours",
    "promoCode": "WELCOME10"
}'

{"orderId":"8a9af5ba-9dce-4d32-ac97-856b02ec7416","status":
"COMPLETED","message":"Order processed successfully","items":
```

CHAPTER 6   ESTABLISHING OBSERVABILITY FOUNDATIONS IN ISTIO: INFRASTRUCTURE, TRACING, AND METRICS

```
[{"productId":"PROD-001","quantity":1,"unitPrice":1299.99,
"subtotal":null,"productName":null,"productCategory":null},
{"productId":"PROD-008","quantity":2,"unitPrice":49.99,"subtotal"
:null,"productName":null,"productCategory":null}],"totalAmount":
1399.97,"createdAt":"2025-01-01T05:00:24.828019221","traceId":
null,"requestId":null}
```

7. Since we have to test Istio's observability feature, we have to go through Istio's ingress gateway. As mentioned in Chapter 4, start Kind's cloud provider that provides an external IP address to your ingress gateway:

```
sudo cloud-provider-kind
```

8. Create the virtual services and destinations rules. Navigate to the kubernetes-manifests folder and apply the virtual services and destination rules. Note that we changed the URI paths in virtual services:

```
kubectl apply -f .
```

9. Finally, you should start seeing an external IP address for your services as shown in Figure 6-3 and should be able to create an order using the below curl.

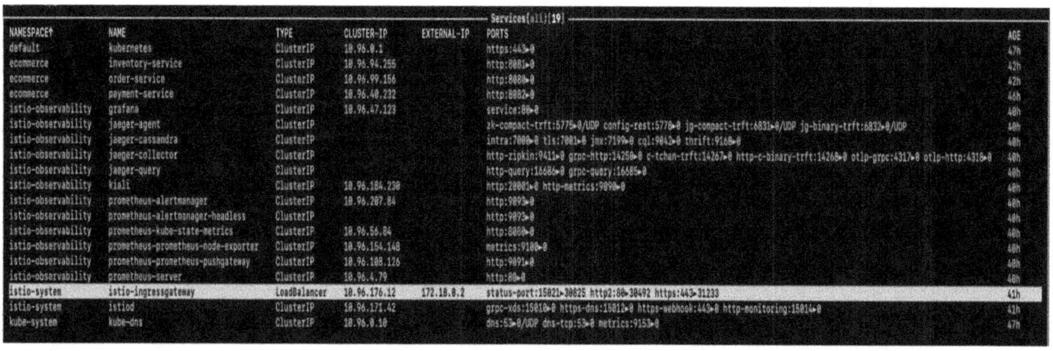

Figure 6-3. External IP address assignment for services in the cluster

```
curl -X POST 'http://172.18.0.2/orders/api' \
-H 'Content-Type: application/json' \
```

```
    -d '{
        "customerId": "CUST-001",
        "items": [
            {
                "productId": "PROD-001",
                "quantity": 1,
                "unitPrice": 1299.99,
                "productName": "Dell XPS 13 Laptop",
                "productCategory": "Electronics"
            },
            {
                "productId": "PROD-008",
                "quantity": 2,
                "unitPrice": 49.99,
                "productName": "Java Programming Guide",
                "productCategory": "Books"
            }
        ],
        "customerNote": "Please deliver during business hours",
        "promoCode": "WELCOME10"
    }'
```

Telemetry API

Before we start our journey with the observability stack, we need to understand why we need Istio's Telemetry API. The Telemetry API represents a revolutionary approach to managing observability within Istio service meshes. Rather than wrestling with scattered configurations across various components, it provides a unified, declarative method for handling all aspects of observability through Kubernetes custom resources. This centralized approach significantly simplifies the complexity that typically comes with monitoring distributed systems.

At its foundation, the API is built on several key components that work together to provide thorough observability. The foundation is built on Kubernetes custom resources, which enable us to manage telemetry settings in a way that is both familiar to Kubernetes users and robust enough to handle sophisticated observability requirements. Also, this method is ideally aligned with modern infrastructure-as-code (IaC) practices, allowing us to version control our observability configurations and easily replicate them across several environments.

Prior to the Telemetry API, configuring observability in Istio involved working with multiple disconnected configurations, which frequently required changes in multiple places to meet a single observability target. The Telemetry API addresses this by providing a unified, Kubernetes-native approach to managing all aspects of observability.

The extensibility of the Telemetry API is what makes it extremely powerful. While we'll go into metrics, tracing, and logging setups in greater detail in subsequent sections, it's worth noting that the API provides a consistent approach to configure all of these features. This consistency makes it easier to learn and use while maintaining the flexibility required for complicated observability requirements.

In the upcoming sections, we will delve deeper into specific configurations for tracing, monitoring, and logging. We'll also look at how to leverage the Telemetry API to create advanced observability patterns and integrate with multiple backends, but for the time being, the main takeaway is that the Telemetry API offers a uniform, Kubernetes-native mechanism to handle observability settings.

Distributed Tracing

Distributed tracing is one of the most powerful weapons in our observability armory, particularly when working with microservices architectures. Consider it a GPS system for your requests; it follows a request's full route as it passes through several services, providing precise information about where it went, how long it stayed at each stop, and what transpired along the way. In our ecommerce application, this is particularly helpful because a single order placing requires numerous services to function together.

Let's look at what happens when a customer places an order using our system. The request initiates a lengthy route that includes using the order service, checking availability using the inventory service, and eventually processing payment with the payment service. Understanding this flow without distributed tracing would be like attempting to put together a story from fragments; you might see parts of what happened in each service's logs, but you'd miss the big picture.

Remember our mesh-config.yaml from our earlier sections that we have provided as input to our istioctl install. This is where you will be defining your trace provider configuration. We will be later referring this provider by name when we want to set up and further customize our configuration:

```
extensionProviders:
  - name: jaeger
    opentelemetry:
      port: 4317
      service: jaeger-collector.istio-observability.svc.cluster.local
  - name: prometheus
    prometheus: {}
```

You can read more about extensionProviders and other configurations in Istio's MeshConfig documentation (https://istio.io/latest/docs/reference/config/istio.mesh.v1alpha1/#MeshConfig).

In distributed tracing, meaningful observability is built on the ability to correlate spans across various services. While Istio's proxies generate individual spans for service-to-service communication, obtaining a complete end-to-end trace necessitates further context propagation through your applications, and this propagation mechanism ensures that separately generated spans can be combined to provide a coherent narrative of request flow.

A set of standardized HTTP headers serves as the foundation for trace context propagation. These headers function as a digital thread, linking separate spans into a single trace, and when a request enters your service mesh, it includes these trace context headers. Your applications must carefully preserve this context by passing these headers to any subsequent outbound requests they make. This forwarding approach establishes an unbroken chain of context, allowing tracing backends to recreate the whole course of a request.

In our ecommerce application, for example, consider what happens when a customer places an order. The initial request might hit our order service, which then communicates with both the inventory service for checking the inventory and the payment service for connecting with the payment gateway. To maintain trace continuity, each service must propagate the trace context headers they receive. In the case of our Spring Boot microservices, we use the TraceContextFilter that extracts the context from the incoming request and makes the extracted context current, and here is how that looks like in practice:

```
@Override
public void doFilter(ServletRequest request, ServletResponse response,
FilterChain chain)
        throws IOException, ServletException {
  HttpServletRequest httpRequest = (HttpServletRequest) request;

  // Extract the context from the incoming request
  Context extractedContext = openTelemetry.getPropagators().
  getTextMapPropagator()
          .extract(Context.current(), httpRequest, getter);

  // Make the extracted context current
  try (Scope scope = extractedContext.makeCurrent()) {
      chain.doFilter(request, response);
  }
}
```

The specific headers that need propagation depend on your chosen tracing backend. For most modern deployments, the W3C Trace Context standard headers form the primary mechanism:

- traceparent: Carries the core trace identification and parent span information
- tracestate: Provides additional vendor-specific trace correlation data

Istio's proxy (Envoy) also relies on its own header:

- x-request-id: Enables consistent sampling decisions and log correlation across the mesh

If you're using Zipkin as your tracing backend, you'll need to propagate additional B3-format headers that carry Zipkin-specific trace correlation data:

- x-b3-traceid: The overarching trace identifier
- x-b3-spanid: The current span's identifier
- x-b3-parentspanid: The identifier of the parent span
- x-b3-sampled: Indicates whether this trace should be sampled
- x-b3-flags: Carries debug and other trace flags

Understanding and implementing adequate trace context propagation transforms distributed tracing from a collection of disconnected spans to an effective tool for analyzing request flow through your system. In the following sections, we'll look at how to efficiently use this traced data to monitor and debug the issues in your service mesh.

Configuring Tracing

Using Telemetry API

Istio's tracing configuration takes a layered approach, giving you both high-level and granular control over your tracing infrastructure. In this section, we'll look at two complementary methods for configuring tracing: the Telemetry API, which provides a declarative, Kubernetes-native way to manage tracing configurations, and the MeshConfig approach combined with pod annotations, which provides fine-grained control over tracing behavior. Understanding these configuration approaches is critical to developing a comprehensive observability strategy that meets your system's requirements.

The Telemetry API that we discussed earlier provides a declarative way to configure tracing across your service mesh. Here's how we configure tracing in our ecommerce application:

```
apiVersion: telemetry.istio.io/v1
kind: Telemetry
metadata:
 name: mesh-default
 namespace: istio-system
spec:
 tracing:
 - providers:
   - name: jaeger
   randomSamplingPercentage: 100.00
   customTags:
     provider:
       literal:
         value: "jaeger"
     environment:
```

```
          literal:
            value: "ecommerce-istio-trace"
        service_version:
          literal:
            value: "2.0.4"
```

In this configuration, we've made several important decisions. First, we're utilizing Jaeger as our tracing provider, which is a reliable distributed tracing solution that works well with Istio. We have set the sampling percentage to 100%, which means we will capture every request. While this provides maximum visibility, in production scenarios, you may want to lower this percentage to reduce overhead.

The custom tags that we've included serve a vital purpose. The environment tag helps us distinguish between different deployment settings, whereas the service version tag allows us to associate traces with specific versions of our services. These tags are quite useful when diagnosing problems or evaluating request trends.

Using MeshConfig and Pod Annotations

Configuring distributed tracing in Istio involves setting up both mesh-wide parameters and workload-specific settings. Let's explore how to use MeshConfig and pod annotations to establish a robust tracing infrastructure in our ecommerce application.

Understanding MeshConfig for Tracing

MeshConfig provides the foundation for tracing across your entire service mesh. In our application, we configure this through a custom mesh configuration:

```
apiVersion: install.istio.io/v1alpha1
kind: IstioOperator
spec:
 meshConfig:
   enableTracing: true
   defaultConfig:
     tracing: {} # disable MeshConfig tracing options
   extensionProviders:
   - name: jaeger
     opentelemetry:
```

```
      port: 4317
      service: jaeger-collector.istio-observability.svc.cluster.local
  - name: prometheus
    prometheus: {}
```

This configuration establishes several critical components. The 100% sampling rate ensures that we catch every request that passes through our mesh, which is especially useful during the development and testing phases, and the custom tags provide additional context, allowing us to determine where traces originate. In an ecommerce context, understanding the environment and cluster helps us monitor issues across our deployment landscape.

Workload-Specific Tracing Configuration

Individual workloads frequently require unique tracing parameters, while mesh-wide settings serve as a baseline. In our ecommerce application, we accomplish this using pod annotations. (Please note we can also accomplish the same thing using a ProxyConfig resource. We will leave that as an exercise to the readers. Please refer to the documentation https://istio.io/latest/docs/reference/config/networking/proxy-config/ for more information.) Here is how we configure the payment service:

```
proxy.istio.io/config: |
      tracing:
        sampling: 100
        customTags:
          service_type:
            literal:
              value: "payment-processing"
          payment_version:
            environment:
              name: PAYMENT_VERSION
              defaultValue: "2.3.0"
```

We use OpenTelemetry for instrumentation in our application, which integrates seamlessly with Istio's tracing infrastructure. You can learn more about OpenTelemetry and the available APIs at https://opentelemetry.io/. The OpenTelemetryConfig class in our services demonstrates this integration:

```
@Bean
public OpenTelemetry openTelemetry() {
    // Create resource attributes that identify your service
    Resource serviceResource = Resource.getDefault()
            .merge(Resource.create(Attributes.builder()
                    // Add standard service identification attributes
                    .put(ResourceAttributes.SERVICE_NAME, serviceName)
                    .put(ResourceAttributes.SERVICE_NAMESPACE,
                    serviceNamespace)
                    .put(ResourceAttributes.DEPLOYMENT_ENVIRONMENT,
                    deploymentEnvironment)
                    // Add container and kubernetes-specific attributes if
                        available
                    .put(ResourceAttributes.CONTAINER_ID,
                            System.getenv().getOrDefault("HOSTNAME",
                            "unknown"))
                    .put(ResourceAttributes.K8S_POD_NAME,
                            System.getenv().getOrDefault("POD_NAME",
                            "unknown"))
                    .put(ResourceAttributes.K8S_NAMESPACE_NAME,
                            System.getenv().getOrDefault("POD_NAMESPACE",
                            serviceNamespace))
                    .build()));

    // Configure how spans are exported to Jaeger
    OtlpGrpcSpanExporter spanExporter = OtlpGrpcSpanExporter.builder()
            .setEndpoint(jaegerEndpoint)
            .build();

    // Configure the tracer provider with sampling and export settings
    SdkTracerProvider sdkTracerProvider = SdkTracerProvider.builder()
            // Set up sampling strategy - what percentage of traces
                to record
            .setSampler(Sampler.traceIdRatioBased(samplerProbability))
            // Configure batch processing of spans for better performance
```

```
            .addSpanProcessor(BatchSpanProcessor.builder(spanExporter).
            build())
            // Add the resource attributes to all spans
            .setResource(serviceResource)
            .build();

    // Build the OpenTelemetry SDK with all our configuration
    return OpenTelemetrySdk.builder()
            .setTracerProvider(sdkTracerProvider)
            // Configure W3C trace context propagation
            .setPropagators(ContextPropagators.create(W3CTraceContextPropaga
            tor.getInstance()))
            .buildAndRegisterGlobal();
}
```

This configuration ensures our application-level traces integrate properly with Istio's mesh-level tracing, providing a complete picture of request flow through our system.

Once we have configured the openTelemetry bean, we inject the bean into the tracer method in the same class that creates the tracer bean, which is later injected into our services to log the spans:

```
/**
 * Creates a tracer for the application to use when creating spans.
 * This tracer will be used throughout the application to create spans.
 */
@Bean
public Tracer tracer(OpenTelemetry openTelemetry) {
    return openTelemetry.getTracer(serviceName);
}

public class InventoryService {

    ...
    private final Tracer tracer;

    ...
```

```java
// Create span with semantic conventions for inventory operations
Span span = tracer.spanBuilder("inventory.check")
    .setAttribute(SemanticAttributes.CODE_FUNCTION, "checkInventory")
    .setAttribute("inventory.product.id", request.getProductId())
    .setAttribute("inventory.requested.quantity", request.
    getRequestedQuantity())
    .startSpan();
```

Also remember when our order service calls both the payment service and inventory service, we still have to pass the trace context along when this call happens. For this, we will add an interceptor to the `RestTemplateConfig` that intercepts the request and adds the trace context. Figure 6-4 shows the request flow:

```java
// Custom interceptor to handle trace context propagation
private static class OpenTelemetryInterceptor implements
ClientHttpRequestInterceptor {
    private final OpenTelemetry openTelemetry;

    public OpenTelemetryInterceptor(OpenTelemetry openTelemetry) {
        this.openTelemetry = openTelemetry;
    }

    @Override
    public ClientHttpResponse intercept(HttpRequest request, byte[] body,
                                        ClientHttpRequestExecution
                                        execution) throws IOException {
        // Always inject the context, regardless of the current span
        openTelemetry.getPropagators().getTextMapPropagator()
                .inject(Context.current(), request.getHeaders(), SETTER);

        // Execute the request

        return execution.execute(request, body);
    }
}
```

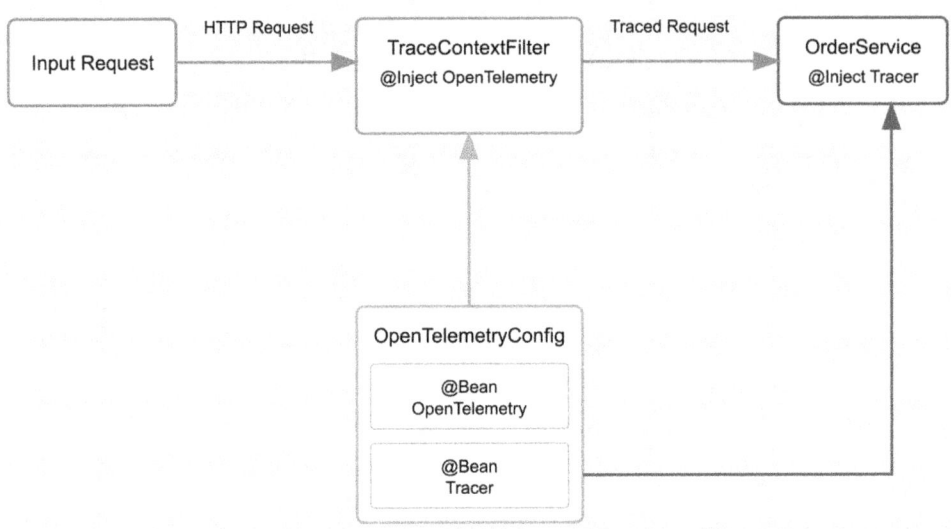

Figure 6-4. Request flow showing trace context propagation through the microservices

Distributed Tracing with Jaeger

Now that we've configured everything, let's have a look at the path of a request using Jaeger. Distributed tracing in a microservices architecture creates new challenges for understanding how requests move through your system. Jaeger addresses these issues by giving a comprehensive picture of request journeys that span service boundaries. In our ecommerce application, this is especially useful because a single client action, such as placing an order, includes many different services working together.

When you visit Jaeger's interface at http://localhost:16686, you'll be provided with a sophisticated suite of tools for examining distributed traces as shown in Figure 6-5. The interface organizes information hierarchically, beginning with service selection. Our ecommerce application includes three primary services: order service, inventory service, and payment service, each of them exposing a variety of operations, including order creation, inventory verification, and payment processing.

CHAPTER 6   ESTABLISHING OBSERVABILITY FOUNDATIONS IN ISTIO: INFRASTRUCTURE, TRACING, AND METRICS

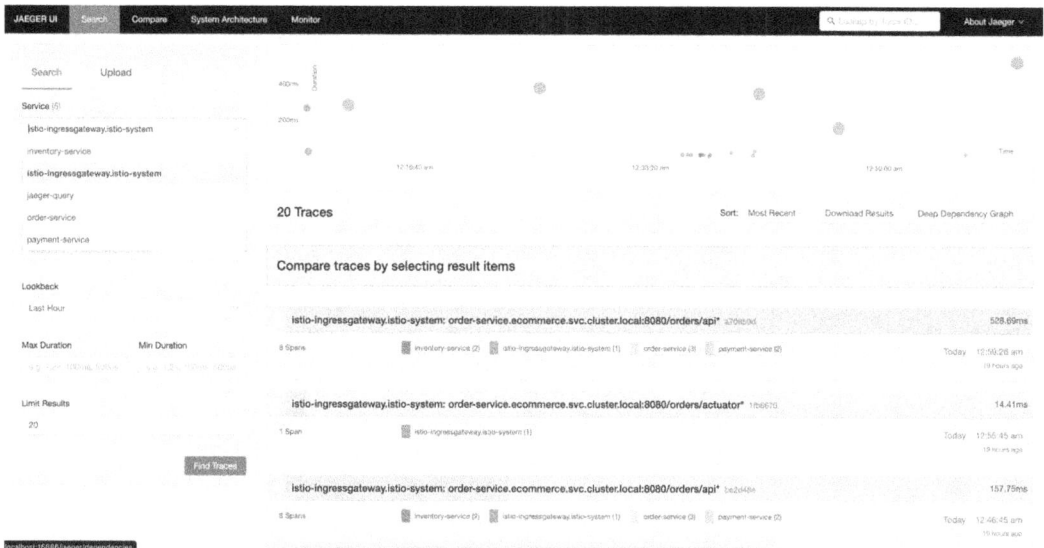

Figure 6-5. *Jaeger's interface providing sophisticated tools for examining distributed traces*

The search interface lets you filter traces based on a variety of factors. For example, while examining a customer complaint about a failed order, you could look for traces with the order ID or filter for traces with errors. This capability is extremely useful when debugging issues in production scenarios.

Analyzing Request Flows

Consider what happens when a customer places an order in our system. The trace begins with the ingress gateway controller. As our curl hits the ingress endpoint `http://<ingress-endpoint>/orders/api`, the ingress gateway forwards the request to OrderController in the order service as shown in Figure 6-6.

CHAPTER 6   ESTABLISHING OBSERVABILITY FOUNDATIONS IN ISTIO: INFRASTRUCTURE, TRACING, AND METRICS

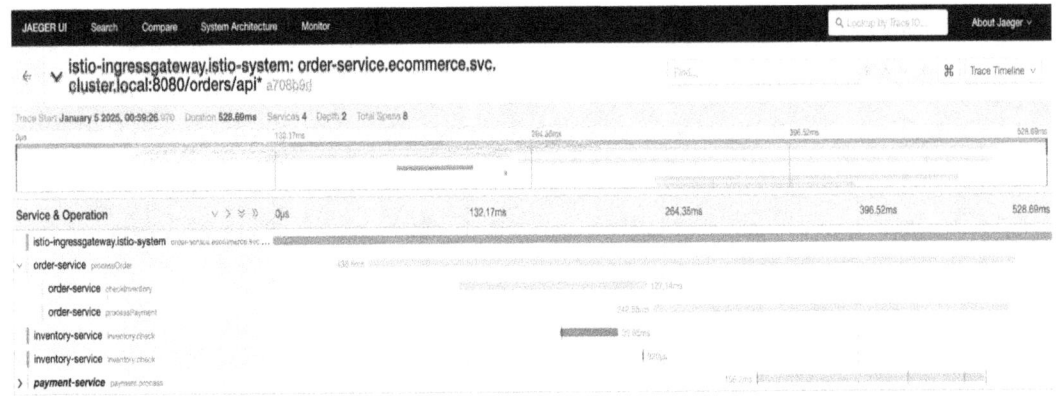

Figure 6-6. *Ingress gateway forwarding request to OrderController in the order service*

From here, Jaeger shows us how the request flows through our system. The following code in OrderService creates a span:

```
@Transactional
public OrderResponse processOrder(OrderRequest orderRequest) {
    ...

    // Create a span using OpenTelemetry's span builder
    Span span = tracer.spanBuilder("processOrder")
            .setAttribute("customerId", orderRequest.getCustomerId())
            .startSpan();

    // Use try-with-resources for proper context management
    try (Scope scope = span.makeCurrent()) {
        ...

    } catch (Exception e) {
        log.error("Error processing order", e);
        // Record error details using OpenTelemetry conventions
        span.setStatus(StatusCode.ERROR, e.getMessage());
        span.recordException(e);

        meterRegistry.counter("order.errors",
                "error_type", e.getClass().getSimpleName()).increment();
```

CHAPTER 6 ESTABLISHING OBSERVABILITY FOUNDATIONS IN ISTIO: INFRASTRUCTURE, TRACING, AND METRICS

```
            return OrderResponse.failure("Order processing failed: " +
            e.getMessage());
        } finally {
            span.end(); // End the span in finally block
        }
    }
}
```

We will continue adding new spans as the request flows through the system. Here OrderService checks for inventory availability and creates a child span as shown in Figure 6-7:

```
private boolean checkInventory(Order order) {
    // Create child span with current context as parent
    Span span = tracer.spanBuilder("checkInventory")
            .setAttribute(SemanticAttributes.CODE_FUNCTION,
            "checkInventory")
            .setAttribute("orderId", order.getOrderId())
            .startSpan();

    try (Scope scope = span.makeCurrent()) {
        ...
```

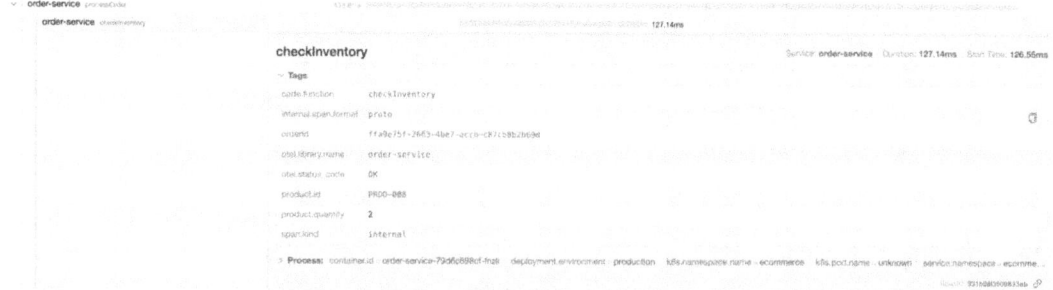

Figure 6-7. *OrderService checking for inventory availability and creating a child span*

The trace continues as the request moves to payment processing as shown in Figure 6-8. Each step adds its span, creating a complete picture of the request's journey:

```
@Transactional
public PaymentResponse processPayment(PaymentRequest request) {
    Span span = tracer.spanBuilder("payment.process")
            .setAttribute("payment.order_id", request.getOrderId())
```

```
.setAttribute("payment.amount", request.getAmount().toString())
.startSpan();
```

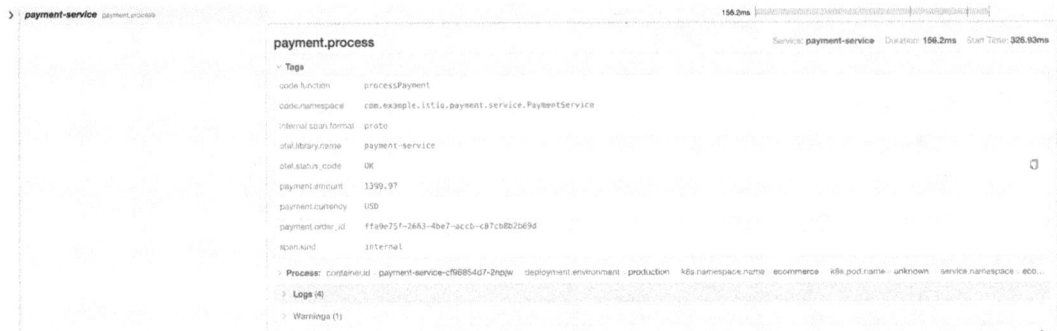

Figure 6-8. Request flow continuing to payment processing with span creation

Enhancing Trace Context

Our tracing method is particularly effective because of the additional context we add to each span. Beyond basic timing and relationship data, we supplement our traces with business-related information. In the payment service, for example, we include information about the transaction:

```
span.setAttribute("payment.order_id", request.getOrderId())
    .setAttribute("payment.amount", request.getAmount().toString())
    .setAttribute("payment.currency", request.getCurrency())
    .setAttribute("payment.method", request.getPaymentMethod());
```

This additional context turns technical traces into useful business insights, and when investigating issues, we can learn not only that a payment failed but also about the specifics of the attempted transaction.

In practice, these traces become invaluable for a variety of operational purposes. When a consumer reports a failed order, we can immediately retrieve the appropriate trace by using the order ID. The trace reveals precisely where the failure occurred, what caused it, and what the system was attempting to perform at the time; this visibility significantly reduces the time required to detect and fix issues.

Furthermore, we can use trace data to identify performance bottlenecks. By analyzing trace durations and patterns, we can spot services or operations that might need optimization. This proactive approach to performance management helps maintain a responsive and efficient system.

Configuring Trace Sampling and Trace Tags

Trace sampling and tag configuration are critical components of distributed tracing that help to combine observability requirements with system performance. The Telemetry API and workload annotations in Istio allow us to customize these settings at different levels. Let's look at how to design effective sampling algorithms and relevant trace tags using our ecommerce application as an example.

Trace Sampling Configuration

Sampling influences the percentage of requests traced in your system. While tracing every request maximizes visibility, it might have an impact on performance and increase storage costs. In our ecommerce application, we configure sampling using the Telemetry API:

```
apiVersion: telemetry.istio.io/v1alpha1
kind: Telemetry
metadata:
  name: tracing-config
  namespace: istio-system
...
    providers:
    - name: jaeger
      randomSamplingPercentage: 100.0
```

This configuration sets a 100% sampling rate, meaning every request flowing through our service mesh gets traced. For production environments, you might want to adjust this based on your traffic volume and observability requirements. For instance, you might reduce it to 1% for high-traffic services while maintaining higher sampling rates for critical paths:

```
apiVersion: telemetry.istio.io/v1alpha1
kind: Telemetry
metadata:
```

```
  name: payment-tracing
  namespace: ecommerce
spec:
  selector:
    matchLabels:
      app: payment-service
  tracing:
  - customTags:
      service_type:
        literal:
          value: "payment-processing"
    providers:
    - name: jaeger
    randomSamplingPercentage: 50.0
```

This configuration applies a 50% sampling rate specifically to our payment service, ensuring we capture more traces for this critical component while maintaining lower sampling rates elsewhere.

Custom Trace Tags

Trace tags offer context to traces, making it easier to link them with business processes and operational metrics. In our ecommerce application, we set up custom tags at the mesh and service levels.

At the mesh level, we can define common tags for all services:

```
apiVersion: telemetry.istio.io/v1alpha1
kind: Telemetry
metadata:
  name: mesh-tracing
  namespace: istio-system
spec:
  tracing:
  - customTags:
      deployment_environment:
        literal:
          value: "production"
```

CHAPTER 6   ESTABLISHING OBSERVABILITY FOUNDATIONS IN ISTIO: INFRASTRUCTURE, TRACING, AND METRICS

```
    service_version:
      environment:
        name: "VERSION"
        defaultValue: "unknown"
```

For specific services, we can add more detailed tags. Here's how we configure tags for our order service in our application:

```
apiVersion: telemetry.istio.io/v1alpha1
kind: Telemetry
metadata:
  name: order-tracing
  namespace: ecommerce
spec:
  selector:
    matchLabels:
      app: order-service
  tracing:
  - customTags:
      order_type:
        literal:
          value: "ecommerce"
      customer_tier:
        header:
          name: "x-customer-tier"
          defaultValue: "standard"
```

We can also add custom tags in our application code using OpenTelemetry instrumentation:

```
Span span = tracer.spanBuilder("processOrder")
    .setAttribute("customerId", orderRequest.getCustomerId())
    .setAttribute("orderAmount", order.getTotalAmount().toString())
    .setAttribute("itemCount", order.getItems().size())
    .startSpan();
```

These tags become invaluable when analyzing traces in Jaeger. For example, while examining a failed order, we can filter traces by customer tier or order amount ranges to find service behavior patterns.

Based on our implementation experience, here are some key recommendations:

1. Start with higher sampling rates during development and testing, and then adjust based on production traffic volumes and performance requirements.

2. Use context-based sampling whenever possible; for crucial business processes, sample more frequently than for routine health checks.

3. Design tags hierarchically—start with broad categories (environment, service) and drill down to specific business contexts (order_type, payment_processor).

4. Include version information in tags to help track issues during deployments.

5. Consider storage implications—while detailed tags provide rich context, they also increase trace storage requirements.

These configurations will allow us to keep extensive insight into our ecommerce system while minimizing the overhead of distributed tracing. The use of thoughtful sample rates and relevant tags means that we can efficiently debug problems and understand system behavior in production.

Metrics Collection with Prometheus

Observability is a critical aspect of managing distributed systems, and metrics form the backbone of any observability strategy. Istio provides extensive support for metrics collection, leveraging Prometheus as the default telemetry backend. By integrating with Prometheus, Istio enables powerful insights into service behavior, application health, and system performance. This section explores how to configure Prometheus for Istio, understand its metrics architecture, and harness these metrics to gain actionable insights.

Understanding Istio's Metrics Architecture

Istio's architecture of metrics revolves around an advanced system of metrics collection points scattered all over your service mesh. Envoy proxies lie at the very center of this—watching all network traffic moving between your services and being very diligent about it. The proxies don't only watch traffic; they actively collect and maintain detailed statistics for every interaction, building a comprehensive view of your service mesh's behavior.

In our ecommerce application, the collection process begins when a request enters the mesh via the Istio ingress gateway, and as the request travels from the gateway to the order service, and possibly to the inventory and payment services, each Envoy proxy along the way collects critical information. These statistics include not just request counts, but also extensive telemetry data like latencies, response codes, and payload sizes.

The metrics collection points in Istio are carefully located at various levels of your infrastructure. Istiod provides metrics on Istio's internal activities via an endpoint at `http://istiod.<namespace>:15014/metrics`. These metrics provide critical insights into Istio's performance, allowing operators to understand everything from configuration processing times to resource distribution patterns and several critical metrics including

- Configuration processing statistics
- Validation operations
- Resource distribution metrics
- Control plane health indicators

`pilot_xds_push_time`, `pilot_proxy_convergence_time`, `pilot_conflict_outbound_listener_tcp_over_current_tcp`, and other Prometheus metrics are examples of those on the control plane.

Every Envoy proxy has its own metrics endpoint at `http://<pod-ip>:15090/stats/prometheus` at the data plane level, and this endpoint provides a glimpse of the real traffic that passes through your services. These endpoints record all of the interactions that take place when a customer puts an order through our ecommerce system: the requests first go through the ingress gateway, then the order service's processing of the request, the inventory check, and finally the payment processing. Metrics produced by

Chapter 6 Establishing Observability Foundations in Istio: Infrastructure, Tracing, and Metrics

each stage aid in our comprehension of the functionality and health of our system. Istio automatically configures this endpoint, which offers comprehensive metrics regarding

- Request counts and latencies
- TCP connection statistics
- Circuit breaker statistics
- Upstream/downstream connections

Examples of these metrics include `istio_requests_total`, `istio_request_duration_milliseconds`, `istio_tcp_connections_closed_total`, etc.

We already installed Prometheus through the Helm charts at the beginning of this chapter, which installs the required CRDs and config maps that we are going to discuss in this section. Prometheus seamlessly integrates with this architecture by means of a meticulously crafted scraping configuration and is preconfigured to automatically discover and collect metrics from all Istio-enabled services in your cluster by default. This configuration is stored in a Kubernetes ConfigMap, which tells Prometheus where to find metrics, how often to collect them, and how to label them for easier querying.

All Envoy proxy metrics are accessible through the primary metrics endpoint at `15090/stats/prometheus` that gives detailed insights into traffic flow through your mesh, including request counts, latencies, and error rates. If enabled, the second endpoint at `15020/metrics` exposes the application's metrics, enabling the collection of both service mesh and application-specific metrics.

What is particularly ingenious about this system is the automatic addition of the requisite Prometheus annotations to your services by Istio:

```
prometheus.io/scrape: "true"
prometheus.io/port: "15090"
prometheus.io/path: "/stats/prometheus"
```

These annotations act as signals to Prometheus, telling it exactly where to find metrics for each service. This automatic configuration means that as soon as you deploy a new service into your mesh, Prometheus knows how to find and collect its metrics without any manual intervention.

The beauty of this system lies in its automation. When you install Prometheus through the standard Helm charts, it comes preconfigured to look for these annotations. The Prometheus configuration includes service discovery rules, which detect services with certain annotations and begin scraping their metrics.

CHAPTER 6   ESTABLISHING OBSERVABILITY FOUNDATIONS IN ISTIO: INFRASTRUCTURE, TRACING, AND METRICS

Because of this automated discovery process, every new service you add to your mesh becomes observable by default. When a request flows through your system, such as from an ingress gateway to several services, Prometheus automatically collects metrics from each hop, providing you with complete visibility into the request's path.

Modifying this configuration allows you to fine-tune your metrics collection strategy. For example, you may want to vary the scrape frequency for different services based on their importance or performance impact. In our ecommerce application, we may require more frequent metrics collecting for the payment service than for less crucial components. This customization is accomplished by modifying the Prometheus ConfigMap in your cluster.

To update the Prometheus configuration, first retrieve the current configuration from your cluster using kubectl, and after making the appropriate changes to the scrape configurations, label selectors, or retention policies, you can apply them to the cluster. However, some changes may necessitate a restart of the Prometheus pod to take effect.

Let's say you want to modify the Prometheus configuration that's already running in your cluster. Here's how to do it.

First, fetch the current configuration:

```
kubectl get configmap prometheus-server -n istio-observability -o yaml > prometheus-config.yaml
```

Edit the configuration, for example, to change the scrape interval and add new job configurations:

```yaml
apiVersion: v1
kind: ConfigMap
metadata:
  name: prometheus-server
  namespace: istio-observability
data:
  prometheus.yml: |
    global:
      scrape_interval: 10s     # Decrease scrape interval from 15s to 10s
      evaluation_interval: 10s

    scrape_configs:
      - job_name: 'istio-mesh'
```

```yaml
      kubernetes_sd_configs:
      - role: endpoints
      relabel_configs:
      - source_labels: [__meta_kubernetes_service_annotation_prometheus_
        io_scrape]
        action: keep
        regex: true
      metric_relabel_configs:
      - source_labels: [__name__]
        regex: 'istio_requests_total|istio_request_duration_.*'  # Only
        keep specific metrics
        action: keep
```

Apply the updated configuration:

```
kubectl apply -f prometheus-config.yaml
```

Restart the Prometheus pod to apply changes:

```
kubectl rollout restart deployment/prometheus-server -n istio-observability
```

You might want to add custom scrape configurations for specific services. Here's how:

```yaml
scrape_configs:
  - job_name: 'custom-service-metrics'
    kubernetes_sd_configs:
    - role: endpoints
      namespaces:
        names:
          - ecommerce  # Target specific namespace
    relabel_configs:
    - source_labels: [__meta_kubernetes_service_label_app]
      regex: 'order-service|payment-service'  # Target specific services
      action: keep
    - source_labels: [__meta_kubernetes_pod_container_port_name]
      regex: 'http-metrics'
      action: keep
```

This configuration would

- Only scrape pods in the 'e-commerce' namespace
- Only target services labeled as 'order-service' or 'payment-service'
- Only scrape ports named 'http-metrics'

When we set up Prometheus monitoring in our service mesh, we have two primary approaches for telling Prometheus what metrics to collect and how to collect them: ConfigMaps and ServiceMonitor and PodMonitor. Consider ConfigMaps to be a detailed written document that provides directions, whereas ServiceMonitors and PodMonitors are automated navigation systems that react to route modifications. While Istio automatically exposes metrics via Envoy proxies, ServiceMonitors and PodMonitors offer a more extensive control over how Prometheus identifies and scrapes these data and provide fine-grained control over your metrics collection strategy. You can learn more about the PrometheusOperator, which contains all these configurations, at https://github.com/prometheus-operator/prometheus-operator.

When troubleshooting metrics collection, understanding the link between Istio's metrics endpoints and Prometheus' scraping configurations is critical. Also, you can confirm that metrics are being collected correctly by visiting the Prometheus targets page, which displays all scraped endpoints and their current status. If metrics are missing, reviewing the Prometheus logs frequently can reveal issues with endpoint accessibility or scraping setups.

Istio and Prometheus work together in this design to provide comprehensive insight into your service mesh. Combining Istio's detailed metrics collection with Prometheus' extensive storage and querying capabilities provides a solid basis for monitoring and analyzing your microservices' activities. This information will be invaluable as you seek to maintain and improve the performance and dependability of your service mesh.

When you start analyzing the collected metrics, you'll realize how powerful this arrangement is. By querying Prometheus, you can discover patterns in service activity, detect performance bottlenecks, and predict future issues before they affect your users, and this proactive approach to monitoring, supported by Istio's complete metrics architecture, contributes to the stability and performance of your microservices system.

Standard Istio Metrics

Understanding Istio's metrics is critical for efficiently monitoring your service mesh. Istio provides a complete collection of metrics at both the proxy and service levels, providing you full visibility into your system's activities. Let's try to skim through some of these important metrics with examples from our ecommerce application. Please refer to the Istio documentation for the complete list of metrics.

Proxy-Level Request Metrics

The Envoy proxies (sidecars) that are deployed alongside your services capture proxy-level metrics. These metrics provide precise insights on the network-level behavior of your services. When a consumer puts an order through our ecommerce system, the request creates several proxy-level metrics as it travels through the mesh.

Metric Name	Type	Description	Use Case Example
istio_requests_total	Counter	Total number of requests handled by an Istio proxy. Includes labels for response code, service name, source/destination workload	Tracks overall service traffic patterns and error rates
istio_request_duration_ milliseconds	Distribution	Time taken to process requests (both service time and network latency)	Monitors service latency and identifies performance bottlenecks
istio_request_bytes	Distribution	Size of HTTP request bodies	Monitors bandwidth usage and identifies large requests
istio_response_bytes	Distribution	Size of HTTP response bodies	Tracks data transfer patterns and optimizes response sizes
istio_request_ messages_total	Counter	Total number of gRPC messages sent	Monitors gRPC communication patterns
istio_response_ messages_total	Counter	Total number of gRPC messages received	Tracks gRPC service responsiveness

The most fundamental metric in your service mesh is `istio_requests_total`. This counter monitors every request that passes through an Istio proxy, delivering detailed information through its extensive labeling system. When you look at this metric, you'll notice labels for the source workload (who made the request), destination service (who received it), and response code (what happened). For example, if we look at our payment service traffic, we may notice this metric indicating that the order service sent 100 successful requests to the payment service in the last five minutes, all with response code 200, and by tracking how this measure evolves over time, we can identify anomalous traffic patterns or rising mistake rates before they affect users.

To understand how quickly your services respond, Istio provides `istio_request_duration_milliseconds`. Unlike simple averages that might hide important patterns, this histogram metric gives you a complete picture of request latency distribution. Think of it like a detailed map of every request's journey time. When your inventory service starts to respond slowly to some queries, this metric might help you determine whether the issue affects all requests or just a subset, and you can use it to monitor your 95th percentile latency, which is a critical indicator of how long the slowest 5% of requests take. This is extremely useful when creating and monitoring service-level objectives (SLOs).

Data volume monitoring comes through the paired metrics `istio_request_bytes` and `istio_response_bytes`. These distribution metrics work together like a two-way traffic counter. The request bytes metric shows you how much data services are receiving, while response bytes reveals how much they're sending back. This becomes very significant when troubleshooting performance issues. For example, if your product catalog service suddenly begins to send significantly larger responses than usual, these metrics will alert you instantly. This could imply a lack of pagination or inefficient data retrieval that has to be optimized.

For services using gRPC, Istio provides the specialized counters: `istio_request_messages_total` and `istio_response_messages_total`. Unlike the traditional HTTP metrics that track request-response pairs, these metrics manage the streaming capabilities of gRPC. They are useful mainly when building real-time features; in our ecommerce platform, we use them to monitor our real-time inventory update system, ensuring that stock level changes propagate correctly across services.

Let's look at a practical example. You can start by monitoring your overall traffic patterns with `istio_requests_total`. This gives you a baseline understanding of service behavior. Watch the error rates by filtering for different response codes. Next, use `istio_request_duration_milliseconds` to ensure your services meet their performance targets. Keep an eye on both average latency and percentiles—a service might have good average performance but still frustrate some users with occasional slow responses.

For data-heavy services, keep an eye on request and response bytes metrics to spot any optimization opportunities: a sudden spike in response size might indicate the opportunity to apply pagination or filtering of responses. Lastly, when using gRPC, track the flow of messages with the messages_total metrics to make sure your streaming communications remain healthy.

Here's a practical example from our ecommerce platform. Assume during a recent flash sale, we are required to monitor our order processing pipeline. We can use the below metrics to achieve it:

```
# Monitor order service request rate and success
rate(istio_requests_total{
  destination_service="order-service.ecommerce.svc.cluster.local",
  response_code=~"2.*"
}[5m])

# Track payment processing latency (95th percentile)
histogram_quantile(0.95,
  rate(istio_request_duration_milliseconds_bucket{
    destination_service="payment-service.ecommerce.svc.cluster.local"
  }[5m])
)

# Monitor inventory update message flow
rate(istio_request_messages_total{
  service_istio_io_canonical_name="inventory-service"
}[5m])
```

This combination of metrics can help us ensure smooth operations during peak traffic, quickly identifying and addressing any bottlenecks that emerge.

Proxy-Level Connection Metrics

In a service mesh, the connection patterns play an important role in understanding how the health and performance of the systems are maintained. The proxy-level connection metrics provide very detailed insight into how the services communicate with each other at the TCP level. Think of these metrics as the dashboard of a network administrator for your service mesh, telling you precisely how many connections are being made, how they're being utilized, and when they're closed.

Metric Name	Type	Description	Use Case Example
istio_tcp_connections_opened_total	Counter	Total number of TCP connections opened	Monitors connection establishment patterns
istio_tcp_connections_closed_total	Counter	Total number of TCP connections closed	Identifies connection lifecycle issues
istio_tcp_received_bytes_total	Counter	Total bytes received over TCP connections	Tracks inbound network traffic
istio_tcp_sent_bytes_total	Counter	Total bytes sent over TCP connections	Monitors outbound network traffic

The `istio_tcp_connections_opened_total` counter tracks each new TCP connection established in your mesh. Consider this metric to be similar to a doorway counter in a crowded store; it indicates how many new connections your services are initiating. For example, when your payment service connects to an external payment gateway, this number is incremented. Monitoring this measure allows you to spot unexpected patterns in connection formation. A quick increase may indicate a connection pool misconfiguration, but a dip could indicate connectivity difficulties.

Its counterpart, `istio_tcp_connections_closed_total`, tells us how connections are being terminated. This metric is particularly valuable for detecting connection leaks. In a healthy system, the number of connections established should roughly equal the number of connections terminated over some time period. A significant difference between these metrics may indicate that your services are not properly closing their connections. For instance, if your inventory service keeps database connections open for too long, you'll see this reflected in the related metrics.

The volume of data flowing through these connections is captured by two important metrics. First, `istio_tcp_received_bytes_total` measures inbound network traffic. This counter helps you understand how much data your services are receiving. Say your order service receives big batches of orders; this metric would help you track the volume of incoming data and plan capacity accordingly. Similarly, the istio_tcp_sent_bytes_total observes the outbound traffic and will show how much data your services are sending.

These metrics become very valuable in troubleshooting performance-related issues or during the planning of network capacity.

The following is a real-world application of these combined metrics in action. Assume you are monitoring the database connection patterns for an ecommerce platform's inventory service:

```
# Monitor connection establishment rate
rate(istio_tcp_connections_opened_total{destination_workload="inventory-mysql"}[5m])

# Compare with connection closure rate
rate(istio_tcp_connections_closed_total{destination_workload="inventory-mysql"}[5m])

# Track data transfer volume
rate(istio_tcp_received_bytes_total{destination_workload="inventory-mysql"}[5m])
```

These queries would help you identify if your inventory service is

- Creating too many new database connections (connection pool issues)
- Properly closing connections after use (resource management)
- Transferring unexpected amounts of data (potential query optimization needs)

Remember to correlate these metrics with application-level metrics for a complete picture. For instance, a surge in TCP connections may occur during a sale event on your ecommerce platform, and these metrics can help you differentiate between typical business operations and possible issues.

Service-Level Traffic Metrics

Understanding that Istio does not directly produce service-level metrics as distinct entities is crucial when talking about service-level metrics in Istio, and what we often call "service-level metrics" are actually generated from the proxy-level metrics that Envoy collects. Understanding this distinction is essential to properly monitoring your services.

The metrics that we frequently consider to be service-level metrics are actually proxy-level data aggregations and transformations, usually carried out using PromQL queries. Let's look at how we can derive these important service-level insights from the proxy-level metrics Istio provides.

Request Rate Monitoring

Instead of a direct istio_requests_rate metric, we calculate the request rate using the istio_requests_total counter. Here's how we would monitor our order service's request rate:

```
rate(istio_requests_total{destination_workload="order-service"}[5m])
```

During our ecommerce application's normal operations, this query might show 50 requests per second, and during high-traffic events like flash sales, we might see this spike to 200 requests per second or more.

Error Rate Analysis

We determine error rate by comparing error responses to total requests, rather than using a pre-calculated metric:

```
sum(rate(istio_requests_total{destination_workload="payment-service",response_code=~"5.*"}[5m]))
/
sum(rate(istio_requests_total{destination_workload="payment-service"}[5m]))
* 100
```

This calculation gives us our service's error rate percentage. In our payment service, we typically aim to keep this below 1% during normal operations. However, during service deterioration, we may see this rise to worrying levels such as 15%, suggesting possible issues that require prompt action.

Request Duration Patterns

We monitor request durations using the istio_request_duration_milliseconds histogram metric:

```
histogram_quantile(0.95,
  rate(istio_request_duration_milliseconds_bucket{
    destination_workload="order-service"
  }[5m])
)
```

This query lets us monitor our 95th percentile latency, which is an important indicator of service performance. At the 95th percentile, we expect our ecommerce platform's order service to process requests in 200 ms or less.

Understanding the link between proxy-level data and service-level insights is critical to effective monitoring. While Istio does not provide pre-calculated service-level metrics, its extensive proxy-level telemetry data, when properly aggregated and analyzed, provides us with all of the information we require to efficiently monitor our services.

This approach is more flexible than using predefined service-level metrics since it allows us to develop custom aggregations and calculations that exactly match our monitoring requirements, for example, in an ecommerce application, we may wish to determine two sorts of error rates, one for technical mistakes (5xx responses) and one for business validation errors (particular 4xx responses), which we can easily do by writing the proper PromQL queries.

Recall that the art of effective service monitoring in Istio goes beyond just knowing what metrics are available; it also means truly understanding how to modify and integrate proxy-level information to arrive at meaningful service-level insights.

Circuit Breaking Metrics

Circuit breaking is a crucial pattern in distributed systems that helps prevent cascading failures. While Istio provides circuit breaking functionality via Envoy proxies, it is crucial to note that, like service-level metrics, there are no direct metrics for circuit breaking. To monitor circuit breaker behavior, we need to look at standard request metrics with specified response flags.

CHAPTER 6 ESTABLISHING OBSERVABILITY FOUNDATIONS IN ISTIO: INFRASTRUCTURE, TRACING, AND METRICS

The `istio_requests_total` counter with the response flag "UO" (Upstream Overflow) is the most significant metric for monitoring circuit breaker activity in Istio; this metric indicates that requests were refused due to circuit breaking conditions. Here's how to check circuit breaker activity:

```
# Track requests rejected by circuit breaking
sum(rate(istio_requests_total{
  destination_service="payment-service.ecommerce.svc.cluster.local",
  response_flags="UO"
}[5m]))
```

In our ecommerce application, this query helps us understand how often our circuit breakers are triggering. For example, if we're seeing a sudden increase in rejected requests during a flash sale, it might indicate that our payment service is receiving more requests than it can handle safely.

To put these rejections in context, we often want to calculate the percentage of requests being rejected by circuit breakers:

```
# Calculate percentage of requests being rejected by circuit breakers
sum(rate(istio_requests_total{
  destination_service="payment-service.ecommerce.svc.cluster.local",
  response_flags="UO"
}[5m])) /
sum(rate(istio_requests_total{
  destination_service="payment-service.ecommerce.svc.cluster.local"
}[5m])) * 100
```

This ratio provides valuable insight into the health of our services. In our ecommerce platform, we typically aim to keep this percentage very low (below 1%) during normal operations. However, seeing this percentage increase during incidents or high-load situations isn't necessarily bad—it indicates our circuit breakers are doing their job by protecting services from being overwhelmed.

It's worth noting that while we might expect to see specific circuit breaker metrics like "circuit_breaker_open" or "circuit_breaker_trips," Istio's approach is to represent this information through standard request metrics with specific response flags. This integration with the regular metrics system allows us to correlate circuit breaker events with other service behaviors easily.

To implement effective circuit breaker monitoring in your service mesh, consider these key practices:

1. Monitor the rate of overflow-flagged requests to understand how often circuit breakers are triggering.

2. Calculate the percentage of rejected requests to gauge the impact on your overall traffic.

3. Correlate circuit breaker events with other service metrics like error rates and latency.

4. Set up alerts for when circuit breaker rejection rates exceed acceptable thresholds.

For example, in our payment service, we might set up an alert when the circuit breaker rejection rate exceeds 5% over a five-minute period, indicating a significant service health issue:

```
# Alert condition for excessive circuit breaking
(sum(rate(istio_requests_total{
  destination_service="payment-service.ecommerce.svc.cluster.local",
  response_flags="UO"
}[5m])) /
sum(rate(istio_requests_total{
  destination_service="payment-service.ecommerce.svc.cluster.local"
}[5m]))) * 100 > 5
```

Understanding how to monitor circuit breaker behavior through these metrics is crucial for maintaining reliable services in your mesh. While the approach might seem indirect compared with dedicated circuit breaker metrics, it provides all the information needed to ensure your services remain resilient under load.

Security Metrics

Security observability is a critical aspect of running a service mesh in production. While Istio provides robust security features like mutual TLS and authorization policies, monitoring their effectiveness requires understanding the specific security-related metrics available to us.

CHAPTER 6   ESTABLISHING OBSERVABILITY FOUNDATIONS IN ISTIO: INFRASTRUCTURE, TRACING, AND METRICS

The primary security-related metrics in Istio focus on mTLS (mutual TLS) status and connection security. Here are the key metrics we can use:

```
Istio_requests_total{connection_security_policy="mutual_tls", destination_service="payment-service.ecommerce.svc.cluster.local" }
```

This metric helps us track the number of requests using mutual TLS. In our ecommerce application, we can use this to ensure all service-to-service communication is properly secured. For example, here's how to calculate the percentage of traffic using mTLS:

```
sum(rate(istio_requests_total{
  connection_security_policy="mutual_tls",
  destination_service="payment-service.ecommerce.svc.cluster.local"
}[5m])) /
sum(rate(istio_requests_total{
  destination_service="payment-service.ecommerce.svc.cluster.local"
}[5m])) * 100
```

For authorization policy monitoring, we can track denied requests:

```
istio_requests_total{
  response_code="403",
  destination_service="payment-service.ecommerce.svc.cluster.local"
}
```

This helps us understand how often requests are being denied due to authorization policies, which is particularly important for sensitive services like our payment processing endpoint.

For comprehensive security monitoring in your service mesh, focus on these key aspects:

1. Monitor mTLS adoption rates across services.

2. Track authorization policy enforcement through 403 response codes.

3. Observe patterns in denied requests to identify potential security issues.

4. Set up alerts for unexpected changes in security-related metrics.

For example, in our payment service, we might want to alert on any non-mTLS traffic:

```
# Alert condition for non-mTLS traffic
sum(rate(istio_requests_total{
  connection_security_policy!="mutual_tls",
  destination_service="payment-service.ecommerce.svc.cluster.local"
}[5m])) > 0
```

By carefully monitoring these metrics and setting appropriate alerts, you can maintain a strong security posture and quickly identify potential security issues before they become serious problems.

Commonly Used Labels

As we have already seen across several examples before this section, all these metrics can be filtered and aggregated using the following standard labels. For the complete list of labels, please refer to the Istio documentation: https://istio.io/latest/docs/reference/config/metrics/.

Label Name	Description	Example Value
source_workload	Name of the source workload	order-service
source_namespace	Namespace of the source workload	ecommerce
destination_workload	Name of the target workload	payment-service
destination_namespace	Namespace of the target workload	ecommerce
request_protocol	Protocol of the request	http, grpc, tcp
response_code	HTTP status code	200, 404, 500
response_flags	Additional context about the response	UH (Upstream Unhealthy)
connection_security_policy	Security policy applied	mutual_tls, none

Standard Envoy Proxy Metrics

Apart from the standard metrics emitted by Istio, the envoy proxies create their own metrics. Understanding Envoy metrics is crucial for comprehensive observability in Istio,

CHAPTER 6   ESTABLISHING OBSERVABILITY FOUNDATIONS IN ISTIO: INFRASTRUCTURE, TRACING, AND METRICS

as Envoy proxies are the workhorses of the service mesh. These proxies generate a rich set of metrics that provide deep insights into the network behavior and performance of your services. Let's explore these metrics in detail.

As discussed earlier, In Istio, each Envoy proxy exposes its metrics through a dedicated port (15090) at the /stats/prometheus endpoint. These metrics are automatically scraped by Prometheus, thanks to the annotations Istio adds to your pods. The raw metrics are exposed in Prometheus format, making them readily available for querying and visualization.

To understand Envoy's metrics, let's first verify what's available. We can do this by port forwarding to any sidecar proxy in our mesh and examining the /stats/prometheus endpoint:

```
kubectl port-forward pod/<your-pod-name> 15090:15090
curl localhost:15090/stats/prometheus
```

This will show us the complete raw list of Envoy metrics as shown in the below Figure 6-9.

```
$curl localhost:15090/stats/prometheus
# TYPE envoy_cluster_assignment_stale counter
envoy_cluster_assignment_stale{cluster_name="xds-grpc"} 0
# TYPE envoy_cluster_assignment_timeout_received counter
envoy_cluster_assignment_timeout_received{cluster_name="xds-grpc"} 0
# TYPE envoy_cluster_assignment_use_cached counter
envoy_cluster_assignment_use_cached{cluster_name="xds-grpc"} 0
# TYPE envoy_cluster_bind_errors counter
envoy_cluster_bind_errors{cluster_name="xds-grpc"} 0
# TYPE envoy_cluster_default_total_match_count counter
envoy_cluster_default_total_match_count{cluster_name="xds-grpc"} 1
# TYPE envoy_cluster_http2_dropped_headers_with_underscores counter
envoy_cluster_http2_dropped_headers_with_underscores{cluster_name="xds-grpc"} 0
# TYPE envoy_cluster_http2_goaway_sent counter
envoy_cluster_http2_goaway_sent{cluster_name="xds-grpc"} 0
# TYPE envoy_cluster_http2_header_overflow counter
envoy_cluster_http2_header_overflow{cluster_name="xds-grpc"} 0
# TYPE envoy_cluster_http2_headers_cb_no_stream counter
envoy_cluster_http2_headers_cb_no_stream{cluster_name="xds-grpc"} 0
# TYPE envoy_cluster_http2_inbound_empty_frames_flood counter
envoy_cluster_http2_inbound_empty_frames_flood{cluster_name="xds-grpc"} 0
# TYPE envoy_cluster_http2_inbound_priority_frames_flood counter
envoy_cluster_http2_inbound_priority_frames_flood{cluster_name="xds-grpc"} 0
# TYPE envoy_cluster_http2_inbound_window_update_frames_flood counter
envoy_cluster_http2_inbound_window_update_frames_flood{cluster_name="xds-grpc"} 0
# TYPE envoy_cluster_http2_keepalive_timeout counter
envoy_cluster_http2_keepalive_timeout{cluster_name="xds-grpc"} 0
# TYPE envoy_cluster_http2_metadata_empty_frames counter
envoy_cluster_http2_metadata_empty_frames{cluster_name="xds-grpc"} 0
# TYPE envoy_cluster_http2_outbound_control_flood counter
envoy_cluster_http2_outbound_control_flood{cluster_name="xds-grpc"} 0
# TYPE envoy_cluster_http2_outbound_flood counter
envoy_cluster_http2_outbound_flood{cluster_name="xds-grpc"} 0
# TYPE envoy_cluster_http2_requests_rejected_with_underscores_in_headers counter
envoy_cluster_http2_requests_rejected_with_underscores_in_headers{cluster_name="xds-grpc"} 0
```

Figure 6-9. *Complete raw list of Envoy metrics displayed in Prometheus format*

Given the extensive list of the metrics available, we will quickly skim over some of the important categories and the metrics in each of these categories. Avid readers can explore the complete list at https://www.envoyproxy.io/docs.

Cluster Metrics (Tracking Upstream Service Communication)

Cluster metrics form the backbone of understanding service-to-service communication in your mesh. These metrics focus on how Envoy proxies handle requests to upstream services—other services that your application depends on.

When Envoy proxies traffic to another service (like when your order service calls the payment service), it creates what it calls a "cluster." Think of a cluster as Envoy's internal representation of an upstream service. Every request your service makes to another service flows through this cluster configuration, generating these metrics. The following are some of the important cluster metrics generated by the envoy proxies.

Metric Name	Type	Description	Example Use Case
envoy_cluster_upstream_rq_total	Counter	Total requests made to the upstream service	Understanding overall traffic patterns to dependencies
envoy_cluster_upstream_rq_active	Gauge	Currently active requests	Monitoring real-time load on upstream services
envoy_cluster_membership_healthy	Gauge	Number of currently healthy hosts	Monitoring service instance health
envoy_cluster_membership_total	Gauge	Total number of cluster members	Understanding cluster capacity
envoy_cluster_upstream_cx_total	Counter	Total connections to upstream	Tracking connection establishment patterns
envoy_cluster_upstream_cx_active	Gauge	Currently active upstream connections	Monitoring connection pool usage
envoy_cluster_upstream_cx_connect_timeout	Counter	Connection timeouts	Identifying connectivity issues

Listener Metrics (Handling Incoming Traffic)

The Envoy listener manager metrics serve as your early warning system and diagnostic toolkit for understanding how network traffic is being handled in your service mesh. Think of these metrics as a dashboard that shows you both the health and configuration status of your network listeners—the components responsible for accepting and routing all incoming traffic to your services. These metrics become invaluable when troubleshooting issues or validating changes in your service mesh. For example, if you're deploying a new version of a service or updating routing rules, you can watch the listener metrics to ensure the changes are being applied correctly: an increase in envoy_listener_manager_listener_modified tells you Istio is updating the configuration, while envoy_listener_manager_total_listeners_warming and envoy_listener_manager_total_listeners_active help confirm that these changes are successfully taking effect. During normal operations, these metrics help you detect potential problems before they impact users—a spike in envoy_listener_manager_listener_create_failure might indicate a configuration issue, while unexpected changes in envoy_listener_manager_total_listeners_active could signal network problems. By monitoring these metrics, operators can maintain confidence in their service mesh's networking layer and quickly respond to any issues that arise, making them essential tools for running a reliable and observable service mesh. The following are some of the important metrics in this category.

Metric Name	Type	Description	Common Use Cases
Lifecycle Metrics			
envoy_listener_manager_listener_added	Counter	Total listeners added through static config or LDS	Tracks listener creation events; monitors configuration changes
envoy_listener_manager_listener_modified	Counter	Total listeners modified via LDS	Monitors dynamic configuration updates; tracks reconfiguration frequency
envoy_listener_manager_listener_removed	Counter	Total listeners removed via LDS	Tracks service removal or configuration cleanup
envoy_listener_manager_listener_stopped	Counter	Total listeners stopped	Monitors graceful shutdown events

(continued)

Metric Name	Type	Description	Common Use Cases
Operational Status			
envoy_listener_manager_listener_create_success	Counter	Total listener objects successfully added to workers	Verifies successful configuration applications
envoy_listener_manager_listener_create_failure	Counter	Total failed listener object additions to workers	Detects configuration issues or resource problems
envoy_listener_manager_listener_in_place_updated	Counter	Total listener objects created for filter chain updates	Tracks efficient listener updates
State Gauges			
envoy_listener_manager_total_listeners_warming	Gauge	Number of currently warming listeners	Monitors listener initialization phase
envoy_listener_manager_total_listeners_active	Gauge	Number of currently active listeners	Tracks operational listener count
envoy_listener_manager_total_listeners_draining	Gauge	Number of currently draining listeners	Monitors graceful shutdown progress
envoy_listener_manager_total_filter_chains_draining	Gauge	Number of currently draining filter chains	Tracks filter chain cleanup
Worker Status			
envoy_listener_manager_workers_started	Gauge	Boolean (1 if started, 0 otherwise) indicating listener initialization status	Basic health check of listener subsystem

These metrics together provide extensive visibility into Envoy's listener management mechanism. As an example, during a configuration update, you may notice

- envoy_listener_manager_listener_modified increment
- envoy_listener_manager_total_listeners_warming temporarily increase
- envoy_listener_manager_listener_create_success increment
- envoy_listener_manager_total_listeners_draining briefly rise
- Finally, envoy_listener_manager_total_listeners_active stabilize at the expected value

Understanding these patterns helps identify both normal operations and potential issues in your service mesh's networking layer.

Server Metrics (Proxy Health and Performance)

Understanding the health and performance of Envoy proxies is critical for ensuring a reliable service mesh. By providing information into how each proxy performs at the system level, operators can ensure the mesh's foundation remains robust. Let's look at the major server metrics that Envoy provides.

Metric Name	Type	Description	Example Use Case
envoy_server_memory_allocated	Gauge	Current memory usage	Monitoring proxy resource usage
envoy_server_uptime	Counter	Server uptime in seconds	Tracking proxy stability
envoy_server_live	Gauge	Server liveness status	Health monitoring
envoy_server_parent_connections	Gauge	Active parent connections	Understanding proxy connectivity
envoy_server_total_connections	Counter	Total connection count	Tracking connection patterns

CHAPTER 6   ESTABLISHING OBSERVABILITY FOUNDATIONS IN ISTIO: INFRASTRUCTURE, TRACING, AND METRICS

These metrics work together to provide a comprehensive view of your proxy's health. By monitoring them collectively, you can ensure your service mesh's foundation remains robust and responsive. For example, during a normal deployment, you might see

- A brief dip in `envoy_server_live` as the proxy restarts
- `envoy_server_live` progress through its states to running (2)
- `envoy_server_memory_heap_size` stabilize at a normal level
- `envoy_server_uptime` begin its count anew

Understanding these patterns helps you maintain a healthy service mesh and quickly identify when things aren't working as expected.

The following are some of the key labels available across metrics:

- cluster_name: Identifies the upstream service (e.g., "outbound|8080||payment-service.default.svc.cluster.local)
- local_cluster: The local service cluster name
- listener_address: The network address the listener is bound to
- listener_port: The port number for the listener
- response_code: HTTP response code (for applicable metrics)
- response_code_class: Grouped response codes (2xx, 3xx, 4xx, 5xx)
- zone: Availability zone (AZ) information
- sub_zone: Sub-zone information
- priority: Priority level of the upstream cluster

You can explore all these metrics using our setup of Prometheus that we have done earlier in this chapter. The following figure shows how you can start typing into the expression text box, and you will start seeing the auto-completion for your PromQL (Figure 6-10).

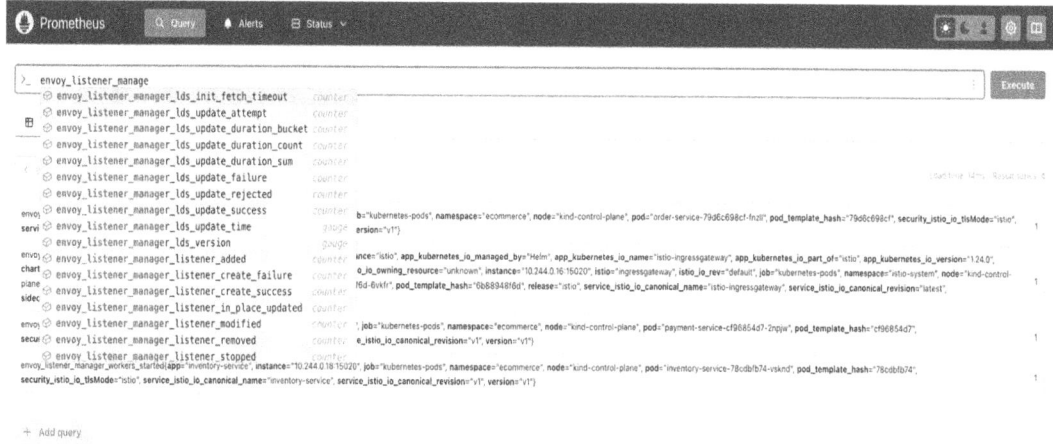

Figure 6-10. Prometheus expression text box showing PromQL auto-completion features

Configuring Custom Metrics

While Istio provides a comprehensive set of default metrics, organizations often need to customize their metrics collection to better align with their specific monitoring requirements. Istio offers powerful capabilities to modify existing metrics and create new ones through its Telemetry API.

Let's explore how to customize metrics in Istio, starting with metric modifications and progressing to creating entirely new metrics.

Understanding Istio's Telemetry API

The key to customizing metrics in Istio lies in its Telemetry API. However, it's important to understand that this API works differently from traditional metrics systems. Instead of creating entirely new metrics, Istio allows you to

- Customize existing metrics with additional tags.
- Modify metrics collection behavior.
- Configure different providers.
- Apply customizations selectively to specific workloads.

355

CHAPTER 6   ESTABLISHING OBSERVABILITY FOUNDATIONS IN ISTIO: INFRASTRUCTURE, TRACING, AND METRICS

Let's start with a basic example. Assume we want to track the inventory status on our ecommerce platform. Here's how we can enhance Istio's request count metric to include inventory-related information:

```
apiVersion: telemetry.istio.io/v1alpha1
kind: Telemetry
metadata:
 name: inventory-metrics
 namespace: ecommerce
spec:
 selector:
   matchLabels:
     app: inventory-service
 metrics:
   - providers:
     - name: prometheus
     overrides:
     - match:
         metric: REQUEST_COUNT
         mode: CLIENT_AND_SERVER
       tagOverrides:
         response_code:
           value: "response.code"
         inventory_status:
           value: "response.headers['x-inventory-status']"
         category:
           value: "response.headers['x-product-category']"
```

This configuration enriches Istio's REQUEST_COUNT metric with two additional dimensions: inventory_status and product_category. But where do these values come from? They come from HTTP headers that we set in our application code:

```
public ResponseEntity<InventoryResponse> checkInventory(
      @PathVariable String productId,
      @RequestParam() Integer quantity,
      HttpServletResponse httpServletResponse) {

   . . .
```

CHAPTER 6   ESTABLISHING OBSERVABILITY FOUNDATIONS IN ISTIO: INFRASTRUCTURE, TRACING, AND METRICS

```
        InventoryResponse response = inventoryService.
        checkInventory(request);

        // Set headers for Istio metrics based on the response
        httpServletResponse.setHeader("x-product-category", response.
        getCategory());
        httpServletResponse.setHeader("x-inventory-status",
                response.getAvailableQuantity() <= lowStockThreshold ?
                "low_stock" : "normal");
        httpServletResponse.setHeader("x-availability-status",
                String.valueOf(response.isAvailable()));

        ...
        return ResponseEntity.ok(response);
    } catch (Exception e) {
        log.error("Error checking inventory for product: {}", productId, e);

        // Record the error in metrics
        meterRegistry.counter("inventory.errors",
                    "error_type", e.getClass().getSimpleName(),
                    "product_id", productId)
            .increment();

        return ResponseEntity
                .internalServerError()
                .body(InventoryResponse.unavailable(productId, null,
                    "Error checking inventory: " + e.getMessage()));
    }
}
```

To validate this metric in Prometheus, you can use the below PromQL query and Figure 6-11:

```
# Total requests by inventory status
istio_requests_total{app="inventory-service"}
```

Figure 6-11. Prometheus metric validation showing custom inventory metrics

Istio provides several standard metrics that you can customize. Here are the available metric types and how each of the Istio metrics maps to an equivalent metric in Prometheus.

Istio Metric Type	Prometheus Metric	Description	Metric Type
REQUEST_COUNT	istio_requests_total	Total number of HTTP requests	Counter
REQUEST_DURATION	istio_request_duration_milliseconds	Time taken to process requests	Histogram
REQUEST_SIZE	istio_request_bytes	Size of HTTP request bodies	Distribution
RESPONSE_SIZE	istio_response_bytes	Size of HTTP response bodies	Distribution
TCP_OPENED_CONNECTIONS	istio_tcp_connections_opened_total	Total number of TCP connections opened	Counter
TCP_CLOSED_CONNECTIONS	istio_tcp_connections_closed_total	Total number of TCP connections closed	Counter
TCP_SENT_BYTES	istio_tcp_sent_bytes_total	Total bytes sent over TCP connections	Counter
TCP_RECEIVED_BYTES	istio_tcp_received_bytes_total	Total bytes received over TCP connections	Counter

Understanding Metric Value Expressions

When configuring metrics in Istio, you'll work with expressions that determine metric values and tags. These expressions provide access to various attributes about your services and their interactions, following specific syntax rules that help you capture exactly the data you need. At its core, the expression system uses a JSON-style format, requiring double quotes for string values. This might seem like a small detail, but it's crucial for proper configuration.

The expression language supports conditional operations through the ? operator, which proves invaluable when you need to handle cases where data might be missing or when you want to provide default values. For instance, when capturing host information, you might write an expression like has(request.host) ? request.host : 'unknown'. This ensures that your metrics always have a value, even when the expected data isn't available.

One of the most powerful features of Istio's metric configuration is its ability to access metadata about communicating services. This metadata is accessible through peer attributes, with upstream_peer used for outbound traffic and downstream_peer for inbound traffic. This distinction is important because it allows you to understand both sides of any service interaction. In our ecommerce application, this becomes particularly valuable when tracking interactions between services.

Consider a scenario where the order service communicates with the payment service. The payment service can access information about the calling order service through the upstream peer metadata. This includes the application name, version, service instance details, and even Kubernetes namespace. For example, when configuring metrics for the payment service, we can capture information about which service is making the request and what version of that service is being used.

This peer metadata system provides a rich set of fields that you can use in your metric configurations. You can access the application name through the app field, version information via the version field, and even cluster-level details using the cluster field. Each field serves a specific purpose in helping you understand your service mesh's behavior. For instance, the namespace field helps track cross-namespace communication, while the workload field identifies specific instances of your services.

In practice, this means you can create very detailed metric configurations that capture the exact information you need. You might track requests from the order service to the payment service by checking if upstream_peer.app equals 'order-service'. Or you could monitor traffic between different versions of services by examining the upstream_ peer.version field. The system is flexible enough to handle complex scenarios while remaining straightforward to configure.

When working with these expressions in our ecommerce context, we often use them to track service-to-service interactions. For example, the payment service might use expressions to monitor which versions of the order service are making requests, helping us understand the impact of deployments and updates. Similarly, we can track cross-namespace requests, which becomes crucial when services are deployed across different namespaces for security or organizational reasons.

The expression system isn't limited to just peer metadata. You can also access request and response attributes, headers, and other contextual information. This means you can create metrics that combine service metadata with request-specific details, giving you a complete picture of your service mesh's behavior. For instance, you might combine peer metadata with response codes to track error rates between specific service versions.

Remember that while these expressions provide powerful capabilities, they should be used judiciously. Each additional tag or dimension you add to your metrics increases the cardinality of your metrics data, which can impact storage and query performance. Focus on capturing the information that provides actionable insights for your specific use cases.

You can read about the complete expression syntax at https://github.com/google/cel-spec. Istio exposes all standard Envoy attributes (https://www.envoyproxy.io/docs/envoy/latest/intro/arch_overview/advanced/attributes) that you can use as part of the value expressions.

Understanding Mode Configuration

The mode field in metric customization is crucial as it determines where and how Istio collects metrics. Istio supports three modes:

1. CLIENT: Metrics are collected only when the service acts as a client (making requests).

2. SERVER: Metrics are collected only when the service receives requests.

3. CLIENT_AND_SERVER: Metrics are collected in both scenarios.

CHAPTER 6 ESTABLISHING OBSERVABILITY FOUNDATIONS IN ISTIO: INFRASTRUCTURE, TRACING, AND METRICS

For example, in our order service's interaction with the inventory service, we want to capture metrics at both ends:

```yaml
apiVersion: telemetry.istio.io/v1alpha1
kind: Telemetry
metadata:
  name: order-service-metrics
spec:
  selector:
    matchLabels:
      app: order-service
  metrics:
    - providers:
      - name: prometheus
      overrides:
      - match:
          metric: REQUEST_DURATION
          mode: CLIENT_AND_SERVER   # Capture latency at both ends
        tagOverrides:
          order_status:
            value: "request.headers['x-order-status']"
```

Here's how to validate the latency metrics:

```
# 95th percentile latency for order service requests
histogram_quantile(0.95, sum(rate(istio_request_duration_milliseconds_
bucket{app="order-service"}[5m])) by (le))

# Average latency by order status
rate(istio_request_duration_milliseconds_sum{app="order-service"}[5m])
  /
rate(istio_request_duration_milliseconds_count{app="order-service"}[5m])
```

If you notice, you will not find the telemetry YAML or the code that adds these headers in the source code of this chapter. We will leave this as an exercise to our readers.

CHAPTER 6   ESTABLISHING OBSERVABILITY FOUNDATIONS IN ISTIO: INFRASTRUCTURE, TRACING, AND METRICS

Disabling Metrics Collection

You may want to disable specific metrics to save resources or focus on metrics that are most important to your use case. Istio lets you disable metrics at different levels.

Disabling Individual Metrics

For example, in our inventory service, we might want to disable response size metrics since they're not critical for inventory monitoring:

```
apiVersion: telemetry.istio.io/v1alpha1
kind: Telemetry
metadata:
  name: inventory-metrics-disable
  namespace: ecommerce
spec:
  selector:
    matchLabels:
      app: inventory-service
  metrics:
    - providers:
      - name: prometheus
      overrides:
      - match:
          metric: RESPONSE_SIZE
          mode: CLIENT_AND_SERVER
        disabled: true
```

Selective Metrics Collection

You can also disable metrics for specific scenarios while keeping them enabled for others. For instance, in our payment service, we might want to collect request duration only for server-side measurements:

```
apiVersion: telemetry.istio.io/v1alpha1
kind: Telemetry
metadata:
  name: payment-metrics
```

```yaml
    namespace: ecommerce
spec:
  selector:
    matchLabels:
      app: payment-service-disable
  metrics:
    - providers:
        - name: prometheus
      overrides:
        - match:
            metric: REQUEST_DURATION
            mode: CLIENT
          disabled: true   # Disable client-side duration metrics
        - match:
            metric: REQUEST_DURATION
            mode: SERVER
          tagOverrides:    # Keep server-side metrics with custom tags
            payment_status:
              value: "response.headers['x-payment-status']"
```

Disabling All Metrics for a Workload

If you have services that don't require metrics collection (like development or test services), you can disable all metrics:

```yaml
apiVersion: telemetry.istio.io/v1alpha1
kind: Telemetry
metadata:
  name: disable-prometheus
  namespace: ecommerce
spec:
  selector:
    matchLabels:
      app: test-service
  metrics:
    - providers:
```

```
- name: prometheus
  overrides:
  - disabled: true
```

Best Practices for Metrics Collection in Istio

As we've explored Istio's observability capabilities throughout this chapter, it's crucial to establish solid practices for metrics collection. Let me share the key practices we've found most effective when implementing metrics in service mesh environments.

Understanding Istio's Default Metrics

Before adding any custom metrics, you should thoroughly understand what Istio provides out of the box. Istio automatically collects a comprehensive set of metrics through Envoy proxies, including request counts, latencies, and error rates. We've seen many teams duplicate effort by implementing custom metrics for data that Istio already provides. For example, rather than creating your own request counting mechanism, leverage the existing "istio_requests_total" metric that comes with useful labels already attached.

Label Management and Cardinality

Label management deserves special attention in Istio deployments. Istio's standard labels follow a consistent pattern—they include "destination_service," "source_workload," and "response_code." When adding custom metrics through your applications, maintain this consistency. For instance, if you're implementing business metrics in your services, follow similar naming patterns:

```
# Istio's standard metric
istio_requests_total{destination_service="payment-service.ecommerce.svc.cluster.local"}

# Your custom business metric following similar patterns
business_transactions_total{service="payment-service.ecommerce.svc.cluster.local"}
```

However, be cautious about cardinality. I've seen deployments struggle when teams add high-cardinality labels like user IDs or session IDs. These can quickly overwhelm your monitoring system. Instead, focus on labels that provide meaningful aggregation points while maintaining reasonable cardinality.

Sampling Configuration

Configuring optimal sampling rates is critical for preserving system performance, and the Telemetry API allows you to change sample rates for various types of telemetry data. Here is a baseline configuration that we recommend for production environments:

```
apiVersion: telemetry.istio.io/v1alpha1
kind: Telemetry
metadata:
  name: metrics-config
spec:
  metrics:
    - providers:
        - name: prometheus
      overrides:
        - match:
            metric: REQUEST_COUNT
            mode: CLIENT_AND_SERVER
          disabled: false
          sampleRate: 0.1  # Sample 10% of requests for high-traffic
          services
```

Resource Usage Optimization

Understanding and optimizing resource usage is critical. Each Envoy proxy exposes metrics that Prometheus scrapes, and we recommend

- Setting appropriate scrape intervals (15 seconds is typically a good balance)
- Configuring retention periods based on your needs
- Monitoring proxy resource usage
- Implementing recording rules for frequently used queries

Integration with Other Telemetry Sources

Your metrics strategy should complement Istio's other telemetry features. While traces excel at capturing individual request journeys and logs provide detailed event information, metrics are best suited for aggregate patterns and trends. Design your metrics collection to work harmoniously with these other telemetry sources.

Version Management

When making significant changes to metrics collection, use Istio's revision-based upgrade feature. This allows for smooth transitions while maintaining observability. I recommend

- Running old and new metric configurations in parallel during transitions
- Validating new metrics before deprecating old ones
- Documenting metric changes and their impact on dashboards and alerts

Monitoring the Monitoring

Finally, implement monitoring for your monitoring system itself. Configure alerts for

- Prometheus scrape failures, especially for control plane metrics
- Resource usage of proxies and Prometheus instances
- Metrics collection latency and drops

These practices have proven valuable across numerous Istio deployments we have worked with. While you should adjust them based on your specific needs, they provide a solid foundation for effective metrics collection in your service mesh.

Conclusion

Throughout this chapter, we've covered the core building blocks of observability in Istio service meshes. Starting with theoretical understanding, we have progressed to actual application and started building a thorough observability stack, meticulously customizing each component, from Prometheus and Jaeger to Grafana and Kiali. This foundation

CHAPTER 6   ESTABLISHING OBSERVABILITY FOUNDATIONS IN ISTIO: INFRASTRUCTURE, TRACING, AND METRICS

allowed us to create distributed tracing and metrics collecting, as seen in our ecommerce application. The change from traditional monitoring to current observability became evident as we investigated Istio's telemetry architecture, which features a Mixerless design with a distributed network of Envoy proxies for efficient and scalable telemetry gathering. Working with OpenTelemetry demonstrated how modern instrumentation standards can provide valuable context while remaining compatible with existing tools.

The metrics collection system, based on Prometheus, demonstrated how precisely telemetry data can be captured and analyzed without affecting system performance. We developed a multi-layered method to understand system behavior, beginning with proxy-level metrics that reveal the fine-grained details of service communication and ending with aggregated service-level insights. We built a framework that balances comprehensive visibility and operational efficiency by carefully examining elements such as sampling rates, label management, and resource optimization. This foundation does more than just allow us to collect data; it also provides the visibility required to develop and manage dependable, performant distributed systems. In the following chapter, we will look at visualization and analysis tools, and the solid framework we've built will serve as the base for more sophisticated observability techniques, such as extensive performance analysis and automatic anomaly identification.

CHAPTER 7

Visualizing and Analyzing Service Mesh Data: Grafana, Kiali, and Logging

Introduction

Building upon the observability foundations established in Chapter 6, we now turn our attention to transforming raw telemetry data into actionable insights through visualization and analysis. While collecting metrics, traces, and logs is essential, the true value of observability emerges when we can effectively interpret this data to understand system behavior, predict potential issues, and make informed decisions about our service mesh.

In this chapter, we'll look at how Grafana, Kiali, and advanced logging techniques work together to provide a comprehensive observability solution. Using our ecommerce application as an example, we'll see how to use Grafana's rich dashboarding capabilities for metrics visualization, Kiali to understand service topology and traffic trends, and effective logging techniques that correlate with metrics and traces. Whether you're monitoring order processing latency, visualizing service dependencies, or debugging failed transactions, you'll learn how to use these tools to obtain a better understanding of your service mesh operations.

CHAPTER 7   VISUALIZING AND ANALYZING SERVICE MESH DATA: GRAFANA, KIALI, AND LOGGING

Visualization with Grafana

Understanding metrics is critical in a service mesh environment, but raw numbers can be overwhelming and difficult to analyze. Grafana converts these metrics into simple visualizations that allow operators to quickly understand system performance and identify trends or issues. Grafana, a very flexible and powerful visualization tool, acts as our window into the metrics collected by Prometheus, enabling both real-time monitoring and historical analysis of our service mesh.

Think of Grafana as a sophisticated dashboard of a car. While the engine (your services) and sensors (Prometheus) collect data, Grafana shows this information in a way that allows us to quickly assess how our system is working by displaying service latencies, request rates, error percentages, and other important metrics in visually appealing and useful ways, similar to how a car's dashboard displays speed, fuel level, and engine temperature.

Setting Up Grafana with Istio

Let's start by confirming that our Grafana installation from Chapter 6 is properly configured to communicate with our Istio service mesh. While we installed Grafana in the previous chapter, we will now focus on the exact configurations that allow for seamless interaction with Istio's telemetry pipeline and ensure that Grafana can correctly display the metrics collected by Prometheus from our service mesh.

Let's start by verifying our Prometheus data source configuration in Grafana. Check the data source settings on Grafana's web interface (usually accessible at http://localhost:3000 if port forwarding is enabled; please refer to the previous chapter on how to bring up Grafana on your local machine). To recall we used the grafana-values.yaml to set up Grafana in our cluster using Helm:

```
...
datasources:
 datasources.yaml:
    apiVersion: 1
    datasources:
    - name: Prometheus
      type: prometheus
      url: http://prometheus-server.istio-observability.svc.cluster.local
```

```
isDefault: true
access: proxy
editable: true
```

This configuration tells Grafana where to find the Prometheus server that's collecting our service mesh metrics. The URL points to our Prometheus service in the Kubernetes cluster, allowing Grafana to retrieve our metrics data, and setting `isDefault` to true makes this Prometheus instance the primary data source, which is especially useful when working with Istio's predefined dashboards that can setup separately. We will discuss more about these dashboards in the further sections.

Next, we should validate that Grafana can successfully connect to Prometheus and query our service mesh metrics. Navigate to Data Sources. Click "Explore" beside the Prometheus data source, select "code" on the right top, and enter your query and click "Run query." A simple test query for Istio's request metrics should confirm the connection:

```
rate(istio_requests_total{destination_service="order-service.ecommerce.svc.cluster.local"}[5m])
```

As shown in Figure 7-1, if this query returns results, we have a functional setup; otherwise, we will need to troubleshoot the connection between Grafana and Prometheus by reviewing the required network policies and service accounts to permit this connection in our Kubernetes cluster.

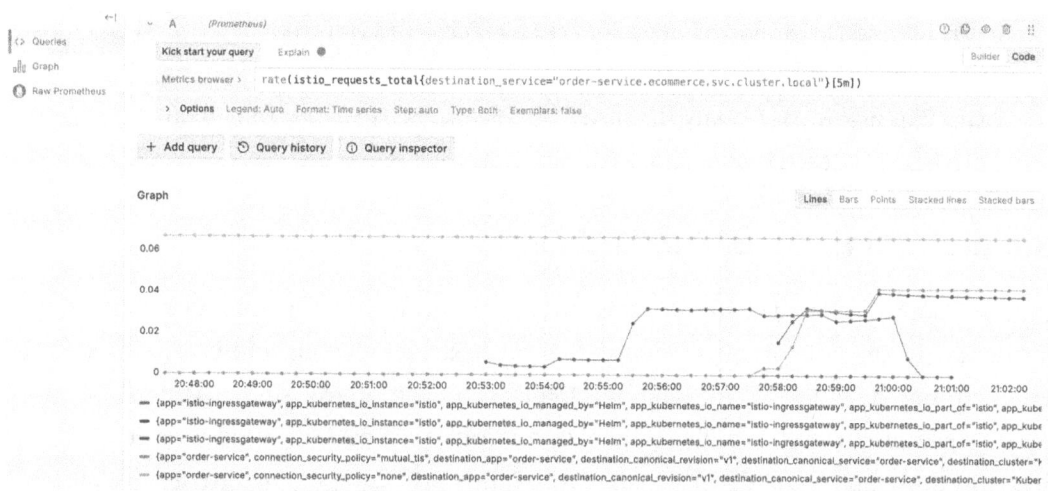

Figure 7-1. *Grafana query interface showing successful connection to Prometheus with query results*

Understanding Default Istio Dashboards

Before we start the technical installation steps, let's look at what makes Istio's default dashboards so valuable for monitoring your service mesh. These dashboards represent years of operational experience from the Istio community and have been carefully designed to provide immediate visibility into the most critical parts of your mesh's behavior.

Let's walk through the process of installing Istio's default dashboards in Grafana. When you install Istio and Grafana separately (rather than using istioctl's demo profile), you need to manually configure these dashboards. To quickly import the Istio dashboards to an existing Grafana instance, you can use the Import button in the Grafana UI to add the dashboard links. Please refer to Istio and Grafana documentations for other ways to import the default dashboards. When you import the dashboards, note that you must select a Prometheus data source. The following are the default dashboards and their corresponding links that you can import into Grafana:

Mesh Dashboard: https://grafana.com/grafana/dashboards/7639-istio-mesh-dashboard/
Service Dashboard: https://grafana.com/grafana/dashboards/7636-istio-service-dashboard/
Workload Dashboard: https://grafana.com/grafana/dashboards/7630-istio-workload-dashboard/
Performance Dashboard: https://grafana.com/grafana/dashboards/11829-istio-performance-dashboard/
Control Plane Dashboard: https://grafana.com/grafana/dashboards/7645-istio-control-plane-dashboard/
Wasm Extension Dashboard: https://grafana.com/grafana/dashboards/13277-istio-wasm-extension-dashboard/

Istio Control Plane Dashboard

The Istio Control Plane Dashboard serves as our window into the operational health of Istio itself—the critical infrastructure that orchestrates all communication in our ecommerce platform. This dashboard allows us to monitor Istiod, the heart of our service mesh, which handles critical operations such as distributing service configuration and handling service discovery and certificate management for secure communication. For our ecommerce application, this is especially critical during deployments and configuration changes. Assume we're updating the routing rules to roll out a new version of the payment service; the Control Plane Dashboard tells us exactly how Istiod processes and distributes these changes across all of our services. We can use metrics like pilot_proxy_convergence_time to ensure that changes to our mesh configuration are applied efficiently across all of our services.

As shown in Figure 7-2, the dashboard's comprehensive view includes more than simply configuration management. It gives precise insights into control plane component resource utilization (CPU and memory), certificate issuance and rotation metrics for secure service-to-service communication, and mesh configuration validation statistics. For example, when our ecommerce platform gets a spike in traffic during a flash sale, we can see how efficiently Istiod handles the increased volume of service discovery requests and configuration distribution. The dashboard also allows us to monitor the health of our webhook validations, ensuring that any changes we make to our service mesh configuration (such as altering traffic rules between the order and payment services) are properly validated before they are applied. We can ensure that our control plane remains healthy and responsive by using panels that display memory usage patterns and xDS push metrics. This is critical to ensuring smooth operations across our whole ecommerce business, and here's an example screenshot of the Control Plane Dashboard.

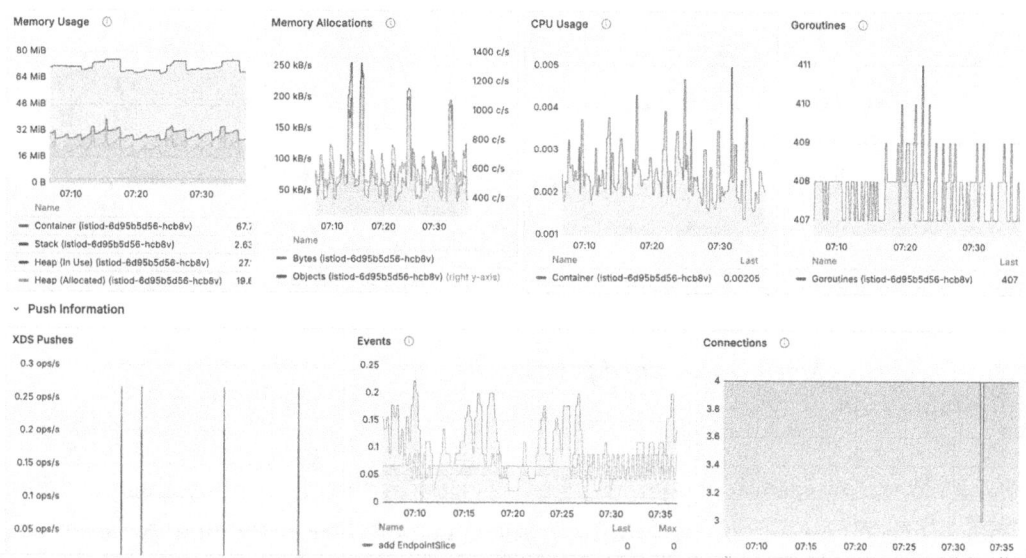

Figure 7-2. Istio Control Plane Dashboard displaying control plane component health and metrics

CHAPTER 7   VISUALIZING AND ANALYZING SERVICE MESH DATA: GRAFANA, KIALI, AND LOGGING

Istio Mesh Dashboard

The Istio Mesh Dashboard as shown in Figure 7-3, gives us an overall view of the operational state of our service mesh, basically telling us the story of how our microservices are communicating in real time. When monitoring our ecommerce application, this dashboard starts with the Service Mesh Overview panel, which gives us critical high-level metrics. What makes this particularly valuable is its capability to show us both global request volume and success rates across our entire platform. For example, in normal operation we can easily see a steady flow of requests as customers browse products through our inventory service, add items to cart, and complete purchases through our payment service. These global request metrics therefore help us make sense of the abovementioned traffic and enable us to pinpoint anomalies instantly, such as sudden spikes in error rates indicative of issues in our flow of order processing.

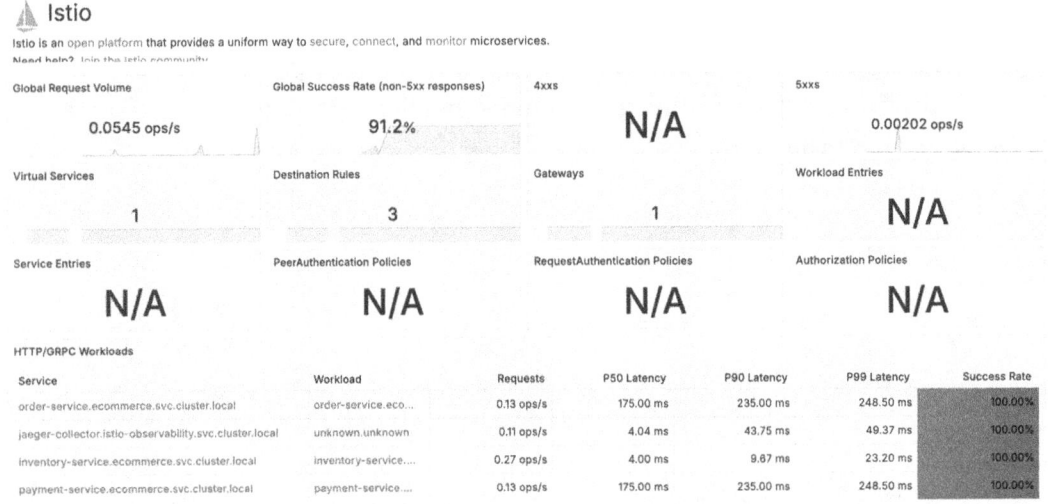

Figure 7-3. Istio Mesh Dashboard providing overall view of service mesh operational state

The Workloads section further enriches this view by showing us how the individual instances of each service are performing, which becomes crucial when we've scaled our services to handle increased load. Through this layered approach to metrics visualization, the Mesh Dashboard serves as our first line of defense in maintaining the health of our ecommerce platform, helping us ensure that every customer interaction flows smoothly through our service mesh. Below is the sample view of the dashboard for the ecommerce application. You will find N/A for "Service Entries" and authentication and authorization policies as these screenshots were captured when we did not have any of these resources defined in the cluster.

Istio Performance Dashboard

The Istio Performance Dashboard as shown in Figures 7-4 and 7-5, serves as our detailed diagnostic tool for understanding resource utilization and efficiency of our service mesh components. In our ecommerce application, this dashboard will be particularly valuable when we need to understand how well our mesh infrastructure handles the workload. Also, this dashboard focuses on the system metrics that influence our mesh's performance. For example, it demonstrates how efficiently the Envoy proxies (sidecars) and our order, payment, and inventory services use resources like CPU and memory. This visibility is especially important during peak traffic periods, when we need to ensure that our infrastructure can handle the extra load properly.

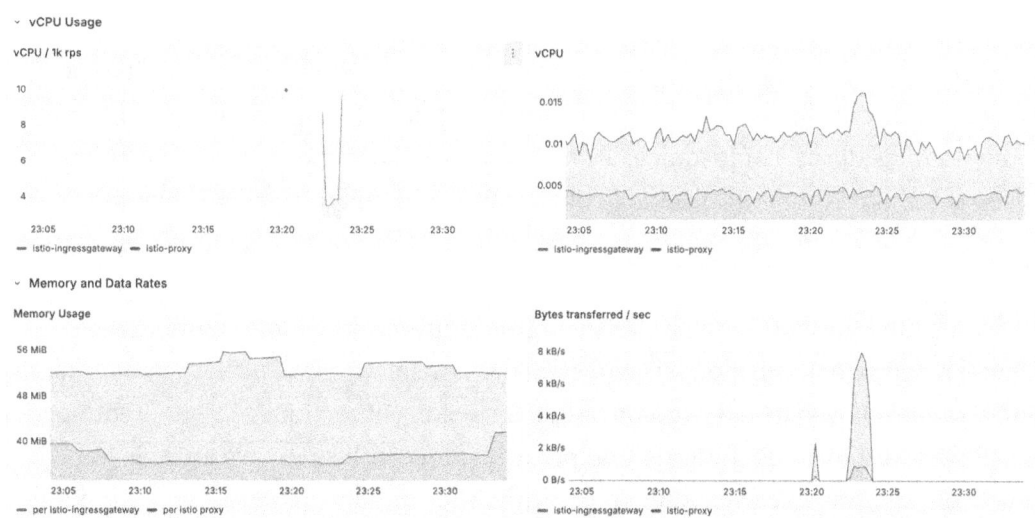

Figure 7-4. Istio Performance Dashboard showing resource utilization and efficiency metrics (part 1)

CHAPTER 7   VISUALIZING AND ANALYZING SERVICE MESH DATA: GRAFANA, KIALI, AND LOGGING

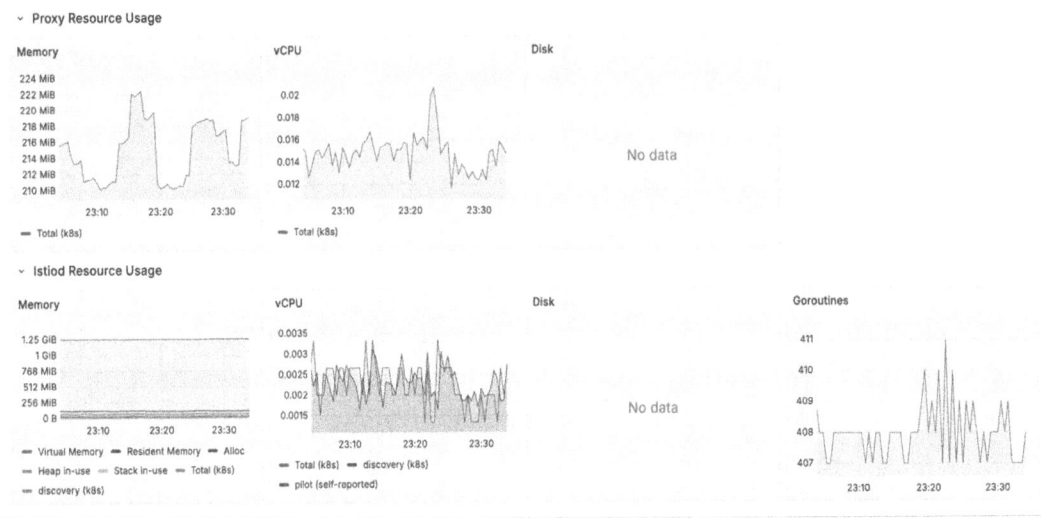

Figure 7-5. *Istio Performance Dashboard showing resource utilization and efficiency metrics (part 2)*

Think of the Performance Dashboard as providing the vital signs for our service mesh's health at a more technical level. It allows us to have detailed insights into proxy workload metrics, which helps us understand if our sidecars are optimally configured for our traffic patterns. For instance, if we see an increase in the latency of payment processing, this dashboard will enable us to realize whether the problem lies within the payment service itself or whether the resource contention is at the proxy level. It also includes useful metrics in the control plane for efficiency, like configuration processing times and proxy push statistics. This helps us understand how quickly changes propagate through our system, which is crucial when we need to update service configurations during peak shopping hours. By looking at sections that show connection pools, memory allocation patterns, and proxy resource utilization, we are able to proactively identify potential bottlenecks before they impact our customers' shopping experience. Having this level of transparency into the performance attributes of our mesh makes it significantly easier to both maintain optimal configurations and allocate resources properly across our platform. Below is a screenshot of the different sections of the Performance Dashboard of our ecommerce application.

CHAPTER 7   VISUALIZING AND ANALYZING SERVICE MESH DATA: GRAFANA, KIALI, AND LOGGING

Istio Service Dashboard

The Istio Service Dashboard is our specialized tool for understanding the behavior and performance of individual services in our ecommerce platform. As shown in Figures 7-6, 7-7 and 7-8 when opened, this dashboard gives us clear visibility into a selected service from two crucial perspectives: how this service handles requests (server-side) and how other services experience it (client-side). For instance, if we select our payment service, the dashboard immediately shows us metrics about payment processing operations, including request volume, success rates, and response times. The client-side metrics tell us about how the order service experiences the payment processing: whether it is getting timely responses trying to complete customer purchases. Meanwhile, the server-side metrics reveal how well the payment service itself is handling these incoming transaction requests.

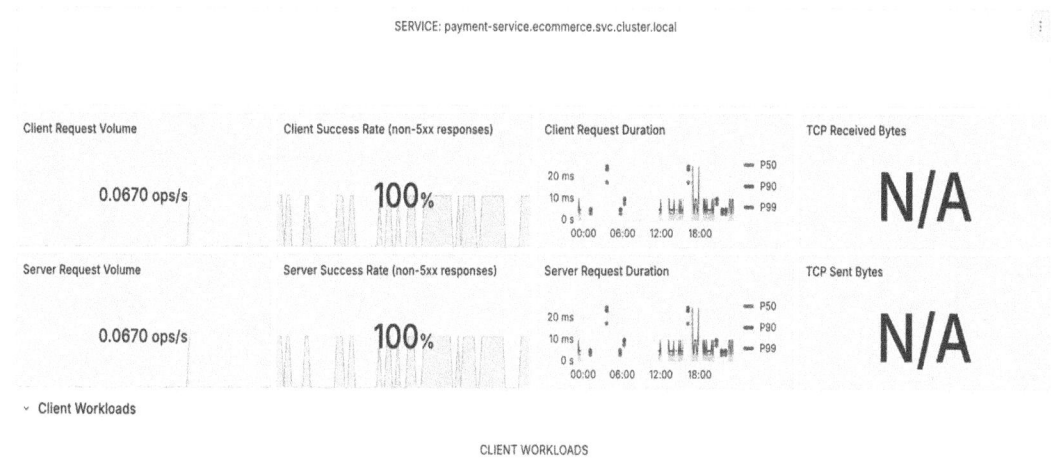

Figure 7-6. Istio Service Dashboard showing individual service behavior and performance (part 1)

CHAPTER 7   VISUALIZING AND ANALYZING SERVICE MESH DATA: GRAFANA, KIALI, AND LOGGING

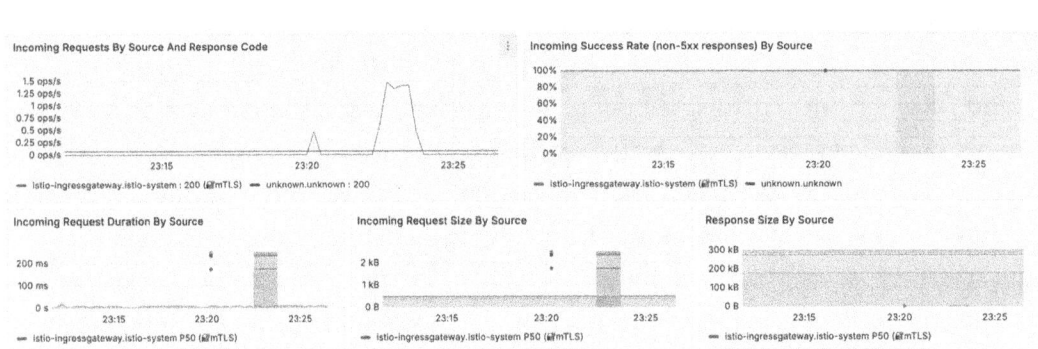

Figure 7-7. Istio Service Dashboard showing individual service behavior and performance (part 2)

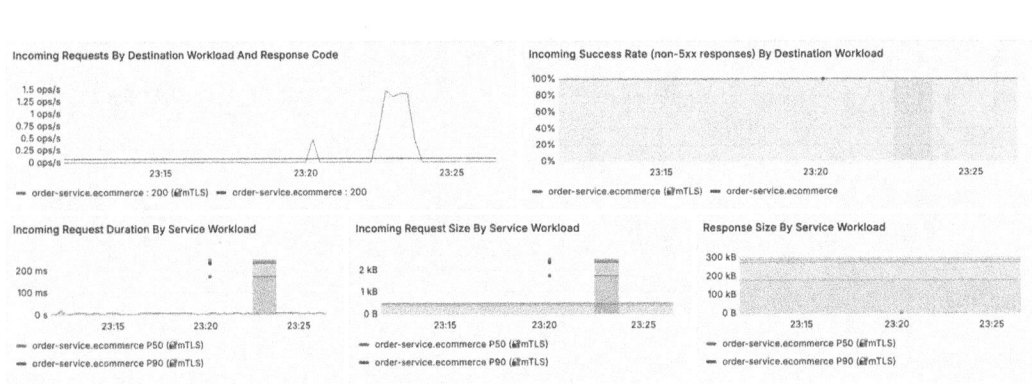

Figure 7-8. Istio Service Dashboard showing individual service behavior and performance (part 3)

What makes this dashboard particularly special is that, through its duration percentiles, it has the capability of showing us extremely detailed latency distributions. When any reports come through about slow payment processing, it can show not just the average response times, but the 95th and 99th percentiles too, which lets us know if all customers are experiencing similar performance or if some transactions take much longer than others. It further breaks down the traffic by response code on the dashboard to immediately find the pattern for failed transactions. Are we seeing an increase in 5xx errors, indicating server problems, or 4xx errors, suggesting invalid payment attempts? That's huge for our ecommerce platform. We can spot right away when payment processing success rates drop below acceptable levels or response times begin to creep up and may start to affect the checkout experience for customers. Furthermore, the dashboard provides TCP metrics when applicable to give insight into connection-level behavior, which can become particularly important when tracking persistent connections either to payment gateways or to database services. Below are the screenshots depicting different sections of the Service Dashboard for our ecommerce application.

Istio Wasm Dashboard

The Istio Wasm Extension Dashboard provides insights into the performance and behavior of the WebAssembly (Wasm) extensions that we've deployed in our service mesh. In the context of our ecommerce application, Wasm extensions enable us to add additional functionality to our service proxies without changing our main services. For example, we could utilize a Wasm extension to add specialized authentication logic for high-value transactions in our payment service, or we could set rate limiting restrictions to protect our inventory service during flash sales. The dashboard allows us to monitor how these custom extensions are behaving, ensuring that they do not introduce unexpected latency or consume excessive resources.

When observing the Wasm Extension Dashboard, we see metrics that help us understand both the operational health and performance impact of our extensions. For each extension deployed across our services, we can monitor its resource consumption patterns, including memory usage and CPU utilization. This becomes particularly important as extensions run in our service proxies—if an extension starts to get too greedy in resources, it could have a cascading effect on the performance of our service mesh as a whole. The dashboard also shows the execution metrics like how often our extensions get invoked and what is the duration taken by each of them to serve the request. For example, if we have a custom fraud detection extension for our payment service, the above metrics would allow us to ensure that it makes decisions quickly without introducing appreciable latency in the payment process. These would give us confidence that our custom mesh extensions are enhancing the capability of our ecommerce platform with no compromise on performance.

Istio Workload Dashboard

The Istio Workload Dashboard brings us to the most detailed level of monitoring our service mesh: the instance, or pod, level of our services. Whereas the Service Dashboard showed us the aggregated service behavior, this dashboard will show how each replica of our services is doing. In our ecommerce application, this becomes important when we have horizontally scaled our services in order to cope with the load. For example, during high-volume shopping events when we run multiple instances of the payment service, this dashboard will inform us whether each instance is processing its fair share of transactions efficiently and consistently. The dashboard breaks this down into two main perspectives: inbound traffic (requests coming into the workload) and outbound traffic (requests this workload makes to other services).

As shown in Figures 7-9 and 7-10, the detailed metrics on this dashboard help us spot instance-specific issues that might be hidden in service-level aggregates. The inbound metrics will provide us request volumes, success rates, and latency distributions for each pod. For example, if one instance of our inventory service is experiencing higher latency than others, we can quickly identify the particular instance and examine whether the latency is due to resource constraints or because of the deployment on a less performant node. The outbound metrics are just as useful, showing us how each instance interacts with other services. Assume one of our order service instances is failing more frequently when invoking the payment service than its siblings; it becomes immediately obvious. The dashboard also displays detailed resource utilization metrics, connection pool status, and request processing metrics for each workload instance. The latter broad view helps us maintain consistent performance across all of our service replicas so that the service is experienced reliably by customers, regardless of which instance is serving their request.

CHAPTER 7   VISUALIZING AND ANALYZING SERVICE MESH DATA: GRAFANA, KIALI, AND LOGGING

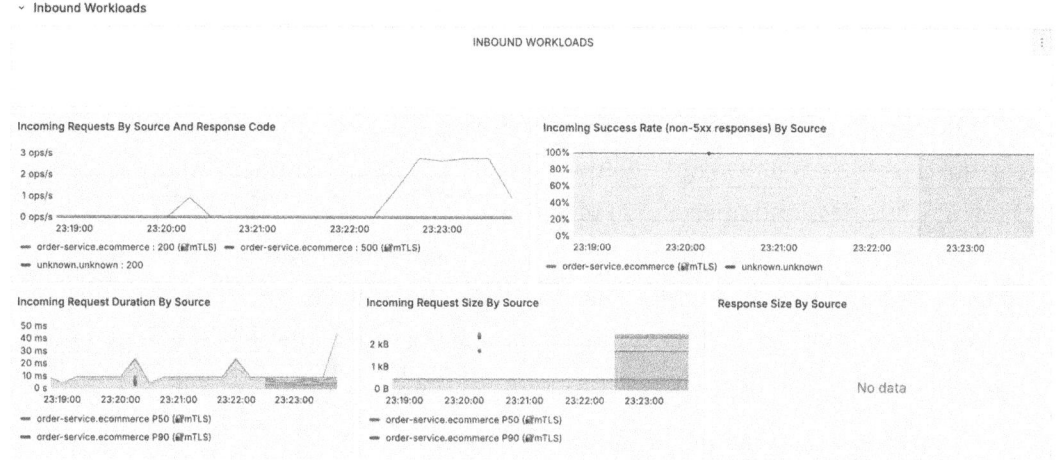

Figure 7-9. *Istio Workload Dashboard displaying inbound traffic metrics for workload instances*

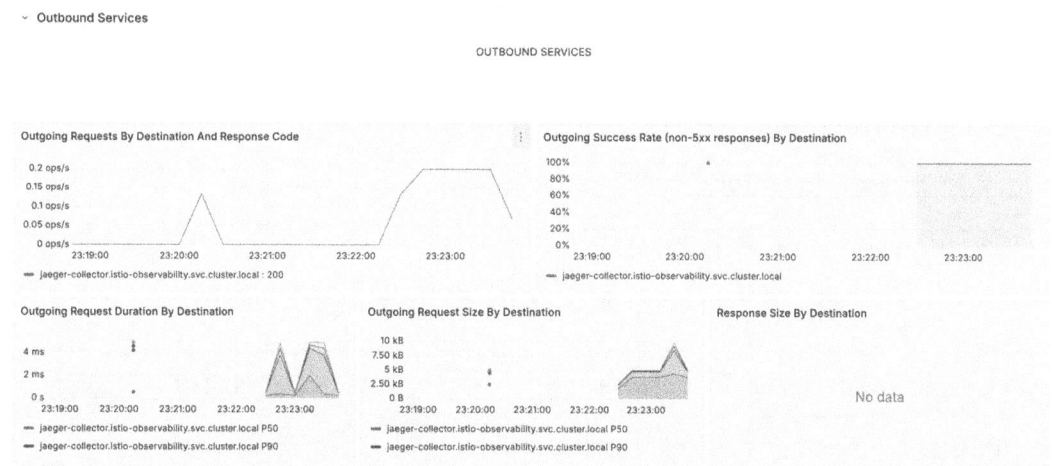

Figure 7-10. *Istio Workload Dashboard displaying outbound traffic metrics for workload instances*

This level of data is extremely useful during scaling events, deployments, and troubleshooting exercises. For example, during the gradual rollout of a new version of our order service, we may compare the performance metrics of the old and new instances side by side to ensure that the new version maintains or improves on the old one's performance. The screenshots below show the inbound and outbound areas of the Workload Dashboard for our ecommerce application.

381

Creating Custom Dashboards for Specific Use Cases

While the default dashboards provided by Istio give excellent coverage for service mesh metrics, our ecommerce application has monitoring needs that are best addressed by custom dashboards. Let's explore how to create targeted dashboards that help us monitor key business and operational metrics unique to our application. You can find all the dashboards under the grafana-dashboards folder of the source code. There are several ways in which we can create dashboards in Grafana. For our demonstration we will choose importing the JSONs into Grafana. To create a new dashboard in your Grafana instance, follow the below steps:

- Log into your Grafana instance.
- Click the "+" icon in the side menu.
- Select "Import."
- Upload a JSON file, or paste JSON content directly.
- Set a unique dashboard name (or keep existing).
- Select the Prometheus data source.
- Choose a folder (optional).
- Click "Import."

Here's a quick comparison between default and custom dashboards.

Aspect	Default Istio Dashboards	Custom Dashboards
Ideal use cases	General service mesh health monitoring, troubleshooting standard mesh behaviors, monitoring Istio components	Business-specific metrics, application-domain monitoring, specialized workflows, executive reporting
Strengths	Preconfigured and tested, comprehensive coverage of mesh internals, maintained by the Istio community, automatically updated with Istio releases	Tailored to specific business needs, focused on relevant metrics only, can combine mesh and application data, customizable visualization types

(continued)

Aspect	Default Istio Dashboards	Custom Dashboards
Limitations	Generic views not specific to your business domain, sometimes include unnecessary information, fixed visualization types	Require manual creation and maintenance, may need updating when Istio changes, require deeper understanding of metrics
Setup effort	Minimal—simply import from provided JSON or URLs	Moderate to high—requires metrics understanding, dashboard design, and regular updates

Business Metrics Dashboard

Our first custom dashboard will focus on business-critical metrics enabling us to keep track of the health of our ecommerce operations. By having this dashboard with the metrics that we already collect via instrumentation of services, we will have complete insight into business performance inside the service mesh environment. This is a bridge between technical metrics and business outcomes, and it helps technical teams and business stakeholders understand what their system performance means in the real world.

For instance, if the Order Success Rate gauge falls below expected thresholds, it immediately flags the possibility of some issues in our order processing pipeline, and when combined with the Payment Processing Rate time series, this metric gives a complete picture about the health of our transaction pipeline. Importantly, the dashboard makes use of metrics emitted from both our OrderService and PaymentService components, which have been carefully instrumented to capture these critical business events:

```
{
    "title": "E-commerce Business Metrics",
    "panels": [
        {
            "title": "Order Success Rate",
            "type": "gauge",
            "datasource": "Prometheus",
            "targets": [
                {
```

```
                "expr": "sum(rate(order_status_total{status=\
                "COMPLETED\"}[5m])) / sum(rate(order_status_total
                {status=~\"COMPLETED|FAILED\"}[5m])) * 100"
            }
        ]
    },
    {
        "title": "Payment Processing Rate",
        "type": "timeseries",
        "datasource": "Prometheus",
        "targets": [
            {
                "expr": "sum(rate(payment_processing_time_seconds_count
                [5m])) by (status)"
            }
        ]
    }
  ]
}
```

The instrumentation in our services plays a critical role in feeding this dashboard with meaningful data. If we look at our codebase, we can see these metrics being emitted through strategic placement of monitoring code:

```
// From OrderService.java
meterRegistry.counter("order.status",
        "status", response.getStatus().toString(),
        "customer_id", request.getCustomerId())
.increment();
```

```
// From PaymentService.java
Timer.Sample timer = Timer.start(meterRegistry);
timer.stop(meterRegistry.timer("payment.processing.time",
        "status", "success",
        "customer_id", order.getCustomerId()));
```

The order service tracks each order's status through a counter metric, enabling us to calculate success rates and identify patterns in order failures. Meanwhile, the payment

CHAPTER 7 VISUALIZING AND ANALYZING SERVICE MESH DATA: GRAFANA, KIALI, AND LOGGING

service employs timer metrics in order to monitor the processing duration, and this allows us to ensure our payment processing stays within an acceptable time bound. These metrics, when visualized together in Grafana, provide immediate insights into the business performance of our platform.

Below Figure 7-11 is how the Business Metrics Dashboard looks in Grafana after import. The gauge visualization gives an immediate sense of our order success rate, while the time-series graph shows the pattern of payment processing over time to highlight trends and potential issues before they affect our business operations.

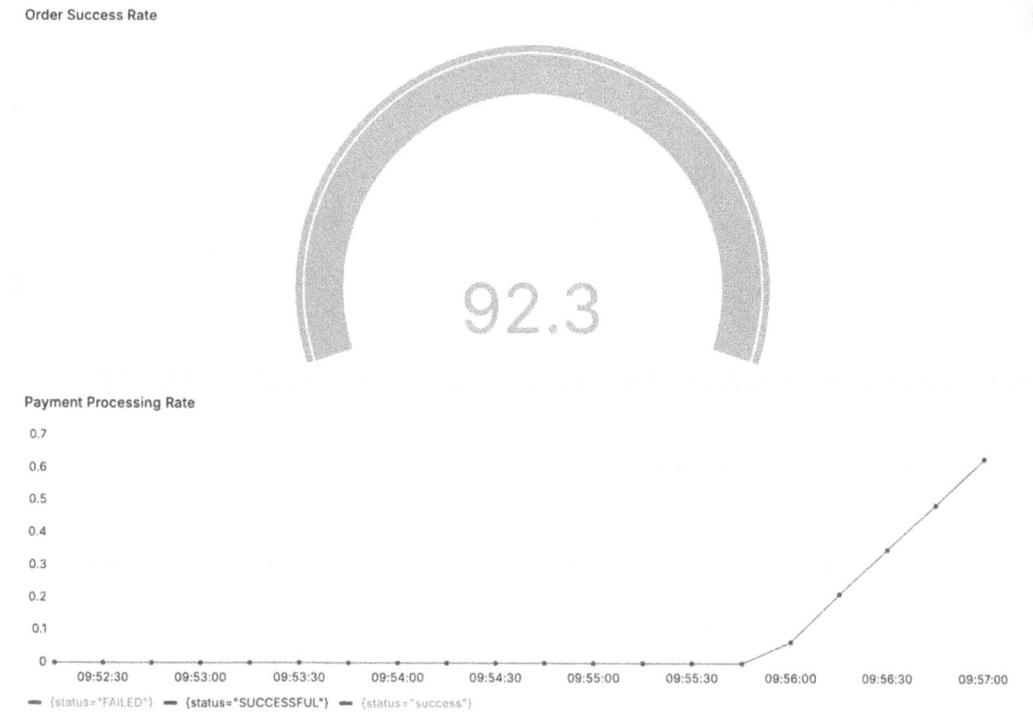

Figure 7-11. Business Metrics Dashboard in Grafana showing order success rate and payment processing metrics

Inventory Health Dashboard

Our Inventory Health Dashboard is a major operational tool in preventing stockouts and helping us maintain optimum inventory levels on our ecommerce platform. This dashboard consolidates real-time inventory metrics and request patterns to give a full view of how well our stock management system is working. It enables us to proactively pinpoint any potential issues with inventory well in advance of customers and sales performance.

CHAPTER 7 VISUALIZING AND ANALYZING SERVICE MESH DATA: GRAFANA, KIALI, AND LOGGING

The dashboard configuration reflects the two primary concerns in inventory management: stock levels and system performance. Here's how we structure this vital monitoring tool:

```
{
  "title": "Inventory Health Dashboard",
  "panels": [
    {
      "title": "Low Stock Items",
      "type": "table",
      "datasource": "Prometheus",
      "targets": [
        {
          "expr": "inventory_lowStock"
        }
      ]
    },
    {
      "title": "Inventory Request Rate",
      "type": "heatmap",
      "datasource": "Prometheus",
      "targets": [
        {
          "expr": "rate(inventory_check_time_seconds_count[5m])"
        }
      ]
    }
  ]
}
```

The dashboard's effectiveness relies on careful instrumentation within our Inventory Service and InventoryController. Let's examine how we capture these crucial metrics:

```
meterRegistry.counter("inventory.lowStock",
            "product_id", inventory.getProductId(),
            "category", inventory.getCategory())
    .increment();
```

```
@Timed(value = "inventory.check.time", description = "Time taken to check
            inventory")
public ResponseEntity<InventoryResponse> checkInventory(
        @PathVariable String productId,
        @RequestParam() Integer quantity,
        HttpServletResponse httpServletResponse) {
```

The Inventory Request Rate panel leverages a heatmap to illustrate the intensity of inventory checks over time. This is an extremely powerful visualization because it helps us understand the patterns in the inventory query loads. The heatmap shows

- Peak request periods that might indicate high-traffic shopping times

- Unusual spikes that could suggest system issues or potential inventory-related problems

- Regular patterns that can inform inventory check optimization strategies

Our @Timed annotation on the checkInventory endpoint automatically tracks the duration of inventory checks, giving us insight into how quickly we can respond to stock inquiries. This becomes especially important during high-traffic periods when quick inventory responses are crucial for maintaining smooth checkout processes.

The dashboard's metrics are especially useful in scenarios such as

- Flash sales, where rapid inventory depletion needs to be closely monitored

- Holiday seasons, in which we should be prepared to handle increased demand with the available stock levels

- New product launches, where we wish to track the pattern of initial inventory movement

Below Figure 7-12 is how the inventory request rate appears in Grafana. The heatmap's color intensity provides an intuitive visualization of request patterns, making it easy for operators to identify both normal traffic patterns and anomalies that might require attention.

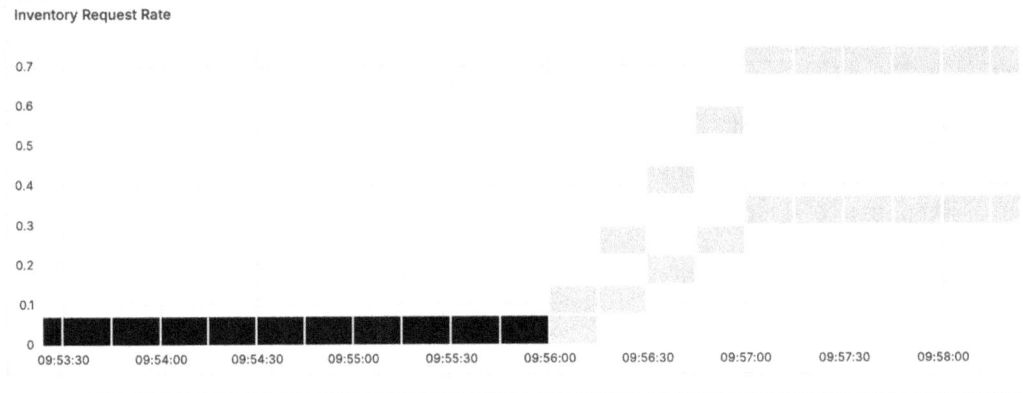

Figure 7-12. *Inventory Health Dashboard heatmap visualization showing inventory request rate patterns*

As you can see, we skipped the "Low Stock Items" dashboard. We leave that as an exercise to our readers. Please refer to the source code attached to this chapter.

Service Mesh Performance Dashboard

While Istio provides comprehensive performance metrics out of the box, our custom Service Mesh Performance Dashboard takes monitoring to the next level by combining both mesh-level and application-level performance indicators. This integration gives us a holistic view of our system's performance, allowing us to correlate service mesh behavior with actual application outcomes. The dashboard helps us understand how service mesh configurations and behaviors directly impact our ecommerce platform's performance:

The dashboard configuration represents this integrated approach to performance monitoring:

```
{
  "title": "E-commerce Service Mesh Performance",
  "panels": [
    {
      "title": "End-to-End Order Processing Time",
      "type": "timeseries",
      "datasource": "Prometheus",
      "targets": [
```

```
          {
            "expr": "histogram_quantile(0.95, sum(rate(istio_request_
            duration_milliseconds_bucket{source_app=\"order-service\",
            destination_app=\"payment-service\"}[5m])) by (le))"
          }
        ]
      },
      {
        "title": "Circuit Breaker Status",
        "type": "stat",
        "datasource": "Prometheus",
        "targets": [
          {
            "expr": "sum(rate(istio_requests_total{response_code=\"503\",
            response_flags=\"UO\"}[5m])) by (destination_app)"
          }
        ]
      }
    ]
}
```

As shown in Figure 7-13, this dashboard brings together the out-of-the-box metrics from Istio and our application metrics into one place for a holistic view of system performance. The End-to-End Order Processing Time panel follows the complete lifecycle of orders as they flow through our system, measuring the time from initial order placement through payment processing. Meanwhile, the Circuit Breaker Status panel monitors the health of our service interactions, alerting us when services become overwhelmed and circuit breakers activate to prevent cascading failures.

CHAPTER 7   VISUALIZING AND ANALYZING SERVICE MESH DATA: GRAFANA, KIALI, AND LOGGING

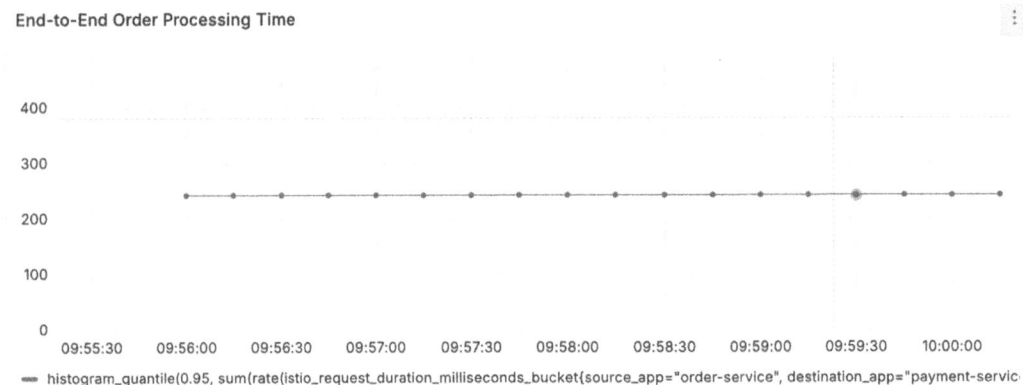

Figure 7-13. *Service Mesh Performance Dashboard combining mesh-level and application-level performance indicators*

Error Tracking Dashboard

Given our sophisticated error handling and logging, let's construct a dashboard dedicated to tracking payment issues. Payment processing is one of the most crucial transaction channels on our ecommerce platform, with any failures having a direct influence on revenue and customer satisfaction. The Error Tracking Dashboard provides real-time visibility into various sorts of payment processing failures, allowing us to identify and resolve issues before they have a substantial impact on our company operations.

The dashboard configuration reflects our focus on payment-related error patterns:

```
{
  "title": "E-commerce Error Tracking",
  "panels": [
    {
      "title": "Payment Processing Errors",
      "type": "timeseries",
      "datasource": "Prometheus",
      "targets": [
        {
```

CHAPTER 7 VISUALIZING AND ANALYZING SERVICE MESH DATA: GRAFANA, KIALI, AND LOGGING

```
          "expr": "sum(rate(payment_errors_total{error_type!=\"\"}[5m])) by
          (error_type)"
        }
      ]
    }
  ]
}
```

As shown in Figure 7-14, this will show up in Grafana as a time-series graph that highlights error patterns and trends clearly over time. Labeling with error_type allows differentiation of types of failures, such as network timeouts, validation errors, or problems with the third-party payment provider. This granular view allows our operations team to quickly find the source of issues in payment processing and take proper corrective action.

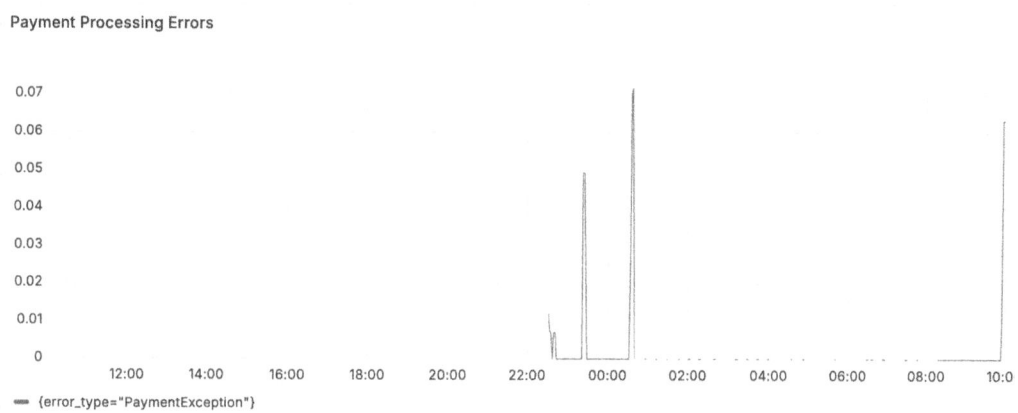

Figure 7-14. Error Tracking Dashboard displaying payment processing error patterns over time

These panels utilize error metrics from our services to provide granular visibility into error patterns. The implementation in our PaymentService demonstrates how we capture detailed error information:

```
// From PaymentService.java
meterRegistry.counter("payment.errors",
    "error_type", e.getClass().getSimpleName(),
    "order_id", request.getOrderId()).increment();
```

CHAPTER 7   VISUALIZING AND ANALYZING SERVICE MESH DATA: GRAFANA, KIALI, AND LOGGING

Embracing the Power of Visualization with Grafana

The integration of Grafana with Istio provides an indispensable window into the operational health and performance of our service mesh. Both preconfigured and custom visualizations in Grafana make the complex telemetry data from our ecommerce platform directly actionable. All default Istio dashboards, from the high-level Mesh Dashboard to the granular Workload Dashboard, provide immediate visibility into critical service mesh metrics, and our custom dashboards bridge the gap between technical metrics and business outcomes.

Our journey through Grafana's capabilities has shown how well it can cover the monitoring of different aspects of our service mesh. The Control Plane Dashboard ensures that the core components of Istio are properly working, and the Performance Dashboard goes deep into resource utilization and efficiency. The Service and Workload Dashboards give complementary views of the behavior of our application, from service-level aggregates to individual pod performance. Grafana provides a comprehensive observability solution that incorporates custom dashboards tracking business metrics, inventory health, and error patterns to serve both technical and business stakeholders.

Grafana's power rests not just in its visualization capabilities, but also in its capacity to assist us in identifying and diagnosing issues before they affect our consumers. Grafana's configurable dashboarding allows us to maintain optimal service mesh performance while supporting our business objectives, whether we're monitoring payment processing latency or inventory levels or evaluating error patterns; and, as our service mesh grows and evolves, these visualization capabilities will play an increasingly important role in guaranteeing the stability and efficiency of our ecommerce platform.

Moving forward, we'll look at how Grafana's insights complement Kiali's service topology visualization and our logging infrastructure, creating a more comprehensive approach to service mesh observability. This integrated perspective will improve our ability to manage, debug, and optimize our service mesh environment.

Service Mesh Visualization with Kiali

As we get beyond the metrics and tracing capabilities covered in our observability stack, we encounter a fundamental requirement: understanding how our services interact as a whole. This is where Kiali, Istio's native visualization platform, plays a very crucial role. While our previous tools excelled at displaying specific components of our system (Grafana for metrics trends, Jaeger for request tracing), Kiali offers something fundamentally different: a dynamic, real-time depiction of our complete service mesh topology.

Consider operating a service mesh without visualization to be similar to navigating a complex city without a map: you may be aware of individual streets (services), but understanding how they link and flow together is difficult. Kiali addresses this by offering an interactive map of your service mesh that includes real-time traffic flows, health indicators, and configuration status, and for our ecommerce platform, this means we can physically observe how consumer orders travel through our system, from the first request to ultimate delivery.

In the following sections, we'll look at how to use Kiali's visualization capabilities, from understanding its basic role in mesh management to implementing advanced traffic analysis tools. We'll show how it converts abstract ideas like service mesh into intuitive, actionable visuals that help us maintain and optimize our ecommerce platform.

Understanding Kiali's Role in Service Mesh Management

Kiali acts as a sophisticated control center for your Istio service mesh, providing capabilities far beyond basic visualization. At its core, Kiali serves three primary functions: mesh visualization, configuration validation, and health monitoring. This combination helps operators understand not just what their mesh looks like, but how well it's functioning and whether it's correctly configured.

Kiali's involvement in our ecommerce application becomes evident when we examine complex operations such as customer order processing. As requests travel between services, from order to inventory to payment, Kiali gives real-time visual feedback on the status of these interactions. Are services communicating as intended? Are there any errors or latency issues? Are our traffic routing rules operating properly? Kiali's accessible interface provides answers to these questions.

Kiali builds on the telemetry foundation we laid in Chapter 6 to turn raw observability data into actionable insights. When we examine any service in our mesh, Kiali presents not only just metrics and traces but also their relationships, dependencies, and configuration state. Kiali's contextual awareness makes it a valuable tool for both daily operations and troubleshooting configurations.

Setting Up and Configuring Kiali

While we already installed Kiali using Helm charts in Chapter 6 as part of our observability stack deployment, let's look at what that setup accomplished and why each configuration decision is important. Our installation connected Kiali to the other observability components we deployed, including Prometheus for metrics collection, Grafana for detailed metrics visualization, and Jaeger for distributed tracing. This integration enables Kiali to deliver a full perspective of our service mesh.

The configuration we implemented in Chapter 6 was centered on three essential features. First, we enabled Kiali to access our ecommerce namespace, letting it to discover and visualize all of our services, including the order service, inventory service, and payment service. Second, we connected Kiali to our observability backends, allowing it to correlate traffic patterns with metrics and traces, and finally third, we enabled anonymous authentication in our development environment; nevertheless, a more secure authentication technique is often used in production environments.

Remember that Kiali uses the telemetry data we configured before, such as the Prometheus metrics, Jaeger traces, and our logging infrastructure. Kiali builds on this basis, transforming raw observability data into simple visualizations that help us understand service interactions, verify configurations, and debug issues in our service mesh. This setup generates a robust observability console that combines all aspects of our mesh's behavior into a single unified interface.

Service Topology Visualization

One of Kiali's most powerful capabilities is the ability to generate and dynamically update visual representations of your service mesh topology. For our ecommerce application, this representation reveals a complicated web of connections between services that would otherwise remain abstract. Consider tracking a customer's order as it goes through your system, from the moment it enters your ingress gateway to order processing, inventory checks, and payment completion. Kiali makes this journey visible and understandable.

To see these visualizations, first, go to Kiali's web interface (usually `http://localhost:20001` if you've configured port forwarding as we did in Chapter 6). Once logged in, choose "Traffic Graph" from the left navigation menu. To focus on our application's services, select the "ecommerce" namespace from the menu at the top of the page. The graph will immediately populate with nodes representing our services and edges depicting their interconnections. You can adjust the time period for the visualization using the option in the top-right corner; this will help you understand how traffic patterns change over time.

The service topology view, as shown in the Figure 7-15, represents each service as a node in an interactive graph, with edges reflecting traffic flow between services, and we can track how the request travels through our services in real time as and when a customer places an order on our ecommerce platform. The order service receives the first request and then makes synchronous calls to both the inventory service (to confirm stock availability) and the payment service (to complete the transaction). Kiali enriches this visualization with vital metadata. The thickness of connecting lines represents traffic volume, colors indicate health status (green for healthy, red for mistakes), and superimposed metrics display request rates and latencies.

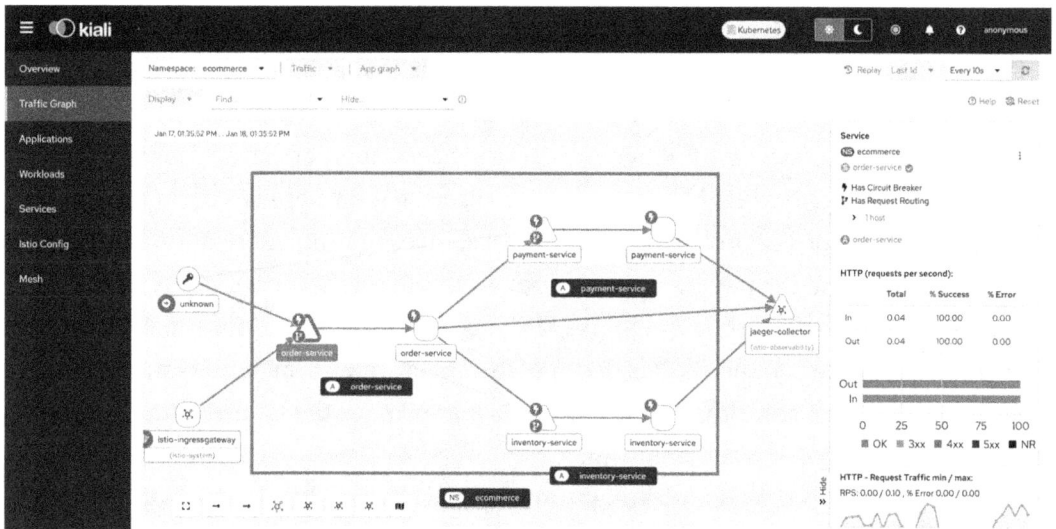

Figure 7-15. Kiali service topology view showing interactive graph of service relationships and traffic flow

To further explore the visualization, try these interactive features:

- Click any node to see detailed metrics about that service in the side panel.

- Double-click a node to focus the graph on that service and its immediate connections.

- Use the mouse wheel to zoom in and out.

- Click and drag the background to pan around the visualization.

- Use the "Display" dropdown in the top menu to toggle different visual elements like traffic animation, service names, or background traffic.

The visualization becomes even more powerful through its customization options. In the top menu bar, you'll find controls for

- "Display": Select the information to show on the graph.

- "Find": Search for specific services.

- "Hide": Remove certain types of nodes or edges from view.

- "Legend" (This is at the bottom of the page): Recognize what each color and shape represents.

This visualization is extremely important due to its dynamic nature and richness of information. When you click a service node, the right-hand panel displays detailed information about the service's activity, such as success rates, error rates, and response time distributions. The edges between services disclose if the services communicate using HTTP, gRPC, or TCP protocols. For instance, investigating the relationship between our order service and the payment service not only shows that the services are talking to each other, but also the protocol in use, the success rate of the communications, and any latency between them. This depth of insight elevates Kiali far beyond a mere visualization tool to a comprehensive diagnosis platform for the investigation and root cause analysis of service mesh behavior.

Kiali's rich visual context and straightforward navigation allow us to confidently manage and optimize our service mesh, ensuring our ecommerce platform's reliability and performance. Whether we're deploying new service versions, diagnosing difficulties, or planning capacity increases, the topology visualization guides us through the complexities of our distributed system.

Traffic Management Features

While we've already explored service topology visualization, let's take a closer look at how to use Kiali's traffic management capabilities effectively. These tools are very useful for implementing and validating complex routing scenarios in your service mesh.

To access Kiali's traffic management validation features, navigate to the "Istio Config" section on the left sidebar. This view displays a complete list of your Istio traffic management resources. Let's go over how to use this interface effectively.

Filter options at the top of the screen allow you to narrow down your search to specific resource types or namespaces. For our ecommerce application, you might wish to filter to only see VirtualServices under the "ecommerce" namespace. The interface shows several important bits of information for each configuration:

1. Configuration Status: Each resource displays a colored icon indicating its validation status:

    a. Green Checkmark: Configuration is valid and working.

    b. Yellow Triangle: Potential issues detected.

    c. Red Circle: Critical configuration errors.

2. Detail View: Clicking any configuration entry opens a detailed view with three important tabs:

    a. "Overview" shows the resource's basic information and status.

    b. "YAML" displays and allows editing of the raw configuration.

    c. "Actions" provides options to delete or update the resource.

For example, when examining our ecommerce VirtualService, you might click its entry to verify the traffic routing rules. The detail view immediately shows if your configuration correctly references existing service versions and if the routing weights add up to 100%.

To see this in action, let's examine a specific route configuration. From the Istio Config view as shown in Figure 7-16, locate your VirtualService for the ecommerce virtual service.

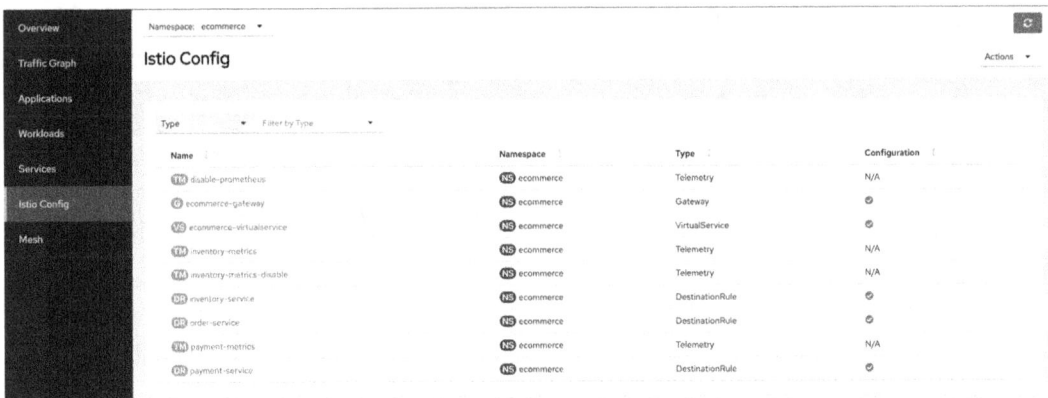

***Figure 7-16.** Kiali Istio Config view displaying list of traffic management resources with validation status*

As shown in Figure 7-17, Kiali validates this configuration in real time, checking that both service versions exist and that weights sum to 100%. Any issues are immediately highlighted in the interface. This integration between configuration and visualization helps you understand exactly how your routing rules impact service communication.

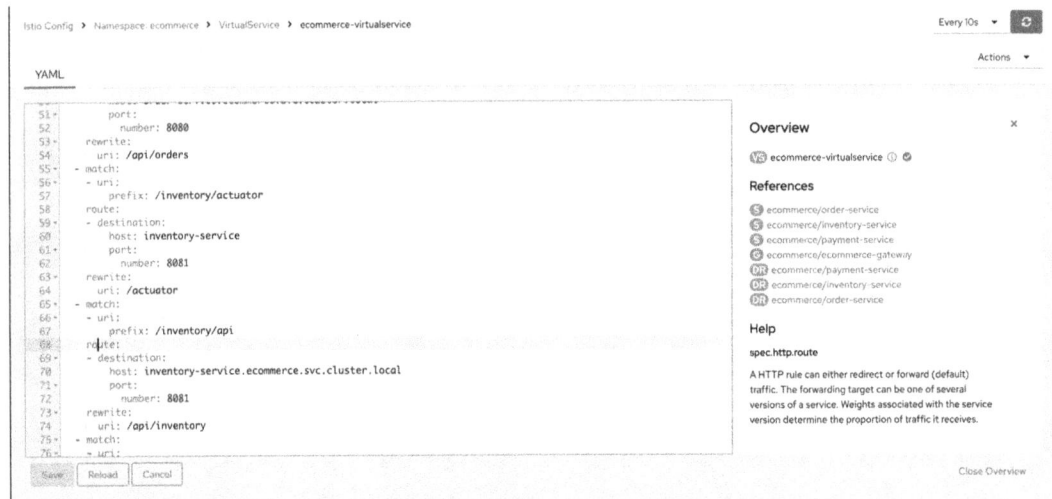

***Figure 7-17.** Kiali configuration detail view showing VirtualService validation and routing rules*

When troubleshooting routing issues, you can use the "Workloads" tab (accessible from the left sidebar) to verify that all service versions referenced in your VirtualService actually exist and are healthy. This cross-referencing capability helps quickly identify common configuration mistakes, such as referencing a service version that hasn't been deployed yet.

The true potential of this interface is revealed during deployments. For example, during a canary release of a new payment service version, you can:

1. Monitor the status of your configuration as you make changes in real time.

2. Ensure that the traffic distribution matches the percentages you expected.

3. Quickly change weights by modifying the YAML directly in Kiali.

4. Observe the impact of your changes in the graph view.

This integrated approach to traffic management ensures that your routing configurations work properly while ensuring service dependability in complex deployment circumstances.

Workload Management and Analysis

Kiali's workload management capabilities provide deep insights into how individual instances of your services are performing within the mesh. While the service-level view shows aggregate behavior, the workload view lets you examine the actual pods running your services. This granular visibility becomes crucial when troubleshooting performance issues or validating deployment configurations.

As shown in Figure 7-18, to access workload-level information in Kiali, click Workloads in the left navbar. That brings you to a list view of all of the workload instances in your mesh. Using our ecommerce example application, you should see one entry for each running pod of the order, payment, and inventory services.

CHAPTER 7   VISUALIZING AND ANALYZING SERVICE MESH DATA: GRAFANA, KIALI, AND LOGGING

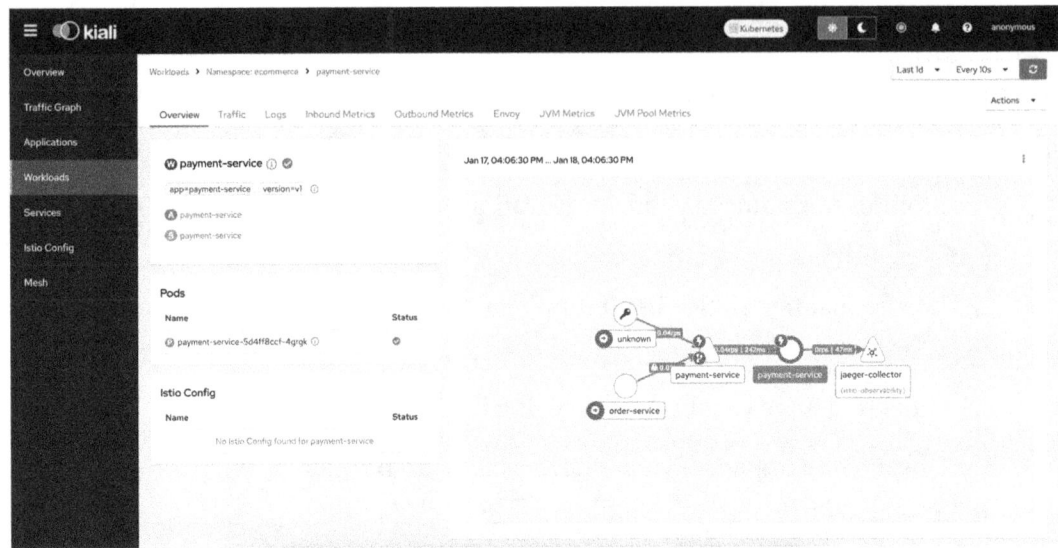

Figure 7-18. *Kiali Workloads list view showing individual service instances and their health status*

The following important pieces of information are available directly from the workload list:

1. Health Status: Each workload displays a colored icon indicating its current health:

    a. Green indicates a healthy workload.

    b. Yellow suggests potential issues.

    c. Red signals critical problems.

2. Application Labels: You'll see the Kubernetes labels associated with each workload, which help identify different versions or deployment configurations. For example, you might see labels like `app=payment-service` and `version=v2`.

Clicking any workload entry brings up a detailed view with various essential tabs. Let's look at how to use each one effectively.

The "Overview" tab offers important information regarding the workload:

- Pod status and readiness
- Container information

- Resource usage metrics (CPU and memory)
- Istio sidecar status
- Applied Istio configurations

The "Traffic" page gives detailed metrics regarding requests that travel through this specific workload instance:

- Inbound and outbound request rates
- Success and error percentages
- Response time distributions
- Protocol-specific metrics (HTTP, gRPC, TCP)

You can better understand the performance of each instance of your service with this level of information. For example, a payment service pod may have higher latencies than others, which could be a sign of a configuration issue or resource constraint.

When managing numerous service iterations, the workload perspective is extremely helpful. Imagine that during a canary deployment, you are running two iterations of the payment service. This is how to evaluate their performance:

1. Navigate to the workload list and look for pods with different version labels.
2. Compare their traffic metrics side by side using the "Traffic" tab.
3. Examine their resource usage patterns in the "Overview" tab.
4. Check their logging output in the "Logs" tab for any discrepancies.

This comparison helps ensure your new version performs as expected before increasing its traffic share. For instance, you might observe that `payment-service-v2` pods show slightly higher latency than `payment-service-v1`, prompting investigation before proceeding with the rollout.

The workload view excels at helping you diagnose issues. When a problem arises

1. Check the "Logs" tab to see real-time logging output from both the application and Istio proxy containers. This helps correlate application behavior with mesh-level events.
2. Use the "Envoy" tab to inspect the proxy configuration and metrics for this specific workload. This can reveal issues with routing rules or network policies.

3. Review the "Metrics" tab for detailed performance graphs, helping identify when problems began and their impact on service behavior.

This detailed visibility at the workload level transforms complex troubleshooting tasks into manageable investigations, helping you maintain reliable service operations across your mesh.

Best Practices for Kiali Usage

To utilize Kiali effectively, you must take a thoughtful and systematic approach that goes beyond simply learning its features. Consider Kiali's interface to be a sophisticated control center for your service mesh; while it gives significant visibility and control, its true value comes when you build clear strategies for leveraging these capabilities. The key is to establish consistent methods that allow you to maintain clarity and efficiency in your daily operations, whether you're troubleshooting issues, managing deployments, or monitoring service performance.

When monitoring your service mesh with Kiali, begin with focused, purpose-built views that meet your operational requirements. This includes configuring specific views for critical flows like payment processing and inventory management on our ecommerce platform, creating tailored visualizations that include only relevant services and their dependencies, and save these configurations for easy access during incidents or routine monitoring. This method elevates Kiali from a general-purpose tool to a precise instrument for analyzing and controlling your individual service mesh deployment. During deployments, these focused views are extremely useful for validating traffic shifting, verifying proper sidecar injection, and monitoring health metrics across service versions. You can learn more about customizing Kiali in their documentation at `https://kiali.io/docs/configuration/custom-dashboard/`.

The most effective Kiali deployments are built on a foundation of systematic troubleshooting and knowledge sharing. Create a methodical strategy to investigation that begins with the service graph for initial problem scoping and then drill down to specific services or workloads as needed. Use Kiali's integration with other observability tools, such as Jaeger for trace analysis and Grafana for metric exploration, document these investigation patterns, and share them with your team to provide a shared knowledge of how to best leverage Kiali's capabilities. This collaborative approach not

CHAPTER 7   VISUALIZING AND ANALYZING SERVICE MESH DATA: GRAFANA, KIALI, AND LOGGING

only increases incident response times, but it also helps your entire team to develop expertise in service mesh operations.

Log Aggregation and Analysis

Log aggregation and analysis are critical components of observability in your service mesh, complementing the metrics and tracing capabilities we've previously addressed. When combined with Istio's extensive telemetry tools, a well-designed logging strategy helps in the development of a comprehensive understanding of your system's behavior, especially during troubleshooting circumstances that necessitate full information about individual requests or events.

Let's look at how Istio's logging architecture works with our ecommerce application's logging strategy. Assume a scenario when a customer is placing an order. This single action generates logs from various services and proxies. The order service records the initial request, the inventory service logs the stock checks, the payment service documents transaction processing, and finally Istio proxies generate their own access logs for each service-to-service communication. Without adequate aggregation and correlation, these distinct log streams might tell disparate stories about the same user behavior.

Istio's access logs serve as the foundation of mesh-level logging, capturing detailed information about every request that flows through your service proxies. Each access log entry tells us which services communicated, the result of that communication, and how long it took. For example, when our order service calls the payment service to process a transaction, the access log captures essential details about this interaction:

```
{
  "timestamp": "2025-01-18T10:15:30.123Z",
  "source": {"workload": "order-service","namespace": "ecommerce"},
  "destination": {"workload": "payment-service", "namespace": "ecommerce"},
  "request": {
    "method": "POST",
    "path": "/api/payments/process",
    "size": 245
  },
  "response": {
```

403

```
    "code": 200,
    "size": 158,
    "latency": "85ms"
  },
  "connection": {
    "protocol": "HTTP/1.1",
    "tls": true
  }
}
```

For auditing purposes, Istio provides audit logs of security-relevant events in your mesh. These logs contain a record of authentication attempts, authorization decisions, and configuration changes that are very important for doing security analysis and meeting compliance requirements. Let's consider an example of an authorization failure while trying to access a protected endpoint:

```
{
  "level": "warn",
  "timestamp": "2025-01-18T10:15:31.456Z",
  "audit": {
    "event": "authorization_denied",
    "source_workload": "inventory-service",
    "destination_workload": "payment-service",
    "reason": "jwt_token_expired"
  }
}
```

We'll explore how to effectively set up, manage, and analyze these logs to gain meaningful insights from your service mesh deployment. The key lies not just in collecting logs but in making them easily searchable and correlatable with other observability data to create a complete picture of your system's behavior.

Understanding Istio's Logging Architecture

At its foundation, Istio's logging architecture is a complex system for capturing and managing observability data throughout your service mesh. Think of it as a network of interconnected observers, each monitoring and recording distinct aspects of your

CHAPTER 7   VISUALIZING AND ANALYZING SERVICE MESH DATA: GRAFANA, KIALI, AND LOGGING

system's behavior. This distributed logging solution operates at numerous levels at once, providing a full view of your service mesh operations.

The architecture is made up of three core logging components that work together seamlessly. First, Envoy sidecars create proxy-level logs, which contain precise information about each request that passes through your mesh. These logs record the fundamental interactions between services, including who spoke with whom, how long it took, and the outcome. Second, Istio's control plane generates its own logs, which record mesh configuration changes, policy decisions, and system events. Finally, the application logs from your services provide critical business context for these technical interactions. For our ecommerce platform, this means we can track a customer's order from the moment it hits our mesh through each service interaction to completion.

What makes Istio's logging architecture particularly powerful is its integration with Kubernetes. When you deploy a service to your mesh, Istio automatically configures the Envoy proxy to emit logs in a standard format. These logs are saved to particular directories in the container filesystem, making them available to your logging infrastructure. The proxy's logging configuration is maintained via Istio's Telemetry API, which allows you to change log levels, formats, and destinations without changing your application code. For example, when our payment service processes a transaction, both the application container and its sidecar proxy generate logs that provide separate viewpoints on the same operation:

```
# Application container log
2025-01-18T10:15:30.123Z INFO [payment-service] Processing payment for
order: ORD-123 amount: $156.78

# Envoy proxy access log
[2025-01-18T10:15:30.123Z] "POST /api/payments/process HTTP/1.1" 200 -
"-" "-" 0 158 85 - "order-service-v1-74d95f4756-xr8vq" "payment-service.
ecommerce.svc.cluster.local" "10.0.0.12:8080" outbound|8080||payment-service.
ecommerce.svc.cluster.local 10.0.0.15:56789 10.0.0.12:8080 10.0.0.11:45678
```

One of the most innovative features of Istio's logging architecture is its built-in support for distributed tracing context. Each log entry can be correlated to traces and metrics using shared identifiers such as request IDs and trace headers. This correlation is quite useful when investigating issues, as you can effortlessly transition from high-level metrics and granular traces to specific log entries. This design automatically propagates the correlation IDs across service boundaries, ensuring that you preserve observability context even during complex microservice interactions.

Understanding this architecture will allow you to better use Istio's logging capabilities to acquire deep insights into your service mesh activity, and this expertise is especially important when setting log aggregation solutions or solving complex issues that necessitate correlation analysis across numerous observability signals.

Configuring Access Logs

Access logs provide critical visibility into your service mesh's operations, but their true value emerges only with proper configuration. Istio provides sophisticated mechanisms for controlling what gets logged, when, and in what format. Think of this configuration as setting up a comprehensive surveillance system for your mesh—you need to carefully position your cameras (log collection points) and decide what details to record.

Let's start with access logs, which document every request flowing through your mesh. In Istio, we configure access logging through the Telemetry API. This configuration determines what information gets captured for each request passing through an Envoy proxy.

We start with setting up the provider in the mesh config file; remember this file needs to be provided as input during installation of Istio. We have explained in detail about how to set up Istio with the mesh config file in section "Reinstalling Istio with Observability Configuration" of Chapter 6. Envoy proxies can be configured to export access logs in the OpenTelemetry format. In this example, the proxies forward access logs to an OpenTelemetry collector, which is set up to output the logs to standard output. You can then access the OpenTelemetry collector's standard output using the `kubectl logs` command:

```
spec:
  meshConfig:
    accessLogFile: /dev/stdout
    extensionProviders:
    - name: otel
      envoyOtelAls:
        service: jaeger-collector.istio-observability.svc.cluster.local
        port: 4317
    defaultProviders:
```

```
  accessLogging:
    - envoy
    - otel
```

Remember we are using the Jaeger collector here, but you can also use the OpenTelemetry collector. Please see the OpenTelemetry collection documentation (https://opentelemetry.io/docs/collector/installation/#kubernetes) for instructions on how to do this. There are other ways to configure access logs in Istio; however, the Telemetry API is the recommended technique. Let's begin with a simple configuration that allows access logging for our ecommerce services:

```
apiVersion: telemetry.istio.io/v1
kind: Telemetry
metadata:
 name: mesh-default
 namespace: istio-system
spec:
 accessLogging:
   - providers:
     - name: otel
```

This configuration enables access logging across our ecommerce namespace, capturing all service interactions. You should start seeing the logs in the istio-proxy container of your pods. For example, for order service pods, when you run the below command, you should start seeing the logs:

```
kubectl logs  order-service-8646c56856-qv24v -n ecommerce -c istio-proxy

[2025-01-19T03:19:15.248Z] "GET /api/inventory/check/PROD-001?quantity=10 HTTP/1.1" 200 - via_upstream - "-" 0 196 4 4 "-" "okhttp/4.12.0" "5c64b86c-4b3c-4107-8965-558a968a9311" "inventory-service.ecommerce.svc.cluster.local:8081" "10.244.0.51:8081" outbound|8081||inventory-service.ecommerce.svc.cluster.local 10.244.0.49:51786 10.96.181.93:8081 10.244.0.49:34876 - default
[2025-01-19T03:19:15.253Z] "GET /api/inventory/check/PROD-008?quantity=20 HTTP/1.1" 200 - via_upstream - "-" 0 190 3 3 "-" "okhttp/4.12.0" "c7de339e-fd71-48a7-a9c4-9d9eb193df05" "inventory-service.ecommerce.svc.cluster.local:8081" "10.244.0.51:8081" outbound|8081||inventory-
```

service.ecommerce.svc.cluster.local 10.244.0.49:51786 10.96.181.93:8081
10.244.0.49:34876 - default
[2025-01-19T03:19:15.260Z] "POST /api/payments/process HTTP/1.1" 200 -
via_upstream - "-" 153 420 107 106 "-" "okhttp/4.12.0" "bff334b4-289c-4df9-
a063-0d68dec8c08e" "payment-service.ecommerce.svc.cluster.local:8082"
"10.244.0.50:8082" outbound|8082||payment-service.ecommerce.svc.cluster.local
10.244.0.49:57866 10.96.87.221:8082 10.244.0.49:58900 - default
[2025-01-19T03:19:15.241Z] "POST /orders/api HTTP/1.1" 200 - via_upstream -
"-" 567 453 135 135 "10.244.0.1" "curl/8.7.1" "b54be7f8-
cc83-475a-9fb4-9ef4b02805f8" "172.18.0.2" "10.244.0.49:8080"
inbound|8080|| 127.0.0.6:38569 10.244.0.49:8080 10.244.0.1:0
invalid:outbound_.8080_._.order-service.ecommerce.svc.cluster.local default

In the upcoming sections, we will try to explore the configurations that enable and disable these access logs in different ways.

Filtering Logs Based on Response Codes

Filtering logs based on response codes provides a powerful mechanism for managing observability in a production service mesh environment. By examining HTTP status codes and related attributes like request duration and URL paths, we can implement intelligent filtering rules that capture significant events while reducing noise from routine operations. This approach becomes especially valuable in high-traffic systems where comprehensive logging of all requests would be impractical and potentially detrimental to performance. Status codes serve as reliable indicators of service health and behavior—with 5xx codes signaling server-side failures requiring immediate attention, 4xx codes highlighting client-side issues or API misuse, and unusual patterns in 2xx responses potentially revealing subtle problems like performance degradation:

```
apiVersion: telemetry.istio.io/v1alpha1
kind: Telemetry
metadata:
 name: payment-service-logging
 namespace: ecommerce
spec:
 selector:
```

```
    matchLabels:
      app: payment-service
  accessLogging:
  - providers:
    - name: otel
    filter:
      expression: "response.code >= 400" # Only log errors
```

The real power of response code filtering emerges when combined with other contextual attributes available in the service mesh. By crafting expressions that consider not just the status code but also the request duration, URL path, headers, and connection termination details, we can build sophisticated logging rules that align precisely with our observability needs. This multidimensional filtering strategy ensures we maintain visibility into critical issues and business-significant operations while keeping log volumes manageable. Whether capturing failed requests, monitoring performance thresholds, or tracking specific business transactions, response code filtering provides the foundation for a balanced and effective logging strategy that supports both day-to-day operations and incident investigation without overwhelming our logging infrastructure. Please refer to Istio's documentation for complete documentation on what all can go inside the expression attribute at https://istio.io/latest/docs/tasks/observability/metrics/customize-metrics/#use-expressions-for-values.

Disabling Access Logs for Specific Services

In service mesh environments, the ability to selectively disable access logging for specific workloads gives you critical control over observability granularity and resource utilization. This capability is especially useful in production installations, where certain services generate large amounts of everyday traffic that may not require extensive logging. Administrators can use Istio's Telemetry API to construct exact rules that disable access logging depending on workload selectors, allowing for effective log volume management while keeping visibility into where it matters most. This selective approach optimizes system resources and lowers storage costs while ensuring that key services continue to provide audit trails for monitoring, troubleshooting, and compliance:

```
apiVersion: telemetry.istio.io/v1alpha1
kind: Telemetry
metadata:
```

```yaml
  name: disable-inventory-logging
  namespace: ecommerce
spec:
  selector:
    matchLabels:
      app: inventory-service  # Matches our inventory service label
  accessLogging:
  - providers:
    - name: otel
      disabled: true
```

This option disables access logging for the inventory service. We utilize the selector to match the `app: inventory-service` label that we specified in our inventory service deployment. The implementation uses Kubernetes label selectors to target individual workloads, making it easy to apply logging policies that are consistent with deployment methodologies or organizational needs. When paired with namespace-level restrictions, this technology provides a hierarchical approach to log management that scales well across large deployments. The ability to disable access logs for specific services provides the granular control required to maintain an efficient and manageable observability infrastructure, whether working with health check endpoints that generate constant traffic, internal system services that require minimal auditing, or development environments where detailed logging is unnecessary, and this functionality is especially useful in microservices architectures because distinct services may have different logging requirements depending on their business criticality, security requirements, or operational features.

Selective Logging Based on Traffic Direction

In contemporary service mesh architectures, the ability to distinguish between inbound (server-side) and outbound (client-side) traffic patterns is an important aspect of controlling access logging behavior. This directional logging capability is especially useful for controlling observability in complicated microservices systems, where services behave as both clients and servers in different contexts. The Telemetry API enables administrators to customize logging policies based on traffic direction, allowing for advanced logging strategies that can capture inbound requests while not necessarily logging the accompanying outbound calls or vice versa. This granular control allows for clear visibility into service interactions while optimizing the amount of logs emitted and avoiding redundant entries that could complicate troubleshooting efforts:

```
apiVersion: telemetry.istio.io/v1alpha1
kind: Telemetry
metadata:
  name: payment-inbound-logging
  namespace: ecommerce
spec:
  selector:
    matchLabels:
      app: payment-service  # Matches our payment service label
  accessLogging:
  - providers:
    - name: otel
    match:
      mode: CLIENT  # Only disable outbound logging
    disabled: true
```

Traffic direction–based logging leverages Istio's understanding of service mesh topology to make intelligent decisions about what gets logged. By specifying the traffic mode in logging configurations, organizations can implement nuanced policies that reflect their observability requirements for different types of service interactions. This approach proves especially valuable when dealing with scenarios where internal service-to-service communication generates high volumes of logs, but only the entry and exit points of a transaction flow need detailed logging. Whether focusing on external client requests, internal service communications, or specific patterns of interaction, directional logging provides the precision needed to maintain effective observability while managing system resources efficiently. The ability to selectively enable or disable logging based on traffic direction becomes a powerful tool in building scalable and maintainable service mesh observability strategies.

Setting Default Exception Logging

In a service mesh environment, establishing default exception logging patterns provides a critical safety net for capturing unexpected behaviors and error conditions across all services. The ability to configure mesh-wide logging rules that focus on exceptional scenarios ensures important issues are never missed, even if service-specific logging policies are more restrictive. These default configurations typically target high-impact events like server errors (5xx status codes), failed route lookups, connection terminations, and unusually slow requests—scenarios that almost always warrant investigation regardless of which service they occur in. Default exception logging serves as a foundational layer of observability that complements more specific, service-level logging policies, ensuring critical issues are consistently captured while still maintaining control over overall log volumes:

```yaml
apiVersion: telemetry.istio.io/v1alpha1
kind: Telemetry
metadata:
  name: ecommerce-default-logging
  namespace: istio-system
spec:
  accessLogging:
  - providers:
    - name: jaeger
    filter:
      expression: |
        response.code >= 500 ||
        xds.cluster_name == 'BlackHoleCluster' ||
        (has(response.duration) && response.duration >= 2000) ||
        (!has(response.code) && has(connection.termination_details))
```

The strength of default exception logging stems from its ability to set standard observability policies throughout the mesh without requiring individual service configurations. By specifying these baseline logging rules at the mesh level, organizations can ensure that critical issues are visible even as new services are introduced or existing ones are modified, and this method is especially useful in dynamic situations where services are frequently deployed or modified, as it establishes a solid foundation for incident detection and troubleshooting. The configuration expressions can combine numerous conditions to create sophisticated exception detection rules, guaranteeing that, while regular traffic generates few logs, any significant deviations from expected behavior are automatically collected and saved for examination. This blend of comprehensive error tracking and logging efficiency makes default exception logging a critical component of any production service mesh observability strategy. Remember that these expressions are evaluated for each request, so overly complicated filters can degrade speed, and it is critical to balance logging requirements with system performance, particularly in production environments.

Configuring Access Log Output and Format

Effective access logging in Istio begins with properly configuring log output, encoding, and format. When first deploying Istio, administrators must make key decisions regarding where logs will be stored and how they will be structured. These configurations are the foundation of your service mesh's observability strategy, deciding not only what data is collected, but also how readily it can be processed and analyzed later.

Istio includes three primary configuration settings that influence access logging behavior. The `accessLogFile` setting specifies the location of log output, with /dev/stdout being a common option that permits logs to be recorded by container runtime logging drivers. The `accessLogEncoding` option allows you to select either JSON format, which gives structured data perfect for automated processing, or TEXT format, which provides human-readable output useful for direct inspection. The `accessLogFormat` parameter provides you with precise control over log content, allowing you to choose which fields show in each log entry and how they are organized. This flexibility is especially useful when connecting with existing logging infrastructure or meeting certain compliance needs.

The default access log format covers all request attributes, including timing, protocol details, response codes, and network information. Every field in this format has a unique observability function, ranging from basic request identification to comprehensive topological mapping within your service mesh. The format includes critical information such as the start time, HTTP method, path, response code, and numerous identifiers that aid in the traceability of requests throughout the system. Examining these logs allows you to reconstruct the whole path of a request through your mesh, including both the client- and server-side perspectives of each interaction. This dual-sided logging is very useful for studying service-to-service communication or performance concerns.

Istio will use the following default access log format if `accessLogFormat` is not specified:

```
[%START_TIME%] \"%REQ(:METHOD)% %REQ(X-ENVOY-ORIGINAL-PATH?:PATH)%
%PROTOCOL%\" %RESPONSE_CODE% %RESPONSE_FLAGS% %RESPONSE_CODE_DETAILS%
%CONNECTION_TERMINATION_DETAILS%
```

CHAPTER 7   VISUALIZING AND ANALYZING SERVICE MESH DATA: GRAFANA, KIALI, AND LOGGING

```
\"%UPSTREAM_TRANSPORT_FAILURE_REASON%\" %BYTES_RECEIVED% %BYTES_SENT%
%DURATION% %RESP(X-ENVOY-UPSTREAM-SERVICE-TIME)% \"%REQ(X-FORWARDED-FOR)%\"
\"%REQ(USER-AGENT)%\" \"%REQ(X-REQUEST-ID)%\"
\"%REQ(:AUTHORITY)%\" \"%UPSTREAM_HOST%\" %UPSTREAM_CLUSTER% %UPSTREAM_
LOCAL_ADDRESS% %DOWNSTREAM_LOCAL_ADDRESS% %DOWNSTREAM_REMOTE_ADDRESS%
%REQUESTED_SERVER_NAME% %ROUTE_NAME%\n
```

The log format begins with the timestamp [%START_TIME%], which records the exact time the request began. This time information is critical when examining issues or analyzing request patterns. The basic request information is recorded as follows: \"%REQ(:METHOD)%%REQ(X-ENVOY-ORIGINAL-PATH?:PATH)%%PROTOCOL%\". This section describes the type of request (GET, POST, etc.), the specific path requested, and the protocol utilized. For example, in our ecommerce application, a request might look like "POST /api/orders HTTP/1.1", indicating that a new order is being created.

The next section focuses on the response data: %RESPONSE_CODE%%RESPONSE_FLAGS%%RESPONSE_CODE_DETAILS%%CONNECTION_TERMINATION_DETAILS%. These fields help us understand what happened during request processing, and the response code signals success or failure (e.g., 200 for success or 500 for server faults), whereas response flags and details provide additional context about any special handling or concerns. When debugging unsuccessful payments in our application, these fields can help determine if the failure was caused by invalid input (400-level codes) or a system issue (500-level codes).

Network-level metrics follow: %BYTES_RECEIVED% %BYTES_SENT% %DURATION% %RESP(X-ENVOY-UPSTREAM-SERVICE-TIME)%. These measurements help understand the size of requests and responses, along with timing information. The duration field is particularly valuable for identifying performance issues—for instance, if payment processing starts taking longer than usual, it would be reflected in these metrics.

The format also captures important contextual information: \"%REQ(X-FORWARDED-FOR)%\" \"%REQ(USER-AGENT)%\" \"%REQ(X-REQUEST-ID)%\". The X-Request-ID, for example, allows us to trace a single request across multiple services in our mesh. When a customer places an order that involves our order, inventory, and payment services, this ID helps us follow the entire transaction chain.

Finally, the log includes detailed routing information: \"%UPSTREAM_HOST%\" %UPSTREAM_CLUSTER% %UPSTREAM_LOCAL_ADDRESS% %DOWNSTREAM_LOCAL_ADDRESS%. These fields reveal exactly how the request was routed through our service mesh, which becomes invaluable when debugging routing issues or understanding traffic patterns.

For instance, we can see whether a payment request properly reached the payment service or was mistakenly routed elsewhere.

The beauty of this format lies in its comprehensiveness—it captures everything from high-level HTTP information to low-level network details, providing a complete picture of each request. When investigating issues in our ecommerce platform, these logs give us all the context we need, whether we're tracking down a failed payment, investigating slow order processing, or understanding traffic patterns during peak shopping periods.

To modify these settings after initial deployment, you must take care to use the appropriate configuration method based on your installation approach. For operator-based installations, modifications to the `IstioOperator` resource allow for declarative configuration management. Alternatively, when using `istioctl` for direct installation, command-line flags provide immediate configuration updates. Regardless of the method chosen, changes to these fundamental logging parameters should be managed carefully, ideally tested in a staging environment before being applied to production systems. Understanding the relationship between log configuration and system observability helps ensure your service mesh remains both observable and manageable as it scales.

Conclusion and Future Trends

In this chapter, we have seen how the powerful trio of Grafana, Kiali, and sophisticated logging forms a complete observability foundation for contemporary service mesh infrastructures. Grafana's visualization capabilities turn the raw metrics into actionable information, allowing both real-time monitoring and historical analysis of everything from business metrics to system performance. Kiali's view of service topology offers another highly crucial feature in the form of a real-time, dynamic service interaction view that allows operators to learn and debug the complex choreography of microservices communications. Our deep dive into logging best practices demonstrated how proper configuration and management of access logs complete the observability picture by offering profound insight into system behavior without overconsumption of resources.

Looking forward, service mesh observability's landscape is continuing to evolve at a fast pace as systems become increasingly complex and distributed. The trend toward more automated analysis, intelligent alerting, and unified observability platforms suggests a promising future where operators can focus more on optimization and spend less hours on basic monitoring. Also, practices and patterns that we've discussed

CHAPTER 7　VISUALIZING AND ANALYZING SERVICE MESH DATA: GRAFANA, KIALI, AND LOGGING

here provide a strong foundation for building observable, maintainable service mesh deployments that support both business objectives and technical operations. By thoughtfully combining metrics visualization, topology mapping, and log analysis with a regular review and update of these tools to meet changing needs, organizations can maintain clear visibility into the behavior of their system, enabling quick problem resolution and data-driven decision-making for continuous optimization in their service mesh development.

CHAPTER 8

Deploying Istio in Production

Introduction

Deploying Istio in a production environment is much more than installing a service mesh. It's about engineering a resilient system that effectively manages microservices communications, security, and observability at scale. In today's cloud-native landscape, Istio stands out by offering advanced capabilities for traffic control, policy enforcement, and performance monitoring. However, making Istio work smoothly in production requires careful planning around resource distribution, tight integration with Kubernetes workloads, and robust security measures.

Automation plays a crucial role in this process. Leveraging tools such as Helm and Terraform not only streamlines the deployment process but also ensures consistency across diverse environments. Once Istio is up and running, scaling it to accommodate growing traffic becomes the next major challenge. Both the control plane (Istiod) and the data plane (Envoy proxies) must be tuned through horizontal and vertical scaling approaches to avoid performance bottlenecks while maintaining cost-effectiveness. This chapter lays out a comprehensive framework for scaling Istio, optimizing resource usage, and troubleshooting performance issues in high-demand scenarios.

In this chapter, we will first demonstrate the single-cluster deployment model using Helm and Terraform on Amazon EKS. After that we will examine various deployment models such as multi-cluster federated architectures and remote cluster integrations to help you choose the strategy that best aligns with your operational needs.

CHAPTER 8   DEPLOYING ISTIO IN PRODUCTION

Objective

By the end of this chapter, you will

- Understand the key considerations for deploying Istio in a production environment.
- Learn how to automate Istio deployments using Helm and Terraform for consistency and repeatability.
- Explore scaling strategies to handle high-traffic loads while maintaining performance.
- Implement horizontal and vertical scaling techniques for optimized resource allocation.

Outline

To deploy Istio effectively in a production environment, it is essential to focus on practical deployment strategies and performance considerations. This chapter begins by discussing the deployment of Istio in Kubernetes, covering best practices for installation, configuration, and monitoring. We will explore how to set up Istio efficiently and ensure a stable and reliable deployment that meets production requirements.

Once Istio is deployed, scaling becomes a critical factor for maintaining performance in high-traffic environments. We will examine horizontal and vertical scaling strategies for both the control plane (Istiod) and the data plane (Envoy proxies) to optimize resource utilization. Additionally, we will discuss cost management techniques to prevent unnecessary resource overhead and ensure an efficient, cost-effective Istio deployment.

Single-Cluster Deployment

Imagine a scenario where all the components of your service mesh—both the brain (control plane) and the brawn (data plane)—reside within a single Kubernetes cluster. This is the essence of a single-cluster deployment as shown in Figure 8-1. It's an excellent starting point for development, testing, or small production environments. Here, simplicity is the virtue: with a unified system, administrative overhead is minimized, and integration with native Kubernetes tools is straightforward.

CHAPTER 8 DEPLOYING ISTIO IN PRODUCTION

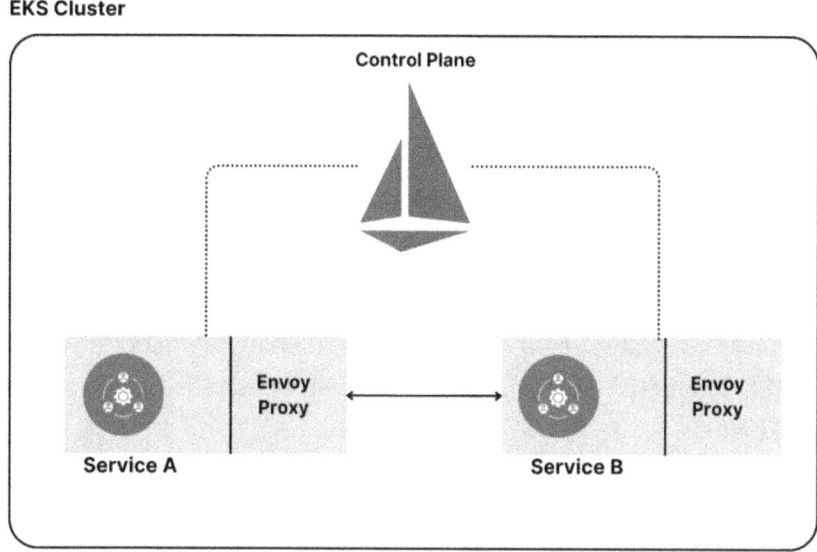

Figure 8-1. *Architecture of Istio in a single cluster*

Furthermore, deploying Istio within a single cluster on EKS provides a cost-effective and scalable solution while leveraging AWS's fully managed Kubernetes capabilities. With EKS handling control plane provisioning, networking, and security, organizations can focus on optimizing Istio's traffic management, observability, and security features rather than dealing with the complexities of managing an entire Kubernetes infrastructure manually.

Introduction to Amazon EKS

Amazon Elastic Kubernetes Service (EKS) is a managed Kubernetes service that simplifies the deployment, scaling, and operation of Kubernetes clusters on AWS. By offloading control plane management to AWS, EKS provides a highly available, secure, and scalable platform for running Kubernetes workloads. In a production environment, maintaining infrastructure that is scalable, resilient, and cost-effective presents significant challenges. EKS simplifies Kubernetes operations while providing deep integrations with AWS services, making it an excellent platform for running Istio at scale. Below are the key benefits of using EKS for Istio:

- Managed Control Plane: AWS takes care of control plane provisioning, scaling, and patching, ensuring high availability and reducing operational overhead.

- Security and IAM Integration: EKS integrates natively with AWS IAM, enabling fine-grained access control and secure service-to-service authentication.

- Scalability: With autoscaling capabilities for worker nodes and seamless integration with AWS Application Load Balancer/Network Load Balancer (ALB/NLB), EKS can efficiently handle dynamic workloads.

- Multi-AZ Resilience: EKS clusters can be deployed across multiple AWS availability zones, improving fault tolerance and reducing downtime.

- Networking and Observability: Deep integration with AWS VPC, Prometheus, CloudWatch, and OpenTelemetry ensures enhanced monitoring and troubleshooting capabilities.

- Simplified Deployment with Terraform and Helm: Using infrastructure-as-code (IaC) tools like Terraform and Helm, you can automate the provisioning and configuration of EKS clusters and Istio components.

Setting Up the Development Environment

In order to run an Amazon Elastic Kubernetes Service (EKS) cluster, it first needs to be deployed into an AWS account. So you need to have an AWS account first, if you don't have it already. EKS can be deployed using multiple methods, including AWS Management Console, AWS CLI, AWS CDK, Terraform, etc. Among these, Terraform [1] is a preferred choice for automating infrastructure deployment due to its declarative approach, repeatability, and scalability. In order to deploy an EKS cluster, ensure you have the following installed on your local machine:

AWS Account

If you don't have an AWS account, sign up at `aws.amazon.com`. Once registered, you will be redirected to the AWS Management Console dashboard as seen in Figure 8-2.

CHAPTER 8 DEPLOYING ISTIO IN PRODUCTION

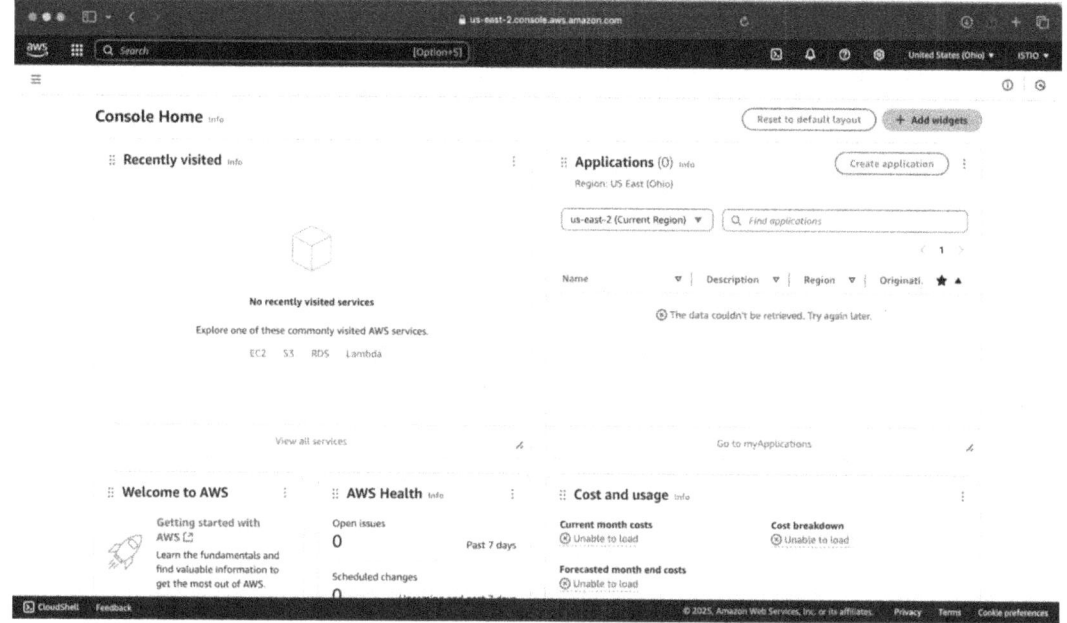

***Figure 8-2.** AWS Management Console dashboard*

AWS CLI

AWS CLI is required for authentication and interaction with AWS services. To install AWS CLI, follow these steps:

For macOS:

brew install awscli

For Linux:

curl "https://awscli.amazonaws.com/AWSCLIV2.pkg" -o "AWSCLIV2.pkg" sudo installer -pkg AWSCLIV2.pkg -target /

Verify Installation:

aws --version

 # Expected Output
aws-cli/2.24.1 Python/3.12.9 Darwin/23.2.0 source/arm64

Configure AWS CLI:

To configure AWS CLI, you must create an IAM user. Once the user is created, you need to create an access key and copy the key ID and secret access key to configure AWS CLI:

```
aws configure
```

```
AWS Access Key ID [None]: <Enter your access key id here>
AWS Secret Access Key [None]: <Enter your secret access key here>
Default region name [None]: <enter desired region name>
Default output format [None]: <enter output format>
```

Terraform

To install Terraform follow the below steps:

For macOS:

```
brew tap hashicorp/tap
brew install hashicorp/tap/terraform
```

For Linux:

```
curl -fsSL https://apt.releases.hashicorp.com/gpg | sudo apt-key add -
sudo apt-add-repository "deb [arch=amd64] https://apt.releases.hashicorp.com $(lsb_release -cs) main"
sudo apt-get update && sudo apt-get install terraform
```

Verify Installation:

```
terraform -v

# Expected Output
Terraform v1.10.5
on darwin_arm64
```

Deploying an EKS Cluster Using Terraform

Now that we have successfully configured our development environment, it is time to define the EKS cluster in code using Terraform, making it easy to version control, audit, and manage.

CHAPTER 8 DEPLOYING ISTIO IN PRODUCTION

Add `variable.tf`, which holds all necessary variables required in this module:

```
variable "cluster_name" {
  description = "istio-eks"
  type        = string
  default     = "istio-eks"
}
variable "region" {
    type = string
    default = "us-west-2"
}
```

Also, let's add a `provider.tf` file to define and configure the cloud provider that Terraform will interact with AWS:

```
provider "aws" {
  region = var.region
}
terraform {
  required_providers {
    aws = {
      source  = "hashicorp/aws"
      version = "~> 5.0"
    }
  }
}
```

To utilize the outputs generated by Terraform, you need to define them in an `outputs.tf` file. This file specifies the variables that Terraform should display or expose after resource creation:

```
output "cluster_endpoint" {
  description = "Endpoint for EKS control plane"
  value       = module.eks.cluster_endpoint
}
output "cluster_security_group_id" {
  description = "Security group ids attached to the cluster control plane"
  value       = module.eks.cluster_security_group_id
```

```
}
output "region" {
  description = "AWS region"
  value       = var.region
}
output "cluster_name" {
  description = "Kubernetes Cluster Name"
  value       = module.eks.cluster_name
}
```

Since EKS requires a VPC with private and public subnets, define the VPC and networking settings in a separate `vpc.tf` file:

```
module "vpc" {
  source  = "terraform-aws-modules/vpc/aws"
  version = "~> 5.0"

  name = "eks_vpc"
  cidr = "10.0.0.0/16"

  azs             = ["us-west-2a", "us-west-2b"]
  private_subnets = ["10.0.0.0/19", "10.0.32.0/19"]
  public_subnets  = ["10.0.64.0/19", "10.0.96.0/19"]

  enable_nat_gateway = true
  single_nat_gateway = true

  public_subnet_tags = {
    "kubernetes.io/role/elb" = "1"
  }

  private_subnet_tags = {
    "kubernetes.io/role/internal-elb" = "1"
  }

  tags = {
    Environment = "Production"
  }
}
```

CHAPTER 8　DEPLOYING ISTIO IN PRODUCTION

Now, define the EKS cluster using Terraform's eks module [2] and associate it with the created VPC in eks.tf:

```
module "eks" {
  source  = "terraform-aws-modules/eks/aws"
  version = "~> 20.0"

  cluster_name    = var.cluster_name
  cluster_version = "1.31"
  cluster_endpoint_private_access = true
  cluster_endpoint_public_access            = true
  enable_cluster_creator_admin_permissions = true

  # EKS Addons
  cluster_addons = {
    coredns                = {}
    eks-pod-identity-agent = {}
    kube-proxy             = {}
    vpc-cni                = {}
  }

  vpc_id     = module.vpc.vpc_id
  subnet_ids = module.vpc.private_subnets

  eks_managed_node_group_defaults = {
    create_launch_template = true
    launch_template_name   = "eks-launch-template"
    ami_type               = "BOTTLEROCKET_x86_64"
    disk_size              = 50
    instance_types         = ["t3.small", "t3.medium"]
  }

  eks_managed_node_groups = {
    nodegroup1 = {
      labels = {
        NodeGroup = "nodegroup1"
      }
      min_size = 1
      max_size = 3
```

```
      desired_size = 2

      instance_types = ["t3.medium"]
      capacity_type  = "SPOT"
    }
  }

  node_security_group_additional_rules = {
    ingress_15017 = {
      description                   = "Cluster API - Istio Webhook
                                      namespace.sidecar-injector.istio.io"
      protocol                      = "TCP"
      from_port                     = 15017
      to_port                       = 15017
      type                          = "ingress"
      source_cluster_security_group = true
    }
    ingress_15012 = {
      description                   = "Cluster API to nodes ports/
                                      protocols"
      protocol                      = "TCP"
      from_port                     = 15012
      to_port                       = 15012
      type                          = "ingress"
      source_cluster_security_group = true
    }
  }
  tags = {
    Environment = "Production"
  }
}
```

Using the above eks module, we will be provisioning an AWS managed control plane, and the node group configuration ensures autoscaling. Now that all the configurations are in place, let's initialize Terraform using the following command:

terraform init

You should see the output as shown in Figure 8-3.

```
(base) karanbirsingh@Karanbirs-MacBook-Pro deploy-eks-using-tf % terraform init
Initializing the backend...
Initializing modules...
Initializing provider plugins...
- Reusing previous version of hashicorp/tls from the dependency lock file
- Reusing previous version of hashicorp/kubernetes from the dependency lock file
- Reusing previous version of hashicorp/time from the dependency lock file
- Reusing previous version of hashicorp/cloudinit from the dependency lock file
- Reusing previous version of hashicorp/helm from the dependency lock file
- Reusing previous version of cloudposse/utils from the dependency lock file
- Reusing previous version of hashicorp/aws from the dependency lock file
- Using previously-installed hashicorp/aws v5.86.1
- Using previously-installed hashicorp/tls v4.0.6
- Using previously-installed hashicorp/kubernetes v2.35.1
- Using previously-installed hashicorp/time v0.12.1
- Using previously-installed hashicorp/cloudinit v2.3.5
- Using previously-installed hashicorp/helm v2.17.0
- Using previously-installed cloudposse/utils v1.28.0
Terraform has made some changes to the provider dependency selections recorded
in the .terraform.lock.hcl file. Review those changes and commit them to your
version control system if they represent changes you intended to make.

Terraform has been successfully initialized!

You may now begin working with Terraform. Try running "terraform plan" to see
any changes that are required for your infrastructure. All Terraform commands
should now work.

If you ever set or change modules or backend configuration for Terraform,
rerun this command to reinitialize your working directory. If you forget, other
commands will detect it and remind you to do so if necessary.
```

Figure 8-3. *Output of the terraform init command*

Now that Terraform has successfully initialized, let's run the plan command to preview the changes Terraform will make before actually applying them. It helps in understanding what resources will be created, modified, or destroyed without making any real changes to the infrastructure:

```
terraform plan
```

When executing the `terraform plan` command, Terraform generates a detailed output outlining the proposed changes to the infrastructure. Given the complexity of cloud infrastructure, this output can be extensive. Figure 8-4 depicts that Terraform indicates that it is planning to create a node group for the Amazon EKS cluster.

CHAPTER 8   DEPLOYING ISTIO IN PRODUCTION

```
# module.eks.module.eks_managed_node_group["general"].aws_eks_node_group.this[0] will be created
+ resource "aws_eks_node_group" "this" {
    + ami_type                = (known after apply)
    + arn                     = (known after apply)
    + capacity_type           = "ON_DEMAND"
    + cluster_name            = "istio-eks"
    + disk_size               = (known after apply)
    + id                      = (known after apply)
    + instance_types          = [
        + "t2.medium",
      ]
    + labels                  = {
        + "role" = "general"
      }
    + node_group_name         = (known after apply)
    + node_group_name_prefix  = "general-"
    + node_role_arn           = (known after apply)
    + release_version         = (known after apply)
    + resources               = (known after apply)
    + status                  = (known after apply)
    + subnet_ids              = (known after apply)
    + tags                    = {
        + "Environment" = "Production"
        + "Name"        = "general"
      }
    + tags_all                = {
        + "Environment" = "Production"
        + "Name"        = "general"
      }
    + version                 = "1.24"
```

Figure 8-4. *Output of the terraform plan command showing a node group will be created for EKS*

Now that we have inspected the `terraform plan`, it's time to deploy the EKS cluster using the following command:

`terraform apply --auto-approve`

Normally, when you run `terraform apply`, Terraform prompts you to review and confirm the proposed infrastructure changes before applying them, but when you execute the `terraform apply` command with the --auto-approve flag, the command automatically applies Terraform changes without requiring user confirmation. Deploying a new EKS cluster should take around ten minutes, and once the command is fully executed, you should be able to see Apply complete! as an output as shown in Figure 8-5.

```
module.eks.module.eks_managed_node_group["one"].aws_eks_node_group.this[0]: Still creating... [1m30s el
apsed]
module.eks.module.eks_managed_node_group["two"].aws_eks_node_group.this[0]: Still creating... [1m30s el
apsed]
module.eks.module.eks_managed_node_group["one"].aws_eks_node_group.this[0]: Creation complete after 2m7
s [id=istio:node-group-1-20250214093122829500000001b]
module.eks.module.eks_managed_node_group["two"].aws_eks_node_group.this[0]: Creation complete after 2m7
s [id=istio:node-group-2-20250214093122829400000019]
module.eks.aws_eks_addon.this["vpc-cni"]: Creating...
module.eks.aws_eks_addon.this["eks-pod-identity-agent"]: Creating...
module.eks.aws_eks_addon.this["coredns"]: Creating...
module.eks.aws_eks_addon.this["kube-proxy"]: Creating...
module.eks.aws_eks_addon.this["kube-proxy"]: Creation complete after 8s [id=istio:kube-proxy]
module.eks.aws_eks_addon.this["coredns"]: Still creating... [10s elapsed]
module.eks.aws_eks_addon.this["vpc-cni"]: Still creating... [10s elapsed]
module.eks.aws_eks_addon.this["eks-pod-identity-agent"]: Still creating... [10s elapsed]
module.eks.aws_eks_addon.this["coredns"]: Creation complete after 14s [id=istio:coredns]
module.eks.aws_eks_addon.this["eks-pod-identity-agent"]: Still creating... [20s elapsed]
module.eks.aws_eks_addon.this["vpc-cni"]: Still creating... [20s elapsed]
module.eks.aws_eks_addon.this["vpc-cni"]: Still creating... [30s elapsed]
module.eks.aws_eks_addon.this["eks-pod-identity-agent"]: Still creating... [30s elapsed]
module.eks.aws_eks_addon.this["eks-pod-identity-agent"]: Still creating... [40s elapsed]
module.eks.aws_eks_addon.this["vpc-cni"]: Still creating... [40s elapsed]
module.eks.aws_eks_addon.this["vpc-cni"]: Creation complete after 45s [id=istio:vpc-cni]
module.eks.aws_eks_addon.this["eks-pod-identity-agent"]: Creation complete after 45s [id=istio:eks-pod-
identity-agent]

Apply complete! Resources: 66 added, 0 changed, 0 destroyed.

Outputs:

cluster_endpoint = "https://5A81BF537801DDD14FD7CC9725398363.gr7.us-west-2.eks.amazonaws.com"
cluster_name = "istio"
cluster_security_group_id = "sg-0edc89349e9662773"
region = "us-west-2"
```

Figure 8-5. *Output of the terraform apply command showing a successful deploy of the EKS cluster*

Now that the cluster is up and running, it is time to configure kubectl so that we can start working with the cluster by executing the following command. Figure 8-6 depicts the output of the command:

```
aws eks --region $(terraform output -raw region) update-kubeconfig \
    --name $(terraform output -raw cluster_name)
```

```
(base) karanbirsingh@Karanbirs-MacBook-Pro deploy-eks-using-tf % aws eks --region $(terra
form output -raw region) update-kubeconfig \
    --name $(terraform output -raw cluster_name)
Updated context arn:aws:eks:us-west-2:651706777003:cluster/istio in /Users/karanbirsingh/
.kube/config
(base) karanbirsingh@Karanbirs-MacBook-Pro deploy-eks-using-tf % []
```

Figure 8-6. *Output of the kubeconfig update command*

Finally, let's make sure we are able to connect to our EKS cluster using kubectl by running the following command:

```
kubectl cluster-info
```

kubectl cluster-info provides more information about the cluster as shown in Figure 8-7.

```
(base) karanbirsingh@Karanbirs-MacBook-Pro deploy-eks-using-tf % kubectl cluster-info
Kubernetes control plane is running at https://154110DDCC43B09D02A4833594B64A95.sk1.us-west-2.eks.amazonaws.com
CoreDNS is running at https://154110DDCC43B09D02A4833594B64A95.sk1.us-west-2.eks.amazonaws.com/api/v1/namespaces/k
ube-system/services/kube-dns:dns/proxy

To further debug and diagnose cluster problems, use 'kubectl cluster-info dump'.
(base) karanbirsingh@Karanbirs-MacBook-Pro deploy-eks-using-tf %
```

Figure 8-7. Output of the kubectl cluster-info command

kubectl get nodes

The command kubectl get nodes provides information about the nodes and their health status as shown in Figure 8-8.

```
(base) karanbirsingh@Karanbirs-MacBook-Pro deploy-eks-using-tf % kubectl get nodes
NAME                                         STATUS   ROLES    AGE     VERSION
ip-10-0-10-224.us-west-2.compute.internal    Ready    <none>   3m42s   v1.31.4-eks-0f56d01
ip-10-0-36-230.us-west-2.compute.internal    Ready    <none>   3m40s   v1.31.4-eks-0f56d01
(base) karanbirsingh@Karanbirs-MacBook-Pro deploy-eks-using-tf %
```

Figure 8-8. Output of the kubectl get nodes command

Deploying Istio on the EKS Cluster

Now that the EKS cluster is running, we can install Istio using Helm to configure traffic management, security, and observability.

Add the Istio Helm repository. You should be able to see the output as shown in Figure 8-9:

```
helm repo add istio https://istio-release.storage.googleapis.com/charts
helm repo update
```

```
(base) karanbirsingh@Karanbirs-MacBook-Pro deploy-eks-using-tf % helm repo add istio https://istio-release.storage
.googleapis.com/charts
"istio" already exists with the same configuration, skipping
(base) karanbirsingh@Karanbirs-MacBook-Pro deploy-eks-using-tf % helm repo update
Hang tight while we grab the latest from your chart repositories...
...Successfully got an update from the "istio" chart repository
Update Complete. *Happy Helming!*
(base) karanbirsingh@Karanbirs-MacBook-Pro deploy-eks-using-tf %
```

Figure 8-9. Output of the helm repo add command

CHAPTER 8 DEPLOYING ISTIO IN PRODUCTION

Finally, install Istio-base and Istiod to the istio-system namespace using Helm. The commands should run without any error and expect a similar output as shown in Figures 8-10 and 8-11:

```
helm install istio-base istio/base -n istio-system --create-namespace
helm install istiod istio/istiod -n istio-system
```

```
(base) karanbirsingh@Karanbirs-MacBook-Pro deploy-eks-using-tf % helm install istio-base istio/base -n istio-syste
m --create-namespace
NAME: istio-base
LAST DEPLOYED: Tue Mar  4 00:55:58 2025
NAMESPACE: istio-system
STATUS: deployed
REVISION: 1
TEST SUITE: None
NOTES:
Istio base successfully installed!

To learn more about the release, try:
  $ helm status istio-base -n istio-system
  $ helm get all istio-base -n istio-system
```

Figure 8-10. Output of the `helm install istio base` *command*

```
(base) karanbirsingh@Karanbirs-MacBook-Pro deploy-eks-using-tf % helm install istiod istio/istiod -n istio-system
NAME: istiod
LAST DEPLOYED: Tue Mar  4 00:56:56 2025
NAMESPACE: istio-system
STATUS: deployed
REVISION: 1
TEST SUITE: None
NOTES:
"istiod" successfully installed!

To learn more about the release, try:
  $ helm status istiod -n istio-system
  $ helm get all istiod -n istio-system

Next steps:
  * Deploy a Gateway: https://istio.io/latest/docs/setup/additional-setup/gateway/
  * Try out our tasks to get started on common configurations:
    * https://istio.io/latest/docs/tasks/traffic-management
    * https://istio.io/latest/docs/tasks/security/
    * https://istio.io/latest/docs/tasks/policy-enforcement/
  * Review the list of actively supported releases, CVE publications and our hardening guide:
    * https://istio.io/latest/docs/releases/supported-releases/
    * https://istio.io/latest/news/security/
    * https://istio.io/latest/docs/ops/best-practices/security/

For further documentation see https://istio.io website
```

Figure 8-11. Output of the `helm install istiod` *command*

Verify that Istio is running by running the following kubectl command, which should print everything that is associated with the istio-system namespace as shown in Figure 8-12:

```
kubectl get all -n istio-system
```

```
(base) karanbirsingh@Karanbirs-MacBook-Pro deploy-eks-using-tf % kubectl get all -n istio-system
NAME                                 READY   STATUS    RESTARTS   AGE
pod/istiod-5668b4464f-g6kck          1/1     Running   0          97s

NAME              TYPE        CLUSTER-IP       EXTERNAL-IP   PORT(S)                                 AGE
service/istiod   ClusterIP   172.20.159.128   <none>        15010/TCP,15012/TCP,443/TCP,15014/TCP   98s

NAME                      READY   UP-TO-DATE   AVAILABLE   AGE
deployment.apps/istiod    1/1     1            1           98s

NAME                                DESIRED   CURRENT   READY   AGE
replicaset.apps/istiod-5668b4464f   1         1         1       98s

NAME                                                 REFERENCE           TARGETS             MINPODS   MAXPODS   REPLICAS   AGE
horizontalpodautoscaler.autoscaling/istiod           Deployment/istiod   cpu: <unknown>/80%  1         5         1          98s
(base) karanbirsingh@Karanbirs-MacBook-Pro deploy-eks-using-tf %
```

Figure 8-12. Output of the `kubectl get all -n istio-system` *command*

Deploying the Istio Ingress Gateway

In an Istio service mesh, the ingress gateway serves as the primary entry point for external traffic. It routes incoming requests to internal services while enforcing security, observability, and traffic management policies. To deploy the Istio ingress gateway, we must configure it to use AWS Network Load Balancer (NLB) and make it publicly accessible. We achieve this by customizing the `values.yaml` file.

Modify the `istio-ingress/values.yaml` file with the following settings:

```
service:
  annotations:
     service.beta.kubernetes.io/aws-load-balancer-type: "nlb"
     service.beta.kubernetes.io/aws-load-balancer-scheme: "internet-facing"
     service.beta.kubernetes.io/aws-load-balancer-attributes:   "load_
balancing.cross_zone.enabled=true"
```

Let's install the ingress gateway in its own namespace using the following commands. You should be able to see output of the commands as shown in Figure 8-13:

```
kubectl create namespace istio-ingress
helm install istio-ingress istio/gateway -n istio-ingress -f istio-ingress/
values.yaml
```

CHAPTER 8   DEPLOYING ISTIO IN PRODUCTION

```
(base) karanbirsingh@Karanbirs-MacBook-Pro deploy-eks-using-tf % helm install istio-ingress istio/gateway -n istio
-ingress -f istio-ingress/values.yaml
NAME: istio-ingress
LAST DEPLOYED: Tue Mar  4 02:32:00 2025
NAMESPACE: istio-ingress
STATUS: deployed
REVISION: 1
TEST SUITE: None
NOTES:
"istio-ingress" successfully installed!

To learn more about the release, try:
  $ helm status istio-ingress -n istio-ingress
  $ helm get all istio-ingress -n istio-ingress

Next steps:
  * Deploy an HTTP Gateway: https://istio.io/latest/docs/tasks/traffic-management/ingress/ingress-control/
  * Deploy an HTTPS Gateway: https://istio.io/latest/docs/tasks/traffic-management/ingress/secure-ingress/
(base) karanbirsingh@Karanbirs-MacBook-Pro deploy-eks-using-tf %
```

Figure 8-13. Output of the `helm install istio-ingress` *command*

Verify that the ingress gateway is up and running by using the following kubectl command, which should print everything that is associated with the istio-ingress namespace as shown in Figure 8-14:

```
kubectl get all -n istio-ingress
```

```
(base) karanbirsingh@Karanbirs-MacBook-Pro deploy-eks-using-tf % kubectl get all -n istio-ingress
NAME                                  READY   STATUS    RESTARTS   AGE
pod/istio-ingress-694797cb69-fr754    1/1     Running   0          58s

NAME                    TYPE           CLUSTER-IP       EXTERNAL-IP
                        PORT(S)                                                                           AGE
service/istio-ingress   LoadBalancer   172.20.113.25    a33d2ac466a3e4f8688c2d4f3e293386-7e90b3696dc50fde.elb.us-we
st-2.amazonaws.com      15021:31846/TCP,80:32240/TCP,443:31017/TCP                                        58s

NAME                            READY   UP-TO-DATE   AVAILABLE   AGE
deployment.apps/istio-ingress   1/1     1            1           58s

NAME                                       DESIRED   CURRENT   READY   AGE
replicaset.apps/istio-ingress-694797cb69   1         1         1       58s

NAME                                                         REFERENCE                 TARGETS           MINPODS   MAXP
ODS   REPLICAS   AGE
horizontalpodautoscaler.autoscaling/istio-ingress            Deployment/istio-ingress  cpu: <unknown>/80%   1        5
1     59s
(base) karanbirsingh@Karanbirs-MacBook-Pro deploy-eks-using-tf %
```

Figure 8-14. Output of the `kubectl get all -n istio-ingress` *command*

With this step, we have successfully deployed Istio on a single EKS cluster, and now we have a production-ready service mesh that enables secure, observable, and scalable microservices communication. This setup provides a solid foundation for managing workloads efficiently while leveraging AWS's powerful infrastructure.

Fine-Tuning in Single-Cluster Mode

Deploying Istio in production is only the first step. As traffic loads increase and service dependencies grow, ensuring that Istio scales efficiently becomes critical. Scaling Istio involves optimizing both the control plane (Istiod) and the data plane (Envoy proxies) to handle high throughput while maintaining performance, reliability, and cost-effectiveness. Istio's performance is influenced by multiple factors, including

- The number of services and workloads in the mesh
- The rate of configuration updates (e.g., new deployments, scaling services)
- The volume of incoming and outgoing requests handled by the Istio ingress gateway
- Resource limits set for Istiod

So let's discuss horizontal and vertical scaling strategies for Istiod and the Istio ingress gateway to maintain high performance in production environments.

Scaling the Control Plane (Istiod)

Horizontal Scaling

As we can see in the last section, HPA is already enabled for Istiod by default. Kubernetes automatically increases or decreases the number of Istiod replicas based on CPU utilization. According to the documentation, a single Istiod instance can support up to 1,000 services, 2,000 sidecars with one vCPU, and 1.5 GB of memory [3]. However, if you need to fine-tune scaling, consider adjusting the HPA thresholds based on observed Istiod CPU and memory usage. Increase the minimum replicas to handle bursts in traffic and avoid cold starts.

Vertical Scaling

Beyond autoscaling, optimizing Istiod's resource requests and limits is essential. A well-tuned Istiod should have sufficient CPU and memory to handle service discovery and configuration propagation efficiently. Also, it should have predefined resource requests and limits to prevent excessive throttling. Here are recommended settings for large-scale deployments:

```
resources:
  requests:
    cpu: "2"
    memory: "4Gi"
  limits:
    cpu: "4"
    memory: "8Gi"
```

Scaling the Ingress Gateway

Similarly, for the ingress gateway HPA is already enabled by default, so K8s should automatically scale it out, but if you need to fine-tune, consider adjustments in the HPA thresholds. Also, make sure there are enough resources such as CPU and memory allocated for it.

Scaling Istio Beyond Single-Cluster Mode

As applications scale, deploying them into multiple Kubernetes clusters becomes necessary. Relying solely on a single-cluster Istio setup might lead to performance bottlenecks, limiting scalability and resilience. Scaling Istio beyond a single Kubernetes cluster involves understanding and leveraging different deployment models to ensure robust, scalable, and resilient service mesh architectures. In a multi-cluster production environment, Istio can be deployed using various deployment models, each catering to different operational needs and requirements.

Primary–Remote Deployment Model

In this model, one cluster hosts the control plane, while remote clusters run only the data plane components (Envoy proxies) as shown in Figure 8-15. The control plane manages configurations, policies, and certificates for the entire mesh, centralizing administrative control. The main advantages of this model are simplified configuration and policy management. Also, it reduces resource overhead, as remote clusters require fewer resources. On the other hand, network latency and reliability between primary and remote clusters must be managed carefully. The primary cluster, i.e., the cluster with the control plane, should be highly available to avoid a single point of failure.

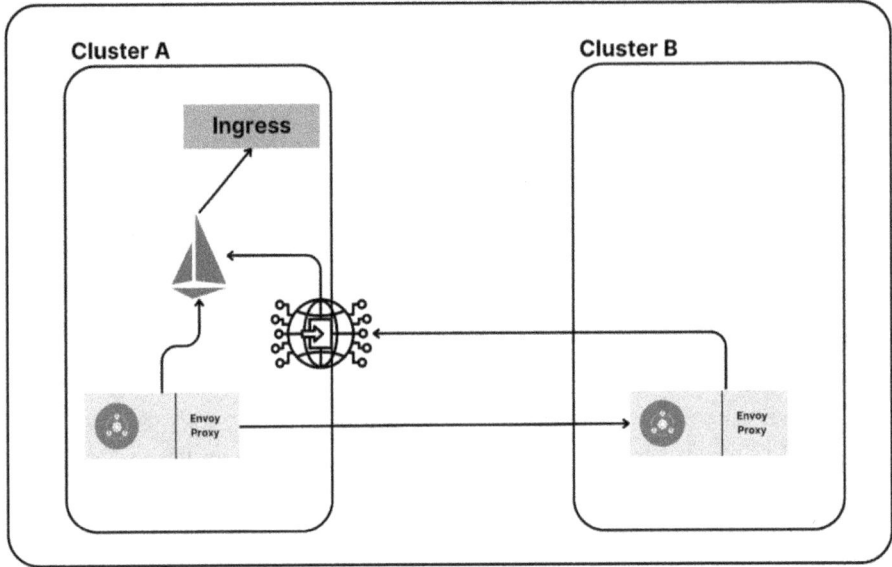

Figure 8-15. *Architecture of primary–remote Istio deployment*

Multi-primary Deployment Model

The multi-primary model features independent primary control planes across clusters, each managing its own workloads but capable of inter-cluster communication as depicted in Figure 8-16. This model is ideal for high-availability and geographically distributed scenarios. The pros of this approach are that it provides enhanced fault tolerance and resilience and failure of one control plane doesn't impact others. Also, latency is reduced due to management of local traffic within clusters. The main cons of this approach are that it requires synchronization mechanisms for configurations and policies between clusters. It has higher administrative head due to the independent management of multiple control planes. To synchronize these control planes, use a shared root CA and GitOps-based config management to ensure consistent identity and policies.

CHAPTER 8 DEPLOYING ISTIO IN PRODUCTION

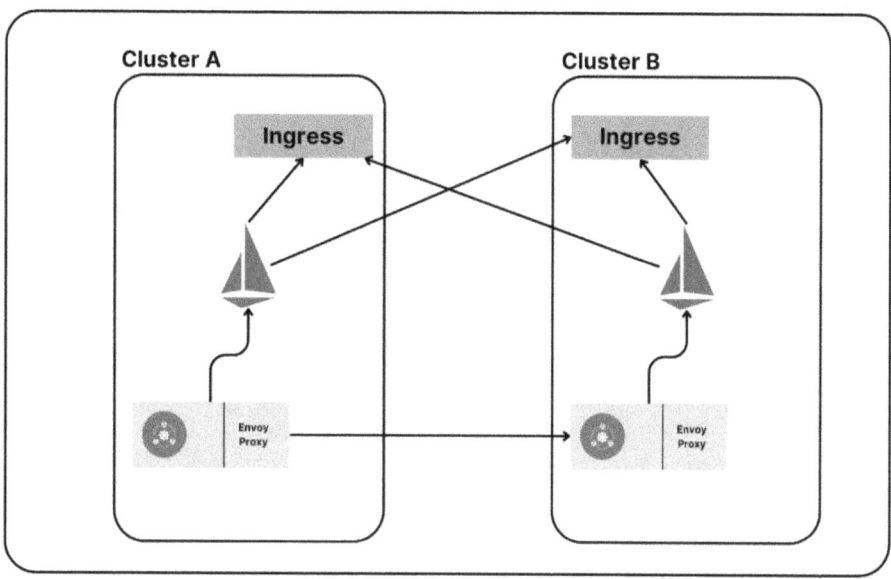

Figure 8-16. Architecture of multi-primary Istio deployment

Multi-network Deployment

In multi-network deployments, clusters reside in separate networks, connected through gateways that securely route traffic between them. Each cluster can have its own primary or remote control plane, providing maximum flexibility and isolation. Figure 8-17 shows primary–remote configuration in different networks. However, there is an increase in complexity in network configuration and management. It also requires careful management of inter-cluster gateways and security rules.

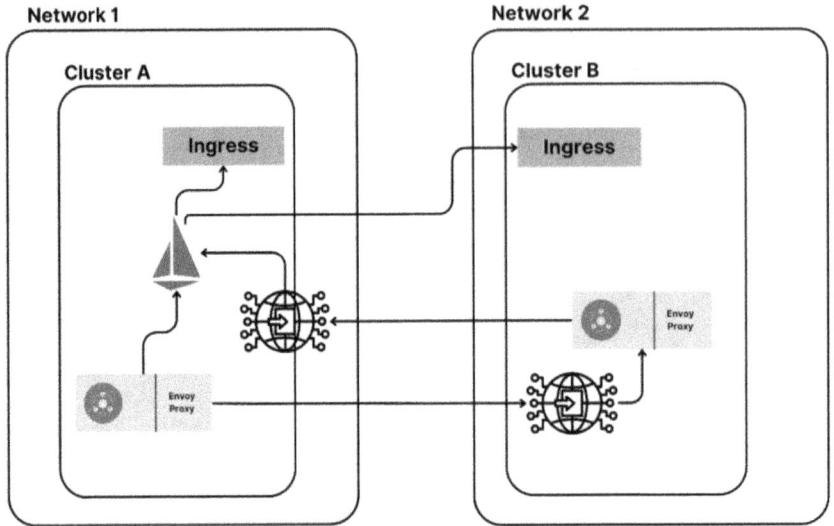

Figure 8-17. Primary–remote configuration in different networks

Determining the Best Fit

Selecting an appropriate deployment model is a balancing act. For small-scale applications or early development phases, a single-cluster setup offers clarity and ease. As operational demands grow, moving to a multi-primary arrangement (whether across multiple clusters in the same network or across diverse networks) can provide the necessary resilience and scalability. In cases where centralized management is paramount, remote clusters offer a strategic compromise. Ultimately, the ideal model depends on several factors, including the scale of the application, the intricacies of the network infrastructure, and the operational philosophies of the organization. By carefully considering these aspects, engineers and architects can harness the full power of Istio to build secure, efficient, and resilient service meshes.

Conclusion

Deploying Istio in production environments involves meticulous planning, execution, and continuous fine-tuning. Whether adopting a single-cluster deployment for simplicity or leveraging multi-cluster architectures for scalability and resilience, understanding the nuances of each deployment model is crucial. Automation through tools like Terraform and Helm significantly enhances consistency and reduces human error, enabling faster, repeatable deployments. Effective scaling strategies for both Istiod and Envoy proxies ensure optimal performance even under high-traffic loads. Ultimately, the success of an Istio deployment hinges upon aligning the chosen architecture and scaling strategies with the organization's operational requirements, infrastructure constraints, and long-term growth plans. By carefully addressing these considerations, teams can build robust, secure, and efficient service meshes that drive sustainable cloud-native applications.

References

[1] https://developer.hashicorp.com/terraform
[2] https://github.com/terraform-aws-modules/terraform-aws-eks
[3] https://istio.io/latest/docs/ops/deployment/performance-and-scalability/

CHAPTER 9

Extending Istio with Custom Plugins

Introduction

While Istio offers complete service mesh capabilities out of the box, organizations often need to extend their functionalities to meet specific requirements. This chapter explores how to extend Istio with WebAssembly plugins, with a focus on the practical elements of creating, deploying, and managing these extensions. We'll also look at Istio's extensibility points using WebAssembly, with a primary focus on C++ examples since it is the most mature and well-documented language for Istio extensions. While Rust and AssemblyScript are also supported for WebAssembly development, we'll stick with C++ code samples to provide clear, actionable guidance. Given that this book is intended for DevOps engineers and platform architects who are already aware with Istio's key concepts, we will focus on practical implementation details with relevant code snippets rather than in-depth theoretical discussions, giving you the hands-on knowledge you need to tailor Istio to your organization's specific requirements.

Istio Extensibility

Istio's extensibility framework has come a long way since its inception. In earlier releases (prior to 1.5), Istio used the Mixer component as the primary extension point for enforcing policies and collecting the telemetry data. Istio's new architecture has dropped the use of Mixer in favor of WebAssembly (Wasm) extensions that are executed directly within the Envoy proxy and removed the additional network hops for better performance.

Istio's current extensibility paradigm operates at two levels: the data plane and the control plane. At the data plane level, WebAssembly modules integrate directly with Envoy proxies, allowing you to modify or enhance network traffic behavior as it flows through the mesh, and these extensions can intercept requests and responses, add or change headers, execute custom authentication or authorization, and edit payload data.

This architecture's strength comes from its flexibility and performance. WebAssembly modules run in a sandboxed environment within the Envoy proxy, providing strong security promise while delivering near-native performance. The modules are dynamically loadable, which allows you to deploy and update extensions without restarting the proxy. This is particularly useful in production environments where downtime must be minimized.

Consider the following scenario: You need to develop a custom rate limiting solution that takes into account both HTTP headers and external metadata. Using a WebAssembly extension, you can intercept proxy requests, evaluate them against your custom logic, and make rate limiting decisions without incurring additional network latency. Also, the extension can maintain its own state, interface with external services as appropriate, and enforce your specific rate limiting guidelines directly within the mesh.

Understanding the extensibility model is critical since it serves as the foundation for all custom development explored in this chapter, and whether you're building custom security controls, providing specialized logging, or integrating with external systems, you'll use this framework to extend Istio's capabilities.

Understanding Istio's Extension Points

Istio provides two basic layers for extending its functionality: data plane and control plane. Understanding these extension points is critical for adding custom behaviors in your service mesh.

At the data plane level, Istio takes advantage of the Envoy proxy's extensibility via WebAssembly modules. These modules can be added to Envoy's HTTP filter chain, allowing them to interact with and modify traffic at various stages of request processing. The HTTP filter chain in Envoy processes requests in a certain sequence, and your WebAssembly module can be placed at any point in this chain. This location is critical because it defines when your custom logic is executed in relation to Istio's built-in functionality, such as authentication, authorization, and routing. Figure 9-1 shows the architecture of the WebAssembly plugin. Don't worry if you don't understand everything yet. We will discuss each of these concepts in more detail in the upcoming sections.

CHAPTER 9   EXTENDING ISTIO WITH CUSTOM PLUGINS

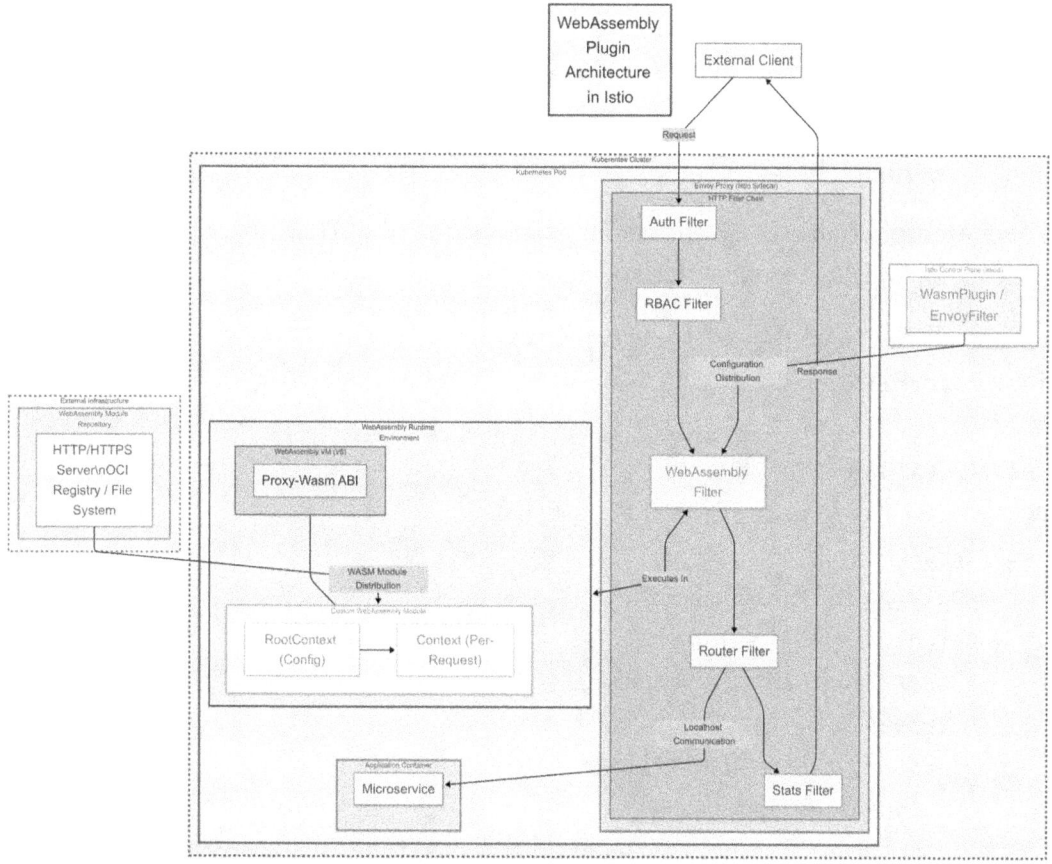

***Figure 9-1.** Architecture of the WebAssembly plugin*

The data plane extension capabilities include

- Modifying HTTP headers, method, or URL
- Accessing and modifying the request/response body
- Adding custom metrics and logging
- Implementing custom authentication or authorization logic
- Integrating with external services for request processing

At the control plane level, Istio offers two primary extension mechanisms:

EnvoyFilter Resource: This is a powerful configuration object that lets you change how Istio configures Envoy proxies. Its capabilities include

- Inserting new filters into the HTTP filter chain
- Modifying existing filter configurations

- Removing default filters when needed
- Configuring your WebAssembly modules with custom parameters
- Applying these changes selectively based on workload labels, ports, or routing rules

For example, to insert a WebAssembly module into the HTTP filter chain, you would create an EnvoyFilter resource that specifies

```
apiVersion: networking.istio.io/v1alpha3
kind: EnvoyFilter
metadata:
  name: custom-wasm-filter
spec:
  configPatches:
    - applyTo: HTTP_FILTER
      patch:
        operation: INSERT_BEFORE
        value:
          name: custom-wasm-filter
          typed_config:
            "@type": type.googleapis.com/udpa.type.v1.TypedStruct
            type_url: type.googleapis.com/envoy.extensions.filters.http.
                     wasm.v3.Wasm
```

Don't worry if you don't understand this right away. We will discuss more about this in the upcoming sections.

Custom Resource Definitions (CRDs): These augment Istio's API (and, in general, introduce additional objects into your Kubernetes namespace) by adding new resource types to the control plane and are very useful to

- Define configuration schemas for your custom extensions.
- Create new APIs that integrate with Istio's control plane.
- Manage complex configuration requirements through Kubernetes-native resources.
- Implement custom controllers that react to these resources.

CHAPTER 9 EXTENDING ISTIO WITH CUSTOM PLUGINS

The combination of these extension points enables powerful customizations. For instance, you might create a custom CRD to define the configuration for your WebAssembly module, use an EnvoyFilter to inject the module into the appropriate location in the filter chain, and then have the module implement your custom processing logic.

These extension points are designed to maintain the stability and security of your service mesh while providing the flexibility required to handle specific requirements. In the upcoming sections, we'll look at how WebAssembly supports these extensions and provide practical examples of how to add custom functionality.

WebAssembly and Its Role in Istio

WebAssembly (Wasm) has been integrated into Istio's extensibility paradigm since version 1.5. It is a low-level binary instruction format intended to execute at near-native speeds in a memory-safe, sandboxed environment. In Istio's case, WebAssembly allows developers to create customized extensions that operate directly within the Envoy proxy, removing the need for external processes or services.

The primary benefits of adopting WebAssembly in Istio are security isolation, performance, and language flexibility. The sandboxed environment ensures that extensions do not compromise the proxy's reliability or security, and because WebAssembly modules run directly in the proxy, they eliminate the latency overhead associated with the prior Mixer-based architecture. Furthermore, developers can create extensions in languages that compile to WebAssembly, with C++ being the most mature and well-documented option in Istio's ecosystem.

When an HTTP request flows through an Envoy proxy in Istio, the WebAssembly module can interact with it at various stages of processing. The module gets callbacks for various events such as request headers, request body chunks, response headers, and response body chunks. This enables fine-grained control over traffic processing while keeping the performance characteristics required for production deployments.

Use Cases for Extending Istio

Organizations adopt Istio extensions to address specific requirements that go beyond Istio's built-in capabilities. Common use cases for extending Istio focus on security, compliance, and integration with existing systems.

Custom authentication and authorization are common use cases in which organizations need to validate specialized tokens or implement complicated access control rules. For example, a financial institution may need to validate custom security tokens containing transaction-specific metadata before allowing requests to proceed, and this validation must occur within the mesh to ensure that security controls are uniform across all services.

Compliance and auditing requirements frequently drive the demand for extensions, especially in regulated industries. Organizations may need to capture specific transaction details, log them in a predefined format, or ensure that certain headers appear on all requests. WebAssembly extension can inspect and log the necessary information directly at the proxy level, ensuring consistent compliance across the service mesh.

Integration with legacy systems is another common case. Many organizations operate in hybrid environments in which current microservices must interact with legacy applications, and extensions can help bridge this gap by transforming protocols, adding necessary headers, or modifying request patterns to assure compatibility.

Performance optimization and custom rate limits are also driving extension development. Organizations may need to create specialized rate limiting algorithms based on business requirements or change requests to optimize performance for certain use situations. These customizations can be effectively implemented with WebAssembly extensions that run directly in the proxy.

WebAssembly Plugins in Istio

Istio's WebAssembly extensions integrate directly with Envoy's filter chain, enabling custom network traffic processing. This architecture, first introduced in Istio 1.5, defines the interface between Envoy proxies and WebAssembly modules using the Proxy-Wasm specification.

The Proxy-Wasm specification defines a standardized Application Binary Interface (ABI) that enables WebAssembly modules to interact with the Envoy proxy, and this standardization ensures that Istio behaves consistently across several deployments and versions. When an extension is deployed, it runs in a sandboxed environment within the Envoy proxy that ensures memory safety and resource isolation to prevent extensions from impacting the proxy's overall stability.

CHAPTER 9   EXTENDING ISTIO WITH CUSTOM PLUGINS

WebAssembly modules are distributed in the form of .wasm files, which are loaded into Envoy proxy from either the local filesystem or a remote HTTP/HTTPS server. From the deployment perspective, the EnvoyFilter resource in Istio is used to handle the configuration for loading these modules, and the following is an example of how a WebAssembly module is loaded in Istio:

```
apiVersion: networking.istio.io/v1alpha3
kind: EnvoyFilter
metadata:
  name: wasm-example
spec:
  configPatches:
    - applyTo: HTTP_FILTER
      match:
        context: SIDECAR_INBOUND
      patch:
        operation: INSERT_BEFORE
        value:
          name: wasm-example
          config_discovery:
            config_source:
              abi_versions: "v1"
              uri: "file:///etc/istio/extensions/example.wasm"
```

The WebAssembly extension lifecycle in Istio includes several key phases:

1. Initialization: When the module is first loaded by Envoy

2. Configuration: Where the module receives its configuration from the EnvoyFilter resource

3. Request Processing: When the module handles HTTP requests and responses

4. Termination: When the module is being unloaded

During request processing, the extension can interact with traffic through a series of callbacks defined by the Proxy-Wasm ABI, including

- Request header processing
- Request body processing
- Response header processing
- Response body processing

This architecture enables extensions to perform various operations such as header modification, traffic filtering, custom authentication, and metrics collection, all while maintaining the performance and security characteristics required for production environments.

> **Note** Starting with Istio 1.9, you no longer need to use EnvoyFilter resources to add custom Wasm modules to your proxies. Instead, you can now use a WasmPlugin resource. In the upcoming sections, we will go into greater detail regarding the new WasmPlugin.

WebAssembly Fundamentals

WebAssembly (often abbreviated as Wasm) is a substantial leap in how we run code in constrained environments. Originally designed for web browsers, WebAssembly has grown into a formidable technology for running efficient, sandboxed code across several platforms, including service meshes such as Istio.

> **Note** This section provides a high-level overview of developing and building a WebAssembly (Wasm) bundle. While we cover the fundamentals, this is only the beginning of knowing Wasm's full capabilities. For a more in-depth exploration, particularly when utilizing C++ with Wasm, we recommend consulting the official Wasm documentation and C++ development guide.

WebAssembly is a binary instruction format that is designed to run at near-native speeds while providing high-security guarantees. Consider it a low-level assembly language for a conceptual machine, rather than a specific hardware configuration, and this abstraction enables WebAssembly to deliver consistent performance across platforms while retaining security via its sandboxed execution environment.

Istio's WebAssembly module compilation is primarily reliant on the LLVM compiler infrastructure. LLVM (formerly Low Level Virtual Machine) is the core of current compilation tools, offering a set of modular compiler components and toolchain technologies. This Intermediate Representation (IR) serves as a bridge between source code and target machine code and is important to LLVM's architecture that includes numerous crucial components for WebAssembly compilation.

Clang is LLVM's C/C++ frontend, which parses source code and generates LLVM IR. It uses the Proxy-Wasm headers to compile C++ source code for Istio WebAssembly modules:

```
// Example C++ source using Proxy-Wasm headers
#include "proxy_wasm_intrinsics.h"
```

The WebAssembly compilation process consists of multiple steps. Let's consider how a C++ extension for Istio is turned into a WebAssembly module:

```
// Example C++ source code for an Istio extension
#include "proxy_wasm_intrinsics.h"

class MyExtension : public Context {
public:
    virtual FilterHeadersStatus onRequestHeaders(uint32_t headers) {
        logDebug("Processing request headers");
        return FilterHeadersStatus::Continue;
    }
};
```

This code goes through the following compilation stages:

Source to LLVM IR: First, the C++ code is compiled to LLVM Intermediate Representation (IR) using Clang.

```
# Compilation command example
em++ -c myextension.cc -I/proxy_wasm_cpp_sdk
```

LLVM IR to WebAssembly: The IR is then converted to WebAssembly binary format using Emscripten.

```
# Linking and generating WebAssembly
em++ myextension.o -o myextension.wasm
```

The resulting .wasm file includes the compiled binary, which can then be deployed to Istio. Also, to make this process easier, most developers use Docker-based build environments that include all necessary tools:

```
FROM wasmsdk/cpp-sdk:latest

COPY . /work
WORKDIR /work

RUN cmake . && make
```

The compilation environment requires several key components:

1. Emscripten SDK: This provides the toolchain necessary to compile C++ to WebAssembly.

    ```
    git clone https://github.com/emscripten-core/emsdk.git
    cd emsdk
    ./emsdk install latest
    ./emsdk activate latest
    source ./emsdk_env.sh
    ```

2. Proxy-Wasm C++ SDK: Contains the headers and interfaces for developing Istio extensions.

    ```
    git clone https://github.com/proxy-wasm/proxy-wasm-cpp-sdk.git

    cd proxy-wasm-cpp-sdk
    ```

3. LLVM and Clang: Usually bundled with Emscripten, but for standalone installation.

    ```
    # For Ubuntu/Debian
    apt-get install llvm clang

    # For macOS
    brew install llvm
    ```

4. Build Tools: CMake, Make, and other standard build utilities.

   ```
   # Ubuntu/Debian
   apt-get install build-essential cmake ninja-build

   # macOS
   brew install cmake ninja
   ```

One of WebAssembly's primary advantages in the context of Istio is its ability to retain consistent behavior across many different environments and function equally whether it is running in a development mode on a local machine or in a production environment across thousands of proxies, thanks to its standardized runtime environment.

With this understanding of WebAssembly fundamentals and compilation, we can now explore how Proxy-Wasm builds upon these concepts to provide a standardized interface for Istio extensions.

Introduction to Proxy-Wasm

Proxy-Wasm supports a standardized interface between WebAssembly modules and proxy servers such as Envoy, and it is an important part of Istio's extensibility model. While WebAssembly is the foundational technology for efficiently running sandboxed code, Proxy-Wasm defines the exact interaction patterns between this code and the proxy environment using a well-defined Application Binary Interface (ABI).

The Proxy-Wasm ABI establishes a contract between extensions and the proxy server, defining available functions and needed callbacks. This standardization guarantees consistent behavior across proxy implementations and deployment scenarios. Also, ABI introduces a hierarchical context system modeled after proxy server request handling, with three core context levels: root context for plugin initialization and configuration, stream context for network connection handling, and HTTP context for request/response processing.

For example, a basic authentication plugin implementation using Proxy-Wasm would structure its contexts like this:

```
class AuthRootContext : public RootContext {
public:
    bool onConfigure(size_t size) override {
```

```
        // Plugin initialization and configuration loading
        auto conf = getConfiguration();
        return true;
    }
};

class AuthHttpContext : public Context {
public:
    FilterHeadersStatus onRequestHeaders(uint32_t headers) override {
        // Per-request authentication logic
        auto token = getRequestHeader("Authorization");
        return validateToken(token);
    }
};
```

Proxy-Wasm provides essential capabilities for service mesh extensions through its host functions, including HTTP traffic manipulation, network operations, metrics collection, and logging. These functions allow extensions to interact with their environment in a controlled manner while still maintaining the WebAssembly sandbox's security guarantees. The ABI enforces very strict memory safety by requiring all memory interactions to take place via predefined function calls that the host environment can monitor and regulate.

In Istio's implementation, Proxy-Wasm is directly integrated with Envoy's filter chain, allowing WebAssembly modules to process traffic alongside built-in filters. This integration allows extensions to access and change request/response data, interact with Envoy's internal systems, and ensure configuration consistency with other components of the service mesh.

The specification carefully balances functionality and performance, utilizing shared memory buffers whenever possible to minimize data copying between the host and WebAssembly module. This design choice ensures that extensions may handle traffic fast enough for production deployments while still maintaining the security benefits of the WebAssembly sandbox.

This standardized approach to proxy extension via Proxy-Wasm lays the groundwork for the more detailed implementation patterns and deployment methodologies discussed in the upcoming sections. As we progress, we'll look at how these ideas translate into real solutions for extending Istio's capabilities in production settings.

CHAPTER 9   EXTENDING ISTIO WITH CUSTOM PLUGINS

The WebAssembly Architecture in Istio

WebAssembly in Istio uses an integration model based on Envoy's filter chain mechanism. This architecture is made up of three main components: the Envoy proxy, the WebAssembly runtime environment, and extension modules. The approach balances security and flexibility by running each WebAssembly module in its own isolated virtual machine within the Envoy proxy. Figure 9-2 shows the high-level WebAssembly architecture.

WebAssembly Plugin Architecture in Istio

```
Envoy Proxy
┌─────────────────────────────────────────────────────────────┐
│                  Host-Guest Architecture                     │
│  ┌──────────────────┐  ┌──────────┐  ┌──────────────────┐  │
│  │  Host (Envoy)    │◄─│Proxy-Wasm│─►│Guest (WebAssembly)│  │
│  │ • Proxy-Wasm host│  │   ABI    │  │ • Custom extension│  │
│  │   functions      │  │          │  │   logic          │  │
│  │ • Memory mgmt    │  │          │  │ • Sandboxed exec │  │
│  │ • HTTP filter    │◄─│standardized│─►│ • Context-based  │  │
│  │   chain          │  │ interface│  │   processing     │  │
│  └──────────────────┘  └──────────┘  └──────────────────┘  │
│                                                              │
│                        Memory Model                          │
│  ┌──────────────────┐   Data Copy   ┌──────────────────┐   │
│  │  Envoy Memory    │──────────────►│ WebAssembly Memory│   │
│  │• Native data     │               │• Linear memory    │   │
│  │  structures      │               │  space            │   │
│  │• Request/response│◄──────────────│• Isolated from    │   │
│  │  buffers         │ Buffer Access │  host             │   │
│  └──────────────────┘               └──────────────────┘   │
│                                                              │
│                  Request Processing Callbacks                │
│  ┌────────────┐ ┌────────────┐ ┌────────────┐ ┌────────────┐ ┌────────────┐ │
│  │onRequest   │►│onRequest   │►│onRequest   │►│onResponse  │►│onResponse  │ │
│  │Headers     │ │Body        │ │Trailers    │ │Headers     │ │Body        │ │
│  └────────────┘ └────────────┘ └────────────┘ └────────────┘ └────────────┘ │
│   Flow managed by Envoy based on HTTP request/response processing stages    │
│                                                              │
│  RootContext:   Configuration, global state  Context:  Per-request state │
└─────────────────────────────────────────────────────────────┘
```

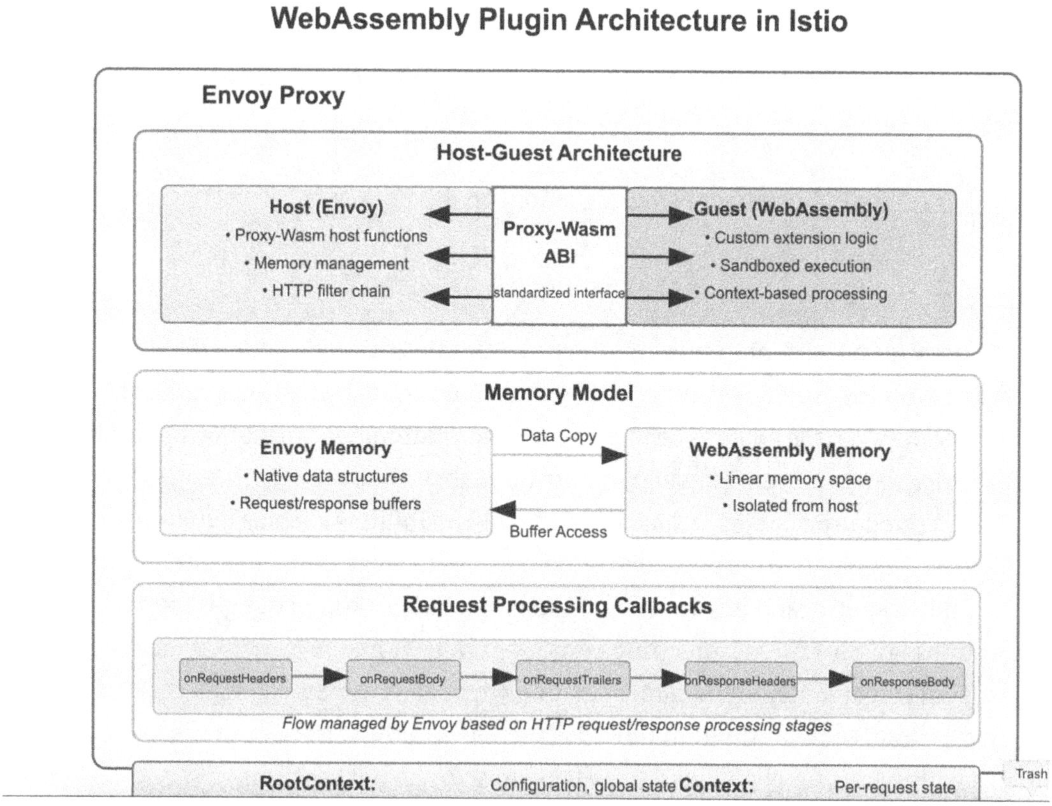

Figure 9-2. High-level WebAssembly architecture

When Istio deploys a WebAssembly extension, the process begins with configuration loading through the EnvoyFilter resource. This configuration affects the module's position in the filter chain, as well as its working parameters. The WebAssembly module then starts up within its virtual machine, establishing its root context, and prepares for request processing.

453

The design follows a host-guest pattern, with Envoy serving as the host environment and WebAssembly modules as guests. Their communication takes place through the Proxy-Wasm ABI, which offers structured interfaces for interaction. For example, a basic extension that integrates with this architecture may look like this:

```cpp
class CustomFilter : public Context {
    FilterHeadersStatus onRequestHeaders(uint32_t headers) {
        // Process incoming request headers
        auto token = getRequestHeader("Authorization");
        if (!validateToken(token)) {
            sendLocalResponse(403, "Unauthorized", "", {});
            return FilterHeadersStatus::StopIteration;
        }
        return FilterHeadersStatus::Continue;
    }
};
```

Memory management in this architecture operates through a controlled interface. Extensions use the host environment's structured memory operations, rather than direct memory access, as this ensures security while maintaining performance by minimizing unnecessary data transfers between the host and extensions.

The architecture enables critical operational capabilities such as dynamic extension loading without proxy restarts, resource isolation between extensions, and secure execution in a sandboxed environment. Also, the configuration changes pass through Istio's control plane (Istiod), ensuring consistent behavior across the service mesh while allowing for targeted deployment to specified workloads or namespaces.

This architectural foundation provides the basis for how Envoy utilizes WebAssembly plugins within its filter chain, which we'll explore in the next section.

How Envoy Uses WebAssembly Plugins

To understand how Envoy uses WebAssembly plugins, consider the fundamental model of how Envoy processes network traffic. Envoy routes requests via a series of filters, each of which can examine and modify the traffic that passes through it. Think of this as an assembly line, with each station (filter) inspecting and modifying the product (request/response) as it moves through.

WebAssembly plugins integrate into this system by acting as HTTP filters in Envoy's filter chain. When you deploy a WebAssembly plugin, it becomes one of the assembly line stations. The main distinction is that WebAssembly plugins run in a sandboxed environment, whereas Envoy's built-in filters are compiled directly into the proxy. The Proxy-Wasm specification governs the interaction of Envoy and WebAssembly plugins, and this specification functions similarly to a well-defined contract, describing exactly how Envoy and the plugin can communicate with one another; when Envoy needs to process a request, it establishes a new context for the request and utilizes this contract to send information to the plugin and receive instructions in return.

Let us look at a practical illustration of how this works. When a new request arrives at Envoy, various things happen in sequence:

First, Envoy generates a new context for the request. This context behaves similarly to a clean workspace, allowing the plugin to carry out this single request without interfering with other requests. The plugin gets request information via callbacks defined in the Proxy-Wasm specification, and as the request travels through the filter chain, the plugin can inspect and adjust its various components. When request headers arrive, Envoy calls the plugin's header processing method. The plugin can check for specific headers, create new ones, or completely block the request. Similar interactions take place with the request body, response headers, and response body.

The host–guest relationship between Envoy and the plugin is what gives this system its unique strength. Envoy acts as the host, providing a controlled environment in which the WebAssembly module (the guest) can run safely. This means that, while plugins can execute sophisticated traffic operations, they can only do so via Envoy's properly defined interfaces. Also, as discussed this architecture prevents plugins from accidentally or maliciously harming the proxy or other system components.

A request through a WebAssembly plugin goes through multiple key stages. When the request arrives, the plugin receives a notification and begins processing. The plugin receives callbacks for each stage of the request, which includes headers, body chunks, and finally the response. This enables the plugin to make decisions or changes based on the entire context of the request. From a practical sense, developers working with WebAssembly plugins in Envoy must get a grasp of this callback-based model. Their plugins must be designed to handle the various stages of request processing, implementing the required functions for each type of callback they expect to receive, and the plugin may choose to ignore some callbacks and focus solely on certain components of the request, such as header manipulation or body transformation.

This design strikes a powerful balance between flexibility and security. Organizations can use custom code to improve Envoy's capabilities while keeping their proxy layer stable and secure. The WebAssembly sandbox ensures that even if a plugin contains bugs or crashes, it will not bring down the entire proxy or interfere with other requests being processed by different plugin instances.

Supported Programming Languages (C++, Rust, AssemblyScript)

Three primary languages are available to developers when creating WebAssembly plugins for Istio: C++, Rust, and AssemblyScript. Each one of these languages compiles to WebAssembly and offers different advantages and trade-offs that developers should consider while building extensions for their service mesh.

C++ remains the most mature and well-documented option for creating Istio extensions. This maturity is seen in the robust tooling and copious documentation for C++ WebAssembly development. The Proxy-Wasm C++ SDK includes a comprehensive set of APIs and tools built primarily for developing Envoy extensions. When working with C++, developers benefit from the language's direct memory management features and close-to-hardware performance, which are especially useful in proxy extensions where performance is critical.

The C++ development workflow mainly relies on the LLVM compiler infrastructure and Emscripten toolchain. This setup enables developers to create regular C++ programs with WebAssembly as the compilation target. The compilation method transforms C++ source code to LLVM's Intermediate Representation (IR) before finally producing WebAssembly binary format.

Rust has emerged as a compelling alternative for WebAssembly development, providing robust memory safety guarantees while maintaining excellent performance. The Rust ecosystem has tools specifically designed for WebAssembly compilation, and its ownership model helps to minimize common memory-related problems that could affect plugin stability. However, developers should be aware that, while Rust support is expanding, the environment for Istio-specific development is less mature than C++.

AssemblyScript provides a unique option for developers with a JavaScript/TypeScript background. As a TypeScript variation designed specifically for WebAssembly compilation, it provides a familiar syntax while creating efficient WebAssembly code. AssemblyScript is especially appealing for teams with JavaScript expertise that want to create Istio extensions without diving into systems programming languages like C++ or Rust.

CHAPTER 9   EXTENDING ISTIO WITH CUSTOM PLUGINS

When selecting between these languages, developers must consider a variety of factors:

> Development Team Expertise: C++ may be the ideal solution for teams with systems programming knowledge, but AssemblyScript may be more appropriate for JavaScript developers.
>
> Performance Requirements: All three languages generate efficient WebAssembly code, but C++and Rust often provide more direct control over performance optimizations.
>
> Tooling Requirements: C++ offers the most advanced tooling ecosystem for Istio development, which can have a significant impact on development velocity and debugging skills.
>
> Project Complexity: C++ or Rust may be better suited to sophisticated additions that demand fine-grained memory management or high speed than AssemblyScript.

The programming language you use can have a major impact on both the development experience and the overall performance of your Istio extensions. While C++ is still the most extensively documented and tested option, the expanding support for Rust and AssemblyScript offers developers viable alternatives that may better match their team's skills or project requirements.

Developing Envoy WebAssembly Plugins

The ability to extend Istio's functionality with WebAssembly plugins is a valuable feature for enterprises looking to customize their service mesh implementation. This section offers an in-depth tutorial to creating Envoy WebAssembly plugins, covering everything from setting up the development environment to implementation and deployment considerations.

Setting Up the Development Environment

Creating a WebAssembly plugin for Istio necessitates a specialized development environment that includes several critical components. Although in this section, we'll set up a development environment on macOS, similar principles apply to other platforms with appropriate adjustments.

At its core, the environment requires key compilation tools that serve as the foundation for development capabilities:

- CMake and Ninja: These build system generators create platform-agnostic build configurations. CMake is a high-level description language for specifying how software components should be built, whereas Ninja optimizes build execution for speed and efficiency. They work together to abstract platform-specific building complexities.

- LLVM: This modular compiler infrastructure serves as the backbone of the WebAssembly compilation process. LLVM's Intermediate Representation (IR) enables source code to be platform agnostic until final code generation, making it ideal for targeting the WebAssembly virtual instruction set.

- Git and Version Control: Essential for collaborative development and code change management, particularly important when working with dependencies that evolve over time.

```
# Install Homebrew if not already installed
/bin/bash -c "$(curl -fsSL https://raw.githubusercontent.com/
Homebrew/install/HEAD/install.sh)"

# Install required dependencies
brew install cmake ninja llvm wget git

# Ensure Xcode command line tools are installed
xcode-select --install
```

Emscripten serves as an important link between traditional C++ code and WebAssembly output. From a theoretical standpoint, Emscripten functions as a specialized compiler and runtime environment with several important capabilities:

1. Source Transformation: It transforms C/C++ source code into LLVM Intermediate Representation.

2. Wasm Code Generation: It compiles LLVM IR into WebAssembly binary format (.wasm files).

CHAPTER 9　EXTENDING ISTIO WITH CUSTOM PLUGINS

3. Runtime Library: It provides JavaScript implementations of standard C/C++ libraries that the WebAssembly module can interact with.

4. Memory Management: It establishes the memory model that WebAssembly modules use, configured through specific compilation flags such as TOTAL_MEMORY and ALLOW_MEMORY_GROWTH.

```
# Create a development directory
mkdir -p ~/istio-wasm-dev
cd ~/istio-wasm-dev

# Clone the Emscripten repository
git clone https://github.com/emscripten-core/emsdk.git
cd emsdk

# Install and activate the latest SDK version
./emsdk install latest
./emsdk activate latest

# Set up the environment variables
source ./emsdk_env.sh

# Add this to your shell profile for persistence
echo 'source "'$(pwd)'/emsdk_env.sh"' >> ~/.zshrc   # or ~/.bash_profile for bash

# Navigate back to the development directory
cd ..
```

The setup process shown in the chapter follows a dependency graph approach, where each component builds upon previously established elements:

System Compiler Tools ➤ Emscripten SDK ➤ Proxy-Wasm C++ SDK ➤ Project Structure

Now we need to set up the Proxy-Wasm C++ SDK, which provides the framework for interacting with Envoy:

```
# Clone the Proxy-Wasm C++ SDK
cd ~/istio-wasm-dev
```

459

CHAPTER 9 EXTENDING ISTIO WITH CUSTOM PLUGINS

```
git clone https://github.com/proxy-wasm/proxy-wasm-cpp-sdk.git
cd proxy-wasm-cpp-sdk

# Make note of this directory path for later use
export PROXY_WASM_CPP_SDK=$(pwd)
echo "export PROXY_WASM_CPP_SDK=$(pwd)" >> ~/.zshrc   # or ~/.bash_profile
for bash

# Go back to the development directory
cd ..
```

Let's create a project structure for our header plugin:

```
# Create project directory
mkdir -p ~/istio-wasm-dev/header-plugin
cd ~/istio-wasm-dev/header-plugin
mkdir -p src
mkdir -p build
mkdir -p k8s
```

Using the Proxy-Wasm C++ SDK

This SDK functions as an abstraction layer that hides the complexity of direct WebAssembly-to-Envoy communication, and from an implementation perspective, it implements the Proxy-Wasm ABI (Application Binary Interface) specification through a set of C++ classes and interfaces. This SDK provides

1. Context Classes: Envoy's request processing is modeled using a hierarchical context architecture, with `RootContext` for global state and initialization and `Context` for per-request processing.

2. Type-Safe Interfaces: C++ templates and classes that ensure type safety while working with the untyped WebAssembly memory model.

3. Extension Points: Clear callback methods are implemented by plugins to intercept various stages of HTTP request processing.

CHAPTER 9　EXTENDING ISTIO WITH CUSTOM PLUGINS

Now we'll write our WebAssembly plugin that adds a custom header to HTTP requests:

```cpp
// src/header_plugin.cc
#include "proxy_wasm_intrinsics.h"

class HeaderPluginRootContext : public RootContext {
public:
  explicit HeaderPluginRootContext(uint32_t id, std::string_view root_id)
      : RootContext(id, root_id) {}

  bool onConfigure(size_t configuration_size) override {
    // Access the configuration data if available
    if (configuration_size > 0) {
      auto configuration = getBufferBytes(WasmBufferType::PluginConfiguration,
        0, configuration_size);
      std::string config_string(configuration->view());

      // Parse the configuration string (expect "header_name:header_value")
      auto delimiter_pos = config_string.find(':');
      if (delimiter_pos != std::string::npos) {
        header_name_ = config_string.substr(0, delimiter_pos);
        header_value_ = config_string.substr(delimiter_pos + 1);
        LOG_INFO("Configured HeaderPlugin with " + header_name_ + ":" +
        header_value_);
        return true;
      } else {
        LOG_WARN("Invalid configuration format, Expected 'header_name:
        header_value'");
      }
    }

    // Use defaults if no valid configuration is provided
    header_name_ = "x-wasm-custom";
    header_value_ = "istio-plugin-example";
    LOG_INFO("Using default configuration: " + header_name_ + ":" +
    header_value_);
    return true;
```

461

CHAPTER 9   EXTENDING ISTIO WITH CUSTOM PLUGINS

```cpp
  }

  std::string header_name_;
  std::string header_value_;
};

class HeaderPluginContext : public Context {
public:
  explicit HeaderPluginContext(uint32_t id, RootContext* root)
      : Context(id, root), root_(static_cast<HeaderPluginRootContext*>
      (root)) {}

  FilterHeadersStatus onRequestHeaders(uint32_t, bool) override {
    // Add the configured header to outgoing requests
    addRequestHeader(root_->header_name_, root_->header_value_);
    LOG_INFO("Added header " + root_->header_name_ + ":" + root_->
    header_value_);
    return FilterHeadersStatus::Continue;
  }

private:
  HeaderPluginRootContext* root_;
};

static RegisterContextFactory register_HeaderPlugin(
    CONTEXT_FACTORY(HeaderPluginContext),
    ROOT_FACTORY(HeaderPluginRootContext),
    "header_plugin");
```

This code snippet showcases a basic WebAssembly plugin for Istio that adds a custom HTTP header to requests passing through the service mesh. Let us break down the code section by section to understand how it works and why each component is important.

The Header File Inclusion

```cpp
#include "proxy_wasm_intrinsics.h"
```

This line imports the Proxy-Wasm SDK's basic functionality. The `proxy_wasm_intrinsics.h` header contains all of the interfaces required for communicating with the Envoy proxy, including classes for handling requests, retrieving headers, and logging, making it an essential link between your code and the Envoy environment.

The RootContext Class

The RootContext class represents your plugin's global and long-lived context. When your plugin loads, it generates a single instance of this class, which lives throughout the plugin's lifetime, making it ideal for storing configuration and shared data.

```
class HeaderPluginRootContext : public RootContext {
```

The constructor takes two parameters:

```
explicit HeaderPluginRootContext(uint32_t id, std::string_view root_id)
  : RootContext(id, root_id) {}
```

Here, Envoy assigns a unique identification called id and root_id is a string that identifies this particular root context, and the constructor simply sends these values to the parent RootContext class.

Configuration Handling

The onConfigure method is a critical part of any Istio plugin:

```
bool onConfigure(size_t configuration_size) override {
```

This method is called when the plugin is loaded and whenever its configuration changes. It receives the size of the configuration data provided through Istio's resources (like an EnvoyFilter or WasmPlugin custom resource).

The configuration processing logic follows a clear pattern:

1. Check if configuration data is available:

    ```
    if (configuration_size > 0) {
    ```

2. Retrieve the configuration bytes using the Proxy-Wasm API:

    ```
    auto configuration = getBufferBytes(WasmBufferType::PluginConfiguration, 0, configuration_size);
    ```

CHAPTER 9   EXTENDING ISTIO WITH CUSTOM PLUGINS

```
std::string config_string(configuration->view());
```

The getBufferBytes is a Proxy-Wasm API method that enables plugins to read data buffers offered by Envoy.

3. A simple "header_name:header_value" format is expected to be used for the configuration string, which must be parsed as follows:

```
auto delimiter_pos = config_string.find(':');
if (delimiter_pos != std::string::npos) {
  header_name_ = config_string.substr(0, delimiter_pos);
  header_value_ = config_string.substr(delimiter_pos + 1);
  LOG_INFO("Configured HeaderPlugin with " + header_name_ + ":"
  + header_value_);
  return true;
}
```

4. If no configuration is provided or if parsing fails, fall back to default values:

```
header_name_ = "x-wasm-custom";
header_value_ = "istio-plugin-example";
LOG_INFO("Using default configuration: " + header_name_ + ":" +
header_value_);
return true;
```

The configuration information is stored in member variables:

```
std::string header_name_;
std::string header_value_;
```

Because they are part of the RootContext class, these variables remain constant during the plugin's lifetime, making the configuration available to all request contexts.

The Request Context Class

While the RootContext handles global state, the Context class processes individual HTTP requests. Envoy creates a new instance of this class for each request that passes through the proxy:

```
class HeaderPluginContext : public Context {
```

CHAPTER 9 EXTENDING ISTIO WITH CUSTOM PLUGINS

The constructor captures a reference to the parent RootContext:

```
explicit HeaderPluginContext(uint32_t id, RootContext* root)
  : Context(id, root), root_(static_cast<HeaderPluginRootContext*>
  (root)) {}
```

This gives each request context access to the shared configuration stored in the root context, and the `static_cast` is necessary because we need to access members specific to our `HeaderPluginRootContext` class.

Request Processing

The core functionality happens in the `onRequestHeaders` method:

```
FilterHeadersStatus onRequestHeaders(uint32_t, bool) override {
  // Add the configured header to outgoing requests
  addRequestHeader(root_->header_name_, root_->header_value_);
  LOG_INFO("Added header " + root_->header_name_ + ":" + root_->
  header_value_);
  return FilterHeadersStatus::Continue;
}
```

This method is invoked whenever Envoy acquires the headers for a new request. Our implementation

1. Uses the `addRequestHeader` function (provided by the Proxy-Wasm API) to add our own header to the request

2. Logs an informational message about the header being added

3. Returns `FilterHeadersStatus::Continue` to instruct Envoy to proceed with normal request processing

The parameters (header count and end-of-stream flag) aren't used in this simple example, which is why they're unnamed in the method signature.

Plugin Registration

The final piece of the puzzle is registering our plugin with the Proxy-Wasm framework:

```
static RegisterContextFactory register_HeaderPlugin(
```

```
    CONTEXT_FACTORY(HeaderPluginContext),
    ROOT_FACTORY(HeaderPluginRootContext),
    "header_plugin");
```

This creates a global registration object that associates the HeaderPluginContext class with the HeaderPluginRootContext class. This plugin is assigned the root ID "header_plugin".

This registration is required for Envoy to correctly load and initialize our plugin. The `CONTEXT_FACTORY` and `ROOT_FACTORY` macros handle the intricacies of building the necessary factory objects.

This WebAssembly plugin exemplifies the primary pattern for expanding Istio's behavior:

1. A root context manages the configuration and global state.
2. A request context executes each HTTP request.
3. Request processing callbacks modify or inspect traffic.
4. Registration connects everything to the Proxy-Wasm framework.

The plugin shows a small but real use case: adding custom headers to service mesh requests. This capability is useful for identifying request origins, implementing feature flags, and assigning correlation IDs for distributed tracing.

Building and Deploying Plugins

Building the Plugin

As an alternative to using a complex Makefile, we will develop a powerful shell script in order to manage the build process:

```
cat > build.sh << 'EOF'
#!/bin/bash
set -e

# Configuration
SDK_PATH="${PROXY_WASM_CPP_SDK:-$HOME/istio-wasm-dev/proxy-wasm-cpp-sdk}"
OUTPUT_NAME="header_plugin.wasm"

# Ensure we have all the tools we need
```

CHAPTER 9 EXTENDING ISTIO WITH CUSTOM PLUGINS

```
if ! command -v emcc &> /dev/null; then
   echo "Error: Emscripten compiler (emcc) not found!"
   echo "Please install and activate Emscripten SDK first."
   exit 1
fi

if [ ! -d "$SDK_PATH" ]; then
   echo "Error: Proxy-Wasm C++ SDK not found at $SDK_PATH"
   echo "Please set PROXY_WASM_CPP_SDK to the correct path or clone
   the SDK:"
   echo "git clone https://github.com/proxy-wasm/proxy-wasm-cpp-sdk.git"
   exit 1
fi

echo "=== Building WebAssembly Plugin ==="
echo "SDK Path: $SDK_PATH"

# Create build directory
mkdir -p build

# Compile the plugin
echo "Compiling plugin..."
emcc -s WASM=1 \
    -s TOTAL_MEMORY=65536 \
    -s TOTAL_STACK=10240 \
    -s ALLOW_MEMORY_GROWTH=0 \
    -s WASM_BIGINT=1 \
    -s ERROR_ON_UNDEFINED_SYMBOLS=0 \
    -s INITIAL_MEMORY=65536 \
    -s "EXPORTED_FUNCTIONS=['_malloc']" \
    --std=c++17 \
    -O3 \
    -flto \
    -fno-exceptions \
    -fno-rtti \
    -DNDEBUG \
    -I"$SDK_PATH" \
```

```
    src/header_plugin.cc \
    -o build/$OUTPUT_NAME

if [ $? -eq 0 ]; then
    echo "=== Build Successful ==="
    echo "Output: build/$OUTPUT_NAME"
    ls -la build/$OUTPUT_NAME
else
    echo "=== Build Failed ==="
    exit 1
fi

EOF

chmod +x build.sh
```

The build script contains several essential configurations that enable successful compilation:

1. Detection of SDK Path: The script checks the SDK environment variable or defaults to a predetermined location.

2. WebAssembly Memory Configuration: `-s TOTAL_MEMORY=65536` and related flags configure the memory constraints for the WebAssembly module.

3. Error Handling for Undefined Symbols: `-s ERROR_ON_UNDEFINED_SYMBOLS=0` is crucial because it allows the compiler to accept external symbols (like `proxy_log`) that will be provided by the Envoy runtime environment.

4. Optimization Flags: Better performance can be achieved by enabling aggressive optimization and link-time optimization with the `-O3 -flto` arguments.

5. C++ Settings: Flags like `-fno-exceptions` and `-fno-rtti` disable exception handling and runtime type information, reducing the size of the WebAssembly binary.

Now we can build our WebAssembly plugin:

```
cd ~/istio-wasm-dev/header-plugin
./build.sh
```

If successful, this will generate a header_plugin.wasm file in the build directory.

Deploying the WasmPlugin

The WasmPlugin resource offers an evolution in Istio's extensibility model, giving a more streamlined approach to installing WebAssembly modules compared with the earlier EnvoyFilter method. This custom resource, introduced in Istio 1.9, provides a specialized API for managing WebAssembly extensions within your service mesh.

WasmPlugin vs. EnvoyFilter

Before getting into the specifics, it's worth understanding how WasmPlugin differs from EnvoyFilter:

1. Simplified Configuration: WasmPlugin abstracts away many of the low-level Envoy configuration elements required by EnvoyFilter.

2. Focused Purpose: While EnvoyFilter can change any component of Envoy's configuration, WasmPlugin is specifically built to manage WebAssembly modules.

3. Enhanced Safety: When compared to the more powerful but complex EnvoyFilter resource, the more tailored API reduces the risk of misconfiguration.

Anatomy of the WasmPlugin Resource

The WasmPlugin resource follows the standard Kubernetes custom resource pattern, which includes metadata and a section defining the extension's behavior. Let's go over each component in detail.

Resource Identity and Scope

The resource declaration begins with normal Kubernetes fields like the API version (extensions.istio.io/v1alpha1) and the resource kind (WasmPlugin). The metadata section explains the plugin's identity and scope:

```yaml
apiVersion: extensions.istio.io/v1alpha1
kind: WasmPlugin
metadata:
  name: header-plugin
  namespace: istio-system
```

The namespace placement has profound implications for the plugin's scope of influence:

- Namespace-Scoped Deployment: When deployed in a specific workload namespace, the plugin applies only to proxies within that namespace, creating a boundary that prevents unintended effects on other parts of the system.

- Mesh-Wide Deployment: When deployed in the istio-system namespace (as in our example), the plugin potentially applies across the whole mesh, subject to the selector's constraints.

This namespace-based scoping approach is consistent with Kubernetes' resource paradigm, offering a familiar and clear method for controlling extension boundaries. Organizations with multi-team environments can use this functionality to delegate extension maintenance to particular teams while avoiding mesh-wide impact.

Targeted Workload Selection

The selector field employs Kubernetes label selectors to determine which workloads should receive the WebAssembly plugin. This targeted approach enables sophisticated deployment strategies:

- Canary Deployments: By selecting a subset of services or specific versions, operators can gradually roll out extensions to validate behavior before wider adoption.

- Service-Specific Customization: Different services may require different customizations; selectors enable tailoring extensions to specific workload requirements.

- Performance Optimization: By limiting plugin deployment to only the services that need custom behavior, operators can minimize resource overhead across the mesh.

The selector system offers the same flexibility as other Kubernetes resources, supporting complex match expressions beyond simple label equality. For instance, you could target multiple services with expressions like

```
selector:
  matchExpressions:
    - key: app
      operator: In
      values: [payment-service, order-service, inventory-service]
```

This flexibility enables precise targeting of extensions to exactly the workloads that need them, minimizing overhead and potential disruption to other services.

Module Source and Versioning

The url field specifies the location from which Istio should retrieve the WebAssembly module. This field supports multiple source types, each with distinct characteristics and use cases:

```
url: <path-to-your-wasm-file>
```

- HTTP/HTTPS URLs: Remote hosting enables centralized management of extension modules, simplifying updates across multiple clusters, for example, https://extensions.example.com/plugins/header-modifier.wasm.

- OCI (Open Container Initiative) URLs: Container registries provide versioning, access control, and integration with existing CI/CD pipelines, for example, oci://registry.example.com/wasm-plugins/header-modifier:v1.2.3.

- Local File Paths: For environments with strict network policies or air-gapped deployments, modules can be pre-deployed to the Envoy container's filesystem, for example, file:///var/local/plugins/header-modifier.wasm.

The URL field plays a crucial role in version management and upgrade strategies. When using container registries, teams can follow established versioning patterns:

- Semantic Versioning: Tags like v1.2.3 enable precise version control.

- Immutable References: Digest-based references (sha256:abc123...) prevent unintended updates.

- Channel-Based Deployments: Tags like `stable`, `beta`, or `latest` facilitate different update cadences.

Organizations should establish clear versioning policies for WebAssembly modules, particularly for production environments where uncoordinated updates could impact service reliability.

Execution Phase and Filter Chain Positioning

The `phase` field determines where in Envoy's HTTP filter chain the WebAssembly module will be inserted. This positioning is critical as it affects the module's visibility into the request/response flow and its ability to interact with other filters:

phase: AUTHN

Istio provides several predefined phases:

- AUTHN: Executes during the authentication phase, before Istio's built-in authentication processes. Extensions in this phase can influence authentication decisions by modifying request properties or implementing custom authentication schemes.

- AUTHZ: Runs during the authorization phase, allowing custom authorization logic to complement Istio's built-in access control. This phase is appropriate for extensions that implement specialized access control requirements.

- STATS: Positioned in the statistics and monitoring phase, enabling custom metrics collection and telemetry processing. Extensions in this phase typically focus on observability rather than active request modification.

- UNSPECIFIED_PHASE: The default placement in Envoy's HTTP filter chain, typically after built-in Istio functionality. This phase is suitable for general-purpose extensions that don't need to influence Istio's core behaviors.

The phase selection has significant implications for the extension's behavior and its interaction with Istio's built-in features. For example, our header plugin uses the AUTHN phase, which means it runs before Istio's authentication processes. This positioning enables the plugin to add headers that might influence authentication decisions or provide context for downstream authentication filters.

In more advanced scenarios, organizations might deploy multiple WasmPlugin resources targeting the same workloads but in different phases, creating a comprehensive extension pipeline that addresses various aspects of request processing.

Plugin Configuration

The `pluginConfig` field provides a structured mechanism to supply configuration data to the WebAssembly module. This data is serialized to JSON and passed to the module's `onConfigure` method during initialization.

This structured approach offers several advantages over simple string-based configuration:

- Type Safety: Different configuration values can use appropriate types (strings, numbers, booleans, arrays, objects).

- Hierarchical Configuration: Complex settings can be organized in a nested structure.

- Schema Validation: The structure can be validated against a schema, reducing configuration errors.

For our header plugin example, the provided configuration is relatively simple, specifying a custom header name and value. However, in more sophisticated extensions, the configuration might include complex properties:

```
pluginConfig:
  headers:
    - name: x-tenant-id
      value: "{{ .Labels.tenant_id }}"
    - name: x-environment
      value: "production"
```

CHAPTER 9 EXTENDING ISTIO WITH CUSTOM PLUGINS

```
  rateLimit:
    requestsPerSecond: 100
    burstSize: 50
  logging:
    level: info
    destination: stdout
```

This structured approach enables extensions to receive precisely the configuration they need while maintaining readability and manageability for operators.

Configuration Processing

When Istio deploys our WebAssembly module using the WasmPlugin resource, it passes the `pluginConfig` part to the module's `onConfigure` method. This is where the Kubernetes resource's structured configuration interacts with the module's initialization logic.

Our original C++ code expected a straightforward string format:

```cpp
bool onConfigure(size_t configuration_size) override {
  if (configuration_size > 0) {
    auto configuration = getBufferBytes(WasmBufferType::PluginConfigurati
                    on, 0, configuration_size);
    std::string config_string(configuration->view());

    // Parse the configuration string (expect "header_name:header_value")
    auto delimiter_pos = config_string.find(':');
    if (delimiter_pos != std::string::npos) {
      header_name_ = config_string.substr(0, delimiter_pos);
      header_value_ = config_string.substr(delimiter_pos + 1);
      LOG_INFO("Configured HeaderPlugin with " + header_name_ + ":"
      + header_value_);
      return true;
    } else {
      LOG_WARN("Invalid configuration format. Expected 'header_name:
      header_value'");
    }
  }
}
```

CHAPTER 9   EXTENDING ISTIO WITH CUSTOM PLUGINS

```cpp
    // Use defaults if no valid configuration is provided
    header_name_ = "x-wasm-custom";
    header_value_ = "istio-plugin-example";
    LOG_INFO("Using default configuration: " + header_name_ + ":" +
    header_value_);
    return true;
}
```

To work with the structured configuration from the WasmPlugin resource, we would need to update this code to parse JSON. A more robust implementation might look like

```cpp
bool onConfigure(size_t configuration_size) override {
  // Default configuration
  header_name_ = "x-wasm-custom";
  header_value_ = "istio-plugin-example";

  if (configuration_size > 0) {
    // Get configuration data
    auto configuration = getBufferBytes(WasmBufferType::PluginConfigurati
                    on, 0, configuration_size);
    std::string json_string(configuration->view());

    // In a production plugin, we would use a proper JSON parser here
    // This simplified example just looks for the expected structure
    if (json_string.find("x-custom-header") != std::string::npos) {
      // Extract header name and value from the JSON structure
      // This is a simplified approach; real implementation would use
         proper JSON parsing
      header_name_ = "x-custom-header";

      // Find the value by looking for pattern: "x-custom-header": "value"
      size_t value_start = json_string.find("\"x-custom-header\"");
      if (value_start != std::string::npos) {
        value_start = json_string.find(":", value_start) + 1;
        // Skip whitespace
        while (value_start < json_string.length() && std::isspace(json_
        string[value_start])) value_start++;
        // Skip opening quote
```

475

```
      if (json_string[value_start] == '"') value_start++;
      size_t value_end = json_string.find("\"", value_start);
      if (value_end != std::string::npos) {
        header_value_ = json_string.substr(value_start, value_end -
                          value_start);
        LOG_INFO("Configured HeaderPlugin with " + header_name_ + ":"
        + header_value_);
        return true;
      }
    }
    LOG_WARN("Failed to parse header value from JSON configuration");
  }
}
LOG_INFO("Using default configuration: " + header_name_ + ":" +
header_value_);
return true;
}
```

In production, developers would likely utilize a suitable JSON parsing library to handle configuration more robustly. The WebAssembly ecosystem has begun to provide similar libraries; however, they frequently must be compiled alongside the extension code.

Execution Context and Timing

The phase: AUTHN setting in our WasmPlugin resource has profound implications for when and how our WebAssembly module executes. In order to accurately estimate how the extension will interact with other components in the service mesh, it is essential to have a solid understanding of this timing.

When we specify the AUTHN phase, our module is added to the filter chain of Envoy, which comes before the authentication filters that are already included into Istio automatically, and this means that our onRequestHeaders method is executed at an early stage in the request preparation pipeline:

```
FilterHeadersStatus onRequestHeaders(uint32_t, bool) override {
```

```
// Add the configured header to outgoing requests
addRequestHeader(root_->header_name_, root_->header_value_);
LOG_INFO("Added header " + root_->header_name_ + ":" + root_->header_
value_);
  return FilterHeadersStatus::Continue;
}
```

This early execution provides several advantages:

1. Pre-authentication Processing: Our added headers can influence Istio's authentication decisions. For example, we might add tenant identifiers or context information that authentication policies can reference.

2. Consistent Header Presence: Since our headers are added before most other processing occurs, downstream filters and the target service can rely on their presence.

3. Potential Optimization: Early filter execution can short-circuit unnecessary processing if the extension determines a request should be rejected.

However, this positioning also introduces considerations:

1. Limited Context: At the authentication phase, certain information (like routing decisions) may not yet be available to the extension.

2. Responsibility for Security: Extensions in the authentication phase need careful design to avoid undermining security guarantees.

3. Performance Impact: Since the extension runs for every request that matches the selector, inefficient code can create a bottleneck early in the processing pipeline.

Different phases offer different trade-offs. For example, placing an extension in the STATS phase would provide access to the complete request and response, but would not allow modifying either for normal processing.

CHAPTER 9   EXTENDING ISTIO WITH CUSTOM PLUGINS

Deployment Scope and Targeting

The combination of namespace placement and label selector in our WasmPlugin resource creates a targeted deployment scope for our extension. This targeting affects both functionality and resource utilization.

With our example configuration, the extension will be deployed to all Envoy proxies associated with pods that have the label `app: my-service`, regardless of which namespace those pods reside in (because our WasmPlugin is in the istio-system namespace).

This targeting enables several sophisticated deployment patterns:

1. Service-Specific Customization: Different services might require different headers. By creating multiple WasmPlugin resources with different selectors and configurations, operators can tailor the behavior to each service's needs.

2. Progressive Rollout: During initial deployment or updates, operators can target a subset of services to validate the extension's behavior before wider rollout.

3. Environment Separation: By deploying different configurations in development, staging, and production namespaces, teams can adapt extension behavior to each environment's requirements.

4. Multi-tenancy Support: In multi-tenant clusters, extensions can be deployed to specific tenant namespaces without affecting others.

This targeted approach allows organizations to balance customization needs with operational complexity, deploying extensions only where they provide value while maintaining a clean configuration model.

Finally, putting everything together, we will create the Kubernetes resources needed to deploy the plugin to an Istio service mesh:

```
apiVersion: extensions.istio.io/v1alpha1
kind: WasmPlugin
metadata:
 name: header-plugin
 namespace: istio-system
spec:
```

```
  selector:
    matchLabels:
      app: my-service # Target specific applications
  url: <path-to-your-wasm-file>
  phase: AUTHN # Execute during authentication phase
  pluginConfig:
    x-custom-header: my-custom-value # Configuration for the plugin
```

After deployment, you can verify the plugin is working correctly as shown below:

```
# Create a test pod if needed
kubectl apply -f - <<EOF
apiVersion: v1
kind: Pod
metadata:
  name: curl-test
  labels:
    app: curl-test
spec:
  containers:
  - name: curl
    image: curlimages/curl
    command: ["sleep", "3600"]
EOF

# Wait for the pod to be ready
kubectl wait --for=condition=Ready pod/curl-test

# Test with curl to see if our header is being applied
kubectl exec curl-test -- curl -v http://my-service.default.svc.cluster.local
```

Deep Dive into the WebAssembly Plugin Architecture

WebAssembly extensions in Istio represent a sophisticated architectural pattern that balances security, performance, and flexibility. This architecture enables organizations to extend Istio's capabilities while maintaining the performance and security characteristics essential for production environments. In this section, we'll explore the underlying mechanisms that power this architecture, going beyond basic implementation details to understand the intricate interactions between components within Istio's extensibility framework.

Understanding the Proxy-Wasm ABI

The Proxy-Wasm Application Binary Interface (ABI) is the underlying contract between WebAssembly modules and the Envoy proxy environment. Unlike high-level programming interfaces, an ABI functions at a lower level, specifying the precise binary interactions required for secure and efficient communication across the WebAssembly sandbox boundary.

The ABI defines several categories of functions that plugins can utilize to interact with the Envoy host environment:

> Memory Management Functions: Proxy_alloc and proxy_dealloc are functions that govern memory allocation and deallocation within WebAssembly's linear memory space, respectively. These functions are critical because WebAssembly modules run in a sandboxed memory model, requiring all external interactions to pass through controlled interfaces.
>
> Here's an example for when storing a header value in your plugin:
>
> ```
> // When storing header value in the plugin
> const std::string& value = getRequestHeader("authorization").value_or("");
> char* buffer = static_cast<char*>(proxy_alloc(value.size() + 1));
> std::memcpy(buffer, value.data(), value.size());
> buffer[value.size()] = '\0';  // Null-terminate the string
>
> // Later, when done with the buffer
> proxy_dealloc(buffer);
> ```
>
> Buffer Access Functions: Functions like proxy_get_buffer_bytes and proxy_set_buffer_bytes enable interaction with data buffers such as request bodies or configuration data. These functions

implement a controlled data exchange mechanism that maintains the WebAssembly sandbox's integrity while allowing plugins to process potentially large data payloads efficiently.

HTTP Traffic Functions: These functions facilitate HTTP traffic manipulation, including adding, retrieving, modifying, or removing headers through functions like `proxy_add_header_map_value` and `proxy_get_header_map_value`. By abstracting the complex internal representation of HTTP messages, these functions provide plugins with a straightforward interface for traffic manipulation without exposing Envoy's internal data structures.

Logging and Metrics Functions: The ABI provides observability through functions like `proxy_log` for sending log messages to Envoy's logging system, as well as `proxy_define_metric`, `proxy_increment_metric`, and `proxy_record_metric` for custom metrics collection. These functions integrate with Envoy's existing telemetry infrastructure, ensuring that custom extensions can leverage the same observability patterns as built-in components.

State Management Functions: Data retrieval and persistence across request contexts are supported by functions such as `proxy_get_property`, `proxy_set_shared_data`, and `proxy_get_shared_data`. These functions maintain the security limits necessary for production deployments while enabling complex state management patterns, such as cross-request data sharing and integration with external systems.

Understanding the layered architecture of the Proxy-Wasm interaction is essential for effective plugin development:

1. Your plugin logic sits at the top, using the Proxy-Wasm SDK to provide a user-friendly C++ API.

2. The SDK abstracts the underlying ABI calls, translating high-level C++ method calls into the appropriate low-level function invocations.

3. The standardized Proxy-Wasm ABI functions form the middle layer.

4. These ABI functions are implemented by Envoy's host functions, which integrate with Envoy's core proxy functionality.

This layered approach ensures both security and performance while maintaining a clean separation of concerns between the plugin developer's code and the proxy infrastructure.

Data marshaling—the process of converting between WebAssembly's linear memory representation and Envoy's native data structures—is one of the more sophisticated aspects of the Proxy-Wasm ABI. This process involves

1. Serializing complex structures like headers into a binary format
2. Allocating space in WebAssembly memory
3. Transferring the serialized data
4. Deserializing it within the WebAssembly module

Despite the complexity, this mechanism is designed to maintain strict memory safety while minimizing performance overhead through techniques like zero-copy operations for large data payloads and buffer reuse for frequently accessed data.

The Proxy-Wasm ABI employs semantic versioning to manage compatibility between different implementations. For production deployments, explicitly specifying the ABI version in your EnvoyFilter or WasmPlugin resources is essential to prevent unexpected compatibility issues during upgrades.

Plugin Lifecycle and Execution Context

A WebAssembly plugin in Istio follows a specific lifecycle that mirrors the operational phases of the Envoy proxy itself, ensuring that extensions integrate seamlessly with Envoy's event-driven architecture. Figure 9-3 shows the high-level view of plugin lifecycle.

CHAPTER 9 EXTENDING ISTIO WITH CUSTOM PLUGINS

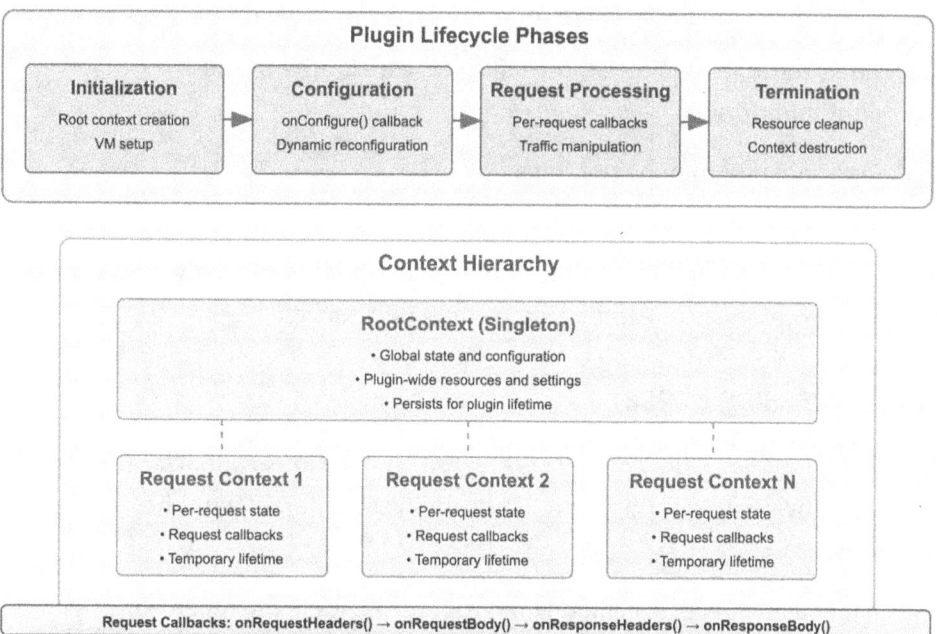

Figure 9-3. *High-level view of plugin lifecycle*

Initialization Phase

When the plugin is first loaded, the Envoy proxy creates a root context that handles configuration and global state. This initialization process includes validating the WebAssembly binary, setting up the execution environment, and establishing the communication channels between the proxy and the plugin.

During initialization, the plugin can establish connections to external systems, precompute frequently used values, or initialize internal data structures. Since this phase occurs only once per plugin instance, it's an ideal place for expensive setup operations that shouldn't be repeated for each request.

Configuration Phase

After initialization, the onConfigure method is called with the configuration data from Istio's resources. This separation between initialization and configuration enables dynamic reconfiguration without restarting the proxy or reloading the plugin, which is essential for production environments where downtime must be minimized.

483

The configuration data typically includes

- Plugin-specific parameters from the EnvoyFilter or WasmPlugin resource
- Environment-specific settings like service identity or mesh configuration
- Optional plugin behavior flags

Since reconfiguration can occur throughout the plugin's lifecycle, the onConfigure method should be designed to handle incremental updates correctly, preserving existing state when appropriate and resetting state when necessary.

Request Processing Phase

For each HTTP request, a new context is created, and various callbacks are triggered as the request flows through the proxy. The plugin can interact with the request at multiple points:

- onRequestHeaders: Called when request headers are received, allowing the plugin to examine or modify headers before they are processed by downstream filters or forwarded to the target service. This callback provides access to metadata like request method, path, and client information.
- onRequestBody: Called for each request body chunk, enabling the plugin to process body content incrementally rather than requiring the entire body to be buffered. This design supports efficient processing of large uploads or streaming data.
- onRequestTrailers: Called when request trailers are received, providing access to any trailing headers in the HTTP request.

The response path follows a similar pattern with corresponding callbacks:

- onResponseHeaders: Called when response headers from the upstream service are received
- onResponseBody: Called for each response body chunk from the upstream service
- onResponseTrailers: Called when response trailers from the upstream service are received

CHAPTER 9 EXTENDING ISTIO WITH CUSTOM PLUGINS

These callbacks form a comprehensive request processing pipeline that gives plugins visibility into the complete HTTP transaction while maintaining efficient memory usage through an incremental processing model.

Termination Phase

When the plugin is unloaded (e.g., during configuration updates or proxy shutdown), contexts are destroyed, and resources are released. The plugin should implement proper cleanup in its destructors to avoid resource leaks or incomplete operations.

Context Hierarchy in Proxy-Wasm

The Proxy-Wasm SDK defines a hierarchical context model that mirrors the natural structure of HTTP traffic processing:

RootContext: A singleton context created when the plugin is loaded. It handles configuration and maintains global state shared across all requests. The RootContext persists for the lifetime of the plugin and provides a central point for

- Plugin configuration management
- Shared resources like connection pools or caches
- Global statistics and metrics
- Plugin-wide logging and troubleshooting

Context: Created for each HTTP request/response pair. Each context has access to its parent RootContext, allowing it to share configuration and state. This per-request context provides isolation between concurrent requests while still enabling access to shared configuration and resources.

This hierarchy allows for efficient memory usage and clear separation of concerns between global configuration and per-request processing. It enables plugins to maintain state at the appropriate scope:

- Request-specific state in the Context
- Service-wide or plugin-wide state in the RootContext

As an illustration, a plugin that restricts the rate of requests could keep information about the quotas for each client in the RootContext while monitoring the consumption of each request in the Context:

```
class RateLimitRoot : public RootContext {
public:
  // Global quota map shared across all requests
  std::unordered_map<std::string, Quota> client_quotas_;
};

class RateLimitContext : public Context {
public:
  FilterHeadersStatus onRequestHeaders(uint32_t) {
    // Access client ID from request
    auto client_id = getRequestHeader("x-client-id");

    // Access quota from root context
    auto root = static_cast<RateLimitRoot*>(this->root());
    auto& quota = root->client_quotas_[client_id];

    if (quota.remaining <= 0) {
      // Quota exceeded, reject request
      sendLocalResponse(429, "Rate limit exceeded", "", {});
      return FilterHeadersStatus::StopIteration;
    }
    // Consume quota
    quota.remaining--;
    return FilterHeadersStatus::Continue;
  }
};
```

This context hierarchy provides a natural model for expressing common patterns in network proxies, such as per-connection state, per-request processing, and shared configuration, making plugin development more intuitive while ensuring efficient resource usage.

EnvoyFilter and Wasm

The EnvoyFilter resource stands as one of the most powerful extension mechanisms in Istio's architecture, enabling fine-grained customization of the Envoy proxies that constitute Istio's data plane. Unlike most other Istio resources that operate at a higher level of abstraction, EnvoyFilter provides direct access to the underlying Envoy configuration, allowing platform engineers to modify how traffic flows through the mesh at a fundamental level. This capability is particularly valuable when integrating WebAssembly (Wasm) modules, which extend Istio with custom traffic processing logic beyond what's available out of the box.

At its core, the EnvoyFilter resource functions as a surgical instrument for modifying the configuration that Istio's control plane generates and distributes to Envoy proxies. These modifications can insert, replace, remove, or merge configuration elements within Envoy's complex configuration hierarchy. For WebAssembly extensions specifically, EnvoyFilter enables the injection of custom modules into Envoy's HTTP filter chain, where they can intercept and process requests and responses at precisely defined points in the traffic flow.

Key Components and Architecture

The EnvoyFilter resource architecture centers around a patching model with several critical components working together to enable targeted modifications:

The **workloadSelector** component determines which specific Envoy proxies will receive the configuration changes. This targeting mechanism operates through Kubernetes label selectors, allowing engineers to deploy extensions to specific services or service subsets. For instance, you might target only your payment processing services with a specific security extension while leaving other services unmodified. When omitted, the EnvoyFilter applies to all workloads within its namespace, creating an implicit targeting scope.

The **configPatches** array forms the heart of the EnvoyFilter resource, containing one or more patch operations that will be applied to the Envoy configuration. Each patch consists of a matching section that identifies the target configuration element and a patch section that defines the modification to apply. This structure enables multiple related changes to be grouped within a single resource, simplifying management and ensuring consistency.

The **match** section defines precisely which part of the Envoy configuration should be modified, using a hierarchical structure that mirrors Envoy's own configuration model. This targeting can be incredibly specific, drilling down through listeners, filter chains, and individual filters to identify exactly where a WebAssembly module should be inserted. The match section also specifies the context (such as inbound sidecar, outbound sidecar, or gateway), further refining when and where the patch applies.

The **patch** section specifies both the operation to perform (INSERT_BEFORE, INSERT_AFTER, REPLACE, REMOVE, or MERGE) and the configuration content to apply. For WebAssembly modules, this typically involves inserting a Wasm HTTP filter with configuration that defines where to obtain the module binary and how it should be initialized.

Deploying WebAssembly with EnvoyFilter

When utilizing EnvoyFilter to deploy a WebAssembly module, we create a configuration that instructs Envoy to load and run our customized code within its processing pipeline. Imagine a situation in which a high-value API service handling financial transactions requires the implementation of customized rate limiting:

```
apiVersion: networking.istio.io/v1alpha3
kind: EnvoyFilter
metadata:
  name: financial-ratelimiter
  namespace: finance-system
spec:
  workloadSelector:
    labels:
      app: transaction-api
      environment: production
  configPatches:
    - applyTo: HTTP_FILTER
      match:
        context: SIDECAR_INBOUND
        listener:
          filterChain:
            filter:
              name: "envoy.filters.network.http_connection_manager"
              subFilter:
                name: "envoy.filters.http.router"
      patch:
        operation: INSERT_BEFORE
        value:
```

CHAPTER 9   EXTENDING ISTIO WITH CUSTOM PLUGINS

```
    name: envoy.filters.http.wasm
    typed_config:
      "@type": type.googleapis.com/udpa.type.v1.TypedStruct
      type_url: type.googleapis.com/envoy.extensions.filters.http.
                wasm.v3.Wasm
      value:
        config:
          name: "tx_ratelimiter"
          root_id: "finance_rate_limiter"
          vm_config:
            vm_id: "finance_ratelimiter_vm"
            runtime: "envoy.wasm.runtime.v8"
            code:
              remote:
                http_uri:
                  uri: "https://artifacts.company.com/wasm/finance-
                        ratelimiter-v1.2.wasm"
                  sha256: "a72e...d37f"
                  timeout: "5s"
            allow_precompiled: true
          configuration:
            "@type": "type.googleapis.com/google.protobuf.
                      StringValue"
            value: '{"default_limit":100,"premium_limit":500,"burst_
                    multiplier":1.5,"redis_endpoint":"redis.finance-
                    system:6379"}'
```

This sample shows some key aspects of utilizing EnvoyFilter for WebAssembly deployment:

The `workloadSelector` selectively targets transaction API services with defined labels, ensuring that the rate limitation only affects the desired high-value services.

The `match` section places our WebAssembly module in the inbound traffic path, intercepting requests before they reach the service but after they've gone through Istio's standard processing like authentication and authorization.

The `value` section defines a complete Wasm filter configuration, including

- Unique identifiers for the filter, root context, and VM instance
- The V8 runtime specification, which is the standard WebAssembly runtime in Istio
- A remote HTTP source for the WebAssembly binary, with integrity verification via SHA256
- Structured JSON configuration that parametrizes the rate limiter's behavior

The `configuration` field passes business-specific parameters to the WebAssembly module, including different rate limits for standard and premium customers, burst behavior configuration, and a Redis endpoint for distributed rate limit state storage.

Filter Chain Positioning and Operations

The positioning of a WebAssembly filter within Envoy's processing pipeline fundamentally affects its capabilities and behavior. Istio's EnvoyFilter resource provides sophisticated control over this placement through its match and operation fields.

When inserting a WebAssembly module, you have several strategic options for placement:

> Pre-authentication Positioning: Placing your module before Istio's authentication filters allows it to influence or augment authentication decisions. This is valuable for implementing custom identity verification logic or injecting authentication context. For example, a module might extract customer identifiers from legacy headers before Istio's JWT authentication:

```
match:
  context: SIDECAR_INBOUND
  listener:
    filterChain:
      filter:
        name: "envoy.filters.network.http_connection_manager"
```

CHAPTER 9   EXTENDING ISTIO WITH CUSTOM PLUGINS

```
        subFilter:
          name: "envoy.filters.http.jwt_authn"
patch:
  operation: INSERT_BEFORE
```

Post-authentication/Pre-authorization Positioning: Inserting your module after authentication but before authorization lets it use validated identity information to influence authorization decisions. A module in this position might implement fine-grained tenant isolation rules that Istio's built-in RBAC cannot express:

```
match:
  context: SIDECAR_INBOUND
  listener:
    filterChain:
      filter:
        name: "envoy.filters.network.http_connection_manager"
        subFilter:
          name: "envoy.filters.http.rbac"
patch:
  operation: INSERT_BEFORE
```

Pre-router Positioning: Placing your module immediately before the router filter (which forwards requests to their destination) is the most common approach. This position gives the module access to all of Istio's processed metadata while still allowing request modification before it reaches the service:

```
match:
  context: SIDECAR_INBOUND
  listener:
    filterChain:
      filter:
        name: "envoy.filters.network.http_connection_manager"
```

```
            subFilter:
              name: "envoy.filters.http.router"
      patch:
        operation: INSERT_BEFORE
```

The EnvoyFilter resource supports several operations that determine how the configuration is modified:

> INSERT_BEFORE/INSERT_AFTER: These operations add your WebAssembly filter before or after an existing filter in the chain, enabling precise positioning relative to Istio's built-in processing stages.
>
> REPLACE: This operation substitutes an existing filter with your custom implementation, allowing you to completely override Istio's default behavior for specific functions.
>
> REMOVE: This operation eliminates a filter from the chain, which can be useful when you need to disable certain built-in functionality that conflicts with your custom processing.
>
> MERGE: This operation combines your configuration with an existing element, enabling partial modifications to existing filters without complete replacement.

Traffic Direction and Context Types

The traffic direction and context in which your WebAssembly module operates significantly impact its functionality. EnvoyFilter provides fine-grained control over this aspect through the context field in the match section.

SIDECAR_INBOUND context applies your filter to traffic entering the service from the mesh. This is where most service-specific processing occurs, such as request validation, authentication enhancement, or payload transformation before it reaches your application. A content validation module might operate in this context to verify JSON schemas or scan for potential injection attacks before requests reach your application code:

```
match:
  context: SIDECAR_INBOUND
  listener:
    portNumber: 8080
```

SIDECAR_OUTBOUND context applies your filter to traffic leaving the service and heading to other mesh services. This context is valuable for client-side concerns like circuit breaking, request enrichment, or response caching. A WebAssembly module implementing a distributed tracing enhancement might operate in this context to ensure that all outgoing requests contain necessary correlation headers:

```
match:
  context: SIDECAR_OUTBOUND
  listener:
    portNumber: 9090
```

GATEWAY context applies your filter to Istio ingress or egress gateway traffic, handling mesh entry and exit points. This context is ideal for edge functionality like API key validation, global rate limiting, or content filtering. A WebAssembly module providing API key validation might be deployed in this context to verify credentials before requests enter the mesh:

```
match:
  context: GATEWAY
  listener:
    portNumber: 443
```

You can further refine the targeting by specifying port numbers, particular routes, or even specific destination services, creating extremely precise control over where your WebAssembly module executes.

WebAssembly Module Configuration and Initialization

The configuration passed from the EnvoyFilter resource to your WebAssembly module serves as its initialization parameters. This configuration flows through to the module's onConfigure method, allowing you to customize its behavior without recompiling the code.

CHAPTER 9 EXTENDING ISTIO WITH CUSTOM PLUGINS

The configuration typically takes the form of a JSON string, though Istio's architecture can accommodate more complex structures if needed:

```
configuration:
  "@type": "type.googleapis.com/google.protobuf.StringValue"
  value: '{"regions":["us-east-1","eu-west-1"],"default_
  timeout":3000,"retry_attempts":3,"circuit_breaker":{"error_
  threshold":50,"min_requests":10}}'
```

This structured approach to configuration enables several powerful patterns:

> Feature Flagging: Your module can selectively enable or disable features based on configuration, allowing feature rollout without code changes. For example, a security module might enable new detection rules through configuration updates.

> Environmental Adaptation: The same WebAssembly module can behave differently in development, staging, and production environments based on configuration parameters. A rate limiting module might apply strict limits in production but allow unlimited traffic in development.

> Multi-tenancy Support: Configuration can contain tenant-specific settings, enabling a single module to handle different requirements for different customers or business units. A data transformation module might apply different redaction rules for different regulatory jurisdictions.

> Integration Coordination: Configuration can provide endpoints, credentials, or other parameters needed for integration with external systems. A module that enriches requests with account information might receive the account service endpoint and authentication parameters through configuration.

Inside your WebAssembly module, this configuration is accessed during initialization:

```
bool MyFilterRootContext::onConfigure(size_t configuration_size) {
  // Get the configuration JSON string
```

```
  auto configuration_data = getBufferBytes(WasmBufferType::Plugin
                            Configuration, 0, configuration_size);
  auto config_string = configuration_data->toString();

  // Parse JSON (simplified example)
  auto config = parseJson(config_string);

  // Extract and store configuration values
  if (config.hasKey("default_timeout")) {
    default_timeout_ms_ = config.getInteger("default_timeout");
  }

  if (config.hasKey("retry_attempts")) {
    retry_attempts_ = config.getInteger("retry_attempts");
  }

  if (config.hasKey("circuit_breaker")) {
    auto cb_config = config.getObject("circuit_breaker");
    circuit_breaker_threshold_ = cb_config.getInteger("error_threshold");
    circuit_breaker_min_requests_ = cb_config.getInteger("min_requests");
  }

  LOG_INFO("Configured with timeout: " + std::to_string(default_
  timeout_ms_) + "ms, retries: " + std::to_string(retry_attempts_));
  return true;
}
```

This configuration mechanism creates a clean separation between code and configuration, enabling operational changes without requiring new WebAssembly module deployments.

WebAssembly Binary Distribution Options

EnvoyFilter provides several methods for distributing WebAssembly binaries to Envoy proxies, each with distinct advantages and trade-offs:

Remote HTTP/HTTPS distribution enables centralized management of WebAssembly modules through a web server or object storage service:

```
code:
  remote:
    http_uri:
      uri: "https://storage.company.com/wasm-modules/auth-enhancer.wasm"
      sha256: "d7f8a756..."
      timeout: "30s"
```

This approach offers several advantages:

- Centralized deployment and updates without modifying Kubernetes resources
- Ability to roll out new module versions without changing EnvoyFilter definitions
- Support for integrity verification through SHA256 checksums
- Compatibility with CDN distribution for global deployments

However, it requires network connectivity during proxy startup and may not be suitable for air-gapped environments.

Local file distribution pre-positions the WebAssembly binary on the Envoy container's filesystem:

```
code:
  local:
    filename: "/var/local/wasm-modules/data-transformer.wasm"
```

This method provides high reliability by eliminating network dependencies during startup. It's particularly valuable in environments with strict network policies or air-gapped deployments. Implementation typically requires customizing the Istio sidecar injection template to mount a volume containing the WebAssembly binaries.

OCI registry distribution leverages container registries to store and distribute WebAssembly modules:

```
code:
  remote:
    http_uri:
      uri: "oci://registry.company.com/wasm-modules/metrics-enhancer:v1.2.3"
      timeout: "30s"
```

This approach integrates WebAssembly module distribution with existing container image workflows, providing

- Familiar versioning through image tags
- Access control via registry authentication
- Integration with existing CI/CD pipelines
- Compatibility with Kubernetes image pull secrets for authentication

For production deployments, the choice of distribution method should consider factors such as

- Network reliability and security requirements
- Operational processes for updates and rollbacks
- Integration with existing CI/CD infrastructure
- Disaster recovery and availability requirements

Namespace Scoping and Mesh-Wide Deployment

The namespace placement of an EnvoyFilter resource has profound implications for its sphere of influence within the service mesh. This namespace-based scoping model aligns with Kubernetes' resource management paradigm while providing flexible deployment options.

When an EnvoyFilter is deployed in Istio's root namespace (typically istio-system), it can potentially affect all workloads throughout the mesh, subject to its workloadSelector. This root namespace placement enables mesh-wide extensions that implement cross-cutting concerns such as security controls, compliance requirements, or global observability enhancements.

Consider a scenario where a financial services organization needs to implement data loss prevention (DLP) scanning for all APIs that might handle sensitive information:

```
apiVersion: networking.istio.io/v1alpha3
kind: EnvoyFilter
metadata:
  name: global-dlp-scanner
  namespace: istio-system  # Root namespace for mesh-wide effect
```

```
spec:
  workloadSelector:
    labels:
      api-security-tier: sensitive  # Only applies to labeled services
  configPatches:
    # WebAssembly filter configuration for DLP scanning
```

This EnvoyFilter would apply to all workloads across all namespaces that have the specified label, creating a consistent security control throughout the mesh without requiring deployment to each namespace.

Conversely, when an EnvoyFilter is deployed in a service-specific namespace, it affects only the workloads within that namespace. This namespace-scoped deployment model enables

> Team Autonomy: Each team can manage their own extensions without affecting other services in the mesh. For example, a payment processing team might implement specialized handling for credit card data without impacting other services.

> Isolation for Testing: New extensions can be tested in development or staging namespaces before being promoted to production or mesh-wide deployment.

> Multi-tenant Separation: In multi-tenant clusters, each tenant's customizations can be isolated to their own namespace, preventing cross-tenant interference.

```
apiVersion: networking.istio.io/v1alpha3
kind: EnvoyFilter
metadata:
  name: team-specific-transformer
  namespace: payment-system  # Service-specific namespace
spec:
  workloadSelector:
    labels:
      app: payment-processor
  configPatches:
    # Team-specific WebAssembly filter configuration
```

This namespace-scoped EnvoyFilter would only affect the payment processor services within the payment-system namespace, providing targeted functionality without impacting other services.

The combination of namespace placement and workloadSelector creates a flexible targeting system that supports both broad mesh-wide policies and narrow service-specific customizations. This dual-layer scoping enables organizations to implement governance models where central platform teams manage mesh-wide extensions while service teams maintain autonomy for service-specific customizations.

Handling Multiple EnvoyFilters and Precedence

When multiple EnvoyFilter resources target the same Envoy proxies, understanding their evaluation order and interaction becomes crucial for predictable behavior. Istio applies a well-defined precedence model that determines how overlapping or conflicting EnvoyFilters are processed.

The evaluation order follows these key principles:

> Namespace Hierarchy: EnvoyFilters in the root namespace (typically `istio-system`) are evaluated before those in service-specific namespaces. This hierarchy enables mesh-wide defaults that can be overridden by namespace-specific customizations.
>
> Alphabetical Ordering: Within the same namespace, EnvoyFilters are evaluated in alphabetical order based on their names. This predictable ordering enables engineers to control precedence through naming conventions.

```
apiVersion: networking.istio.io/v1alpha3
kind: EnvoyFilter
metadata:
  name: a-auth-enhancement  # Evaluated first due to alphabetical ordering
  namespace: retail-system
spec:
  # Configuration for authentication enhancement
---
```

```
apiVersion: networking.istio.io/v1alpha3
kind: EnvoyFilter
metadata:
  name: b-request-transformation   # Evaluated second
  namespace: retail-system
spec:
  # Configuration for request transformation
```

For insertions of WebAssembly filters, this evaluation order creates a sequential insertion pattern that determines the final order of filters in the chain. The first evaluated EnvoyFilter inserts its filter, then the second inserts relative to existing filters (which now include the first insertion), and so on.

This ordering mechanism enables sophisticated filter chain construction where multiple WebAssembly modules work together in a coordinated sequence. For example, a data processing pipeline might consist of multiple modules handling different aspects of the request:

1. A validation module verifies request structure and content.
2. A transformation module converts data formats or protocols.
3. An enrichment module adds additional context from external systems.
4. A security module applies final access control checks.

By carefully naming the EnvoyFilter resources and specifying their insertion points, platform engineers can ensure that these modules execute in the correct sequence despite being deployed through separate resources.

When multiple EnvoyFilters attempt to modify the same exact configuration element (rather than inserting new elements), the last evaluated filter takes precedence. This "last writer wins" approach allows higher-priority configurations to override lower-priority ones, enabling patterns like

> Base Configuration with Overrides: A default configuration in the root namespace can be selectively overridden by namespace-specific configurations.

Progressive Enhancement: Generic configurations can be enhanced with additional settings for specific services or environments.

Configuration Layering: Different teams can contribute different aspects of a configuration that are merged into the final result.

Understanding these precedence rules is essential when implementing complex extension scenarios involving multiple WebAssembly modules or when overriding default Istio behaviors.

Practical Application Patterns

EnvoyFilter-based WebAssembly extensions offer a variety of useful patterns that address common service mesh deployment requirements, and these patterns use EnvoyFilter's precision control and placement capabilities to implement customizations that extend beyond Istio's built-in functionality.

Enhanced security controls provide specialized authentication or authorization logic to complement Istio's built-in security capabilities. An example of this would be a healthcare institution that, prior to allowing access to medical records, implements a HIPAA compliance filter that verifies the patient consent tokens:

```
apiVersion: networking.istio.io/v1alpha3
kind: EnvoyFilter
metadata:
  name: hipaa-consent-validator
  namespace: healthcare-system
spec:
  workloadSelector:
    labels:
      data-classification: phi   # Protected Health Information
  configPatches:
  - applyTo: HTTP_FILTER
    match:
      context: SIDECAR_INBOUND
      listener:
        filterChain:
```

```
    filter:
      name: "envoy.filters.network.http_connection_manager"
      subFilter:
        name: "envoy.filters.http.jwt_authn"  # After JWT
              validation
patch:
  operation: INSERT_AFTER
  # WebAssembly filter that validates consent tokens
```

This pattern positions the consent validation immediately after Istio's JWT authentication, ensuring that identity is verified before consent is checked, creating a layered security approach.

Protocol adapters enable integration between services using different communication protocols or data formats. For instance, a financial services company might deploy a protocol adapter that converts between a legacy XML-based protocol and modern JSON APIs:

```
apiVersion: networking.istio.io/v1alpha3
kind: EnvoyFilter
metadata:
  name: xml-json-adapter
  namespace: integration
spec:
  workloadSelector:
    labels:
      app: legacy-gateway
  configPatches:
    - applyTo: HTTP_FILTER
      match:
        context: SIDECAR_OUTBOUND
        listener:
          portNumber: 8080  # Specific port for the API service
      patch:
        operation: INSERT_BEFORE
        value:
          name: envoy.filters.http.wasm
          # WebAssembly filter that transforms between XML and JSON
```

CHAPTER 9   EXTENDING ISTIO WITH CUSTOM PLUGINS

This adapter enables modern services to communicate with legacy systems without requiring either to change, facilitating incremental modernization strategies.

Advanced traffic management implements sophisticated routing, load balancing, or traffic shaping beyond what Istio provides natively. A retail platform might deploy a seasonal traffic manager that implements dynamic routing based on real-time inventory levels:

```
apiVersion: networking.istio.io/v1alpha3
kind: EnvoyFilter
metadata:
  name: inventory-aware-router
  namespace: retail
spec:
  workloadSelector:
    labels:
      app: product-api
  configPatches:
    - applyTo: HTTP_FILTER
      match:
        context: SIDECAR_OUTBOUND
      patch:
        operation: INSERT_BEFORE
        # WebAssembly filter that routes based on inventory levels
```

This extension could query inventory services in real time and adjust routing decisions to balance load across different catalog systems during high-traffic sales events.

Custom observability augments Istio's telemetry with business-specific metrics or logging. A payment processor might deploy a transaction monitor that captures financial metrics without exposing sensitive details:

```
apiVersion: networking.istio.io/v1alpha3
kind: EnvoyFilter
metadata:
  name: transaction-metrics
  namespace: payments
spec:
```

CHAPTER 9   EXTENDING ISTIO WITH CUSTOM PLUGINS

```
  workloadSelector:
    labels:
      app: payment-gateway
  configPatches:
    - applyTo: HTTP_FILTER
      match:
        context: SIDECAR_INBOUND
      patch:
        operation: INSERT_BEFORE
        # WebAssembly filter that extracts and reports transaction metrics
```

This observability extension could implement domain-specific metrics like transaction volume, approval rates, or average transaction value while redacting sensitive financial details.

Configuration externalization patterns separate WebAssembly module behavior from deployment details by sourcing configuration from external systems rather than embedding it directly in the EnvoyFilter. A multi-region deployment might implement dynamic configuration based on the deployment region:

```
apiVersion: networking.istio.io/v1alpha3
kind: EnvoyFilter
metadata:
  name: regional-adapter
  namespace: global-services
spec:
  workloadSelector:
    labels:
      app: multi-region-api
  configPatches:
    - applyTo: HTTP_FILTER
      match:
        context: SIDECAR_INBOUND
      patch:
        operation: INSERT_BEFORE
        value:
          name: envoy.filters.http.wasm
```

```yaml
            typed_config:
              "@type": type.googleapis.com/udpa.type.v1.TypedStruct
              type_url: type.googleapis.com/envoy.extensions.filters.http.
                        wasm.v3.Wasm
              value:
                config:
                  vm_config:
                    code:
                      remote:
                        http_uri:
                          uri: "https://storage.company.com/wasm/regional-
                                adapter.wasm"
                    configuration:
                      "@type": "type.googleapis.com/google.protobuf.
                                StringValue"
                      value: '{"config_service":"https://config.company.com/
                              api/v1/regional-config"}'
```

Instead of hardcoding region-specific behavior, this WebAssembly module would fetch its configuration from an external service at runtime, enabling centralized management of regional differences.

These patterns demonstrate how EnvoyFilter-based WebAssembly extensions can address sophisticated requirements while maintaining the security, performance, and reliability characteristics essential for production deployments.

Implementation and Troubleshooting

Implementing and deploying WebAssembly plugins in Istio requires careful planning and execution. This section explores practical aspects of bringing your WebAssembly extensions from development to production, covering testing methodologies, deployment strategies, monitoring approaches, and best practices that ensure reliable operation in production environments.

CHAPTER 9 EXTENDING ISTIO WITH CUSTOM PLUGINS

Testing WebAssembly Plugins

Testing WebAssembly plugins thoroughly before deployment is essential to prevent service disruptions in your mesh. Unlike application code that might fail in isolation, proxy extensions can impact all traffic flowing through the mesh, making rigorous testing particularly important.

Unit Testing Extensions

Unit testing forms the foundation of a robust testing strategy for WebAssembly plugins. While testing WebAssembly modules presents unique challenges compared with regular applications, several approaches can help ensure your extensions function correctly:

Testing the core logic independently from the Proxy-Wasm integration allows you to verify business logic functionality separately from the integration points. Consider this pattern for a header validation plugin:

```cpp
// Extract core validation logic into a separate function
bool validateHeaderFormat(const std::string& header_value) {
  // Core validation logic that can be tested independently
  if (header_value.empty()) return false;

  // Check for required format (e.g., "tenant-id:region:environment")
  std::vector<std::string> parts = split(header_value, ':');
  return parts.size() == 3 && !parts[0].empty() && !parts[1].empty() && !parts[2].empty();
}

// In the WebAssembly plugin class
FilterHeadersStatus onRequestHeaders(uint32_t, bool) {
  auto header = getRequestHeader("x-context-id").value_or("");
  if (!validateHeaderFormat(header)) {
    sendLocalResponse(400, "Invalid context header format", "", {});
    return FilterHeadersStatus::StopIteration;
  }
  return FilterHeadersStatus::Continue;
}
```

This separation enables you to write focused unit tests for the validation logic without needing to simulate the entire proxy environment.

Mock implementations of the Proxy-Wasm interfaces allow you to test extension behavior in isolation. The Proxy-Wasm ecosystem includes mocking frameworks that simulate the host environment for testing:

```
TEST_F(HeaderValidatorTest, RejectsInvalidHeaders) {
  // Setup mock expectations
  EXPECT_CALL(*mock_, getRequestHeader("x-context-id"))
      .WillOnce(Return(WasmResult::Ok, "invalid-format"));

  EXPECT_CALL(*mock_, sendLocalResponse(400, _, _, _))
      .WillOnce(Return(WasmResult::Ok));

  // Execute the filter callback
  EXPECT_EQ(FilterHeadersStatus::StopIteration,
          context_->onRequestHeaders(0, false));
}
```

These tests verify that your extension correctly handles various input scenarios without requiring a live proxy environment.

Integration Testing with Envoy

While unit tests validate individual components, integration testing ensures your WebAssembly plugin functions correctly within Envoy. The Envoy project provides tooling specifically designed for testing WebAssembly extensions:

The Envoy WebAssembly test framework enables testing extensions against an actual Envoy instance in a controlled environment. This approach verifies that your plugin integrates correctly with Envoy's filter chain:

```
# Example of using envoy's testing framework
bazel test //test/extensions/filters/http/wasm:wasm_filter_integration_test
```

Docker-based integration testing creates lightweight environments for testing your extensions without a full Kubernetes deployment. This approach uses Docker Compose to create a minimal Envoy + WebAssembly environment:

```
# docker-compose.yaml for testing
```

```yaml
version: '3'
services:
  envoy:
    image: envoyproxy/envoy:v1.20.0
    volumes:
      - ./envoy.yaml:/etc/envoy/envoy.yaml
      - ./build/my_extension.wasm:/etc/envoy/extensions/my_extension.wasm
    ports:
      - "9901:9901"
      - "10000:10000"

  test-backend:
    image: kennethreitz/httpbin
    ports:
      - "8080:80"
```

This setup allows you to send test traffic through Envoy with your WebAssembly plugin and verify the behavior without a full mesh deployment.

End-to-End Testing in a Mesh Environment

Before production deployment, end-to-end testing in a realistic mesh environment helps identify integration issues that might not appear in more isolated tests:

Kubernetes-based testing environments provide a realistic platform for validating WebAssembly extensions. Using a dedicated test namespace, you can deploy your extension alongside representative services:

```
# Create a test namespace with Istio injection
kubectl create ns wasm-test
kubectl label namespace wasm-test istio-injection=enabled

# Deploy test services
kubectl apply -f test-services.yaml -n wasm-test

# Deploy your WebAssembly plugin
kubectl apply -f wasmPlugin.yaml -n wasm-test

# Run automated tests against the environment
go test ./e2e/... -mesh-namespace=wasm-test
```

Canary testing with traffic splitting enables gradual validation of extensions with real traffic patterns. By applying your WebAssembly plugin to a subset of services and comparing behavior with unmodified services, you can identify potential issues before full deployment:

```
apiVersion: networking.istio.io/v1alpha3
kind: VirtualService
metadata:
  name: canary-test
spec:
  hosts:
    - service-a
  http:
    - route:
      - destination:
          host: service-a-control
          subset: v1
        weight: 90
      - destination:
          host: service-a-wasm
          subset: v1
        weight: 10
```

This approach lets you observe how your extension behaves with a small percentage of real traffic before committing to full deployment.

Monitoring and Troubleshooting

Effective monitoring and troubleshooting capabilities are essential for operating WebAssembly extensions in production environments. Since extensions operate within the critical path of service communication, visibility into their behavior is crucial for maintaining reliability.

CHAPTER 9   EXTENDING ISTIO WITH CUSTOM PLUGINS

Metrics and Telemetry

Custom metrics from WebAssembly extensions provide visibility into their operational behavior. Extensions can emit metrics through Envoy's metrics subsystem to track key indicators:

```
// In the extension code
void MyContext::incrementRequestCounter(const std::string& type) {
  incrementMetric({"requests", type}, 1);
}

// Usage in request processing
FilterHeadersStatus MyContext::onRequestHeaders(uint32_t, bool) {
  auto path = getRequestHeader(":path").value_or("");
  if (path.find("/api/v1/") != std::string::npos) {
    incrementRequestCounter("api_v1");
  } else if (path.find("/api/v2/") != std::string::npos) {
    incrementRequestCounter("api_v2");
  } else {
    incrementRequestCounter("other");
  }
  return FilterHeadersStatus::Continue;
}
```

These metrics are then accessible through Istio's telemetry collection and can be visualized in dashboards for operational monitoring.

Performance impact monitoring is especially important since WebAssembly extensions add processing overhead to the request path. Tracking key performance indicators helps identify potential bottlenecks:

```
# Prometheus query examples for monitoring WebAssembly performance
# Latency introduced by WebAssembly processing
sum(istio_request_duration_milliseconds_sum{wasm_filter="header_validator"})
by (destination_service) /
sum(istio_request_duration_milliseconds_count{wasm_filter="header_validator"})
by (destination_service)
```

```
# Error rate attributable to WebAssembly filters
sum(rate(istio_requests_total{wasm_filter="header_validator",response_
code=~"5.*"}[5m]))
by (destination_service) /
sum(rate(istio_requests_total{wasm_filter="header_validator"}[5m]))
by (destination_service)
```

These metrics help identify whether WebAssembly extensions are contributing to latency or error conditions.

Integration with distributed tracing adds context to WebAssembly extension behavior. Extensions can add span annotations or tags to provide visibility into their processing:

```
// In the extension code
void addTracingData(const std::string& key, const std::string& value) {
  addResponseHeader("x-tracing-"+key, value);
}

// Usage in request processing
FilterHeadersStatus onRequestHeaders(uint32_t, bool) {
  auto start_time = getCurrentTimeNanoseconds();

  // Perform processing
  bool result = validateRequest();

  // Add tracing information
  auto duration = getCurrentTimeNanoseconds() - start_time;
  addTracingData("validation-result", result ? "pass" : "fail");
  addTracingData("validation-duration-ns", std::to_string(duration));

  return FilterHeadersStatus::Continue;
}
```

These tracing annotations help correlate WebAssembly processing with overall request flow for debugging and performance analysis.

Debugging Techniques

Debugging WebAssembly extensions requires specialized approaches due to their embedded nature. Several techniques facilitate troubleshooting in both development and production environments:

Enhanced logging configuration enables detailed visibility during troubleshooting. WebAssembly extensions can implement configurable logging levels:

```cpp
// In the extension code
void logWithLevel(LogLevel level, const std::string& message) {
  if (level <= configured_log_level_) {
    switch (level) {
      case LogLevel::Debug:
        logDebug(message);
        break;
      case LogLevel::Info:
        logInfo(message);
        break;
      case LogLevel::Warn:
        logWarn(message);
        break;
      case LogLevel::Error:
        logError(message);
        break;
    }
  }
}

// Usage with configuration
bool onConfigure(size_t configuration_size) {
  // Get configuration
  auto configuration = getBufferBytes(WasmBufferType::PluginConfiguration,
0, configuration_size);
  auto config_string = configuration->toString();

  // Parse JSON configuration
  auto config = parseJson(config_string);
```

```
  // Set log level from configuration
  std::string log_level = config["log_level"].getStringValue("info");
  if (log_level == "debug") {
    configured_log_level_ = LogLevel::Debug;
  } else if (log_level == "info") {
    configured_log_level_ = LogLevel::Info;
  } else if (log_level == "warn") {
    configured_log_level_ = LogLevel::Warn;
  } else if (log_level == "error") {
    configured_log_level_ = LogLevel::Error;
  }

  logWithLevel(LogLevel::Info, "Configured with log level: " + log_level);
  return true;
}
```

This approach enables dynamic control of logging verbosity through configuration, allowing detailed logs during troubleshooting without redeploying the extension.

Debug headers provide a mechanism for targeted debugging without increasing log volumes. Extensions can check for specific headers that enable debug mode for individual requests:

```
FilterHeadersStatus onRequestHeaders(uint32_t, bool) {
  // Check for debug header
  bool debug_mode = false;
  auto debug_header = getRequestHeader("x-debug-wasm");
  if (!debug_header->view().empty() && debug_header->view() == "true") {
    debug_mode = true;
    logDebug("Debug mode enabled for request");
  }

  // Process request with enhanced logging if in debug mode
  processRequestWithLogging(debug_mode);

  return FilterHeadersStatus::Continue;
}
```

This pattern allows selective debugging of specific requests without modifying global configuration, making it valuable for production troubleshooting.

Traffic shadowing enables safe analysis of extension behavior with production traffic. By configuring mirror traffic to services with experimental extensions, you can observe how new versions would behave with real-world traffic without affecting production services:

```
apiVersion: networking.istio.io/v1alpha3
kind: VirtualService
metadata:
  name: my-service
spec:
  hosts:
    - my-service
  http:
    - route:
      - destination:
          host: my-service
          subset: production
        mirror:
          host: my-service
          subset: wasm-debug
        mirrorPercentage:
          value: 100.0
```

Combined with a WasmPlugin that targets only the "wasm-debug" subset, this approach provides a realistic testing environment with production traffic patterns.

Rollback Strategies

Despite thorough testing, issues may still occur in production. Having effective rollback strategies ensures quick recovery when WebAssembly extensions cause unexpected behavior:

Rapid configuration rollbacks provide the fastest recovery path by modifying the extension's behavior without removing it entirely. This approach works well for issues related to configuration rather than fundamental extension problems:

Rollback to a previous configuration
kubectl apply -f wasm-plugin-previous-config.yaml

This approach is particularly effective when combined with configuration versioning that maintains previous configurations in a version control system.

Extension removal offers a more decisive rollback option by completely removing the problematic extension from the traffic path. This approach guarantees restoration of pre-extension behavior:

Remove the WebAssembly plugin entirely
kubectl delete wasmplugin header-validator -n production

This method provides a clean recovery but may require reapplying the extension later once the issues are resolved.

Circuit breaking protects against cascading failures by automatically disabling extensions that exceed error thresholds. While Istio doesn't provide this capability natively for extensions, you can implement it within the extension itself:

```
FilterHeadersStatus onRequestHeaders(uint32_t, bool) {
  // Check circuit state in root context
  auto root = static_cast<MyRootContext*>(this->root());

  if (root->isCircuitOpen()) {
    // Circuit is open, skip extension processing
    logWarn("Circuit open, bypassing extension processing");
    return FilterHeadersStatus::Continue;
  }

  try {
    // Normal processing
    return processRequest();
  } catch (const std::exception& e) {
    // Record error and possibly open circuit
    root->recordError(e.what());
    return FilterHeadersStatus::Continue;
  }
}
```

Combined with a mechanism to automatically "open" the circuit after reaching an error threshold, this pattern prevents problematic extensions from impacting service reliability.

Selective disabling provides a middle ground between full removal and continued operation. By modifying the selector to exclude critical services, you can limit the impact of problematic extensions while maintaining functionality for less sensitive workloads:

```
# Original selector targeting all API services
selector:
  matchLabels:
    app: api-service
```

```
# Modified selector excluding critical services
selector:
  matchLabels:
    app: api-service
    tier: non-critical
```

This approach enables a more nuanced response to extension issues, containing the impact while maintaining extension availability where appropriate.

Best Practices

Based on real-world implementation experience, several best practices have emerged for developing and deploying WebAssembly extensions in Istio environments. Following these guidelines helps ensure reliable, maintainable, and efficient extensions.

Development Best Practices

Following sound development practices creates WebAssembly extensions that are robust, maintainable, and perform well in production environments:

Minimize memory allocation and copying to optimize performance. WebAssembly modules operate with limited memory, making efficient memory usage critical for performance:

```
// Inefficient approach with extra copying
std::string getHeaderValue(const std::string& name) {
  std::string result = "";
```

CHAPTER 9   EXTENDING ISTIO WITH CUSTOM PLUGINS

```cpp
  auto header = getRequestHeader(name);
  if (!header->view().empty()) {
    result = std::string(header->view());
  }
  return result;
}

// Improved approach avoiding unnecessary copies
const std::string_view getHeaderValueView(const std::string& name) {
  auto header = getRequestHeader(name);
  return header->view();
}
```

Using string views and avoiding unnecessary copies significantly improves performance, especially for large headers or high-traffic services.

Implement graceful error handling to prevent extension failures from affecting service availability. Robust error handling ensures that extensions fail safely without disrupting the overall traffic flow:

```cpp
FilterHeadersStatus onRequestHeaders(uint32_t, bool) {
  try {
    // Normal processing path
    if (!validateHeaders()) {
      sendLocalResponse(400, "Invalid headers", "", {});
      return FilterHeadersStatus::StopIteration;
    }
    return FilterHeadersStatus::Continue;
  } catch (const std::exception& e) {
    // Exception caught, log and continue
    logError("Error processing headers: " + std::string(e.what()));
    return FilterHeadersStatus::Continue;
  } catch (...) {
    // Unknown exception, log and continue
    logError("Unknown error in header processing");
    return FilterHeadersStatus::Continue;
  }
}
```

CHAPTER 9   EXTENDING ISTIO WITH CUSTOM PLUGINS

This pattern ensures that unexpected errors result in logged information rather than request failures or proxy crashes.

Version your API contracts explicitly to facilitate evolution without breaking compatibility. Clear API versioning helps manage extension upgrades and ensures that configuration changes don't unexpectedly break existing deployments:

```
bool onConfigure(size_t configuration_size) {
  // Get configuration
  auto configuration = getBufferBytes(WasmBufferType::PluginConfiguration,
  0, configuration_size);
  auto config_string = configuration->toString();

  // Parse JSON configuration
  auto config = parseJson(config_string);

  // Check configuration version compatibility
  std::string config_version = config["version"].getStringValue("1.0");
  if (config_version == "1.0") {
    return configureV1(config);
  } else if (config_version == "2.0") {
    return configureV2(config);
  } else {
    logError("Unsupported configuration version: " + config_version);
    return false;
  }
}
```

This approach enables backward compatibility with existing configurations while allowing new features to be added in future versions.

Follow isolation principles by making extensions focused and single-purpose. Rather than creating monolithic extensions that perform multiple functions, develop smaller, focused extensions that do one thing well:

```
// Instead of one large extension that does multiple things:
- authentication
- rate limiting
- payload transformation
- metrics collection
```

```
// Create separate, focused extensions:
- auth-extension.wasm
- rate-limiter.wasm
- transformer.wasm
- metrics-collector.wasm
```

This approach improves testability, simplifies troubleshooting, and allows for more granular deployment control.

Operational Best Practices

Operational best practices focus on how WebAssembly extensions are deployed, managed, and monitored in production environments:

Maintain a registry of approved extensions to prevent uncontrolled proliferation of custom code in the mesh. A structured registry approach includes

1. Version control for WebAssembly module source code
2. CI/CD pipelines for automated building and testing
3. A private registry for storing approved WebAssembly modules
4. Documentation of each extension's purpose, configuration, and operational characteristics
5. Access controls for deploying extensions to production environments

This structured approach prevents "shadow IT" scenarios where undocumented or untested extensions impact service reliability.

Implement progressive resource limits to prevent extensions from consuming excessive resources:

```
apiVersion: extensions.istio.io/v1alpha1
kind: WasmPlugin
metadata:
  name: resource-controlled-plugin
spec:
  selector:
    matchLabels:
```

```yaml
    app: my-service
  url: https://registry.example.com/wasm/my-plugin.wasm
  pluginConfig:
    resources:
      requests:
        memory: "10Mi"
      limits:
        memory: "50Mi"
```

While not currently supported in Istio's WasmPlugin resource, future versions are likely to include resource constraints similar to container specifications, helping prevent resource contention.

Create dashboards specifically for monitoring WebAssembly extension performance:

```
Key dashboard metrics:
1. Extension initialization time
2. Per-request processing latency
3. Memory usage over time
4. Error rates by extension
5. Rejection rates (requests blocked by extensions)
6. Configuration reload events
```

These dashboards provide ongoing visibility into extension behavior and help identify performance trends before they impact service reliability.

Document extension configurations thoroughly to ensure operational knowledge retention:

```yaml
apiVersion: extensions.istio.io/v1alpha1
kind: WasmPlugin
metadata:
  name: well-documented-plugin
  annotations:
    description: "Implements tenant header validation for multi-tenant
    services"
    owner: "platform-team@example.com"
    documentation: "https://internal.docs/istio/extensions/tenant-
    validator"
```

```yaml
    version: "1.2.3"
    last-updated: "2023-04-15"
spec:
  selector:
    matchLabels:
      app: tenant-service
  url: https://registry.example.com/wasm/tenant-validator.wasm
  pluginConfig:
    # Detailed comments explaining each configuration parameter
    validation_mode: "strict"  # Rejects requests with missing tenant headers
    tenant_header: "x-tenant-id"  # Header containing tenant identifier
    log_level: "info"  # Default logging level
```

Thorough documentation enables operational teams to understand extension behavior without needing to examine the source code, particularly important during incident response.

Implement automated tests as part of deployment validation to catch configuration or compatibility issues early:

```bash
#!/bin/bash
# Post-deployment validation script

# Deploy test client
kubectl apply -f test-client.yaml

# Wait for client to be ready
kubectl wait --for=condition=Ready pod/test-client

# Run test requests
echo "Testing basic request..."
RESULT=$(kubectl exec test-client -- curl -s -o /dev/null -w "%{http_code}" http://test-service/api/v1/test)
if [ "$RESULT" != "200" ]; then
  echo "Basic request test failed with status $RESULT"
  exit 1
fi
```

```
echo "Testing invalid request..."
RESULT=$(kubectl exec test-client -- curl -s -o /dev/null -w "%{http_code}"
-H "x-test-trigger: invalid" http://test-service/api/v1/test)
if [ "$RESULT" != "400" ]; then
  echo "Invalid request test failed with status $RESULT"
  exit 1
fi

echo "All tests passed!"
```

These automated tests validate that the extension behaves as expected in the actual deployment environment, providing an early warning system for potential issues.

By following these implementation and deployment best practices, organizations can successfully leverage WebAssembly extensions to customize Istio's behavior while maintaining the reliability, security, and performance characteristics expected in production environments. The combination of rigorous testing, careful deployment strategies, comprehensive monitoring, and operational best practices creates a solid foundation for extending Istio with custom functionality tailored to your specific requirements.

Conclusion

This chapter has explored how to extend Istio's capabilities through WebAssembly plugins, providing DevOps engineers and platform architects with practical knowledge for customizing service mesh functionality. We've examined Istio's evolution from the Mixer-based extension model to the more efficient WebAssembly approach, detailed the Proxy-Wasm architecture that enables secure and high-performance extensions, and provided concrete implementation patterns for common use cases like custom authentication, protocol adaptation, and observability enhancements. The chapter has balanced theoretical understanding with hands-on guidance, covering the complete lifecycle from development environment setup through testing, deployment, monitoring, and troubleshooting. By following the best practices outlined for both development and operations, organizations can confidently extend Istio to meet their specific requirements while maintaining the security, performance, and reliability that production environments demand. WebAssembly extensions represent a powerful capability that allows Istio to be tailored to unique organizational needs without sacrificing the core benefits of a service mesh architecture.

CHAPTER 10

Emerging Trends and the Future of Istio

The complexity of modern distributed systems, the exponential increase in digital business, and the growing demands of these businesses are causing an unprecedented transformation in the landscape of cloud-native technologies. At the heart of this evolution is the reliance on the service mesh ecosystem, with Istio emerging as a leader in enterprise deployment and innovation. Architects, developers, and operational teams must comprehend the future of service mesh technology, as organizations spanning industries are rapidly adopting microservices architectures and distributed systems. This development is more than just a technological advancement; it represents a fundamental shift in how organizations design, deploy, and manage their applications in an increasingly distributed environment. This chapter delves into the strategic considerations, upcoming features, and emerging trends that will shape the future of Istio and the larger service mesh landscape. It gives you the knowledge you need to stay ahead of the curve in this rapidly changing field.

The Current State and Future Roadmap

The evolution of Istio from its initial release to its present state is a remarkable achievement in the field of service mesh technology. Istio has undergone a substantial transformation from a complex but promising platform to a robust and enterprise-ready solution for the management of microservices communications, security, and observability since its inception. The platform has made substantial progress in several critical areas that have historically been a source of frustration for users as we approach 2025. The engineering teams have significantly enhanced performance optimization and reduced resource consumption by employing innovative approaches to proxy management and control plane operations. By optimizing memory usage and reducing CPU overhead, Istio has become more cost-effective and efficient for businesses of all types and sizes.

Intelligent automation and enhanced default configurations have simplified the previously complex and error-prone installation and configuration processes. The IstioOperator API has simplified deployment management, and enhanced configuration validation helps prevent misconfigurations from causing issues in production environments. While maintaining the sophisticated controls that advanced users require, these improvements have substantially diminished the barrier to entry for new users. In response to the increasing demand for service management across distributed environments, multi-cluster support has been enhanced to provide more user-friendly cross-cluster service discovery mechanisms and enhanced federation capabilities.

The Istio roadmap presents a bold vision that has the potential to revolutionize the deployment and management of service meshes. Looking ahead, this vision is evident. The ambient mesh architecture is a game-changing approach that fundamentally reimagines service mesh implementation, and it is one of the most significant developments on the horizon. This innovative architecture introduces a more granular and flexible method of deploying mesh capabilities, transitioning from the traditional sidecar-per-pod model to a more resource-efficient and scalable approach. The mesh architecture clearly distinguishes between the control plane and data plane, enabling organizations to deploy service mesh capabilities selectively following their unique requirements. This division enables organizations to determine which services necessitate full mesh capabilities or if it can operate with minimal overhead, thereby facilitating more efficient resource utilization and scalability.

Istio's future developments focus on:

- Production-Ready Ambient Mesh: Continuing to refine the sidecar-less model for broader adoption

- Deeper Kubernetes Integration: Leveraging native APIs for seamless service mesh functionality

- Enhanced Observability and Security: Building upon zero-trust principles and improving monitoring capabilities

Istio's plans encompass substantial enhancements in operational simplicity, which will address one of the most prevalent criticisms of service mesh technology. The project is currently in the process of creating more user-friendly configuration APIs to assist teams in the management of their service mesh deployments without the need for extensive networking knowledge. The development of improved automation capabilities for common operational tasks is underway, including the implementation of intelligent defaults that are effective in the majority of use cases, automatic protocol detection, and improved service discovery. The development of sophisticated debugging features and troubleshooting tools will aid teams in the identification and resolution of issues in their service mesh deployments. These improvements encompass more detailed performance metrics, improved logging capabilities, and improved traffic flow visualization.

Emerging Technologies and Integration

Several transformative technologies are emerging in the service mesh ecosystem, which is fundamentally changing the way service meshes function and integrate with other systems. WebAssembly (Wasm) is a particularly noteworthy development, as it offers unparalleled flexibility for the extension and customization of service mesh functionality. The Wasm filter ecosystem is being significantly expanded by the Istio community, which has led to a thriving marketplace of extensions that can be safely deployed at runtime without the need for proxy restarts. This emphasis on extensibility allows organizations to customize their service mesh to meet specific requirements while simultaneously ensuring security and performance. Teams can now benefit from WebAssembly's security and performance guarantees by creating custom filters for specialized use cases, such as advanced routing rules, custom authentication mechanisms, or industry-specific protocol handling.

Extended Berkeley Packet Filter (eBPF) technology is another game changer in the service mesh landscape. The integration of Istio and eBPF presents novel opportunities for the enhancement of kernel-level security controls and network performance monitoring. This potent combination offers profound insight into network behavior without the overhead that is typically associated with service mesh implementations. The eBPF integration allows for more efficient load balancing, increased security through kernel-level filtering, and better performance monitoring via direct kernel instrumentation. Organizations can now implement sophisticated network policies and collect detailed metrics with minimal impact on application performance, thus allowing them to maintain robust security and observability while retaining efficiency.

CHAPTER 10   EMERGING TRENDS AND THE FUTURE OF ISTIO

The future of service mesh technology is increasingly focused on supporting diverse runtime environments, reflecting the reality of modern enterprise architectures. As organizations continue to operate in hybrid and multi-cloud environments, the ability to seamlessly integrate with different platforms becomes paramount. Istio is evolving to provide sophisticated support for serverless platforms, enabling consistent security and traffic management policies across functions-as-a-service deployments. Virtual machine support has been enhanced through improved integration with traditional infrastructure, allowing organizations to gradually migrate legacy applications into the mesh. The platform now offers better compatibility with various container runtimes, ensuring that organizations aren't locked into specific technology choices. This multi-runtime support enables organizations to maintain consistent security and observability policies across their entire infrastructure, regardless of where services are deployed or how they're implemented.

Competitive Landscape and Market Evolution

The service mesh market has grown into a diverse ecosystem of solutions, each with its philosophical approach and technical capabilities. Linkerd has carved out a significant niche by positioning itself as a lightweight alternative to Istio, focusing on simplicity and operational ease. Its Rust-based data plane has proven to be a game changer in terms of performance and resource efficiency, with consistently lower latency and memory usage than proxy implementations in other languages. Its simple installation, ease of use, and configuration processes have made it especially appealing to organizations that value simplicity and quick time to value. However, this simplicity comes at a cost; Linkerd's feature set is intentionally more focused than Istio's, and its ecosystem of extensions and integrations, while expanding, is still more limited. Organizations that choose Linkerd frequently prioritize operational simplicity and performance over the breadth of features that Istio offers.

HashiCorp's Consul represents yet another significant approach to service mesh implementation, building on the company's solid foundation in infrastructure management. Consul's greatest strength is its seamless integration into the larger HashiCorp ecosystem, which includes Vault for secret management and Terraform for infrastructure as code. This integration ensures a consistent experience for organizations that have already invested in HashiCorp's tools. Consul performs well in non-Kubernetes environments, providing robust service discovery capabilities and simplified configuration management via its key-value store. However, the platform has limitations when compared with Istio. While its traffic management features are functional, they fall short of Istio's more sophisticated capabilities. A multi-cluster configuration can be more complicated, especially when dealing with complex federation scenarios. The learning curve for advanced features can be steeper, particularly for teams unfamiliar with HashiCorp's infrastructure patterns and terminology.

Edge Computing and IoT Integration

Among the most groundbreaking developments in the field is the growth of service mesh technology to edge computing and IoT environments. The conventional centralized method of service mesh implementation has to change as companies use applications at the edge and link ever-increasing numbers of Internet of Things (IoT) sensors. Utilizing several creative ideas that promise to transform our perspective on service mesh in distributed environments, Istio is actively adjusting to meet these new challenges. Edge computing's special qualities—limited resources, intermittent connectivity, and higher latency—demand basic changes in how service meshes run.

Edge computing environments create special difficulties that are inspiring major advancements in service mesh technology. Usually running with limited resources, unreliable network connections, and strict latency requirements, these environments can make conventional service mesh implementations unworkable. Istio is creating specialized lightweight control plane solutions that can run efficiently in environments with limited resources to help with these difficulties. Among these advances are increased locality-aware load balancing, considering the physical distribution of services, better support for offline operation during network interruptions, and partial mesh capabilities. The platform is also bringing advanced retry mechanisms and circuit breaking capabilities that stop cascading failures, addressing the variable network conditions typical in edge environments.

Istio is developing to meet the special needs of device management and communication at scale in the fast-growing IoT space. The platform is developing advanced features for protocol translation and normalization, facilitating smooth communication between devices running several protocols. In IoT systems, when devices from several manufacturers and generations must interact efficiently, this is especially crucial. Improved device authentication, automated certificate management, and fine-grained access restrictions are among the security elements being added to specifically target the particular vulnerabilities connected with IoT installations. Better support for store-and-forward patterns and offline operation helps the platform to also manage the intermittent connectivity typical in IoT environments.

The Role of Service Mesh in AI and Machine Learning Workloads

A remarkable frontier in cloud-native computing is the junction of artificial intelligence and machine learning with service mesh technology. Service mesh technology is developing to support these specialized workloads with their particular needs and challenges as artificial intelligence and machine learning grow ever more central in modern applications. Leading this change is Istio, creating advanced capabilities especially meant to meet the intricate requirements of artificial intelligence/machine learning applications. These advances include better traffic management systems for model serving that can manage the bursty character of inference requests, enhanced observability capabilities for tracking model performance in production, and tailored support for GPU-enabled workloads requiring careful resource management and scheduling.

Service mesh combined with artificial intelligence/machine learning platforms is creating fascinating new opportunities for intelligent operations and automated management. Utilizing traffic pattern analysis and service health metrics, machine learning models can now be used to maximize routing decisions in real time, enabling intelligent load balancing actions. Employing historical data and real-time metrics, advanced anomaly detection systems can forecast and prevent failures before they affect users. Through automatically changing security policies depending on observed behavior patterns, security posture becomes more dynamic and responsive. More robust and effective distributed systems that can automatically adapt to changing conditions and needs are resulting from this junction of technologies.

MLOps and Istio's Role in Decentralized Machine Learning

One of the most exciting directions of invention in the cloud-native ecosystem is the junction of machine learning operations (MLOps) and service mesh technology. Although conventional MLOps systems usually depend on centralized platforms,

CHAPTER 10 EMERGING TRENDS AND THE FUTURE OF ISTIO

companies are progressively adopting distributed models that enable individual teams while preserving control and operational standards. Emerging as a major enabler of this decentralization, Istio offers distributed ML systems the security controls, observability, and communication infrastructure required.

Direct inspiration for "ML Mesh," first proposed by ML platform engineers at companies like Netflix and Spotify, comes from service mesh architecture. This method keeps central governance and control while distributing ML capabilities all around the company. ML Mesh allows companies to scale their machine learning capabilities horizontally across teams while maintaining consistent security, monitoring, and operational standards. This distributed method tackles a major obstacle in the acceptance of enterprise ML: the conflict between team autonomy and centralized control.

ML Mesh implementations depend critically on Istio's traffic management features. To support strategies, including canary deployments, A/B testing, and progressive rollouts, models in production need complex traffic splitting and routing. As confidence in the model rises, Istio's fine-grained traffic control lets ML engineers monitor performance, allocate a tiny portion of traffic to new model versions, and progressively change traffic distribution. High-stakes ML applications in finance, healthcare, and autonomous systems, where model failures can have major repercussions, especially benefit from this ability.

Another area in which Istio offers essential capability for distributed machine learning is security. Sensitive data processing by ML systems makes security a top issue. While its authentication and authorization features enable fine-grained access control to model endpoints and data services, Istio's mutual TLS implementation guarantees that all communication between ML services is encrypted.

One of the most difficult parts of ML operations is monitoring model performance in production, and this is addressed by Istio's observability. While custom metrics and monitoring can track model-specific metrics including prediction latency, feature drift, and inference quality, Istio's integration with monitoring systems including Prometheus and Grafana provides complete visibility into model serving infrastructure. Maintaining model performance over time and rapidly spotting problems likely to influence business results depend on this observability layer.

Industry acceptance of the ML Mesh concept driven by Istio is quickly increasing. Giants in technology like Google and Microsoft have included aspects of this architecture into their corporate ML systems. Azure Machine Learning, now offered by Microsoft, uses Istio for security and inter-service communication, so it integrates service mesh capabilities. For managing ML microservices, Google Cloud's Vertex AI system has also embraced service mesh concepts. Particularly eager adopters have been financial services companies, such as Goldman Sachs and Capital One, using distributed ML architectures leveraging service mesh technology.

MLOps and Istio collaborate at scale, as shown here. Istio's ML Mesh architecture gives companies a distributed method of machine learning that strikes team autonomy against corporate governance. Fundamentally, this architecture enforces consistent security, observability, and traffic management policies while using Istio's service mesh capabilities to build a communication layer linking independent ML domains—such as fraud detection, recommendation, and risk modeling teams. Though it gains from centralized governance, each domain keeps local control over their ML assets—data, models, pipelines. Likewise, in federated learning systems, Istio offers the safe communication architecture that lets several companies train ML models without distributing private raw data—only encrypted model updates pass the mesh, so data stays local. This method solves the basic conflict in business ML between centralization and autonomy by letting companies scale their ML capabilities horizontally across teams or even organizational boundaries while keeping constant standards, security, and operational excellence.

CHAPTER 10 EMERGING TRENDS AND THE FUTURE OF ISTIO

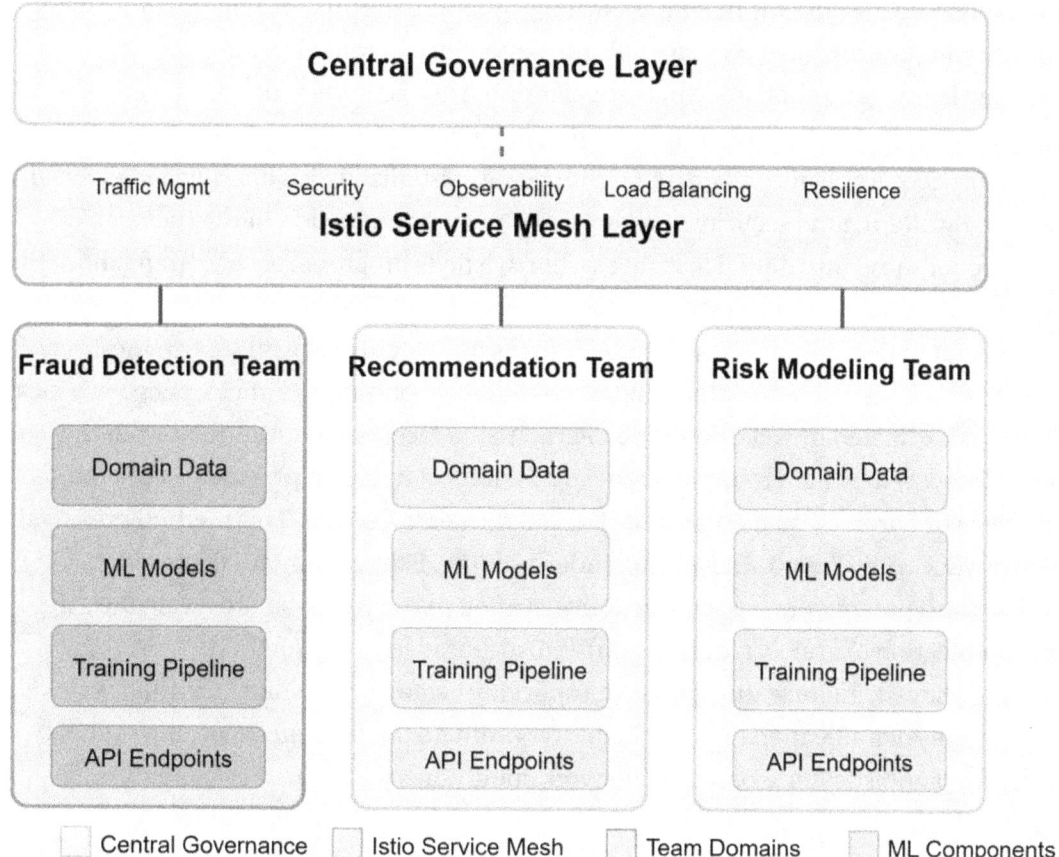

Figure 10-1. Simplified ML Mesh architecture with Istio

ML Mesh implementations depend critically on Istio's traffic management features. To support strategies including canary deployments, A/B testing, and progressive rollouts, models in production need complex traffic splitting and routing. As confidence in the model rises, Istio's fine-grained traffic control lets ML engineers monitor performance, allocate a tiny portion of traffic to new model versions, and progressively change traffic distribution. High-stakes ML applications in finance, healthcare, and autonomous systems where model failures can have major repercussions especially benefit from this ability.

CHAPTER 10   EMERGING TRENDS AND THE FUTURE OF ISTIO

Istio's Role in Federated Learning

A paradigm change in how machine learning systems can run while maintaining data privacy and lowering data movement is presented by federated learning, a distributed machine learning method allowing model training across several decentralized devices or servers holding local data samples. When practical constraints, privacy issues, or regulatory requirements prevent data from being centralized, this approach is especially helpful. By offering the security mechanisms and communication infrastructure required for these distributed learning systems, Istio is progressively becoming more important in allowing strong federated learning implementations.

Federated learning systems' architecture fits quite naturally with service mesh capabilities. Under federated learning, each of several participant nodes, each with local data, is coordinated by a central server. Participants receive model updates from the central server; they then train the model on their local data and provide just the model gradients or parameters, not raw data, back to the central server. This method preserves data privacy while supporting group model building. Istio guarantees that model updates and parameters are sent securely between participants, so providing the safe communication channels required for this distributed learning method.

Istio's several main features make it especially useful for federated learning systems:

Features of traffic management help to coordinate the federated learning process with great sophistication. Based on network conditions, participant availability, and priority, Istio can maximize communications as model updates pass between the central server and participant nodes. In heterogeneous settings where participants might have different computational resources and connectivity, this is especially crucial. Traffic management features of Istio guarantee that, despite these fluctuations, the federated learning process stays effective and strong.

In federated learning, security is critical since model parameters might include sensitive data subject to inference attacks and could be used for advantage. While its authentication and authorization systems stop illegal access to the federated learning network, Istio's mutual TLS encryption guarantees that all interactions between participants are secure. Ensuring that only authorized participants may contribute to and access the model addresses a major issue in federated learning systems.

As federated learning systems grow to involve hundreds or thousands of participants, load balancing features become absolutely vital. By spreading the computational load of aggregating model updates over several central servers, Istio can guarantee effective use

CHAPTER 10 EMERGING TRENDS AND THE FUTURE OF ISTIO

of computational resources and help to avoid congestion. Large-scale federated learning systems—which run across organizational boundaries or worldwide areas—especially depend on this.

Mechanisms for fault tolerance and circuit breaking guard the federated learning process against interruptions brought on by participant failures. Istio can automatically route around a failure and guarantee the learning process proceeds with the remaining participants should a participant become absent or begin delivering corrupted model updates. Maintaining the continuity of federated learning in dynamic, distributed settings requires this resilience.

Early adopters of federated learning with Istio in healthcare industry were institutions such as Mayo Clinic's federated learning systems implemented by Mayo Clinic and Partners HealthCare let cooperative model development across several hospitals without patient data sharing. These systems guarantee compliance with healthcare privacy rules and use Istio to protect communications between cooperating organizations.

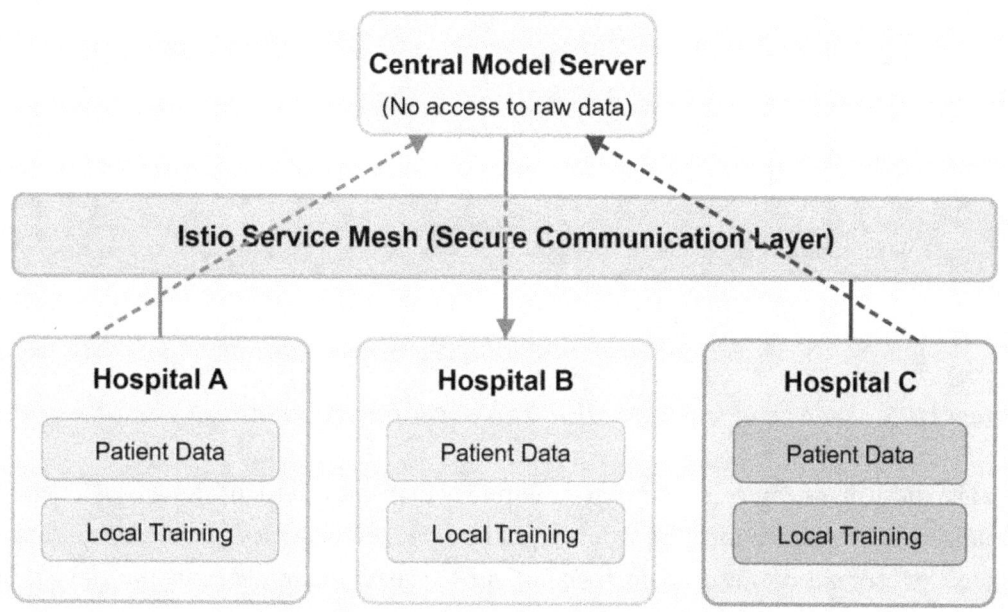

Figure 10-2. Federated learning with Istio in healthcare

Similarly financial institutions are using federated learning with Istio for risk modeling and collaborative fraud detection without distributing sensitive consumer data. Using Istio to protect communications between cooperating banks, a group of European banks under the direction of the European Banking Authority has instituted a federated learning system for anti-money laundering. Maintaining customer data confidentiality and following GDPR guidelines, this system lets the banks create more successful fraud detection models.

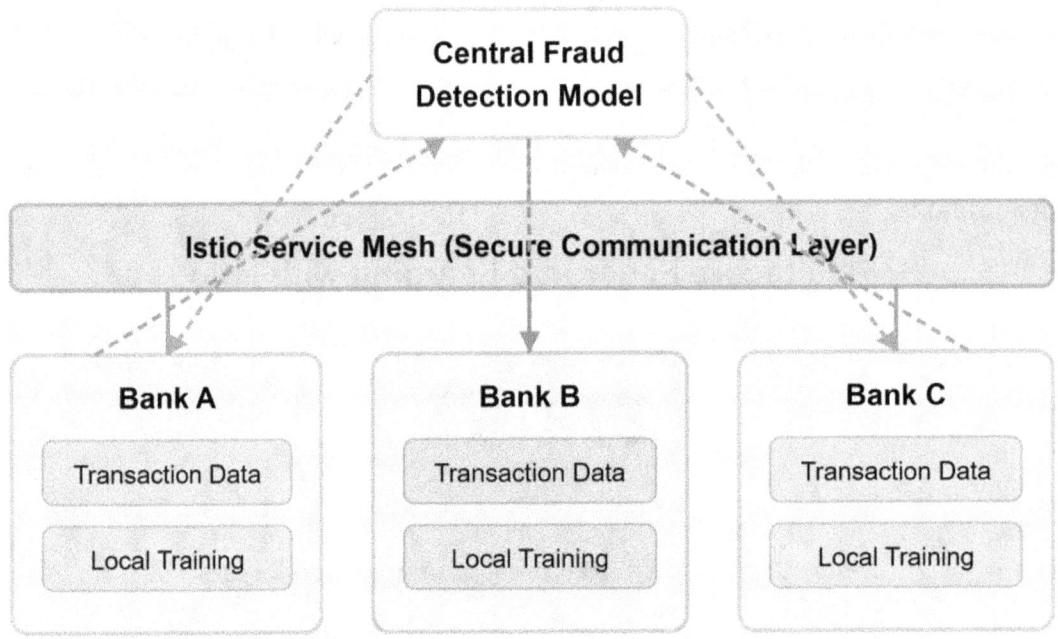

Figure 10-3. Federated learning with Istio in the financial industry

Data mesh architecture, a distributed method of data management along with federated learning, offers further chances for Istio integration. Under a data mesh architecture, data ownership is spread among domain-specific teams instead of centralized in a single data lake or warehouse. This method fits very nicely with federated learning since every domain team can contribute to cooperative model development under control of their data. Enforcing access limits and preserving security, Istio offers the connectivity layer allowing these domain-specific data products to engage in federated learning.

CHAPTER 10 EMERGING TRENDS AND THE FUTURE OF ISTIO

Looking ahead, as companies try to strike a balance between the advantages of collaborative AI and the need of data privacy and sovereignty, the convergence of federated learning, data mesh, and service mesh technologies like Istio is probably going to accelerate. Advanced architectures using service mesh capabilities for next-generation federated learning systems are under investigation in research projects including the MIT Media Lab and Stanford's Center for Research on Foundation Models. Built on the safe communication infrastructure Istio offers, these systems seek to offer even more robust privacy guarantees using approaches including differential privacy and secure multi-party computation.

Combining federated learning with service mesh technology presents a convincing solution for companies who must cooperate on AI development while keeping tight control over their data as regulatory frameworks around artificial intelligence and data privacy change. As the safe, visible, controllable communication infrastructure that makes advanced federated learning feasible in corporate environments, Istio's role in this ecosystem is probably going to expand.

Financial institutions are similarly leveraging federated learning with Istio for collaborative fraud detection and risk modeling without sharing sensitive customer data. A consortium of European banks coordinated by the European Banking Authority has implemented a federated learning system for anti-money laundering that uses Istio to secure communications between participating banks. This system allows the banks to develop more effective fraud detection models while maintaining the confidentiality of their customer data and complying with GDPR requirements.

The intersection of data mesh architecture—a decentralized approach to data management—and federated learning creates additional opportunities for Istio integration. In a data mesh architecture, data ownership is distributed across domain-specific teams rather than centralized in a single data lake or warehouse. This approach aligns well with federated learning, as each domain team can participate in collaborative model development while maintaining control of their data. Istio provides the connectivity layer that enables these domain-specific data products to participate in federated learning while enforcing access controls and maintaining security.

Looking ahead, the convergence of federated learning, data mesh, and service mesh technologies like Istio is likely to accelerate as organizations seek to balance the benefits of collaborative AI with the need for data privacy and sovereignty. Research initiatives at organizations like the MIT Media Lab and Stanford's Center for Research on Foundation Models are exploring advanced architectures that leverage service mesh capabilities for next-generation federated learning systems. These systems aim to provide even stronger privacy guarantees through techniques like differential privacy and secure multi-party computation, all built on the secure communication infrastructure that Istio provides.

As regulatory frameworks around AI and data privacy continue to evolve, the combination of federated learning and service mesh technology offers a compelling approach for organizations that need to collaborate on AI development while maintaining strict control over their data. Istio's role in this ecosystem is likely to grow, providing the secure, observable, and controllable communication infrastructure that makes advanced federated learning practical in enterprise environments.

Skills and Technologies for the Future

The development of the service mesh ecosystem calls for professionals operating in this field to constantly expand their technical expertise. Since most service mesh installations center on Kubernetes and container orchestration, a solid basis in these technologies is still absolutely vital. This covers operator patterns, Custom Resource Definitions (CRDs), and thorough awareness of Kubernetes networking ideas. Professionals must become experts in not only the fundamental ideas of container orchestration but also advanced ideas, including custom controllers, admission webhooks, and extended scheduling capabilities allowing complex service mesh implementations.

As service mesh technology develops, knowing network programming and protocols becomes ever more important. This covers not just conventional TCP/IP networking ideas but also contemporary protocols, including HTTP/2, gRPC, and WebSocket. Professionals must grasp how these protocols interact with advanced traffic management capabilities, protocol-specific load balancing algorithms, and sophisticated retry mechanisms—all of which constitute part of service mesh features. From the application layer down to the transport layer, the ability to troubleshoot network problems at several tiers of the stack is turning into a critical ability.

Particularly, as service meshes are implemented in more important environments and edge locations, security knowledge has become crucial. Professionals must grow knowledgeable in zero-trust systems and know how to apply and sustain safe service-to-service communication in distributed environments. This covers mastery of certificate management systems, knowledge of current cryptographic techniques, and awareness of security best practices for distributed systems. Anyone working with service mesh technology must be able to handle secret management, apply and manage role-based access control (RBAC) policies, and preserve safe configuration practices.

Adapting and Transitioning for Organizations

When transitioning to Istio's new configuration models, particularly with the introduction of ambient mesh and the evolving Gateway API, organizations should adopt several best practices to ensure a smooth and secure migration. Automation plays a central role in this process. By leveraging GitOps workflows and treating configurations as code, teams can manage policy changes consistently and safely across environments. This approach ensures that updates to traffic routing, security policies, and observability settings are version-controlled, auditable, and easily reproducible. As Istio shifts more functionality away from sidecars through features like waypoint proxies and ztunnels, it is advisable to test these new components in staging environments to validate behavior before full deployment. Ensuring secure service-to-service communication is essential, and organizations should enforce mutual TLS (mTLS) across the mesh using PeerAuthentication and DestinationRule resources or ambient mesh policies. It is equally important to implement fine-grained authorization using Istio's AuthorizationPolicy resource, supporting a zero-trust security model. Maintaining robust monitoring, observability, and certificate rotation practices will help align with broader compliance and security requirements. Staying up to date with Istio's release notes and upgrade guidance will further ensure compatibility and prevent potential disruptions as the platform continues to evolve.

Case Studies and Research Initiatives

The adoption of Istio across various industries has led to numerous success stories and innovative implementations. These real-world applications, combined with ongoing research and development activities, provide valuable insights into the practical benefits and future potential of service mesh technology.

Enterprise Case Studies

Financial Services: JPMorgan Chase's Cloud-Native Transformation

CHAPTER 10 EMERGING TRENDS AND THE FUTURE OF ISTIO

JPMorgan Chase's transformation of their global banking infrastructure represents one of the most comprehensive Istio implementations in the financial sector. The bank, processing over 12 million transactions daily across their retail and investment banking platforms, adopted Istio as a cornerstone of their cloud migration strategy. According to James Higginbotham, Executive Director of Cloud Architecture at JPMorgan Chase, "Implementing Istio has been fundamental to our zero-trust security model and has dramatically improved our ability to meet regulatory compliance requirements."

The implementation details revealed at their 2023 technology summit included

- Zero-trust security implementation across 2,300+ microservices with granular policy enforcement
- Reduction in operational overhead by 42% through automated mutual TLS and certificate rotation
- Enhanced observability stack integrating with Prometheus and Grafana, leading to 65% faster incident resolution times
- Successfully implemented circuit breaking patterns that prevented cascading failures during the 2022 market volatility events
- Custom extensions using WebAssembly to implement financial industry-specific compliance monitoring

E-commerce: Target's Peak Season Resilience
Target Corporation implemented an Istio-based service mesh to handle their holiday season traffic and improve their platform security. During their presentation at KubeCon 2023, Luke Snyder, Target's Principal Engineer for Cloud Infrastructure, detailed how their platform scaled to handle Black Friday demand:

> "Our previous infrastructure struggled with the 400% traffic increases during peak shopping days. After implementing Istio, we were able to not only handle these spikes seamlessly but also implement more sophisticated traffic management for our promotional activities."

Their implementation showcased the following:

- Successfully handled 425% traffic increases during Black Friday through intelligent traffic shifting and load balancing
- Implementation of sophisticated A/B testing for their mobile app features across different customer segments

CHAPTER 10   EMERGING TRENDS AND THE FUTURE OF ISTIO

- A 53% reduction in service-to-service authentication overhead while strengthening security posture

- Improved developer productivity through standardized security policies and traffic routing templates

- Custom observability dashboard that reduced mean time to resolution (MTTR) by 58%

- Integration with their existing CI/CD pipeline for automated policy deployment

Healthcare: Teladoc Health's HIPAA-Compliant Service Mesh
Teladoc Health, a leading telemedicine provider serving over 50 million members globally, implemented Istio to ensure HIPAA compliance and improve their virtual care platform reliability. Dr. Claus Jensen, Teladoc Health's Chief Innovation Officer, shared their experience at the Healthcare Information and Management Systems Society (HIMSS) conference:

> "Patient data security and service availability are non-negotiable in healthcare. Our Istio implementation has not only strengthened our security posture but also improved the reliability and performance of our virtual consultations."

Their case study highlighted the following:

- End-to-end encryption for all patient data communications with detailed audit logging for compliance

- Implementation of strict access controls with integration to their identity management system

- 99.996% service availability through advanced traffic management and failover capabilities

- Reduced latency in video consultations by 42% through intelligent routing optimizations

- Custom health check implementations that improved early detection of service degradation

- Seamless integration with their existing Epic electronic health record system through custom adapters

CHAPTER 10   EMERGING TRENDS AND THE FUTURE OF ISTIO

Research and Development Initiatives

Academic Research Projects

The University of California Berkeley's RISELab, led by Professor Ion Stoica, has been conducting groundbreaking research on service mesh optimization. Their "MeshOptimizer" project, funded by a $3.2 million NSF grant, has published several influential papers on next-generation service mesh technology. Professor Stoica explains, "We're fundamentally rethinking how service meshes operate in cloud environments by applying machine learning techniques to optimize every aspect of mesh operations."

The project's latest publications detail innovations in

- Dynamic proxy configuration optimization that reduced CPU overhead by 31% in large-scale deployments

- Machine learning–based traffic routing algorithms that improved response times by 27% under variable loads

- Automated policy generation through behavioral analysis, preventing 94% of common security misconfigurations

- Resource optimization in multi-tenant environments, which increased resource utilization by 42%

- Their open-source AutoMesh framework that was recently adopted by Lyft for production workloads

MIT's Computer Science and Artificial Intelligence Laboratory (CSAIL), under the direction of Professor Arvind Krishnamurthy, is working on the "SecureMesh initiative:

- Novel approaches to service mesh security in zero-trust environments, with a $2.5 million DARPA grant

- Performance optimization through eBPF integration, achieving 48% reduction in latency

- Edge computing adaptations for service mesh architecture, tested in partnership with Verizon's 5G edge network

- Quantum-resistant security protocol implementation for Istio, currently in testing with financial services partners

- Published research on automated anomaly detection using their proprietary DeepMesh algorithm

Industry Research Collaborations

The Cloud Native Computing Foundation (CNCF) has established several influential research initiatives with published findings and ongoing development:

The Service Mesh Performance (SMP) working group, led by Lee Calcote of Layer5 and including engineers from Microsoft, Red Hat, and Solo.io, is

- Developing standardized benchmarks for service mesh performance across different implementations
- Publishing quarterly performance comparison reports between Istio, Linkerd, and Consul
- Creating the Universal Service Mesh Interface (USMI) specification for cross-platform compatibility
- Releasing meshmark, an open source tool for measuring service mesh overhead

The Mesh Security Alliance (MSA), chaired by John Morello of Palo Alto Networks, is conducting the following:

- Research on next-generation mTLS implementations with post-quantum cryptography
- Development of automated security policy generators based on observed traffic patterns
- Vulnerability assessment of service mesh implementations through their Red Team exercises
- Integration standards for service meshes with existing enterprise security frameworks

The Edge Mesh Working Group, co-led by engineers from Red Hat and Intel, is

- Investigating service mesh implementations for edge computing with prototype deployments in smart city infrastructure
- Developing specifications for resource-constrained service mesh deployments

CHAPTER 10   EMERGING TRENDS AND THE FUTURE OF ISTIO

- Testing 5G integration scenarios with AT&T's network edge computing platform

- Publishing edge computing reference architectures using Istio adapted for constrained environments

Google and IBM Research Initiative

In 2023, Google Cloud and IBM Research announced a $15 million joint research project called "Project Quantum Mesh," led by Dr. Donna Dillenberger of IBM Research and Dr. Louis Ryan from Google, a co-founder of the Istio project. The initiative is exploring

- Quantum-resistant security protocols for service mesh with testing in IBM's quantum computing environment

- AI-driven traffic management and anomaly detection that reduced false positives by 87% in early testing

- Advanced observability through machine learning, generating predictive alerts for potential service degradations

- Automated policy generation and optimization that improved security posture scores by 43% in enterprise environments

Their findings are being gradually incorporated into the Istio roadmap, with the first quantum-resistant security features expected in Istio version 1.20.

Emerging Research Areas

Service mesh technology's junction with newly developing fields is providing rich ground for research and invention. Led by Dr. Katherine Guo, Nokia Bell Labs' Advanced Networking Research team is working creatively on service mesh integration with 5G infrastructure. Presented at the 2023 IEEE Conference on Network Function Virtualization, their ground-breaking paper Service Mesh Architectures for 5G Network Slicing" detailed amazing developments, including service mesh architecture adaptations for 5G network slicing that lowered control plane overhead by 64% and integration with network function virtualization frameworks like ONAP. While their automated scaling systems based on real-time network conditions were effectively

CHAPTER 10 EMERGING TRENDS AND THE FUTURE OF ISTIO

tested in collaboration with T-Mobile, their Atlanta testbed attained remarkable edge computing optimizations with sub-10 ms latency for critical applications. Three main telecom companies are currently assessing the reference implementation the team created, "5GMesh." "The integration of service mesh technology with 5G infrastructure marks a basic change in how we manage network services," notes Dr. Guo. At the network edge, this convergence makes security, observability, and control hitherto unheard of possible.

Concurrent with this, Microsoft Research's Autonomous Systems team is working with the Azure Kubernetes Service group to develop self-managing service mesh technology, thus transforming operations. Using AI/ML integration, their "AutoMesh" project has shown amazing self-healing capacity, lowering human interventions by 76% and applying automated policy adaptation depending on security concerns in Microsoft's manufacturing facilities. Along with predictive scaling based on traffic pattern analysis that lowers scaling-related events by 62%, the system achieves dynamic resource allocation and optimization that increases general cluster utilization by 38%. Their paper, "Towards Autonomous Service Mesh Management," won the Best Paper award at USENIX OSDI 2023, attesting to their innovations. "We're moving beyond basic automation to truly autonomous service mesh systems that can reason about complex environments and make high-quality decisions with minimal human intervention," principal researcher Dr. Shu Han says.

With the Sustainable Computing Lab at ETH Zurich, under Professor Anwar Hithnawi, starting a thorough research program on environmentally sustainable service mesh implementations, environmental sustainability has also become a major study focus. Together with resource optimization strategies for a lower carbon footprint, tested in association with Equinix data centers, their work has generated energy-efficient proxy implementations that cut power consumption by 43% compared with standard Envoy configurations. They published a power consumption analysis of various mesh architectures in their widely cited "Energy Footprint of Service Mesh Implementations" study, and the team has recorded sustainable scaling practices in service mesh deployments using their "Green Mesh" framework. Their creation of eMesh, an energy-aware service mesh that dynamically changes resource use depending on carbon intensity signals, is maybe the most original. Professor Hithnowicz emphasizes the importance of this work: "Our studies show that while preserving performance, optimizing service mesh deployments can greatly lower energy consumption. These improvements have significant environmental effect since cloud infrastructure consumes a growing portion of world electricity."

CHAPTER 10   EMERGING TRENDS AND THE FUTURE OF ISTIO

Future Research Directions

Recent papers, conference presentations, and research funding announcements point to several interesting directions for the next work in service mesh technology. These new research directions are pushing the envelope of what is feasible in distributed systems management and helping Istio and the larger service mesh ecosystem to evolve.

An important boundary in service mesh research is the integration of quantum-resistant security. Working with Isovalent, the developers of Cilium, the National Institute of Standards and Technology (NIST) has developed thorough post-quantum cryptography standards for service mesh implementations. Ambitious objectives of this $4.2 million project include Istio using NIST-selected post-quantum cryptographic algorithms by 2026. The effort also centers on building flawless migration routes for current installations to move to quantum-resistant security without disturbance. To guarantee they can be implemented without appreciable performance penalties, researchers are developing complex performance optimization strategies for the computationally demanding quantum-resistant algorithms. Furthermore, benefiting the whole service mesh ecosystem are reference implementations and thorough testing systems the project is developing.

Another important avenue of inquiry is the evolution of federated multi-mesh architectures. Industry leaders, including Google, Microsoft, Red Hat, and VMware, have joined the "FederatedMesh" special interest group that the Linux Foundation's Cloud Native Computing Foundation has announced to be formed. Establishing strong guidelines for mesh federation across organizational boundaries is the main emphasis of this cooperative project, so allowing various companies to securely link their service meshes. The group is creating sophisticated policy reconciliation systems for multi-owner mesh environments, addressing the difficult issues that arise when several companies with different security needs must share services. Their work consists of designing graduated trust models that allow safe cross-organizational service communication while keeping suitable security limits and developing advanced identity management solutions for federated service mesh installations.

Combining machine learning with service mesh technology is creating fascinating new opportunities for intelligent operations. Through open-sourcing their "MeshIntelligence" framework, Netflix's Open Source Technology Center has made major contributions in this field. This novel system shows the possibilities of advanced traffic routing based on complex reinforcement learning algorithms that develop constantly depending on observed performance. Automated canary analysis with statistical confidence scoring is part of the framework to support more dependable and data-driven installations. Especially remarkable are the anomaly detection systems that, using proactive rather than reactive operations, can spot service degradation before consumers are affected. Another innovation is the self-tuning proxy configurations, which automatically maximize performance and dependability using observed traffic patterns, so avoiding human intervention. The development of the WebAssembly ecosystem inside service meshes promises to fundamentally alter the extension and customizing capability of these systems. Comprising technology executives, including Fastly, Google, Mozilla, and Intel, the Bytecode Alliance has created the "Wasm for Service Mesh" working group to forward this technology. Their work centers on creating consistent and interoperable standardized interfaces for WebAssembly modules in service mesh systems. To reduce overhead and maximize flexibility, the group is developing cutting-edge performance optimization methods for Wasm-based filters. They are also developing thorough security guidelines for Wasm extensions to guarantee that mesh security is not compromised by customizing capability. Most importantly, they are creating a rich ecosystem of reusable Wasm modules for common service mesh needs, allowing companies to rapidly expand their service meshes free from the need for custom code.

"WebAssembly is doing for the service mesh what containers did for application deployment—creating a universal, safe, and efficient runtime that will fundamentally change how we extend and customize our infrastructure," Solomon Hykes, co-founder of Docker and current CEO of Dagger, observed. This evaluation reflects the transforming power of WebAssembly in service mesh technology and implies that we might be about to experience a paradigm change in how service meshes are tailored and extended to fit particular organizational needs.

Conclusion

The future of Istio and the broader service mesh ecosystem is defined by rapid innovation and adaptation to new distributed computing challenges. As organizations adopt microservices architectures and distribute their applications across a variety of environments, from cloud to edge, the role of service mesh technology becomes increasingly important. Istio's evolution toward greater simplicity, improved performance, and better support for edge and IoT use cases positions it as a foundational technology for modern distributed systems.

CHAPTER 10 EMERGING TRENDS AND THE FUTURE OF ISTIO

The integration of cutting-edge technologies, such as WebAssembly and eBPF, as well as improved support for AI/ML workloads, demonstrates the platform's ability to adapt to changing requirements and push the boundaries of service mesh technology. While alternatives such as Linkerd and Consul take different approaches to service mesh implementation, Istio's comprehensive feature set, strong community support, and clear vision for the future keep it at the forefront of the space.

Staying current with developments in service mesh technology and maintaining a broad skill set will be critical for success in this rapidly evolving field. The future holds exciting possibilities for service mesh technology, and those who understand and can apply these capabilities will be well-positioned to build and manage tomorrow's distributed systems. As we look ahead, it's clear that service mesh technology will continue to play an important role in shaping the future of cloud-native computing, allowing organizations to create more resilient, secure, and efficient distributed systems capable of meeting the demands of an increasingly connected world.

Index

A

Abort injection, 176, 178
Academic Research Projects, 540
Access control mechanisms, 227
accessLogEncoding parameter, 413
accessLogFile parameter, 413
accessLogFormat parameter, 413
Access logs, 293
Advanced traffic management techniques
    attributes, 132
    blue/green deployment (*see* Blue/green deployment)
    canary deployments
        monitoring and validating releases, 136–139
        progressive rollouts, 133–135
        rolling back, 139–142, 144
    header-based splitting, 132
    health checking, 132
    load balancing, 132
    percentage-based traffic distribution, 132
    session persistence, 132
AI-powered recommendation algorithm, 186
Airbnb, 12
Amazon Elastic Kubernetes Service (EKS)
    benefits, 419
    development environment setting, 420–422
    Istio, 430–433
    offloading control plane management, 419
    Terraform, 422–430
Ambient mesh architecture, 524
Ambient mode, 64–73
Anti-money laundering, 534, 535
API Server, 14
Application Binary Interface (ABI), 446, 451, 480–482
Application logs, 293
Artificial intelligence (AI), 189, 528, 535
AssemblyScript, 456
attempts, 182
Auditing, security events, 273–279
Audit logs, 288, 293
Authentication, 6, 224, 442, 525
    cleanup, 249
    client identities, 242
    frontend and backend service, 242
    implementation, 244–248
    mTLS, 76
    namespace, 243
    peer policies, 242
    request, 242
AuthenticationPolicy, 262
Authorization, 6, 224, 242–249, 446, 529
    external systems, 279
    factors, RBAC, 249
    namespace, 243
    OPA, 77
AuthorizationPolicy, 262
Automated certificate management, 206
Automated tests, 521
Automation, 417, 537

INDEX

AutoMesh, 543
Autonomous service mesh systems, 543
Autoscaling, 16, 17
Autotrader UK, 12
AWS Management Console dashboard, 420, 421

B

baseEjectionTime, 165
Behavior validation, 189
Blue/green deployment
    implementation strategies
        contingency planning, 151
        foundation setup, 146, 147
        health checks, 148, 149
        post-deployment strategy, 151, 152
        pre-deployment validation, 147, 148
        traffic management, 150
        traffic switch, 149, 150
    production environments, 144
    rollback procedures, 155–158
    setting up, 144, 145
    traffic switching between versions
        planning and execution, 152
        pre-switch validation, 154
        progressive switching strategies, 153, 154
Buffer access functions, 480
Business continuity, 289
Business-critical metrics, 383–385
Business metrics, 138, 293

C

Callback-based model, 456
Canary deployments
    monitoring and validating releases, 136–139
    progressive rollouts, 133–135
    rolling back, 139–142, 144
Capacity planning, 189
Cardinality, 364
Cash App, 11
Centralized policy management, 207
Certificate authorities (CAs), 41, 225
Certificate management, 229, 288
Certificate revocation lists (CRL), 225
Cert-manager integration, 77
Circuit breakers, 37
    configuration, 159
        HTTP connection parameters, 162–164
        recommendation service, 160
        TCP connection parameters, 161, 162
    defined, 159
    patterns
        monitoring status, 171–174
        outlier detection, 168
        progressive, 169
        simple, 167, 168
        version-aware, 170, 171
    threshold settings, 164–167
Circuit breaking, 344–346
Clang, 450
Client-side metrics, 375
Cloud computing, 2
Cloud Controller Manager, 15
Cloud migration strategy, 538
Cloud Native Computing Foundation (CNCF), 12, 537
Cluster, 52, 53
Cluster autoscaler, 17
Cluster metrics, 349, 350
CMake, 454

Computer Science and Artificial
    Intelligence Laboratory
    (CSAIL), 540
ConfigMaps, 337
ConfigPatches array, 487
Connection pooling
    benefits, 116, 117
    connectTimeout, 115
    defined, 114
    HTTP-specific and TCP-specific
        configurations, 114
    maxConnections, 115
    trafficPolicy.connectionPool
        section, 114
    use cases, 116
connectTimeout, 161
consecutiveGatewayErrors, 165
consecutiveLocalOriginFailures, 165
consecutive5xxErrors, 165
Consul, 526
Container runtime, 15
Contingency planning, 151
Controller manager, 14
Control plane, 9, 14, 15, 26, 35, 37, 417,
        418, 434, 442, 443
    configuration management, 40
    multi-cluster and hybrid cloud
        support, 43, 44
    observability and telemetry, 42, 43
    policy enforcement, 43
    security management, 41, 42
    service discovery, 40, 41
    traffic control and routing, 42
Cookie-based switch, 153
Cryptographic techniques, 536
Customer order processing, 393
Customer relationship management
    (CRM), 11

Custom metrics, 510, 511
    disabling metrics for
        workload, 363
    disabling individual metrics, 362
    mode configuration, 360, 361
    selective metrics collection, 362
    Telemetry API, 355-358
    value expressions, 359-360
Custom resource definitions (CRDs), 78,
    95, 444, 536
Custom trace tags, 330-332
C++ WebAssembly development, 456

D

DaemonSets, 46
Dashboard metrics, 520
Data loss prevention (DLP), 288, 497
Data marshaling, 482
Data mesh architecture, 534, 535
Data plane, 8, 35, 38, 82, 417, 418, 442, 443
    security, 45
    service mesh architecture, 44
    telemetry, 46
    traffic management, 45
DDoS protection, 207
Debugging, 512-514
Default exception logging, 411, 412
Delay injection, 174-176
Dependency graph approach, 459
DestinationRule, 84
DestinationRule resources, 160, 537
DevSecOps, 227
Differential privacy, 536
Digital certificates, 224
Disaster recovery, 288, 289
Disruptions, 286
Distributed machine learning, 529

INDEX

Distributed security
 challenges, 226
 evolution, 226
 implications, 227
 modern systems
  Istio role in, 228
  need for, 227, 228
Distributed systems, 4, 288
 circuit breaker patterns, 167
 security (*see* Distributed security)
Distributed tracing
 configuration, 316
  MeshConfig, 319, 320
  Telemetry API, 318, 319
  workload, 320–323
 context propagation, 316
 custom trace tags, 330–332
 defined, 315
 Jaeger, 324–329
 observability, 316
 primary mechanism, 317
 sampling configuration, 329, 330
 Zipkin correlation data, 317
Docker, 20, 21
Domain-driven design, 200
Duration patterns, 343, 344
Dynamic service discovery, 45, 52
Dynamic traffic routing, 93

E

E-commerce, 538, 539
Ecommerce namespace, 397
Edge computing, 527, 528
Edge Mesh Working Group, 541
Egress gateway
 configuration, 211
  controlling outbound traffic, 211–214

 external systems, 210
 recommendation service, 210
 service entry configuration, 214–219
 third-party analytics services, 210
Egress traffic security
 cleanup, 272
 cluster communication, 263
 configurations, 261
 high-level example, 262
 implementation, 267, 269
 mechanisms, 261
 monitoring, 271
 sample application, 269, 271
 testing, 271
 TLS, 261
Emscripten, 458
Emscripten SDK, 450
Encrypted storage, 18
Encryption, 229
Endpoint controller, 14
Endpoints component, 215
End-to-end encryption, 287
End-to-end testing, mesh environment, 508, 509
Enterprise case studies
 e-commerce, 538, 539
 financial services, 538
 healthcare, 539
Environmental adaptation, 494
Environmental sustainability, 543
Environment segregation pattern, 202, 203
EnvoyFilter
 binary distribution options, 495–497
 components and architecture, 487, 488
 configuration, 487, 493–495
 deployment, 488–495
 filter chain positioning and operations, 490–492

INDEX

functions, 487
initialization, 493–495
namespace scoping and mesh-wide deployment, 497–499
practical application patterns
  configuration externalization, 504, 505
  custom observability, 503
  enhanced security controls, 501
  protocol adapters, 502
  traffic management, 503
and precedence, 499–501
resource, 443
traffic direction and context types, 492, 493
Envoy proxy, 9, 38, 43, 82
  cluster, 52, 53
  components, 46
  configuration, 47, 48
  extensions and Wasm filters, 56, 57
  filter chains, 51, 52
  installation, 47
  listener, 49, 51
  local setup, 47
  routes, 54, 55
  running, 49
  tracing and observability, 55, 56
  traffic management, 84
Envoy proxy metrics
  cluster metrics, 350
  list, 349
  listener metrics, 350–352
  server metrics, 353, 354
Error detection mechanisms, 165
Error logs, 293
Error propagation, 294
Error rate analysis, 343
Error tracking, 390, 391

European Banking Authority, 534, 535
Extended Berkeley Packet Filter (eBPF) technology, 525
External load balancing, 18
External security systems
  authorization, 279
  capabilities, 280
  certificate management, 279
  implementation, 282–286
  OPA, 280, 281
  SIEM, 279

F

Fault injection, 40, 86, 103
  abort, 176, 178
  network delays, 174–176
  resilience service testing, 178–181
Fault tolerance, 5, 533
Feature drift, 529
Feature flagging, 494
Features-based routing pattern, 200, 201
Federated learning systems, 530, 532–536
FederatedMesh, 544
Federated multi-mesh architectures, 544
Filter chains, 51, 52
Filtering Logs, 408, 409
Financial services, 538
Fine-grained access control, 18, 206
5GMesh, 543

G

Gateway, 85
GATEWAY context, 493
Gateway management
  components, 193
  egress, 210–219

551

Gateway management (*cont.*)
    ingress, 194–210
    load balancing, 194
    monitoring, 194
    protocol support, 194
    security, 194
    version management, 194
Gateway resources, 207
Git, 458
Google and IBM Research Initiative, 542
Gradual mirror implementation, 192
Grafana
    configuration, 299
    custom dashboards
        business metrics, 382–385
        error tracking, 390, 391
        inventory health, 385–388
        operational metrics, 382
        service mesh performance, 388, 389
        steps, 382
    default Istio dashboards, 372–381
    default *vs.* custom dashboards, 382
    integration, 392
    metrics, 271, 370
    setting up Istio, 370, 371
    source code, 298
    visualization capabilities, 392
Granular control, 94, 188
Green Mesh framework, 543

H

Hardware security modules (HSMs), 286
Header-based routing, 122
Header-based validation switch, 153
Healthcare, 539
Healthcare Information and Management Systems Society (HIMSS), 539

Health check implementation, 148, 149
Helm, 24, 25
Helm repositories, 298–303
h2MaxRequests, 162
Horizontal pod autoscaler (HPA), 16
Host-based routing, 207–210
Hosts component, 215
HTTP connection parameters, 162–164
http1MaxPendingRequests, 162
HTTP traffic functions, 481

I

Identity management, 287
    authentication, 76
    authorization, 77
    Cert-manager integration, 77
idleTimeout, 162
Inbound metrics, 380
Industry research collaborations, 541, 542
Inference quality, 529
Infrastructure-as-code (IaC), 315, 420
Ingress gateway, 435
    configuration, 195–198
    exposure patterns
        environment segregation, 202, 203
        features-based routing, 200, 201
        path-based routing, 199, 200
    host-based routing, 207–210
    routing, load balancing, and security features, 194
    SSL/TLS termination
        benefits, 205, 206
        best practices, 206, 207
        configuration, 204, 205
        encryption and decryption, 203
Ingress traffic security
    cleanup, 272

INDEX

cluster communication, 263
configurations, 261
external access, 260
high-level example, 262
implementation, 264–266
mechanisms, 261
monitoring, 271
sample application, 269, 271
testing, 271
TLS, 261
Integration coordination, 494
Integration testing, 507, 508
Inter-cluster communication, 436
Intermediate representation (IR), 449
Internal load balancing, 18
Internet of Things (IoT), 527, 528
interval, 165
InventoryController, 386
Inventory health management, 385–388
InventoryService, 386
Inventory service deployment, 410
Istio
   adapting and transitioning, 537
   add istioctl to path, 26
   architecture, 37, 38
   case studies
      Airbnb, 12
      Autotrader UK, 12
      Mindtickle, 12
      Rappi, 11
      Salesforce, 11
      T-Mobile, 11
   case studies and research initiatives
      emerging research areas, 542, 543
      enterprise, 538, 539
      future research, 544, 545
      research and development initiatives, 540–542
   circuit breakers, 37
   cloud systems, 2
   competitive landscape and market evolution, 526, 527
   components, 8
   control plane, 9, 39–44
   control plane dashboard, 372, 373
   cost management, 418
   creating K8s cluster, 27
   custom-built solutions, 37
   data plane, 8, 39, 44–46
   default dashboards links, 372
   deployment modes, 46
   download, 25
   dynamic environments, 36
   edge computing and IoT integration, 527, 528
   elements, 38
   emerging technologies and integration, 525, 526
   envoy proxy, 9
   evolution, 523
   extensibility (*see* Istio's extensibility framework)
   federated learning, 532–536
   future developments, 524
   helm install istio base command, 431
   helm install istiod command, 431
   helm install istio-ingress command, 433
   helm repo add command, 430
   ingress gateway, 432, 433
   installation, 372
   install control plane, 26
   intelligent automation and default configurations, 524
   K8s (*see* Kubernetes (K8s))

Istio (*cont.*)
    kubectl get all-n istio-ingress command, 433
    kubectl get all-n istio-system command, 431, 432
    load balancing, 75, 76
    local environment setup, 19–24
    mesh dashboard, 374, 375
    MLOps, 528–531
    namespace, 28
    operational simplicity, 525
    performance dashboard, 375, 376
    RBAC (*see* Role-based access control (RBAC))
    roadmap, 524
    scaling, 418
    serverless platforms, 526
    service dashboard, 377, 379
    service discovery, 74, 75
    vs. service mesh solutions, 9, 10
    skills and technologies, 536, 537
    telemetry (*see* Telemetry system)
    traffic applications, 28
    traffic management, 78
    verify installation, 27
    Wasm extension dashboard, 379
    workload dashboard, 380, 381
Istiod, 82
IstioOperator API, 524
IstioOperator resource, 306, 415
Istio's extensibility framework
    CRDs, 444
    data and control plane, 442, 443
    EnvoyFilter resource, 443
    scenario, 442
    telemetry data, 411
    use cases, 445, 446

Wasm (*see* WebAssembly (Wasm))
Istio-system namespace, 27

J

Jaeger, 300, 301, 307
    debugging issues, 325
    interface, 324
    primary services, 324
    request flows, 325–327
    single client action, 324
    trace context, 328
    traces, 332
JPMorgan Chase's transformation, 538

K

Kiali, 302
    best practices, 402
    requirement, 392
    service mesh management, 393
    service topology visualization, 394–396
    setting up and configuration, 394
    traffic management, 396–399
    workload management and analysis, 399–402
kubectl, 21, 22
Kubelet, 15
Kube-proxy, 15
Kubernetes (K8s)
    architecture, 13
    control plane, 14, 15
    custom resources, 295
    defined, 12
    deployment, 309
    features, 16
        automated rollouts and rollbacks, 17

INDEX

    autoscaling, 16, 17
    load balancing, 18
    orchestration and automation, 19
    secure management, 18
    self-healing capabilities, 17
    service-to-service
       communication, 19
  namespace, 359
  scaling options, 16
  worker nodes, 15
  workloads, 12
Kubernetes IN Docker (Kind), 23, 24

L

Label management, 364
Latency information, 294
Latency metrics, 361
Least-request algorithm, 112
Legacy systems, 446
Linkerd, 526
Listener, 49, 51
Listener metrics, 350–353
Load balancing, 6, 18, 45, 75, 76, 147
  defined, 111
    least-request, 112
    random, 112
    round-robin, 111
    weighted, 112–114
Local file distribution, 496
Location component, 215
Log aggregation
  authorization failure, 404
  configuration, 406–408
  default exception, 411, 412
  defined, 403
  filtering, response codes, 408, 409
  Istio's architecture, 404, 406
  mesh-level, 403
  output and format, 413–415
  services and proxies, 403
  specific services, 409, 410
  traffic direction, 410, 411
Logging, 293, 369, 481
Logging system, 273–279
Low level virtual machine (LLVM), 449, 450, 458

M

Machine learning (ML), 189, 528, 544
Machine learning operations (MLOps), 528–531
Match section, 487
maxConnections, 161
maxEjectionPercent, 166
maxRequestsPerConnection, 162
maxRetries, 162
Mean time to resolution (MTTR), 539
Memory management, 454, 480
MeshConfig, 319, 320
MeshIntelligence framework, 544
Mesh-level logging, 403
MeshOptimizer, 540
Mesh Security Alliance (MSA), 541
Mesh-wide deployment, 470, 497–499
Method-based routing, 124
Metrics functions, 481
Metric value expressions, 359, 360
Microsegmentation, 289
Microservices architecture
  business functionality, 2
  challenges
    developer overhead, 33
    with Istio, 35
    observability, 33

555

INDEX

Microservices architecture (*cont.*)
    observability gaps, 4
    operational overhead, 5
    resilience and fault tolerance, 5
    scaling and resilience, 33
    security gaps, 32
    security risks, distributed systems, 4
    traffic management, 4, 32
  characteristics
    decentralization, 3
    fault isolation, 3
    scalability, 3
    separation of concerns, 3
  definition, 2
  drawbacks, 1
  ecommerce, 32
  independent services, 2
  SSL/TLS termination, 203
  traffic mirroring, 189
  without Istio, 32
Microservices environment's foundational security, 224, 225
Mindtickle, 12
minHealthPercent, 166
Mirror percentage, 187
Mirror service, 186
Mixerless architecture, 296
ML Mesh, 529–531
Monitor certificate expiry, 206
Multi-cluster configuration, 527
Multi-cluster deployments, 286–288
Multidimensional filtering strategy, 409
Multi-layered security approach, 288
Multi-network deployments, 437
Multi-party computation, 536
Multi-primary deployment model, 436, 437
Multi-tenancy support, 494

Multi-tenant clusters, 498
Mutual TLS (mTLS), 4, 6, 32, 41, 51, 76, 105, 206, 224, 262, 347, 537
  cleanup, 241
  defined, 228
  handshake process, 229
  implementation, 229, 230
    application services, 235–238
    certificate infrastructure, 231
    certificate rotation and monitoring, 240
    creating namespace, 234, 235
    install cert-manager helm repository, 232, 233
    STRICT mode, 238, 239
  integration and security policies, 230
  namespaces, 230
  operation modes, 229
  service identity and certificate management, 229
  transparent encryption and security, 229
  troubleshooting steps, 241

N

Namespace, 28
Namespace-scoped deployment model, 470, 497–499
National Institute of Standards and Technology (NIST), 544
Network-level metrics, 414
Network Load Balancer (NLB), 432
Network policies, 286
Network security, 226, 289
Ninja, 458
Node controller, 14
Normalization, 527

O

Observability, 4, 7, 37, 78, 94, 207, 291
    application, 309
    architecture overview, 307
    challenges, 33
    configuration, 305–307
    control plane, 42, 43
    deployment process, 309
    distributed tracing, 316
    Envoy proxy, 55, 56
    installing Helm, 297–302
    Kubernetes deployment, 309
    learning objectives, 310–314
    logs, 293
    metrics, 292, 293
    prerequisites and environment setup, 297
    Prometheus (*see* Prometheus)
    service implementation, 308
    tracing, 294
    verification, 302, 304, 305
OCI registry distribution, 496
onConfigure method, 463, 483
Online Certificate Status Protocol (OCSP), 225
onRequestBody, 484
onRequestHeaders, 465, 476, 484
onRequestTrailers, 484
onResponseBody, 484
onResponseHeaders, 484
onResponseTrailers, 484
Open Container Initiative (OCI), 471
Open policy agent (OPA), 41, 43, 45, 77, 280, 281
OpenTelemetry-based tracing pipeline, 307
OpenTelemetryConfig class, 320
Operational knowledge retention, 520
Operational overhead, 5
Outbound metrics, 380
Outbound traffic controlling, 211–214
Outlier detection, 117–120
Outlier detection pattern, 168

P

Patch section, 488
Path-based routing pattern, 199, 200
Payment-related error patterns, 390
Payment service, 399
PeerAuthentication, 537
Peer authentication policies, 242
Performance degradation, 408
Performance impact monitoring, 510
Performance metrics, 293
Performance testing, 188
perTryTimeout, 182
Pod annotations, 320
PodMonitors, 337
Pod restarting, 17
Pods, 15
Policy enforcement, 7, 43, 227
Policy reconciliation systems, 544
Port-based routing, 126, 127, 129
Ports component, 215
Post-authentication positioning, 491
Post-deployment strategy, 151, 152
Post-quantum cryptographic algorithms, 544
Pre-authentication positioning, 490
Pre-authorization positioning, 491
Precedence, 120
Pre-deployment validation, 147, 148
Prediction latency, 529
Pre-router positioning, 491

INDEX

Pre-switch validation, 154
Primary-remote configuration, 437, 438
Primary-remote deployment model, 435, 436
Product catalog service, 3
Production environments, 52, 524
Production-grade deployments, 28
Progressive circuit breaking pattern, 169
Progressive delivery, 219
Progressive deployment, 219
Progressive rollouts
    confidence building, 135
    expanded validation, 135
    initial exposure, 134
    recommendation service, 133, 134
    safety mechanisms, 134
Progressive switching strategies, 153, 154
Project Quantum Mesh, 542
Prometheus
    best practices
        label management and cardinality, 364
        monitoring, 366
        resource usage optimization, 365
        sampling configuration, 364
        telemetry sources, 365
        understanding Istio's default metrics, 363
        version management, 365
    configuring custom metrics, 355–364
    metrics architecture, 332–337
    standard Envoy proxy metrics, 348–354
    standard Istio metrics
        circuit breaking, 344–346
        labels, 348
        proxy-level connection metrics, 340–342
        proxy-level request metrics, 338–340
        security metrics, 346–348
        service-level traffic metrics, 342–344
Prometheus Query Language (PromQL), 172
Protection limits, 166, 167
Protocols, 207
Protocol-specific routing, 86
Protocol translation, 527
Proxy-level connection metrics, 340–342
Proxy-level request metrics, 338–340
Proxy-Wasm
    ABI, 448, 451, 480–482
    authentication plugin implementation, 451
    context hierarchy, 485, 486
    defined, 446, 451
    extension, 452
    host functions, 452
    specification, 452
Proxy-Wasm C++ SDK, 450
    classes and interfaces, 460
    configuration handling, 463, 464
    header file, 463
    HTTP requests, 461, 462
    plugin registration, 465, 466
    request context class, 464
    request processing, 465
    RootContext class, 463
Public key infrastructure (PKI), 224, 225, 286

Q

Quantum-resistant security, 544

R

Random algorithm, 112
Rappi, 11
Rate limiting, 207
Rate monitoring, 343
Real-time monitoring, 191, 192
Regression testing, 189
Reliability, 7
Remote HTTP/HTTPS distribution, 495
Replication controller, 14
Request authentication, 242
Request context, 294
Rescheduling, 17
Resilience, 5, 7, 94
    circuit breakers (*see* Circuit breakers)
    and scaling, 33
    service testing
        building plan, 178, 179
        load testing, 179, 180
        recommendations, 178
        validating recovery patterns, 180, 181
Resolution component, 215
Resource-intensive approach, 73
Resource management, 298
Resource metrics, 292
Resource utilization, 149
Response time distribution, 137
RestTemplateConfig, 323
Retry and timeout policies
    backoff configuration, 183
    best practices, 184, 185
    configuration, 181, 182
    settings, 183
    video streaming platform, 181
retryOn, 182
Role-based access control (RBAC), 18, 45
    authorization policies, 249
    defined, 249
    implementation, 250
        authentication and authorization, 257-259
        cleanup resources, 260
        creating Kubernetes resources, 253-257
        creating namespace, 251
        install Istio, 251
        node applications, 252
        setup verification, 259
        testing rules, 259
    microservices, 250
    policies, 251, 537
Rollback procedures, 155-158
Rollbacks, 17
Rollback strategies, 514, 516
Rolling back canary deployments, 139-142, 144
Rollouts, 17
RootContext class, 463, 465, 485
Round-robin algorithm, 111
Routes, 54, 55
Routine penetration testing, 287
Rust, 456

S

Salesforce, 11
Scheduler, 14
Secure management, 18
SecureMesh, 540
Security audits, 207
Security events, auditing and logging, 273-279
Security gaps, 32
Security information and event management (SIEM), 279, 287

INDEX

Security metrics, 346–348
Self-healing capabilities, 17
Self-tuning proxy configurations, 545
Server metrics, 353, 354
Server Name Indication (SNI), 105
Server-side metrics, 377
Service account controller, 14
Service dependencies, 294
Service discovery, 74, 75, 373
ServiceEntry, 85
Service entry configuration
    Endpoints component, 215
    external dependencies, 214
    Hosts component, 215
    Location component, 215
    mesh-internal services, 214
    Ports component, 215
    resolution and mesh control, 216, 218, 219
Service health metrics, 528
Service identity, 229
Service-level objectives (SLOs), 176, 339
Service-level traffic metrics
    error rate analysis, 343
    PromQL queries, 342
    request duration patterns, 343, 344
    request rate monitoring, 343
Service mesh performance (SMP), 541
Service mesh performance metrics, 388, 389
Service mesh technology, 1, 2, 525
    AI and machine learning workloads, 528
    components, 35
    debugging issues, 36
    definition, 5, 34
    distributed application, 34
    features, 5, 6
    centralized management, 8
    extensibility, 8
    observability, 7
    platform agnostic, 7
    policy enforcement, 7
    resilience and reliability, 7
    security, 6
    traffic management, 6
  role of, 36
ServiceMonitors, 337
Service-to-service communication, 19, 77, 219, 316, 373
Shadow responses, 187
Shadow traffic, see Traffic mirroring
SIDECAR_INBOUND context, 492
Sidecar mode, 57–63, 73
SIDECAR_OUTBOUND context, 493
Sidecar-per-pod model, 524
Simple circuit breaking pattern, 167, 168
Single-cluster deployment
    Amazon EKS (see Amazon Elastic Kubernetes Service (EKS))
    architecture, 418, 419
    best fit, 438
    fine-tuning
        control plane, 434
        factors, 434
        ingress gateway, 435
    multi-network deployments, 437
    multi-primary deployment model, 436, 437
    primary–remote deployment model, 435, 436
Source service, 186
SSL/TLS termination
    benefits, 205, 206
    best practices, 206, 207
    configuration, 204, 205

encryption and decryption, 203
State management functions, 481
Static resolution, 216
Stock management system, 382
Stress-testing, 178
Subnet-based routing, 125, 126

T

Targeted workload selection, 470, 471
Target's Peak Season Resilience, 538, 539
TCP connection parameters, 161, 162
tcpKeepalive, 162
Teladoc Health, 539
Telemetry, 510, 511
Telemetry system
    API, 295, 296, 314, 315, 318, 319, 355–358
    architecture, 294, 295
    configuration, 295, 296
    control plane, 42, 43
    data plane, 46
    integration, 366
    mixer-based architecture, 296
    monitoring, 77
    proxies, 294, 295
    suspicious patterns, 273
Terraform
    cloud provider, 423
    command, 426–428
    EKS cluster, 425, 426
    infrastructure, 427
    kubeconfig update command, 429
    kubectl cluster-info command, 430
    kubectl get nodes command, 430
    node group, 427, 428
    resource creation, 423
    variables, 423

VPC and networking settings, 424
Threshold settings
    configuration, 164
    defined, 164
    error detection mechanisms, 165
    protection limits, 166, 167
Thundering herd problem, 184
T-Mobile, 11
Token validation, 242
Trace sampling configuration, 329, 330
Trace tags, 330–332
Tracing, 55, 56, 294
Traditional monitoring technologies, 4
Traffic direction–based logging, 410, 411
Traffic management, 4, 6, 32, 78, 218, 396–399, 503, 527, 532
    APIs, 84, 85
    architecture, 82, 83
    data plane, 45
    Envoy proxy, 84
    importance, 81, 82
    maintainability and scalability, 220
    patterns, 219, 220
    performance considerations, 221
    recommendation service, 85–92
    route rules, 220
    routing (*see* Traffic routing)
    troubleshooting, 221
    virtual services and destination rules
        benefits, 94
        connection pooling, 114–117
        defined, 92
        fields and significance, 96–100
        load balancing, 111–114
        match conditions and routing rules, 101, 103, 104
        outlier detection, 117–120

INDEX

Traffic management (*cont.*)
    protocol-specific routing
        features, 104–107
    purpose, 93
    purpose and relationship, 108
    strategy, 150
    structure and configuration, 95, 96
    subsets, 108–111
    use cases, 93
Traffic metrics, 292
Traffic mirroring
    concepts, 186, 187
    defined, 185
    implementation, 187, 188
    microservices architecture, 189
    performance monitoring and analysis, 190, 191
    real-time analysis and automation, 191, 192
    testing and validation strategies, 192, 193
    use cases, 188, 189
    versions, 189
Traffic pattern analysis, 528
Traffic routing
    defined, 120
    headers, 122
    method, 124
    port, 126, 127, 129
    rules and precedence, 120
    subnet, 125, 126
    URI, 123
    version, 120
    weighted, 124, 125
Traffic shadowing, 514
Traffic splitting, 40, 86
Traffic switch preparation, 149, 150
Transport layer security (TLS), 224

U

Unit testing, 506, 507
Universal Service Mesh Interface (USMI), 541
Upstream overflow (UO), 345
URI-based routing, 123
Use cases, 445, 446
User-agent header, 122

V

Version-aware circuit breaking pattern, 170, 171
Version management, 366
Vertical pod autoscaler (VPA), 16
Virtual machine, 453, 526
VirtualService, 84
Virtual services, 196, 197
    benefits, 94
    connection pooling, 114–117
    defined, 92
    fields and significance, 96–100
    load balancing, 111–114
    match conditions and routing rules, 101, 103, 104
    outlier detection, 117–120
    protocol-specific routing features, 104–107
    purpose and relationship, 93, 108
    resources, 92
    structure and configuration, 95, 96
    subsets, 108–111
    use cases, 93
Visualization
    Grafana (*see* Grafana)
    Kiali, 392–403

W, X, Y

Wasm for Service Mesh, 545
WasmPlugin *vs.* EnvoyFilter, 469
Waypoint proxies, 537
WebAssembly (Wasm), 51, 441, 525, 545
  benefits, 445
  defined, 445
  development best practices, 516–519
  EnvoyFilter resource (*see* EnvoyFilter)
  Envoy proxy, 56, 57
  events, 445
  operational best practices, 519–522
  plugins (*see* WebAssembly plugins)
WebAssembly plugins
  architecture, 453, 454
  assembly line stations, 455
  building, 466–469
  callbacks, 448
  compilation, 449
  defined, 446
  deployment
    configuration, 473–476
    execution context and timing, 476, 477
    execution phase and filter chain positioning, 472, 473
    module source and versioning, 471, 472
    perspective, 447
    resource identity and scope, 469, 470
    scope and targeting, 478, 479
    targeted workload selection, 470, 471
    WasmPlugin *vs.* EnvoyFilter, 469
  environment development setting, 458–461
  Envoy routes, 454
  flexibility and security, 456
  fundamentals, 448–451
  host–guest relationship, 455
  lifecycle and execution context
    configuration phase, 483
    initialization process, 483
    request processing phase, 484, 485
    termination phase, 485
  monitoring and troubleshooting, 509–516
  phases, 447
  programming languages, 456, 457
  Proxy-Wasm, 451, 485, 486
    ABI, 480–482
    C++ SDK, 460–466
    specification, 446, 455
  stages, 455
  testing, 506–509
Webhook validations, 373
Weight-based routing, 132
Weighted load balancing, 112–114
Weighted routing, 124, 125
Worker nodes, 15
Workload management, 399–402
Workloads, 15
WorkloadSelector component, 487
Workload-specific tracing configuration, 320–323

Z

Zero-trust architectures, 288
Zero-trust security model, 538
Ztunnels, 537

GPSR Compliance

The European Union's (EU) General Product Safety Regulation (GPSR) is a set of rules that requires consumer products to be safe and our obligations to ensure this.

If you have any concerns about our products, you can contact us on

ProductSafety@springernature.com

In case Publisher is established outside the EU, the EU authorized representative is:

Springer Nature Customer Service Center GmbH
Europaplatz 3
69115 Heidelberg, Germany